# The History of South Carolina from Its First European Discovery to Its Erection Into a Republic
by William Gilmore Simms

Address:
HardPress
8345 NW 66TH ST #2561
MIAMI FL 33166-2626
USA
Email: info@hardpress.net

TABLE MOUNTAIN

THE
HISTORY
of
South Carolina

THE
HISTORY
of
South Carolina

THE

# HISTORY

OF

# SOUTH CAROLINA

FROM

## ITS FIRST EUROPEAN DISCOVERY

TO ITS

### ERECTION INTO A REPUBLIC

WITH

### A SUPPLEMENTARY BOOK, BRINGING THE NARRATIVE DOWN
### TO THE PRESENT TIME

BY WILLIAM GILMORE SIMMS,

AUTHOR OF "THE YEMASSEE," "EUTAW," "CASSIQUE OF KIAWAH," "THE SCOUT," ETC.

NEW AND REVISED EDITION.

# REDFIELD
34 BEEKMAN STREET, NEW YORK
1860

SAVAGE & McCREA, STEREOTYPERS,
13 Chambers Street, N. Y.

TO

THE YOUTH OF SOUTH CAROLINA,

THIS RECORD OF THE DEEDS, THE TRIALS, AND THE VIRTUES,

OF THEIR ANCESTORS,

IS RESPECTFULLY AND AFFECTIONATELY INSCRIBED

BY THEIR FRIEND AND COUNTRYMAN,

THE AUTHOR

# CONTENTS.

## BOOK I.
### FRENCH AND SPANISH SETTLEMENTS

## BOOK II.
### THE CAROLINAS UNDER THE LORD-PROPRIETORS.—ENGLISH.

## BOOK III.
### ROYAL GOVERNMENT.—1719 TO 1736.

# BOOK IV.

## PROGRESS TO REVOLUTION.

# BOOK V.

## THE REVOLUTION IN SOUTH CAROLINA.

# BOOK VI.

## SUPPLEMENTARY.

# PREFACE.

THE volume here submitted to the reader, is an attempt to supply what seemed to the writer a popular desideratum. It was written fifteen years ago, and is now revised, with copious additions. It was originally conceived with the view to the instruction of an only daughter in the history of her birthplace. This could not be done with the existing histories. He found it no easy matter to place before her the materials necessary to convey the desired information. He had, it is true, all the several works already devoted to this subject. The various histories of Hewatt, Drayton, Ramsay, Moultrie, etc., were all in his collection; but volumes so cumbrous, and so loaded as they are with prolix disquisition, and unnecessary if not irrelevant detail, he felt convinced were in no respect suited to the unprepared understanding and the ardent temper of the young. These authors wrote, generally, at a period when the doctrines of popular representation, of suffrage, self-government, and many other principles, regarded as essential to the preservation of social liberty, were either of novel suggestion or very imperfectly understood. It seemed necessary, and was, therefore, proper, in that early day, that they should be discussed at length. These discussions, however, overloaded the narrations

1

of the historian and impaired their interest. They were cumbered with opinions now regarded as truisms, which too greatly trespassed on the dominions of simple truth. So soon as the public mind had decided these questions, the discussions upon them necessarily sunk out of sight, and involved in their own oblivion the histories upon which they had been grafted. The latter, accordingly, ceased to be sought after, either for amusement or instruction; and, finally, and by a natural transition, were thrust away into that general lumber-house of

> " Things that on earth were lost or were abused,"

a sort of Astolfo's mansion of the moon,

> " Which safely treasures up
> Whate'er is wasted in our earthly state —"

the upper shelves of the library — where, frowning in immemorial dust and dignity, they enjoy the time-honored epithets of " books of reference " — a classification for which their venerable writers never stipulated, and which would have very imperfectly rewarded the severe toils of elaborate authorship.

Valuable in this point of view, they are scarcely of present value in any other. To the great portion of the reading community they are entirely useless. For this reason, though long since out of print, a republication of them is considered unnecessary, and would, probably, involve in serious pecuniary loss the most cautious publisher. The late reprint of Hewatt, Archdale, and others, in the historical collections of Mr. Carroll, offers no exception to the general justice of this remark. A reluctant subscription failed to pay the expenses of printing, and but for the liberal appropriation of the state legislature, after the risk had been incurred, that enterprising young citizen might have had reason to repent the rashness of his patriotism. He certainly would have gained nothing from his publication beyond the applause which is due to his public spirit.

The cumbrousness of the works, of South Carolina history, already existing, suggests another serious obstacle to their circulation as popular volumes. They are necessarily expensive. Books for schools and for the popular reader — the two objects for which the present history is designed — must be cheap as well as compact. Strange as the fact may appear, this truth seems to have been of recent discovery. It is only of late days that it has been thought advisable to recognise the poor among the other classes of book-readers. A few years back, our authors labored under the ambition of bringing forth big books — corpulent quartos, if possible, but octavos at all events; and with this ambition they seldom stopped short at a single volume. It would seem that they regarded the size of the work as no imperfect token of the writer's merit. It followed, from this ambition — an ambition which, in most cases, effectually defeated its own object — that the quantity of the material furnished but a very uncertain rule in the construction of the volume. Its dimensions being arbitrary, what was wanting in fact was supplied by conjecture, and when conjecture halted, and grew irresolute or blind, opinion came in to her relief; and, between discussion and declamation, she hobbled on through the requisite number of pages to the end of the chapter. The present age, if less ambitious, and no wiser, is certainly more economical in this respect. Small volumes, neat abridgments, and the judicious separation of subjects, not necessarily connected, into their proper classes, realizes all the natural energies of a free press, and places the learning and the wisdom of the past and the present within the reach of the humblest and the poorest of mankind.

Cheap literature to the poor is of scarcely less importance, indeed, than was the discovery of the art of printing to mankind at large. The chief importance of this grand discovery, resting entirely on its power for diffusing knowledge rapidly throughout the world, it necessarily follows that the author who makes his book costly through its cumbrousness, adops a mode of publication which, to a great extent, must defeat the objects of the press. The time occupied in printing, and the expense of the work when printed, lessen greatly the infinite superiority which the modern printer possesses over the ancient scribe. We may instance the valuable work of Johnson, the life of Greene, as incurring, from its plan, some of these objections and disadvantages. That work abounds in materials which, properly classified, would have made a dozen popular volumes. In its present state, the toil of the reader is continual and great to separate the narrative from the discussion, which equally precedes and follows it — which wraps it as in a cloud, and makes it difficult for the memory to compass and retain the several remote but relevant incidents which are necessary to a true comprehension of the subject. The result is, that a work which abounds in copious details and much spirited writing, and which relates to periods of the most exciting interest in our national and domestic history, is seldom read, and almost as unfrequently referred to. And yet no work of American biography, could the author have descended to the humbler task of making an abridgment, would have more amply compensated both publisher and reader, than the same work stripped of its controversial additaments and contracted to the moderate compass of a single duodecimo.

To this work of Johnson, we acknowledge our large indebtedness. We have relied upon it in preference to all others, during that long period, crowded with fluctuating events, which followed the disastrous defeat of Gates at Camden to the close of the Revolutionary war; and though studiously avoiding the expression of any opinion upon the vexed questions — some of them of very small importance to the result — which the venerable author was, perhaps, only too fond of discussing, we freely avow our full confidence in the general fidelity of his statements, and in his habitual desire to discover and to declare the truth.

For the account of the early settlements of the Huguenots, in and about Carolina, as contained in this volume, the simple and affecting narrative of Laudonniere in Hakluyt has been chiefly relied on. The work of Hewatt, the narrations of Archdale, Glenn, and others, contained in the " Historical Collections," and the highly useful and comprehensive sketch of South Carolina, from the first settlement to the Revolution of 1719, which we owe to the patriotism and painstaking of Professor Rives, have furnished the authorities next ensuing, down to the conflict of the colonies with parliament and the repeal of the stamp act. To Moultrie, Ramsay, Drayton, and Johnson, we owe what follows to the close of the Revolution, and the erection of South Carolina, from a rebelling colony, into an independent and republican state. These have been our chief sources of information ; though, in our progress, we have found it advisable to consult Holmes, Bancroft, Grahame, Tarleton, and several other writers.

The pretensions of the present volume are exceedingly moderate. The aim of the writer, as already expressed, has been to provide a volume for the popular reader and for the use of schools ; to supply the rising generation with such a history of the country as will enable them to satisfy their own curiosity and the inquiries of others. It is lamentable to perceive the degree of ignorance in which our people live with regard to those events which made their ancestors famous, and which have given them equal station and security. To say that the great majority of our young people know little or nothing of the history of the state, is to do them no injustice. We may equally charge this deficiency upon the old. This ignorance was inevitable, from the unwieldy cumbrousness and heavy cost of the volumes in which our history was locked up. To steer clear

of the great errors of my predecessors, my first aim was condensation. My work, however, is much more than an abridgment. It is in many respects original, especially in the suggestion of clues; and it embodies much material which has
escaped other historians, and this very material is of a kind
which seems to me absolutely essential to a proper understanding of many details the import of which was confessedly obscure.
Though seeking rather to be useful and sufficient than original,
I have felt it a duty sometimes to be excursive, and occasion-
ally to introduce a conjecture of my own, wherever the subject-
matter would seem to provoke a doubt or to require discussion.
Circumstances, of late days, also seemed to demand that a frequent survey should be made of the general condition of the
country, in order that the reader should be able, of himself, to
decide upon the resources, and so properly to appreciate the
responsibilities, of the state and people. All the clues to argument upon doubtful or disputed points have been indicated; and
though I have forborne unnecessary details, avoiding all prolix-
ity, I believe that nothing has been omitted which is essential,
not only to a knowledge of the history in general, but to the
argument, in the elucidation of particular topics which, improp-
erly understood, might tend to the disparagement of the chief
actors, or the people of the state at large.

In the course of the narrative I have not scrupled to make
occasional use of the very language of my authority, wherever
it seemed particularly comprehensive or felicitous. To place
the facts in a simple form, in a just order; to give them an
expressive and energetic character; to couple events closely, so
that no irrelevant or unnecessary matter should interpose itself
between the legitimate relation of cause and effect; and to be
careful that the regular stream of the narrative should flow on
without interruption to the end of its course, have been with me
primary objects.

To the mind of the youthful reader, the advantages of such a mode of condensation appear to me of obvious importance. The unbroken progress of connected events enchains the attention and beguiles while it informs the thought, until reading ceases to be study, and instruction persuades to industry through the medium of amusement. To say how far I have been successful in this design, must be the business of the reader. To the youthful student — to the children of this growing time — I commend it as a fond, and perhaps a last, tribute from the pen of one who has rarely overlooked their claims to a loving consideration, in everything that he has written.

W. G. S.

WOODLANDS, S. C., *November*, 1859.

THE

# HISTORY OF SOUTH CAROLINA.

## BOOK I.

### FRENCH AND SPANISH SETTLEMENTS.

### CHAPTER I.

#### FORT CHARLES.

THE CAROLINAS, North and South, forming twin provinces under the British dominion in America, were anciently a part of that extensive territory, known to the European world under the several names of Virginia, Florida, and New France. Still more anciently, according to tradition and old chronicles of the Northmen, the region was occupied by a race, or races, of white men, to whom, if these traditions are well-founded, we are to ascribe the tumuli, earthworks, and numerous remains of fortified places in which the whole country abounds, rather than to the nomadi red men who occupied the territory at the time of the discovery, by Columbus and other voyagers, within the modern and historical period. The province thus covered by the two Carolinas, extended northwardly along the coast, until it reached the confines of Virginia; southwardly as far as the bay of Mexico, and stretched away, for many hundred miles, into the dense forests of the interior. Three great nations contended on grounds

1. By what names were the territories of the Carolinas first known to the European world? 2. What was the tradition of the Northmen, as to the inhabitants of this region? 3. To what races are we to ascribe the ancient remains in the country? 4. How far on every hand did the territories of the Carolinas extend?

1*

of nearly equal justice, for the right to, if not the possession of the soil.

England laid claim to it, according to one class of writers, by virtue of a grant from the Roman Pontiff; by others, her right was founded upon a supposed discovery of its shores in 1497–8, by John Cabot, an Italian, and his son, Sebastian — both in the service of Henry the Seventh. The Cabots approached the continent of North America, and penetrated some of its bays and rivers, nearly fourteen months before it was beheld by Columbus; but made no attempt at occupancy.

The pretensions of Spain were based upon similar and equally worthless grounds. Juan Ponce de Leon, under her commission, discovered and traversed a neighboring territory, to which he gave the name of Florida (1512) — a name which, in her ancient spirit of arrogant assumption, was made to cover a region of measureless extent, which she could not compass, and vainly sought to conquer. Ponce was beaten by the natives, and driven from the country in disgrace. He fled to Cuba, where he died of a wound received in his fruitless expedition.

To him succeeded one Velasquez de Ayllon, who sailed from St. Domingo with two ships (1520). He made the shores of South Carolina, at the mouth of a river, to which he gave the name of the Jordan. This river is now known by the Indian name of Combahee. Here he was received by the natives with a shy timidity at first, the natural result of their wonder at the strange ships, and strangely habited visitors. Their timidity soon subsided into kindness, and they treated the Spaniards with good nature and hospitality. The country they called Chiquola, or, as it has since been corrupted, Checora — the latter word being in most frequent use, but the former being the correct one. The red men of the South knew nothing of the letter R. This name was probably conferred upon the region by some wandering tribe, and was not of permanent recognition, since we hear of it no more from subsequent voyagers. An interchange of

5. How many nations of Europe claimed its sovereignty, and upon what grounds? 6. For what power did the Cabots discover? 7. Who discovered for Spain? 8. What were her claims? 9. What of Ponce de Leon? 10. What were his fortunes? 11. Who was Velasquez de Ayllon, and what nation did he represent? 12. What river in South Carolina did he penetrate? 13. How was he received by the natives?

friendly offices soon took place between the red men and their visitors, and the former were easily persuaded to visit the ships in numbers. Watching the moment when their decks were most crowded, the perfidious Spaniards suddenly made sail, carrying nearly two hundred of this innocent aud confiding people into captivity.

Velasquez, insensible to all feelings but those of mercenary exultation at the success of his criminal scheme, pursued his way to St. Domingo, where a slave market had been already established, by the policy of Las Casas, who proposed to supply, with a hardier population, the place and numbers of the feeble natives, who were perishing fast under the unmeasured cruelties of their iron-handed masters.

But his triumph was not entirely without its qualifications. One of his vessels foundered before he reached his port, and captors and captives alike were swallowed up in the seas together. His own vessel survived, but many of his captives sickened and died; and he himself was reserved, for the time, only to suffer a more terrible form of punishment.

Though he had lost more than half of the ill-gotten fruits of his expedition, the profits which remained were still such as to encourage him to a renewal of his enterprise. To this he devoted his whole fortune, and with three large vessels and many hundred men, he once more descended upon the coast of Carolina (1524).

As if the retributive Providence had been watchful of the place, no less than the hour of justice, it so happened that, at the mouth of the very river where his crime had been committed, he was destined to meet his punishment. His largest vessel was stranded ere he reached the point he aimed at, and the infuriate natives, availing themselves of the event, set upon the struggling Spaniards in the sea. Two hundred of them were massacred, and, according to one account, though this has been denied, Velasquez himself, with others of his company, fell victims to the cannibal propensities of the savages. Whatever may be the

14. How did he treat the red men? 15. Did he make a second voyage to the same precinct? 16. What fortune awaited him? 17. What is supposed to have been his fate?

doubts cast upon this latter statement, it is surely not improbable. Nothing is positively known of him after this event, and what we have of conjecture, describes him as living a life of ignominy, and dying miserably at last.

The claim of France to the possession of the Carolinas, rested upon the discoveries of one John Verazzano, a Florentine, who was sent out in 1523, by Francis the First. He reached the coast, somewhere, as is supposed, in the latitude of Wilmington, North Carolina (1524). Here he found the country full of beauty to the eye. The forests were noble, and the various perfumes which reached the seamen from the shore, intoxicated them with a thousand oriental fancies. The yellow sands gave ample promise of gold, which was the prime motive for most of the adventures of the time; and the hospitality of the Indians suffered no obstacle to prevent the free examination of their country by the strangers.

Verazzano describes the natives as "gentle and courteous in their manners; of sweet and pleasant countenance, and comely to behold." Their population, according to the imperfect account which he has given us, was "numerous; well formed in limb; having black and great eyes, with a cheerful and steady look; not strong of body, yet sharp-witted; nimble, and exceeding great runners." The women are described as handsome, and of "comely forms;" and, which seems to have been not unusual among the North American savages, the government of the tribe was in the hands of a woman.

The red men of this region seem to have possessed a more decided civilization than was apparent among the northern tribes. They dwelt in log-houses, so covered with matting as to be impervious to rain and cold; they had boats wrought by flint and fire from mighty trees, some of which were twenty feet in length; and, a better evidence yet in their favor, they treated the European strangers with an urbanity, grace, and kindness, which remind us of the patriarchal virtues enumerated in bible history. One of the crew of Verazzano, attempting to

18. What were the claims of France? 19. Who was Verazzano? 20. In what latitude did he first gain the coast of the Carolinas? 21. How did he describe the country? 22. How the natives? 23. What was the degree of civilization which they enjoyed?

swim ashore, was so much injured in passing through the surf, that he lay senseless on the beach. They ran to his relief, rescued him from the waves, rubbed his limbs, gave him refreshment, and returned him in safety to the vessel.

Thus far, it appears that these three great nations, through their agents, did little more than look upon the country to which they asserted claims, which they strove afterwards to maintain by a resort to every violence and crime. Subsequently, two armies of Spain entered Florida; the first, under Narvaez (1527), well known as an unsuccessful adventurer in Mexico, and destined to be as little prosperous in Florida. He failed, was driven from the country, and perished in his flight, at sea.

He was followed, a few years after, by an abler, if not a braver man. This was Ferdinand de Soto, a gentleman of good birth and fortune, who signalized himself in Peru, under the lead of Pizarro, and was considered one of the most eminent Spanish captains of the time. He projected the invasion of Florida, and, at his own expense, provided a noble armament of seven ships and a thousand men for this object.

The Spaniards reached the bay of Espiritu Santo early in 1539, and had scarcely landed and pitched their tents for the night, when they were attacked, with partial success, by a large body of the natives. This was but a foretaste of what was yet in reserve for them.

Undiscouraged by this reception, they boldly advanced into the country, upon that miserable march, which has been most erroneously styled "a conquest of Florida." Never was human adventure so unhappily misnamed. So far from De Soto conquering Florida, the Floridians conquered him. Harassed at every footstep—yielding bloody tribute at every stream that lay in their path, every thicket that could harbor an enemy or mask an ambush — the Spaniards fought their way onward, entirely hopeless of return. The path before them alone lay

24. How did they display their humanity? 25. Which nation first attempted the conquest of the country? 26. Who led the first invasion of the Spanish? 27. What was the fate of Narvaez? 28. Who was Ferdinand de Soto? 29. What armament did he lead in the invasion of the country? 30. Where did he first land? and when? 31. What was his reception from the red men? 32. What is said of his conquest of Florida?

open but not free.　It was filled with foes no less resolute, than those they had left — as determined as they were strong, and as audacious as they were adroit.　Nothing could exceed their audacity — their froward valor — their sleepless and persevering hate.　De Soto reached the Mississippi, and was buried beneath its waters, a broken-hearted man; having discovered, in the significant language of one of our own historians, nothing in all his progress " so remarkable as his burial-place." In his march he crossed the present state of Georgia, penetrated South Carolina at Silver Bluff, on the Savannah; skirted the gold regions of both states, and is supposed to have worked the mines in both; but he preferred conquest of great cities to obscure labor in the mountains, and we know his career only by weary wandering marches, which his followers traced out with their blood.　The wretched remnant of his army, reduced to half their number, escaped, after a tedious period of suffering, to the shores of the gulf, whence they made their way to the river Panuco.

Nearly thirty years elapsed, after the miscarriage of this enterprise, before either of the three great claimants of the soil renewed the attempt to occupy it.　The strifes of empire at home, and, perhaps, the melancholy results of all previous attempts, served to discourage the rival monarchs, no less than their subjects, from prosecuting adventures which had hitherto been attended by nothing but disaster.

At length, in 1561, the eye of the celebrated Huguenot leader, Coligny, admiral of France, was turned upon the shores of the new world, as a place of refuge to which the Protestants might fly and be secure from those persecutions which they suffered at home, and from the worse evils which he saw awaited them.　With this object in view, he succeeded in obtaining from Charles the Ninth, permission to plant a colony on the borders of Florida.

33. What great river did he reach? 34. What was his fate, and where was he buried? 35. Through what States did he march? 36. Where did he enter South Carolina? 37. What is conjectured of his occupations while in Georgia and Carolina? 38. What became of his surviving followers? 39. How long after Soto's death did the country which he had invaded remain unknown by Europeans? 40. What kept the European monarchs from invasion during this period? 41. Who was Coligny? 42. Why did he desire to colonize in Florida? 43. From whom did he get permission?

This expedition was intrusted to the command of John Ribault, of Dieppe, an experienced seaman, a brave soldier, and a staunch Protestant. He was attended by some few of the young nobility of France, and his troops were mostly veterans. These were all, most probably, voluntary adventurers. Charles was too bigoted a Catholic to contribute to the prosperity of a colony which he did not protect, and refused to avenge. His commission to the colonists, which was sufficiently ample, was simply intended to rid himself of a portion of his subjects, who had shown themselves as stubborn as they were intelligent, and for whom he subsequently devised a more summary mode of removal, on the dreadful day of St. Bartholomew.

With two ships, Ribault set sail from France on the 18th of February, 1562. His aim was to reach the river Combahee, called "the Jordan," to a knowledge of which the French had been already introduced by the discovery and disaster of Velasquez.

Sailing too far to the south, he first made land in the latitude of St. Augustine, where he discovered the river St. John's, to which he gave the name of May river. Thence he pursued a northerly course along the coast, still in search of the Jordan, and naming the various streams which he discovered as he proceeded, after well known rivers of France. The St. Mary's, for the time, became the Seine; The Satilla, the Somme; the Altamaha, the Loire; the Ogechee, the Garonne; and the Isundiga, or Savannah, the Gironde.

The names which he conferred upon the rivers of South Carolina, they still partially retain. The Belle is now the "May," and the Grande, the "Broad." While he proceeded in his search for the "Jordan," his two vessels were separated by a storm, in which one of them was supposed, for a time, to be lost; but she had anchored in a bay which seemed the outlet of some magnificent river. To this bay, "because of the fairnesse and largenesse thereof," Ribault gave the name of Port Royale.

"Here," says the narrative, " wee stroke our sailes, and cast anker at ten fathom of water ; for the depth is such when the sea beginneth to flow, that the greatest shippes of France, yea, the arguzies of Venice, may enter in there."

The delighted Huguenots landed upon the northern bank of the entrance of Port Royal, which they believed to be one of the mouths of the Jordan, and gave themselves up for a time to the contemplation of the aspects of the new world, which seemed to them no less beautiful than strange. The mighty oaks, and the "infinite store of cedars," enforced their wonder, and as they passed through the woods, they saw "turkey cocks flying in the forests, partridges, gray and red, little different from our's but chiefly in bigness ;" they "heard within the woods the voices of stags, of bears, of hyenas, of leopards, and divers other sorts of beasts, unknown unto us." " Being delighted with the place," they set themselves to fishing with nets, and caught such a number of fish that it was wonderful."

Having refreshed themselves with the fruits, the flesh, and the fish of this prolific region, with a curiosity stimulated by what they had already seen, the Huguenots ascended the river about fifteen leagues, in their pinnaces, when they beheld a group of red men, who, at their approach, "fled into the woods, leaving behind them a young lucerne [opossum], which they were turning upon a spit ; for which cause the place was called Cape Lucerne."

Proceeding farther, Ribault came to an arm of the river, which he entered, leaving the main stream. "A little while after, they began to espy divers other Indians, both men and women, half hidden within the woods ;" these "were dismayed at first, but soon after emboldened, for the captain caused stores of merchandize to be showed them openly, whereby they knew that we meant nothing but well unto them, and then they made a sign that we should come on land, which we would not refuse."

50. Where finally did he strike his sails and land ? 51. How did he describe the river of Port Royal ? 52. How did the Huguenots describe the country ? 53. What do they say of the natives, or red men ?

The savages saluted Ribault after their simple fashion, and brought skins, baskets, made of palm leaves, and a few pearls, which they freely bestowed upon the strangers. They even began to build an arbor, to protect their visitors from the sun; but the Huguenots refused to linger.

There is a tradition among the red men, which preserves correctly the events of this meeting between themselves and the Europeans, and the very spot on which it took place is supposed, and with strong probability, to be that now occupied by the village of Coosawhatchie, a name borrowed from the aborigines.

On an island — by some conjectured to be Lemon island, by others, Beaufort, but which, we have now good reason to believe is Paris * island, and where there are still the remains of a fortress which corresponds, in form and size, with the structure raised by the French — Ribault raised a monument of freestone, on which the arms of France were engraved, and took possession of the fertile domain, in the name of his sovereign. Here on a river which the French christened Chenonceau, he built a fortress, " in length but a sixteen fathom, and thirteen in breath, with flanks according to the proportion thereof," in which he placed provisions and warlike munitions, and to which he gave the name of Fort Charles, in honor of the reigning monarch of France. At the persuasion of Ribault, twenty-six of his men consented to garrison this fort, and when he had provided, as he supposed, sufficiently for their safety, he set sail for France, leaving one Captain Albert in command of the colony.

* And, by the way, the name which the island bears, would indicate a French origin. When was it given? By whom, if not the Huguenots?

54. How were they treated by them? 55. Where did they first meet the red men? 56. Where did Ribault raise a pillar and build a fort? 57. How did he name it, and in whose honor? 58. What garrison did he leave, and under whose command?

## CHAPTER II.

### FATE OF THE FIRST COLONY.

Ribault continued his voyage northwardly along the coast, but made no discoveries of any importance, and though he penetrated some rivers in his pinnace, he effected no landing. His crews became impatient for their own country. His officers congratulated him on having discovered "in six weeks, more than the Spaniards had done in two years in the conquest of their New Spaine;" and pleased and satisfied with this conviction, his prows were turned to the east.

He reached France in safety; but the fires of civil war, which the sagacious mind of Coligny had anticipated, were already blazing in that kingdom. The admiral, struggling with dangers at home, and beset by powerful foes, against whom he could barely, and only for a time, maintain himself, was in no condition to send supplies to the colony in Carolina. The forlorn few who remained in that wild country, were left to themselves, to their own enterprise, courage, and industry—qualities which, if exercised, might have amply sustained them among the hospitable natives; but which seem to have been utterly banished from their minds, by rashness, improvidence, and the most unhappy dissentions.

When first left by their companions, the twenty-six Frenchmen, under their captain, Albert, duly impressed with their isolation, proceeded, without intermission of labor, to fortify themselves in their habitations. This done, they proceeded to explore the country, and made allies of several Indian tribes,

1. What farther progress did Ribault make along the coast? 2. What was the boast of his officers? 3. How did he reach France, and in what condition did he find that country? 4. What was the effect of the civil war in France, upon the French colonists in Carolina? 5. What was their conduct? 6. What was their intercourse with the red men ?

north and south of their fortress. Audusta, the king or chief of one of these tribes — a name in which we may recognise the modern Edisto — was in particular their friend. He sent them ambassadors, invited them into his country, furnished them with provisions, and admitted them to a sight of those ceremonies of his religion, which, among the Indian tribes, have been most usually kept secret from strangers. Some of these ceremonies were curious, like those of most savages; an odd mixture of the grotesque and sanguinary. The scene of the performance, and one of their superstitious festivals, is thus described by Laudonniere, one of the lieutenants of Ribault.

"The place was a great circuit of ground, with open prospect, and round in figure. All who were chosen to celebrate the feast, were painted, and trimmed with rich feathers of divers colors. When they had reached the place of Toya — such was the name of their deity — they set themselves in order, following three other Indians, who differed in gait and in gesture from the rest."

"Each of them bore in his hand a tabret, dancing and singing in a lamentable tune, when they entered the sacred circuit. After they had sung and danced awhile, they ran off through the thickest woods, like unbridled horses, where they carried on a portion of their ceremonies in secret from the crowd. The women spent the day in tears, as sad and woful as possible ; and in such rage they cut the arms of the young girls with muscle shells, that the blood followed, which they flung into the air, crying out as they did so, He-Toya—He-Toya—He-Toya."

They had three priests, to whom they gave the name of Iawas. These presided over their sacrifices, were their only physicians, and professed to deal in magic. They held almost unlimited power over the minds of their people, and dictated in all the counsels of the country. It was fortunate for the French that they took no alarm at their presence, and suffered the hospitality of the aborigines to pursue a natural direction.

7. Who was Audusta, and what his relations with the French? 8. What were the religious ceremonies of the red men, and what was the name of their Deity? 9. What the name of their priests? 10. In what did they deal besides religion?

The provisions of the colonist soon failed them, and they were compelled to turn to the Indians for supplies. The humble stock of the savages was freely shared with them; "they gave them part of all the victuals which they had, and kept no more to themselves than would serve to sow their fields."

This excessive liberality had the effect of sending the natives to the woods, that they might live upon roots until the time of harvest: and having thus exhausted the resources of the people of Audusta, the French turned to other tribes — to king Couexis, "a man of might and renown in this province, which maketh his abode toward the south, abounding at all seasons, and replenished with quantity of mill [meal], corn, and beans" — and to "king Ouade, a brother of Couexis, no less wealthy than the former.

" The liberality of Ouade, whose territories lay upon the river Belle (May), was not less than that of Audusta. He received the French kindly, in a house hanged about with tapestry feathers of divers colors." "Moreover, the place where the king took his rest was covered with white coverlets, embroidered with devices of very witty and fine workmanship, and fringed round about with a fringe dyed in the color of scarlet.

This prince commanded their boats to be filled with provisions, and presented them with six coverlets, like those which decorated his couch. The French were not wanting in gratitude, which they testified by similar presents, and the parties separated, equally pleased and satisfied.

The colonists had scarcely returned to the fort, when their barrack was destroyed by fire — a catastrophe which was soon repaired by their Indian neighbors. They hurried to the spot, and with an industry only equalled by their generous enthusiasm, a large company, under the direction of two of their chiefs, rebuilt the fabric in the short space of twelve hours.

But no generosity of the Indians could enable them to supply the continual demands which the colonists made for food. The resources of Ouade failed them in like manner with those

11. From whom did the Huguenots get their food when their own stores failed them ?
12. Who were King Couexis, and King Ouade, and how did they receive the French. 18. With what kindness, in what state ? 14. What calamity happened to the French at Fort Charles ? 15. How repaired and by whom ?

of Audusta, and a portion of the company was sent to explore the country. They were next supplied by Couexis, who added to his gifts a certain number of exceeding fair pearls, some pieces of fine crystal, and certain silver ore. This last gift inflamed the minds of the colonists with new and fatal desires. They eagerly demanded whence the crystal and the silver came, and were told that the "inhabitants of the country did dig the same at the foot of certain high mountains, where they found it in very good quantity."

Hitherto, the French had conducted themselves in a proper and becoming manner. They had dealt justly and gently with the natives, and had been treated kindly. "But," in the language of the old chronicle, from which we quote, "misfortune, or rather the just judgment of God, would have it, that those who could not be overcome by fire nor water, should be undone by their own selves. This is the common fashion of men who can not continue in one state, and had rather overthrow themselves, than not attempt some new thing daily."

The first civil troubles among the colonists began about a common soldier, named Guernache. He was a drummer of the band, and for some offence, the character of which is unknown, but which has been represented as too small to have justified the severity with which he was treated, he was hung without trial, by the orders of Captain Albert.

This commander appears to have been of a stern, uncompromising, and perhaps tyrannical temper. Such, at least is the description given of him by those whom he ruled — a description not to be received without great caution, since it is made to justify their own violent and insubordinate conduct while under him. His usual treatment of his men was said to be harsh and irritating ; and, while they were yet aroused and angry because of his alleged injustice to Guernache, he added still farther to the provocation by degrading another soldier, a favorite of the people, named La Chere. This man he banished to a desert island about nine miles from the fort, and there

16. What dissensions took place among the French? 17. How did Captain Albert treat Guernache? 18. What was the character of Albert? 19. How did he treat La Chere?

left him to starve without provisions; his avowed desire being, that he should perish of hunger.

This tyranny of Albert, if truly reported, might well justify the mutiny which followed. A threat of the imprudent commander, to treat in like manner those who complained of this injustice, precipitated a revolt. The colonists conspired together, rose suddenly in arms and slew him. This done, they brought the banished La Chere back from his place of exile, where they found him almost famished. They then chose a leader from their own ranks, in the person of one Nicholas Barré, a man described by Laudonniere as worthy of commendation, and one who knew so well how to acquit himself of the charge of government, that all rancor and dissension ceased among them. Famine, and the loneliness of their condition, contributed to dispose them peaceably.

Hearing nothing from France, hope sickened within them, and they yearned to return to their homes. They resolved, finally, by unanimous consent, to leave the wilderness in which, however hospitable had been the natives, they had found little besides suffering and privation. Though without artificers of any kind, they commenced building a pinnace. Necessity supplied the deficiencies of art; and the brigantine rose rapidly under their hands. The luxuriant pine forests around them yielded resin and moss for calking. The Indians brought them cordage for tackle; and their own shirts and bed linen furnished the sails. The brigantine was soon ready for sea, and, a fair wind offering, the adventurers prepared to depart.

The Indians, to whom they left all their unnecessary merchandise, beheld their departure with a lively sorrow; while the poor colonists, themselves, "drunken with the too excessive joy which they had conceived for their returning into France, without regarding the inconstancy of the wind, put out to sea, and with so slender a supply of victuals, that the end of their enterprise became unlucky and unfortunate."

20. What followed among the people of the fort? 21. What was the fate of Albert? 22. What became of La Chere? 23. After Albert was slain, who was chosen leader? 24. His character? 25. What made the Huguenots despond? 26. What did they resolve? 27. How did they build and rig their vessel?

For a time, however, fortune smiled upon their progress. They had sailed, without mishap, a full third of their way, when they were surprised by a calm. For three weeks they made but twenty-five leagues; and, to add to their trials, their supplies failed them. Twelve grains of corn, daily, were made to answer the cravings of their hunger; and, even this resource, so carefully computed, lasted but a little while. Their shoes and leathern jerkins became their only remaining food, and death appeared among them, and relieved their misery by thinning their numbers.

The picture of their distress is not yet complete. " Besides this extreme famine, which did so grievously oppress them, they were constrained to cast the water continually out, which, on all sides, entered into their bark."

Each day added to their sufferings, so that, in the simple but strong language of the old chronicler, " being now more out of hope than ever, to escape this extreme peril, they cared not to cast out the water, which now was almost ready to drown them, and, as men, resolved to die, every one fell down backward, and gave themselves over altogether, to the will of the waves."

From this condition of despair, one among their number, the man La Chere, who had been exiled by Captain Albert, and who seems to have been of a character to justify the interest which his people took in his fate, was the first to recover. He encouraged them to take heart, saying they could now have but a little way to sail, and assured them that, if the wind held, they should make land within three days.

This encouragement prompted them to renew their efforts. They recommenced the task of throwing out the water from their sinking vessel, and endured for three days longer without drink or food. At the end of this time, seeing no land, they once more gave themselves up to despair. The want of food was their greatest evil, and the same person, La Chere, whose words had encouraged them so long, again came to their relief.

He proposed that one of their number should die for the

28. What sort of voyage had they? 29. What was they reduced to eat? 30. How did La Chere show himself a hero?

safety of the rest. The lot fell to himself; and, without struggle or reluctance, he bared his neck to the stroke. They greedily drank of his blood, while his flesh, distributed equally among them, enabled them to bear a little longer, until "God of his goodness, using his accustomed favor, changed their sorrow into joy, and showed unto them a sight of land. Whereof they were so exceeding glad, that the pleasure caused them to remain a long time as men without sense; whereby they let the pinnace float this way, or that way, without holding any right way or course."

In this state, they were picked up by an English vessel, which carried the few and feeble survivors of this expedition into England. Thus ended the first effort of the modern European world to found a permanent colony upon that portion of the continent of North America, which is now covered by the confederacy of the United States.

81. What was his fate? 82. What their fate, and whither carried?

# CHAPTER III.

## SECOND COLONY.—FORT CAROLINE.

MEANWHILE, a treacherous peace had been made between the imbecile Charles, and the Protestant portion of his subjects. This peace enabled Coligny to direct his attention to the forlorn colony which had been left in Carolina. Its fate was as yet unknown in France. To relieve the colonists, three ships were given for the service, and placed under the command of Rene Laudonniere; a man of intelligence, a seaman rather than a soldier, who had been upon the American coast in a former voyage, and was supposed to be the most fitting that could be chosen, from many offering, to lead forth the present colony.

Emigrants offered themselves in numbers; for Florida was, at this time, a country of romance. Men dreamed of rich mines of gold and silver in its bowels; they had heard truly of its fruits and flowers; and they believed, in addition, that, under its bland airs and genial influence, the duration of human life was extended. Laudonniere himself tells of natives whom he had seen, who were two hundred and fifty years old, yet had a reasonable hope of living forty or fifty years longer.

These idle fancies, which could only have found credence at a period when the wonderful discoveries of Columbus and other captains, had opened the fountains of the marvellous beyond the control of the ordinary standards of human judgment, readily stimulated the passion for adventure, and the armament of Laudonniere was soon rendered complete and ready for the sea.

A voyage of sixty days brought the voyagers to the shores of New France, which they reached the 25th of June, 1564.

1. How was Coligny at length enabled to send supplies for the colony at Fort Charles? 2. Who was sent to relieve the colony? 3. Who was Laudonniere? 4. What was then thought of Florida in Europe? 5. What does Laudonniere say of the age of the red men? 6. When did Laudonniere reach the shores of New France?

They proceeded to May river, were they were received by the Indians with the warmest shows of friendship.    They carried Laudonniere to see a pillar of stone which Ribault had set up in a former voyage, and the satisfaction of the Europeans may be imagined, when they beheld the pillar crowned with chaplets of laurels and other flowers, while its base was encircled with baskets of provisions, with which these generous children of the forest testified the unqualified warmth of their friendship for their strange visitors.    The Indians had learned glibly to pronounce the French word "ami," signifying "friend;" and with this word in their mouths, men and women followed in crowds the progress of the vessels, as they coasted along the shore, showing a degree of attachment for their visitors, which seems to have had the unusual effect of producing a corresponding kindness in return.

The French did not abuse a confidence so courteously expressed, and the future pages of this narrative, however painful to read where the dealings of the Europeans with each other are recorded, bear few evidences of that cruelty and wrong towards the red man which blacken so many of the histories of European conquest.

Laudonniere, after some delays, in which he seemed to have almost forgotten one of the objects of his voyage, resumed it and proceeded northwardly, until he received tidings of the fate of the colony he came to succor.    The news discouraged him in his design of visiting Port Royal.    He stopped short, and, for various reasons, resolved upon establishing his new settlement on the river May — the present St. John's in Florida. A small hill was chosen, a little retired from the northern bank of the river, upon which he erected the arms of France; and, with favorable auspices, springing rather from his hopes and fancies, than from any obvious superiority in the place of his choice over that which he had resolved to desert, he commenced the foundation of the second European fortress in North America.

7. Where did he land?    8. How did the red men receive him?    9. How did both parties behave?    10. Finding the colony of Fort Charles abandoned, where did Laudonniere found his new settlement?

The site chosen, though greatly inferior to that of Port Royal, had its attractions also. "Upon the top of the hill," in the warm language of Laudonniere, "are nothing else but cedars, palmes, and bay trees, of so sovereign odor, that balme smelleth nothing in comparison. The trees were environed round with vines, bearing grapes in such quantity, that the number would suffice to make the place habitable. Touching the pleasure of the place, the sea may be seen plane and open from it; and more than five great leagues off, near the river Belle, a man may behold the meadows divided asunder into isles and islets, interlacing one another. Briefly, the place is so pleasant, that those which are melancholick, would be forced to change their humour."

The objections to Port Royal, exaggerated by the disastrous termination of the first settlement, are fitly opposed to this glowing description. "On the other side," says the same commander, "if we pass farther north to seek out Port Royal, it would be neither very profitable nor convenient; at least if we should give credit to the report of them which remained there a long time, although the haven were one of the fairest of the West Indies. In this case the question is not so much of the beauty of the place, as of things necessary to sustain life. It is much more needful to us to plant in places plentiful of victual, than in goodly havens, fair, deep, and pleasant to the view. In consideration whereof, I was of opinion to seat ourselves about the river of May; seeing also, that in our first voyage we found the same only among all the rest, to abound in maize and corne, *besides the gold and silver that was found there; a thing that put me in hope of some happy discovery in time to come.*"

The fort was built in shape of a triangle; the landside, which looked westwardly, was faced by a little trench, and "raised with terraces, made in form of a battlement, nine foot high;" the river side was enclosed with "a palisado of planks of timber, after the manner that gabions are made." On the south side there was a bastion, which contained a room for the ammunition. The fabric was built of turf, fagots, and sand, and remains of this primitive fortress are understood to have been since discovered. When finished, it was named with all due ceremo-

11. How does he describe the place?   12. Describe the fort?

nies, La Caroline, in honor of the reigning monarch. The name thus conferred, extended over the whole country, a full century before it was occupied by the English. It remained unchanged, and was adoped by them, as it equally served to distinguish their obligations to Charles II., of England, under whose auspices and charter the first permanent European colony was settled in Carolina.

Like their predecessors, the colonists under Laudonniere, were well received and kindly treated by the natives of the country. At the first, this reception was natural enough. Pleased with the novelty of such an advent, the poor savages did not anticipate the constant drain upon their limited resources, which would follow the coming of the French. Simple and uncalculating, they did not reflect how inadequate would be the supplies of their little corn crops, to meet the wants of so many additional mouths; and it was only when their own utter impoverishment and famine ensued from their unwise hospitality, that they became conscious of their error. When they withheld their stores, the necessities of the strangers overcame all their scruples. Laudonniere took an unbecoming part in their petty wars, robbed their granaries, and made enemies of all around him.

The inevitable consequences of such a condition of things, ensued among the colonists. Disaffection followed, the authority of their leader was defied, and mutinous disorders became frequent. The emigrants to a new country, at its first settlement, are generally of a desperate complexion. Those under Laudonniere were particularly so. The civil wars through which they had just passed in France, had given them a taste for insubordination; and, appreciating their wants and habits, one La Roquette, a common soldier, conceived the idea of deposing his commander.

He claimed to be a magician, and pretended, by reason of his art, to have discovered a mine of gold or silver, at no great distance up the river. He invited his comrades to join with him

18. Its name? 14. What was the subsequent use of this name? 15. What was the conduct of the red men? 16. What of Laudonniere? 17. What of the colonists? 18. Who was La Roquette?

in effecting this discovery. He pledged his life on the issue. Some trifling acquisitions of silver which they had made, by trade among the Indians, strengthened his assurances, which soon became generally believed. He found an active coadjutor in another soldier, named La Genre, who had taken offence at Laudonniere, because he had been denied the command of the packet which returned to France.

These wretches conspired the death of Laudonniere; first by poison, then by an explosion of gunpowder. Their schemes failed, most probably through their own want of courage. Meanwhile, a Captain Bourdet arrived at the settlement, with an additional body of soldiers from France, which timely event perhaps, restrained the more open development of hostility.

Laudonniere, thus strengthened, seized this occasion to examine into the conduct of La Genre, who had shown himself the most active among the discontents. The chief officers were assembled for this purpose, but the criminal fled to the woods, and took shelter with the Indians.

After the departure of Bourdet, the conspirators, no longer restrained by the presence of numbers, resumed their evil practices. Availing themselves of the sickness of their commander, they put themselves in complete armor, and under the guidance of three ringleaders, Fourneaux, La Croix, and Stephen le Genevois, they penetrated his chamber and seized upon his person. Depriving him of his arms, they carried him on board ship, where they extorted from him, under the most atrocious threats, a sort of passport or commission for the seas, which they immediately employed to cover a premeditated course of piracy.

They then seized two of his vessels, and departing for the West India islands, where they succeeded in capturing the governor of Jamaica, and possessing themselves of considerable wealth besides. They demanded a large sum for his ransom, and in order to procure it, permitted him to send messengers to his wife.

The wily governor contrived, by the same messengers, to apprise the captains of his vessels, of his true situation. They

19. Who was La Genre? 20. What did these men conspire to do? 21. What of their schemes? 22. What arrested them? 28. Who were the new conspirators? 24. What did they to Laudonniere? 25. What afterwards?

came to his relief, and so completely were the pirates ensnared, that the governor, with all his ships and treasure, was rescued from their possession. One only of the French vessels escaped under the guidance of the pilot, who had been forced by them from Fort Caroline, and who, without their knowledge, carried her back to May river.

Want of food compelled the pirates to return to the commander whom they had deserted, and the opportunity thus afforded for avenging his own wrong, and punishing the criminals against his authority, was not suffered to escape. Four of the chief conspirators were seized, condemned, and executed, as an example to the rest; and this summary justice done, the discontents and strifes of the colony were ended for a brief period.

Laudonniere was soon after this relieved from some of the cares of his government. Ribault arrived from France in command of a well-appointed fleet, and with a commission to supercede him. Some mutual distrusts and jealousies between the two commanders, were reconciled after a friendly explanation, but the former, though offered equal authority with Ribault, resolved on yielding up his charge.

His successor had scarcely commenced his duties, before he was beset by dangers of a new and formidable character. His fleet had been closely followed from Europe by one under the command of Pedro Melendez de Avilez, a Spanish captain of great renown at that period, a bigoted religionist, but an able soldier. In the command of a far superior force to that of Ribault, Melendez seemed to be advised of all the movements of the latter; and it is the conviction of most historians, that his master, the king of Spain, had been duly informed by Charles IX. of France, that the Huguenot interest in the new world was one which it did not concern him to maintain. The indifference, at least, of the one Catholic monarch, readily surrendered to the tender mercies of another, a people who had audaciously withdrawn themselves from that spiritual control of Rome, which they both equally acknowledged. There is no question that the

26. How were their piracies arrested? 27. What was their fate? 28. Who succeeded Laudonniere in the government? 29. What enemy followed Ribault from Europe? 30. Who was Pedro Melendez? 31. By what European powers was his hostility to the Huguenots encouraged?

Spaniards knew of all the movements, objects, and strength of armament of the Huguenot commander.

Melendez was chosen to conduct an enterprise which was considered of equal importance to the interests of church and state. The French colonists were Protestants, and they were supposed to be trespassers upon a territory to which, under the general name of Florida, the Spaniards asserted an exclusive title. Melendez was invested with the swelling title of a Spanish Adelantado. The hereditary government of the Floridas was conferred upon him, and, at the call of the church, three thousand men volunteered to crowd his armament, which consisted of nearly twenty vessels.

But, deserted by their earthly monarch, the Huguenots were for a time, indirectly, the care of heaven. The fleet of Melendez was met by storms, and his force lessened ere he reached the coasts of Florida, to one third of its original strength.

This disaster, however, did not lessen the confidence of the Spaniard in his own fortune, and the bigotry of his soul gave a degree of enthusiasm to his resolve, which supplied the deficiencies of his armament. He rebuked the council of those who advised, in the shattered state of his vessels, and the diminished force of his crews, that for the present, the expedition should be abandoned. "The Almighty," said he, "has thus reduced our strength that his own may more completely do the work."

Sailing along the coast, he discovered a fine haven and beautiful river, to which he gave the name of St. Augustine, and where he subsequently founded the noble fortress of that place. Continuing his route northwardly, he discovered a portion of the fleet of Ribault. The French, as he approached, demanded his name and object.

. "I am Melendez of Spain," was the reply: "I am sent with strict orders from my king, to gibbet and behead all the Protestants in these regions. The Frenchman who is a Catholic I will spare — every heretic shall die."

82. Why? 83. What government and title were conferred upon him by Spain? 84. What befel his fleet at first? 85. How did he endure its disasters? 86. What did he say in respect to them? 87. How did he name the river which he discovered? 88. What said he to Ribault when the two fleets first encountered?

# CHAPTER IV.

### FATE OF FORT CAROLINE.

THE language of this reply, the uncompromising hate which it expressed, and the threat which it conveyed, struck terror to the hearts of the Huguenots. Feebler in numbers than their foes, and unprepared for battle, such as remained in the ships resolved upon flight. The approach of evening, while it prevented them from doing so in the first moment of their alarm, saved them also, for the night, from their enemies. But, with the dawn of day, they cut their cables, hoisted sail, and stood out to sea. They were closely pursued and fired upon all day, but escaped by superior sailing.

Melendez returned to the harbor of St. Augustine, of which he took possession in the name of Philip II., whom he proclaimed monarch of all America, with the most solemn ceremonies of religion; and under the favoring auspices of partial success, the building of the town, the oldest now in the United States, was begun.

While the Spaniards were thus employed, the colonists at Fort Caroline were neither idle nor apprehensive. Ribault resolved upon the most manly alternative. He prepared to anticipate the assaults of the enemy, and seek Melendez at sea. Crowding his main strength into his vessels, he left but a small garrison behind for the protection of his women and children, the sick of the expedition, and the stores. The garrison under Laudonniere, did not exceed eighty men, and not more than twenty of these were effective. The heavy ships which had fled before Melendez, now joined Ribault, and the French com-

1. What was the effect upon the Huguenots of the reply of Melendez? 2. Upon what did they resolve? 3. What then did Melendez? 4. What ancient town did he establish? 5. What did Ribault resolve? 6. What force did he leave with Laudonniere at Fort Caroline?

mander proceeded south, with almost certain assurances of success.

He found the fleet of Melendez without its complement of men, who were on shore, and moored in a situation that seemed to make its fate inevitable. Two hours would have sufficed for its destruction, and would have placed in the hands of Ribault sufficient means for the annihilation of his enemy; but one of those sudden tempests, so common in those latitudes, suddenly arose, baffled his hopes, and drove his vessels down the gulf of Florida. The storm lasted from the first week in September to the beginning of the following month, and in that time the ships of Ribault were dashed to pieces against the rocks, full fifty leagues south of Fort Caroline. The men escaped only with their lives.

This disaster gave an entirely new aspect to the fortunes of Melendez. Without knowing the extent of Ribault's misfortune, he at least knew, from the violence and long-continuance of the storm, that many days must elapse before Ribault could return to his colony; and of this conviction he availed himself with that promptness and boldness which distinguished his character, and which had shown more worthily in the prosecution of any nobler object. With a fanatical indifference to toil, he led five hundred picked troops, overland through the lakes, wastes, and forests which divided St. Augustine from Fort Caroline, and had sheltered himself from sight in the forests which surround it, before Laudonniere had a suspicion of his having left St. Augustine.

Cruel and dark, if not strange, was the superstition which seems to have clouded the minds, and embittered the hearts of these stern adventurers. The massacre of the French as heretics, had been long before deliberately resolved upon. Solemnly, on bended knee in prayer to the Almighty, did they prepare themselves for this unhallowed sacrifice. From prayer they rushed to slaughter; the feeble garrison was surprised, and

7. How did Ribault find the fleet of Melendez? 8. What saved the latter? 9. What befel the fleet of Ribault? 10. What was the next enterprise of Melendez? 11. What was the dark fanaticism of Melendez? 12. What did he effect at Fort Caroline?

and dreadful was the carnage that ensued. The old, the sick, women, and children, were alike massacred. The humanity of Melendez, after the havoc had raged for some time, tardily interposed to save such of the women and the children under fifteen years, as still survived. But many of the garrison were preserved for a more terrible sacrifice. As if a distinct testimony were needed to show that this atrocious consummation of his crime was an act of faith, and a tribute to that gentle and benignant God who came only to propitiate and save. The living and the dying, after the fury of the fight was over, were hung together upon the boughs of a tree, and left to shrivel in the sun.

An inscription upon a stone beneath, declared the motive of this meritorious deed. "We do this," wrote the fanatic, "not to Frenchmen, but to heretics."

Nearly two hundred persons were massacred. A few, leaping from the parapet when all was lost, escaped into the woods. Among these were Laudonniere, Challus, and Le Moyne, a painter who had been sent out with the colony, with an especial regard to the exercise of his art. From these we gather the horrors of the scene, which was not yet finished. But whither should the fugitives turn? Death was everywhere around them; the forests had no refuge, the sea no hiding-place. "Shall we surrender to the Spaniards, and appeal to their mercy?" became the question among them. "No!" said Challus, "Let us trust in the mercy of God—we can not look for mercy to these men."

Unfortunately, there were some who refused to adopt this resolution. They had hopes that the tiger rage of their conquerors was already sufficiently glutted by the blood which they had drank. They gave themselves up, and shared the fate of their comrades. Those who followed the council of Challus, found their way to the seaside, and were received on board of two French vessels under the command of the son of Ribault, which had lingered in the harbor, and had dropped down the river beyond the reach of cannon, as soon as they discovered the

18. Of what crime was he guilty when he had overcome the garrison? 14. What inscription did he write over the men he murdered? 15. How many were massacred? 16. Who escaped? 17. Who was Le Moyne? 18. What said Challus? 19. What other massacre followed?

fate of the fort. Mass was said when the carnage was over; and while the earth was yet smeared and soaking with the blood of men made in God's likeness, the site was chosen for a church to be dedicated to God.

The work thoroughly finished, the butcher led his soldiers back to St. Augustine in all haste, as he feared the possible retaliation of Ribault upon that post. Of the fate of this unfortunate commander he knew nothing. ' Cast upon the shore with a small supply of provisions, and only in part provided with the weapons of defence, the Frenchmen were almost abandoned to despair. A long stretch of swamp and forest, filled with enemies, heathen and Christian, equally hostile and equally savage, lay between them and their hope of and supposed refuge. It remained for them only to reach Fort Caroline, or surrender themselves to the doubtful mercies of the Spaniards.

They resolved to go forward, and were divided into two bodies for this purpose. It is probable that thus divided they pursued different routes, with the view to the more easy procuring of their food.

One of these bodies, preceding the other, reached the banks of a small river twelve miles south of St. Augustine. Before they could procure the means of effecting the passage, they were encountered by Melendez at the head of forty soldiers. Then, for the first time, he learned the fate of Ribault's fleet.

The shipwrecked men were in a state of helpless weakness, half famished, subdued in spirit, wanting equally in food and water. Melendez invited them to rely on his compassion. His invitation was complied with. The French yielded by capitulation, and were brought across the river by small divisions, in a single boat. As the captives stepped upon the bank occupied by their enemies, their hands were tied behind them; a measure of precaution which probably did not alarm them, as they must have seen the smallness of the Spanish force. Two hundred were transported in this manner, and when brought together in the forests, at some distance from, and out of sight

20. Under what circumstances did Melendez choose a site for a church? 21. What was the condition of the shipwrecked French under Ribault? 22. How did they divide? 23. Where did the first division meet Melendez?

of their companions, who were yet to cross, "at a line marked with his cane upon the sand," and, at a signal from Melendez, they were set upon and butchered. Their carcasses were left unburied where they were slain.

A few days elapsed, when the remaining party, under Ribault himself, appeared at the same river, and were met, like the former, by the inveterate Spaniard. On this occasion, Melendez brought with him a more imposing force. A protracted negotiation followed, and a large ransom was offered by the Frenchmen; but Melendez deliberately pacing the river bank, and permitting the negotiators to come and go at their pleasure, yet varied nothing from his first expressed resolution. He required them to surrender at discretion. He is even said to have set food and refreshments before them, while meditating a cruelty toward them, like that which he had so inflexibly shown their comrades.

Ribault, himself, crossed the river with several of his officers, without restraint, but without moving the stern decision of the Spaniard. He was respectfully received, conducted to the plain, where the carcasses of the slaughtered party which preceded him lay bare to the elements, was informed of the manner of their fate, and of those left in Fort Caroline, and was still required to surrender at discretion.

It was in vain that these wretched men urged that, as the two monarchs of their respective countries were not only at peace, but in alliance, they could not be treated as enemies. The answer was, "the catholic French are our friends and allies; but, with heretics, I wage a war of extermination. In this, I serve both monarchs. I came to Florida to establish the Catholic faith. If you are satisfied to yield yourselves to my mercy, I will do with you as God shall inspire me. If not, choose your own course; but, do not hope from me either peace or friendship."

With this final answer, Ribault returned to his comrades. It is somewhat surprising, that a commander who has been reputed so brave as himself, should have been content to parley with such a monster, after so bold an avowal of his resolves, and after the unstinted revelation which he had made of the treatment of his former captives. It is still more a matter of surprise, that he should at length have delivered himself up, on any terms, to a wretch so bigoted and sanguinary. The exposure of the mangled corses of his countrymen, slain as captives, and under an assurance of mercy, should have provoked, in the surviving French, a resolution to incur any hazards, not merely in maintaining the possession of their arms, but in revenging their slaughtered brethren.

But fatigue and starvation subdue, in time, the boldest natures, and nothing, surely, but the sheer exhaustion of spirit and frame could have reconciled the unfortunate Ribault to the course which he subsequently adopted. Perhaps, indeed, he had some hope from the very audacity of Melendez. He fancied that the object of the Spaniard was to make the merit of his mercy the more — that he was already sated with blood — and simply insisted upon the hard terms which he proposed, for the gratification of a tenacious pride, which nothing short of unqualified surrender could well satisfy.

Whatever may have been the reasonings of the French commander, he resolved to submit himself, with one hundred and fifty of his followers, to his enemy; but, the remainder of his men, two hundred in number, determined, more wisely, to brave every form of danger rather than yield to one who had shown himself so merciless. A melancholy separation of this forlorn band took place. Ribault led his division into the hands of Melendez, and, being tied with ten others, suffered with the rest. The two hundred, who retained their arms, met with a milder fate. Returning to the wrecks of their vessels, they raised a temporary fortress for their defence, and proceeded to build a ship to effect their escape.

But their inhuman enemy was not willing to leave his work unfinished. He pursued them to their place of partial refuge. From this they were driven, and, flying to an elevated piece

28. How was Ribault supposed to reason upon this answer? 29. What was his fate?

of ground, they prepared for the last conflict, resolved to sell their lives dearly if they could not repulse their foe.

Their desperate demeanor and unyielding aspect, together with the advantage of their position, compelled Melendez to abate something of his inveteracy and hate.

A negotiation was opened, and they received a solemn assurance of security and kind treatment — an assurance which, in this case, was followed by no breach of good faith. But no assurance, however solemn, from those who had been so faithless before, could satisfy the commander of this little party. His name is not given us, but his unbending resolution of character merits every encomium. He resolved rather to trust the forest thickets, with their troops of savage men and savage beasts, than such monsters as the Spaniards had shown themselves. With twenty followers, who felt like himself, he separated from the larger company, and disappeared from sight. The Spaniards hunted the fugitives in vain. They were never heard of more. It is just possible that they found security among the red- men, in one of their gentler moods, and became amalgamated with their tribes. Those who received the protection of Melendez, either established themselves in Florida, or found their way, at a remote period, to their several homes.

The French writers assert, that Ribault was flayed alive, his body burnt, and his stuffed skin sent to Europe, as a worthy trophy of the conqueror, and a fitting tribute to the Christian and throned barbarians who then ruled over half the world. The number of the victims is computed at nine hundred. The Spanish authorities diminish this number, but not the atrocity of the deed. Melendez returned to Spain, impoverished but triumphant. He was well received by his sovereign, to whom his services had been of so grateful a character; and his only human punishment, so far as the knowledge has been obtained, is the infamous notoriety which has followed the record of his deeds.

80. Did any of his troop escape this fate? 81. What was the effect of their resolve to fight and not submit? 82. Was there still another party who did not accept terms of the Spaniards? 83. What is supposed to be their fate? 84. What do the French writers assert of the cruelties of Melendez, and the extent of his massacres? 85. How was Melendez received, on his return to Europe?

## CHAPTER V.

### VENGEANCE OF DE GORGUES.

THE tidings of these dreadful massacres, when they reached France, awakened everywhere, save at court, a burning sentiment of indignation. Thither, they carried an odor, such as was offered to the kingly nostrils by the bloody fumes of a like massacre, on the day of St. Bartholomew. The French government heard, with apathy, if not with satisfaction, of an outrage which offended the moral sense of Christian Europe. It did not even offer a remonstrance on the destruction of a colony, which, if maintained, would have given to France an empire in the new continent, before England had yet founded a plantation.

But the feeling of the court was not that of the nation. The people, Catholic no less than Protestant, burned with the desire for vengeance, which they were yet compelled to smother. This sentiment was, at length, embodied into form, and found utterance in the deeds of a gallant Gascon.

The Chevalier Dominique de Gorgues — the very personification of intense heroism and a noble nature — rose up to redress his murdered countrymen and his insulted country. He was a Catholic, born at Mont Marsan, county of Cominges. His youth had been passed in warlike enterprises, and his reputation, as a subaltern officer, was not surpassed by any in France. His life had been a series of surprising adventures. He had passed from service to service, and won reputation in each. He became the captive of the Spaniards, while fighting against them, in Italy; and, his obstinate valor, which would

1. What was the effect upon the French court when these tidings of massacre reached the country? 2. What was the feeling among the people? 3. Who finally embodied the popular feeling in form and action? 4. Who was the Chevalier Dominique de Gorgues? 5. What had been his fortunes?

have met with the admiration of a generous enemy, received but chains from his Spanish captors. He was consigned to the galleys, and was rescued from its oars only to fall into another form of bondage. The prize, in which he rowed, was taken by a Turkish corsair. Redeemed from Algerine slavery, he returned to his country in season to revenge its wrongs. His own treatment, at the hands of his Spanish captors, may have helped to warm his indignation.

By the sale of his property, and the voluntary contributions of his friends, he found means for the equipment of a small fleet of three vessels. With a crew of one hundred and fifty men, he sailed from Bordeaux, on the twenty-second of August, 1567, disguising his real purposes from the public, by the avowed intention of engaging in the slave trade, on the coast of Africa.

Such was the nature of the commission under which he sailed; and, the object which he afterward pursued, seems to have remained entirely unsuspected. De Gorgues, however, had contrived to secure the services of one of the soldiers who had escaped, with Laudonniere, from Florida. When fairly at sea, he declared his true purpose to his soldiers. He painted, in glowing language, the wrongs of his countrymen—the brutality of the Spaniards—the cries of the thousand widows and orphans whom they had made in France—their prayers unheeded—their injuries unredressed. His speech, which is preserved, is a fine specimen of manly eloquence and patriotism. It had the desired effect upon his men. With one voice, they adopted his resolution. They declared their wish to follow him and avenge the murder of their countrymen, and the dishonor done to France.

De Gorgues, himself, had but the one object. He did not seek to colonize; his force was too small for that. But it was sufficient, under his guidance, and moved by his spirit, for the purposes of destruction. Nor was his vengeance long delayed. The shores of Florida soon after rose in sight, and so entirely unsuspicious of danger were the Spaniards, in possession of

6. What did he resolve? 7. How did he equip his fleet? 8. When did he sail, and whence? 9. What was his speech to his followers? 10. What was his single object?

La Caroline, that they gave the fleet of De Gorgues a salute, as it appeared. This salute he returned, the better to confirm them in their dangerous security; and, passing on to the river, by the French, called the Seine, he entered it, and came to a landing with his men.

Here, he was soon discovered by a formidable body of the savages, headed by no less than eight of their principal chiefs. They recognised the French costume and language, and their delight was unmeasured. Before De Gorgues could declare his purpose, they denounced the Spaniards, as well for their murders of the French, as for their own repeated wrongs to themselves, and declared their desire to destroy them.

So desirable an alliance was at once accepted. They were provided with pikes, swords, and daggers, and at once embodied with the French, though still under the command of their own warriors—one of whom, named Olotocara (Holata Cara), greatly distinguished himself, in the assault upon the Spanish forts.

These were three in number; that of La Caroline being strengthened by two similar structures, immediately contiguous. De Gorgues made his approaches with the coolness of a veteran. He sent forth spies, both French and Indian, and regulated his assault by their reports. The defences of the Spaniards were very complete, and, but for the surprise which they experienced, and the terror which they felt at an exaggerated report, which had reached them of the numbers of the French, the results might not have been so favorable to the cause of vengeance.

The two small forts were carried by storm, and the men, not slain in the assault, were carefully reserved for the final sacrifice, which De Gorgues meditated from the first. The avenues, leading to La Caroline, were then occupied by the red men, so that there remained no possibility of escape for the fugitives. This done, De Gorgues proceeded to a deliberate survey of all the difficulties of the enterprise. He soon discov-

11. Where did he land in Florida? 12. What co-operation did he find? 13. Who was the leader of the red men? 14. How did De Gorgues make his approaches to the forts of the Spaniards? 15. How were the two smaller forts carried?

ered that the place must be carried by escalade. It was defended by three hundred men, under a valiant governor, had a large number of culverins, and other cannon, of various sizes, plentiful supplies of ammunition, and provision in abundance.

While the French — having retired to a wood, for shelter from the Spanish cannon, which began to play upon them warmly from the moment when they came in sight — were preparing their ladders for the escalade, the governor of the fort precipitated his own defeat. Under an excess of valor, he imprudently sallied forth, with sixty of his men, and had advanced but a little distance, when he found himself suddenly surrounded by the French, under De Gorgues and his lieutenant, Cazenove, who cut off his return, and slew his party, to a man, on the spot where they were encountered.

The besieged, who beheld this exploit, now left without a commander, were so terrified by the event, that, in their panic, they fled from their defences, and sought shelter in the neighboring thickets. But here they were met by the Indians, under Olotocara, who drove them back upon the French. Death encountered them on all sides, and those who survived the conflict were reserved for a more distinguished and more cruel fate. They were conducted, with those taken at the smaller forts, to the trees on which Melendez had hung the Frenchmen, under Ribault, and suspended to the same boughs. Taking down the inscription of Melendez, De Gorgues put another, much more appropriate, in its place. "I do this," said the writing — which was impressed by a searing-iron upon a pine plank — "I do this, not to Spaniards, nor Catholics; but to traitors, robbers, and murderers."

The victor had sternly carried out his resolution of vengeance. He had proved himself as inflexibly just as he was merciless, since the victims had been the offenders, or had so far approved and participated in the crime for which they were punished, as to leave us little occasion for rebuke or

16. How was La Caroline defended? 17. Of what imprudence was its governor guilty? 18. What was the fate of the sortie which he led? 19. What was the effect upon the garrison of the success of De Gorgues? 20. What fate did De Gorgues reserve for the captives? 21. What was the inscription which he substituted for that of Melendez?

regret. It is, perhaps, only by a terrible retribution like this, that guilt is taught to pause in the career of crime, to doubt its own security, and forbear the deed of blood which may waken up such an avenger.

Having set forth on this single purpose, its completion left the generous Gascon little more to do. He had no selfish objects of conquest or colonization. The stern and undivided desire of his mind was satisfied; and, razing to its foundation the fort which had been the theatre of such a sanguinary story, he returned to France to receive, not the honors and rewards of its monarch, but persecution and exile. The court of France refused its countenance to his deeds; and, pursued by the malignant hostility of Spain, he found a home in Portugal, where he was invited into honorable, and, to him, grateful service, in the wars then waging, by that country, against the Spaniards; but he died of wounded pride, and a painful sense of the ill treatment of his sovereign, ere he entered upon foreign service. His memory can not be forgotton, and his adventures might well become a story of their own.

22. How did France receive the avenger of the Huguenots, and what of his death?

# BOOK II.

## THE CAROLINAS UNDER THE LORD-PROPRIETORS.——ENGLISH.

——•——

## CHAPTER I.

### FIRST SETTLEMENT OF THE ENGLISH ON ASHLEY RIVER.

THUS ended the ill-fated and badly conducted expeditions of the French to Carolina, and the initial attempt of Coligny to provide, in the wildernesses of the new world, a refuge from the tyrannies and persecutions of the old. France not only disowned the expedition of De Gorgues, but relinquished all pretensions to Florida. Spain and Britain continued to assert their claims upon the territory, but the former alone maintained her possession of it.

But the massacres, which De Gorgues had avenged, aroused, in Protestant England, a feeling of indignation, like that which it had awakened in Catholic France. Her eye was drawn to a region, of which tales, equally bloody and attractive, had been told. The wrecked survivors of La Caroline had been, as we will remember, carried into England, and had their story to tell of the country. Sir John Hawkins, besides, a famous English navigator of this period, had visited the colony, under Laudonniere, and could and did make his report, also, of the character of the country, and the imbecility of the French colony.

Walter Raleigh, then fighting the battles of the Huguenots, on the continent, under the banners of Coligny, listened with a keen ear to the strange narratives which, on every hand, he heard of the wild and picturesque regions of Florida. From

1. Did France renew her attempt to colonize in Florida? 2. What nation continued to assert their rights in that territory? 8. How was England roused to the work of colonization? 4. What of Sir John Hawkins? 5. What of Walter Raleigh?

the ideas and feelings thus awakened in his mind, we may trace that passion for adventure in the new world, which led him to the shores of North Carolina.

He obtained a patent, in March, 1584, for such lands as he should discover, not in possession of any Christian prince or people, and sent out two ships the month following. They reached the shores of the western continent, which saluted them with a fragrance which was " as if they had been in the midst of some delicate garden, abounding with all kinds of odoriferous flowers." They ranged the coast, for one hundred and twenty miles, in search of a convenient harbor, entered the first haven which offered, and, landing on the island of Wokoken, the southernmost of the islands forming the Ocracocke inlet, took solemn possession of the country, in the name of the Virgin Queen.

The crews were landed on the fourth day of July; a day that has since been made to distinguish a national epoch in America. A colony was established, and the new continent, for the first time, received the English name of North and South Virginia. All lands lying toward the St. Lawrence, from the northern boundary of the Virginia province, belonged to the northern, and all thence to the southward, as far as the gulf of Florida, to the southern district.

The colony of Raleigh failed, after a painful but short existence of a few years. The settlers disappeared, and no traces of their flight were found, and no knowledge of their fate has ever become known to the historians. They probably sank, under the united assaults of famine and their Indian neighbors.

English discovery now became continuous along the coasts of the continent. The shores, bays, headlands, and harbors, of New England, were successively discovered; and, in 1607, under the genius of the celebrated John Smith, the first permanent colony of England, in America, was planted at James' River.

6. What was the date of his patent for discovery? 7. Where did his ships go? 8. Of what lands did the English take possession, and when? 9. How did they name them? 10. What became of this colony? 11. Where, and when, was the first permanent English colony established, in America?

In 1620, a settlement was effected in New England; and, ten years after, a grant was made to Sir Robert Heath, attorney-general of Charles I., of all that region which stretches southward of the Virginia coast, from the thirty-sixth degree of north latitude, comprehending the Louisiana territory, on the Mississippi, by the name of Carolana. It is said that Sir Robert conveyed his right to the earl of Arundel; that this earl planted several parts of the country, and afterward conveyed his title to a Doctor Cox, who was at great pains to establish his pretensions, explored a part of the country, and subsequently memorialized the crown on the subject of his claims. Heath's charter was, however, declared void, because of the failure of the grantees to comply with certain of its conditions; and, for thirty years after, the territories of Carolina remained unsettled.

At length, in 1663, Edward, earl of Clarendon, and several associates, formed a project for planting a colony there. They obtained from Charles II. a charter conveying all the lands lying between the 31st and 36th degrees of north latitude. The charter states that the applicants, " excited by a laudable and pious zeal for the propagation of the gospel, beg a certain country in the parts of America not yet cultivated and planted, and only inhabited by a barbarous people, having no knowledge of God."

This was the pious pretence of the time, which seems, as a matter of course, to have furnished the burden of every such prayer. It may be said in this place that the efforts were but few and feebly sustained, to promote the professed objects of the memorial. The chartists, beside the earl of Clarendon, were George, duke of Albemarle; William, lord Craven; John, lord Berkeley; Antony, lord Ashley; Sir George Carteret, Sir William Berkeley, and Sir John Colleton.

Neither of these noblemen was of a character to warrant the supposition that any pious purposes entered seriously into their plans for the settlement of their colony. Clarendon, though

12. When was the first settlement made in New England? 13. At what time, and of what region, was a grant made to Sir Robert Heath? 14. Why was his charter declared void? 15. What was the next English charter?—when? 16. To whom?

shrewd and sagacious as a politician, was of a mean, covetous nature; the duke of Albemarle was George Monk, famous for the part which he took in the restoration of the Stuarts — a soldier and selfish politician; Craven was a brave old soldier, but neither a good Christian nor a philosopher; Ashley-Cooper, afterwards earl of Shaftesbury, the most highly endowed, intellectually, of all the proprietors, was a subtle mercurial statesman — a restless intriguer, unstable in aim, and faithless in principle and conduct; Colleton was a royalist, but one of no distinction; the two Berkeleys, Lord John and Sir William — the latter better known as governor of Virginia, were wrong-headed and obstinate personages; Carteret was neither too wise nor too honest.    They represented the cavaliers of that day; but these had sadly degenerated from the period when Charles the First took the field against his subjects.    They were only so many rapacious courtiers, seeking a selfish object, and without either the capital to achieve or the capacity to design a plan of colonial establishment, which should answer their own desires.

The grant which they obtained, comprised a territory of which, subsequently, the several states of South Carolina, North Carolina, and Georgia were composed.    Two years after this grant, it was enlarged by a second, making its boundaries from twenty-nine degrees of north latitude to thirty-six degrees and forty seconds, and from these points on the seacoast westward in parallel lines to the Pacific ocean.

Of this immense region, the king constituted them absolute lords and proprietors, reserving to himself, his heirs, and successors, the simple sovereignty of the country.    He invested them with all the rights, jurisdiction, royalties, privileges, and liberties within the bounds of their province, to hold, use, and enjoy the same, in as ample a manner as the bishop of Durham did in that county-palatine in England.    The Bahama islands were subsequently included in the gift of the monarch.

17. What was the extent of territory which it covered ? 18. By what king conferred ? 19. For what avowed objects ? 20. How are the lord-proprietors described ? 21. What further grants were made them ? 22. What rights did the charters confer upon them ? 23. What was the reservation of power to the crown ? 24. What islands were afterwards included in the grant ?

Agreeably to these powers, the proprietors proceeded to frame a system of laws for the colony which they projected. Locke, the well-known philosopher, was summoned to this work, and the largest expectations were entertained in consequence of his co-operation. Locke, though subsequently one of the proprietors, was, at the beginning, simply the secretary of the earl of Shaftesbury. The probability is, that, in preparing the constitution for the Carolinas, he rather carried out the notions of that versatile nobleman than his own. It may be doubted if his agency extended much beyond that of one chosen as a ready writer to express lucidly a scheme of government which was somewhat chaotically conceived.

The code of laws called the "Fundamental Constitutions," which was devised, and which subsequently became unpopular, in the colony, is not *certainly* the work of his hands. It is ascribed by Oldmixon, a contemporary, to the earl of Shaftesbury, one of the proprietors. The most striking feature in this code provided for the creation of a nobility, consisting of landgraves, cassiques, and barons. These were to be graduated by the landed estates which were granted with the dignity; the eldest of the proprietary lords was to be the superior, with the title of Palatine, and the people were to be serfs. Their tenants, and the issue of their tenants, were to be transferred with the soil, and not at liberty to leave it, but with the lord's permission, under hand and seal.

The whole system was rejected after a few years' experiment, It has been harshly judged as the production of a feeble intellect — the crude conception of a mind conversant rather with books than men — with the abstract rather than the practical in government and society. And this judgment is certainly true of the constitutions in the case in which they were employed. They did not suit the absolute conditions of the country, or the class of people which subsequently made their way to it. But contemplating the institution of domestic slavery, as the proprietors had done from the beginning — a large villanage and a wealthy aristocracy, dominating almost without restraint or re-

25. What is said of Locke's agency? 26. Who is supposed to have formed the code of government? 27. What were the chief features of this code? 27. What is said of it?

sponsibility over the whole — the scheme was not without its plausibilities. But the feudal tenures were everywhere dying out. The time had passed, even in Europe, for such a system; and such could only have been successfully established in the wildernesses of the new world by great wealth, supported by power and the presence of the lord-proprietors themselves. But neither of these was willing to risk his person in the enterprise, and their European necessities left them little wealth to expend. The settlers were generally poor, and the nobility created for the occasion, and from the people, was deficient in all those marks of hereditary importance, which, in the minds of men, are found needful to disguise, if not to justify, the inequalities of fortune. The great destitution of the first settlers left them generally without the means of procuring slaves; and the equal necessities, to which all are subject who peril life and fortune in a savage forest and on a foreign shore, soon made the titular distinctions of the few a miserable mockery, or something worse.

Having devised their plan of government, however, the proprietors began to advertise for settlers, though nothing seems to have been seriously done towards emigration till some time after. A colony was formed upon the river Albemarle, and another at Cape Fear; the last of these two was conducted from Barbadoes, by John Yeamans, afterwards made a baronet, and many of these colonists subsequently found their way to the settlement of Ashley river.

In 1667, an exploring ship was fitted out, and the command given to William Sayle, who was simply commissioned to survey and give some account of the coast. Sayle seems to have been nothing but a sailor. In his passage, he was driven by a storm among the Bahamas, of which he acquired some useful knowledge. By his representations of their value to Carolina, as places of retreat or defence against the Spaniards, the proprietors obtained an additional grant of them from the king.

He sailed along the coast of Carolina, observed several navigable rivers, and a flat country covered with woods. He at-

29. Of the proprietors? 30. Where did they first form colonies? 31. When was Sayle sent out? 32. Whither did he go?

3

tempted to go ashore in his boat, but was discouraged by the
hostile appearance of the savages on the banks.   His report,
on his return to England, was, however, so favorable as to prompt
the energetic action of the proprietors.   Two ships were put under his command, a number of adventurers were embarked, and,
well provided with utensils for building and cultivation, together
with arms and munitions of war, the little armament sailed in
January, 1670.   Twelve thousand pounds was the sum (not
very extravagant, surely) expended on this venture.

The fame of Port Royal, of which the name conferred by
Ribault remained in use among the English, was remembered
at this time; and to this river Sayle directed his course.   He
safely reached his port, and proceeded with all due diligence to
establish himself.   The foundations of a town and government
were laid at the same time.   A parliament was composed and
invested with legislative power.   Already were the laws of
Shaftesbury and Locke departed from; and, deeming it impracticable at the very outset, to execute the model which had
been given them, they determined to follow it as closely as they
could.   As an encouragement to settle at Port Royal, one hundred and fifty acres of land were given, at an easy quit-rent, to
every emigrant; and clothes and provisions bestowed upon all
who could not provide for themselves.   The neighboring red
men were conciliated by presents and pledges of friendship
freely exchanged with their cassiques and warriors.   Here
Sayle died in the midst of his labors, having fallen a victim to
the climate or to fatigue in a warm region, and under unusual responsibilities.

This event happened in less than a year after his arrival.   It
led to the extension of the command of Sir John Yeamans,
who had hitherto ruled the northern plantation about Cape
Fear over that of Sayle; and, gathering the planters together,
"from Clarendon on the north, from Port Royal on the south,"
he resorted, "for the convenience of pasturage and tillage," to
the banks of Ashley river.   There were, probably, other rea-

33. Did he make a settlement?  34. When was he sent out for this purpose, and
with what armament?  35. Where did he first settle?  36. What encouragements
were held out to the colonists?  37. What was their intercourse with the red men?
38. What happened to Sayle?  39. Who succeeded Sayle?

sons which prompted this change of locality. Port Royal was too near the Spanish settlements and too accessible from the sea, while Spain was a great maritime power.

This removal took place in 1671, and in the same year, "on the first highland," was laid the foundations of that settlement which we now distinguish as Old Charlestown.

For some years, this became and continued the capital of the southern settlements; but, as the commerce of the colony increased, the disadvantages of the position were discovered It could not be approached by large vessels at low water. In 1680, by a formal command of the proprietors, a second removal took place, the government literally following the people, who had in numbers anticipated the legislative action; and the seat of government was transferred to a neck of land called Oyster Point, admirably conceived for the purposes of commerce, at the confluence of two spacious and deep rivers, the Kiawah and Etiwan, which, in compliment to Lord Shaftesbury, had already been called after him, Ashley and Cooper.

Here the foundation was laid of the present city of Charleston. In that year thirty houses were built, though this number could have met the wants of but a small portion of the colony. The heads of families at the Port Royal settlement alone, whose names are preserved to us, are forty-eight in number; those brought from Clarendon by Yeamans could not have been less numerous; and the additions which they must have had from the mother-country, during the seven or eight years of their stay at the Ashley river settlement, were likely to have been very considerable.

Roundheads and cavaliers alike sought refuge in Carolina, which, for a long time, remained a pet province of the proprietors. Liberty of conscience, which the charter professed to guaranty, encouraged emigration. The hopes of avarice, the

40. Why was Beaufort abandoned? 41. Whither did the colonists go, and when? 42. What were the objections to the new settlement on Ashley river? 43. By what name is that site now known? 44. Whither was the colony removed, and when? 45. After whom were the two rivers called? 46. What city was founded between these rivers? 47. How many houses were built the first year? 48. What is conjectured of the number of inhabitants? 49. How was emigration from Europe encouraged?

rigor of creditors, the fear of punishment and persecution, were equal incentives to the settlement of this favored but foreign region.  Groups of settlers, following favorite leaders — the victims of some great calamity ; or the enthusiastic, under some general impulse — were no less frequent than individual emigrants.

In 1674, when Nova Belgia, now New York, was conquered by the English, a number of the Dutch from that place sought refuge in Carolina.  The proprietors facilitated their desire, and provided the ships which conveyed them to Charlestown.  They were assigned lands on the southwest side of Ashley river, drew lots for their property, and founded a town which they called Jamestown, but which they afterwards deserted, and spread themselves throughout the country, where they were joined by greater numbers from ancient Belgium.

Two vessels filled with foreign, perhaps French, Protestants, were transported to Carolina, at the expense of Charles II., in 1679 ; and the revocation of the edict of Nantz, a few years afterwards, by which the Huguenots were deprived of the only securities of life, liberty, and fortune, which their previous struggles had left them, contributed still more largely to the infant settlement, and provided Carolina with some of the best portions of her growing population.  The territory which had been soaked with the blood of their countrymen, under Ribault and Laudonniere, was endeared to them, probably, on that very account ; and they naturally turned their prows to a region which so great a sacrifice had so eminently hallowed to the purposes of their liberty and worship.

In 1696, a colony of Congregationalists, from Dorchester in Massachusetts, ascended the Ashley river nearly to its head, and there founded a town, to which they gave the name of that which they had left.  Dorchester became a town of some importance, having a moderately large population and considerable trade.  It is now deserted ; the habitations and inhabitants have alike vanished ; but the reverend spire, rising through

50. In what year and what event brought the Dutch to Charleston?  51. What people came in 1679 ?  52. By whom sent ?  53. What other settlement was made on Ashley river in 1696 ?—where and by whom ?  54. What has been the fate of this settlement ?

the forest trees which surround it, still attests (1840) the place of their worship, and where so many of them yet repose.

Various other countries and causes contributed to the growth and population of the new settlement. After the Restoration, the profligacy of English morals led to constant commotions between the two still great parties of cavaliers and puritans. The former sought to revenge themselves for the hardships which they had suffered during the Protectorate. Having obtained the ascendency, they retaliated by every means which the partiality of the law, or the evil temper of the court toward the puritans, would allow. The latter were uniformly encountered with contempt, and commonly with injustice, and ardently wished for some distant retreat to which they might fly and be secure.

To prevent open strife between these parties, Charles the Second encouraged emigration. Grants of land in Carolina were the lures by which the turbulent were beguiled from home; and hundreds of dissenters, with their families, embracing the proffer, transported themselves to the infant colony. At a later period, the wild, roystering cavaliers, who could not be provided from an exhausted treasury in England, received grants; and the spectacle was no less strange than grateful to behold these parties mingling peacefully in Carolina, who had seldom met but in deadly hostility at home.

Emigrants followed, though slowly, from Switzerland, Germany, and Holland; and the Santee, the Congaree, the Wateree, and Edisto, now listened to the strange voices of several nations, who, in the old world, had scarcely known each other except as foes. These, for a while, mingled harmoniously with the natives;—the French Huguenot and the German Palatine, smoked their pipes in amity with the Westo and the Serattee; and the tastes and habits of the Seine and the Rhine, became familiar to the wondering eyes of the fearless warriors along the Congaree. It was not long before a French violinist had opened a school for dancing, among the red men on the Santee river.

55. What brought the English dissenters to Carolina? 56. What the cavaliers? 57. What other countries contributed to the increase of the colony? 58. How did they live together? 59. What first did the French settlers attempt to teach to the red men of Santee river?

## CHAPTER II.

THE COLONY UNDER THE GOVERNORS, YEAMAN AND WEST,
1670–1682.

THE settlers of Carolina, thus accumulated from so many and, sometimes, conflicting European nations, entered upon their new enterprise with industry and spirit. They seem to have been of a singularly elastic and cheerful temper of mind. At all events, we may assume, for their several parties, a lead ership, distinguished by character, courage, and a direct, manly, good sense, and conservative temper. They could never else have withstood and triumphed over the oppressive influences of the climate, and the constant strifes of near and numerous savages. Though comparatively strong in numbers, by the frequent accession of emigrants, as already shown, they were yet feeble in many of those elements of national strength, in which the best securities of a people are to be found. A common necessity had brought them together; but, when the pressure of external dangers was withdrawn, it was not found so easy for them to harmonize. They were then apt to fall apart; to revive old dislikes — the result of their several European pre-judices — and, if they did not join in actual hostility, to pursue differing objects and interests, which had all the effect of open strife upon the welfare of a small colony.

Many of them were dependants upon the bounty of others; most of them were poor; and, all of them, were so placed — an isolated community, in a savage land — as to need, for a time, at least, the continual and fostering providence of foreign patronage. This necessity, of itself, led to new weaknesses and much humiliation, from which they were only relieved by

1. What is said of the settlers of Carolina? 2. How long did they continue to min-gle and work together harmoniously? 3. What was their condition?

the withdrawal of the reluctant bounty, upon which they had been too willing to depend. This unmanly disposition received its first and becoming rebuke from the proprietors, in a letter, which announced to them their resolution to bestow no more " stock and charges upon the idle."—" We will not," were the words of this epistle, " continue to feed and clothe you without expectation or demand of any return."

Thus, fortunately, forced upon their own resources, the Carolinians received that first lesson of independence which, perhaps, has done much toward giving them that high rank among their countrymen of the sister states, which can not be denied them. A sense of mortified pride co-operated with their necessities to make them address themselves, with earnestness, to their labors. They proceeded to fell the forests, and clear their fields, with a hearty resolution, which, while it amply atoned for past remissness, as sufficiently guarantied the realization of every future good.

New settlers, in all countries, are subjected to many hardships; but those of Carolina seem to have equalled, if they did not surpass, everything of the kind to which men, in any age, have ever been subjected. To subdue the forest to the necessities of civilized man; to build habitations, and clear the ground for raising provisions, while it is always the first, would seem, also, to be the sufficient employment of the emigrant. In a low, flat country, and under a climate so sultry as that of Carolina, the burden of such labors must have been greatly increased. The Europeans soon sank under the fatigue of laboring in the open air, in the low latitudes, and those diseases which are peculiar to level countries, overflowed with water, and subject to the action of a constant, burning sun, soon made their appearance among them, to diminish their strength, enfeeble their spirits, and lessen their numbers. To enhance the evils of such a condition, they were surrounded by Indian enemies, who were eminently irritable and warlike, and who daily became more jealous of the encroachments of their white neighbors.

4. What was the language of the lord-proprietors ? 5. What was the consequence of this language? 6. What were their hardships? 7. What their dangers from the climate? 8. From the red men ?

Carolina is said to have been occupied, at its first settlement, by no less than twenty-eight Indian nations. Perhaps we should speak more justly to describe the larger number of these as mere tribes; the offshoots of the several nations of Muscoghees, Catawbas, Cherokees, Chickasaws, and Choctaws. Their settlements extended from the ocean to the mountains. The Westos, Stonos, Coosaws, and Sewees, occupied the country between Charleston and the Edisto river. They were conquered by the Savannahs, and expelled from the country. The Yemassees and Huspahs held the territory in the neighborhood of Port Royal. The Savannahs, Serannas, Cussobos, and Euchees, occupied the middle country, along the Isundiga, or Savannah river. The Apalachians dwelt at the head-waters of the Savannah and Altamaha, and gave their name to the mountains of Apalachia, and the bay of Apalachicola. The Muscoghees, or Creeks, occupied the south side of Savannah and Broad rivers — the latter, being, at that time, called the Cherokee — and, by this river, they were divided from the Cherokees, a formidable nation, which dwelt upon the territory now included in the districts of Pickens, Anderson, and Greenville. The Congarees, Santees, Waterees, Saludahs, Catawbas, Pedees, and Winyahs, lived along the rivers which bear their names. The Chickasaws and Choctaws dwelt, or roved, westward from the borders of Carolina, to the banks of the Mississippi.

As already said, we should speak more correctly to describe the greater number of these nations, as merely tribal, and some of them as rather wandering over, than dwelling permanently within, the territory. They belonged to a few mighty families which occupied the vast and measureless interior. They were tributaries of one or other of the several nations of Muscoghees, Cherokees, Catawbas, Choctaws, and Chickasaws,

9. By what nations, or tribes, of red men was the country inhabited? 10. What were their several territories? 11. What are the characteristics of the red men? 12. What of the Westos, Stonos, Coosaws, and Sewees? 13. What became of them? 14. What territory did the Yemassees inhabit? 15. What the Huspahs? 16. What tribes skirted the Savannah river? 17. Where dwelt the Apalachians? 18. Where the Muscoghees? 19. What river separated their territory from the Cherokees? 20. What districts have been made from Cherokee territory?

among which the territory of the Carolinas was divided, and, perhaps, frequently disputed. These Indians, united, could probably bring fifty thousand men into the field. The Muscoghees and Catawbas were the most warlike races *within* Carolina ; the Cherokees were as numerous as either, and, perhaps, more civilized, but not esteemed so brave. The Choctaws and Chickasaws seem to have been less stationary than these tribes, and, most probably, resembled those roving bands of the west, who drew their stakes and changed their habitations with the progress of the seasons.

To the infant colony of Carolina, these nations, or the tributary tribes which owned their sway, suggested constant alarm and danger. The Westo and Stono tribes, as they were most contiguous, seem to have been the most troublesome. Their assaults were doubly dangerous and annoying, as it was found so difficult to provide against them. The superiority of the musket over the bow and arrow, in a dense and primitive forest, was very small. Concealed in the thicket, of which he has almost grown a part and is a native, the Indian launches his shaft ere the European has dreamed of the presence of an enemy. Its leaves hide him from the aim, and its mighty trees effectually shield him from the bullet which the angry stranger sends in reply. He ranges the woods in safety, while the invader sleeps ; and the swamps, in the atmosphere of which European life stagnates and perishes, yield a congenial element to him.

Thus circumstanced, in connection with their Indian neighbors, the Carolinians were compelled to stand in a continual posture of defence. While one party slept, an equal number watched. He who felled the tree of the forest, was protected by another, who stood ready with his musket in the shade ; and so persevering were his stealthy enemies, that the settler dared not discard his weapon, even while gathering the oyster

21. Give the places of abode of Congarees, Waterees, Santees, Saludas, Catawbas, Pedees, and Winyahs. 22. Of the Chickasaws and Choctaws. 23. Which of these were the most powerful ? 24. What the number of their warriors ? 25. Which nation was most warlike ? 26. Which were most wandering ? 27. Which most troublesome ? 28. What of the difference of warfare between white and red men ? 29. What of the toils and perils of the whites ?

on the shores of the sea. From the woods he was almost wholly exiled, by reason of the swarms of foes which infested them ; and, but for the fish from the rivers, the colonists must have perished of famine. Their scanty crops were raised, not only by the sweat of their brows, but at the peril of their lives ; and, when raised, were exposed to the plundering assaults of the foe. A single night, frequently, lost to the farmer the dearly bought products of a year of toil.

It is no easy matter to describe the dreadful extremities to which the Carolinians were, at last, reduced by their close neighborhood with the hostile red men. A civil disturbance was the consequence, which threatened the ruin of the colony. Robbed of the slender stock of grain, which their fields had produced, and failing to receive supplies from Europe, they were ready for any measure to which the phrensy of despair might prompt them.

Where·a people are discontented, there will not be long wanting some unruly spirit to take advantage of their sufferings, and stimulate their sedition ; and one Florence O'Sullivan, to whom the island, at the entrance of the harbor, which now bears his name, had been intrusted for defence, deserting his post, joined the discontents of the town ; and the popular fury might have expended itself in violence and bloodshed, but for the prudence and firmness of Sir John Yeamans, the governor.

O'Sullivan was arrested on charges of sedition, and the people, for the time, were quieted, while vessels were despatched, for supplies, to Barbadoes and Virginia. A timely arrival from England, bringing provisions and a number of new settlers, revived the spirits of the people, and cheered them to renewed efforts. Yeamans, sensible of their hardships, readily forgave their commotions ; but Culpepper, the surveyor-general, and a member of the common house of assembly, who had stimulated their excesses — a man afterward prominent in an alleged insurrection in North Carolina — was sent to England to be tried for treasonable conspiracies against the settlement. Culpepper was saved by the testimony of Shaftesbury,

20. What of Florence O'Sullivan ?  21. What of Culpepper ?

who did not scruple at a falsehood, for the safety of one, who, according to some of the historians, was a patriot, resisting an unjust and unwise usurpation, and who, at worst, simply anticipated the revolutionary spirit of 1776.

While these events were in progress, a new enemy started up, to add to the many dangers and annoyances of the Carolinians. The Spaniards, at St. Augustine, had long regarded the settlement of the English at Ashley river, as an encroachment upon the dominions of their monarch. Perhaps, they remembered the ancient conflicts between Ribault, Laudonniere, and Melendez, for supremacy, in the same neighborhood; and, as if the massacres, which they had caused and suffered, had confirmed the right to the soil, which they founded upon the discoveries of De Leon and De Soto, they watched the colony of the English with a keen disquiet, proportioned to their hostility.

Having obtained a knowledge of the miserable condition of the Carolinians, and the discontents which prevailed among them, they advanced, with a well-armed party, to dislodge and destroy the settlers. They reached St. Helena, where they were joined by one Brian Fitzpatrick, a worthless traitor, who had deserted the colony in the moment of its greatest distress, and who now exposed its weaknesses to the invaders. The Spaniards continued to advance, under his guidance; but, in the meantime, the vessel, bringing supplies of men and munitions of war, fortunately arrived in Ashley river.

This re-enforcement enabled the governor to assume the offensive. He despatched, with his ship of war, fifty volunteers, under colonel Godfrey, to meet the invaders; but the Spaniards did not await his attack. They fled at his approach, evacuating St. Helena island, of which they had obtained full possession, and retreated, with all haste, to Augustine. This attempt of the Spaniards, though conducted with little spirit, and distinguished by no combat, was the prelude to a long suc-

82. What of the Spaniards? 83. What feeling did they entertain for the English, at Ashley river? 84. Upon what did they found their claims to the country? 85. Did they assail the settlement, and where? 86. Who betrayed the colony? 87. What was the result of their invasion?

cession of conflicts, between the two colonies, resulting in mutual invasion, and unprofitable and unnecessary loss of blood and treasure.

To conciliate the Indian tribes, and escape from that harassing and constant warfare which they had waged upon the colony, from the beginning, was now the chief object of Governor Yeamans. But, one circumstance, at this time, contributed, more than anything beside, to the peace of the settlement. The Westos, who had always harbored the most unconquerable aversion to the whites, and who were doubly dangerous, from their near neighborhood, were suddenly invaded by the Serannas, a powerful tribe, living on the Isundiga river. A war followed between them, which was waged with so fatal a fury, as to end in the almost complete annihilation of both. The Carolinians, without doubt, as a matter of policy, encouraged the hostile temper of the combatants; at all events, they found security from its continuance, and were finally rid of two fierce neighbors when it ended.

In 1674, under the administration of Sir John Yeamans, the Fundamental Constitutions were formally proclaimed to the people. Hitherto, the colony had been living under a temporary government, rather military than civil, which employed but few of the provisions of that model code, whether of Shaftsbury or Locke, which had been devised for it, from the beginning. But now, the population having, as it was thought, sufficiently increased and expanded, and the lord-proprietors earnestly desiring to put their favorite plan into execution, the more elaborate system was now made of force. The people were assembled, accordingly, and the Constitutions declared to them as so much law, and not submitted for adoption. Under their authority, the province was divided into four counties, called Berkeley, Colleton, Craven, and Carteret. But Colleton and Berkeley, alone, were considered to be sufficiently populous to need or deserve representation, and ten members of assembly were chosen from each.

38. What was the result of their invasion? 39. What of the Westos and Serannas? 40. When were the Fundamental Constitutions formally declared? 41. How was the province subdivided?

This duty done, Sir John abandoned the colony, and went to Barbadoes, where he died. His administration had its partisans and assailants, in nearly equal degree. By one side, his labors for the success of the settlement are spoken of as indefatigable. By another, he is described as unjust, and tyrannical.

He was succeeded by Joseph West, as governor, and, under his rule, the freemen of the colony were called together, at Charlestown, for the purpose of making laws for their government, according to the Fundamental Constitutions. The upper and lower houses of assembly were formed, and, with the governor as its head, took the name of parliament. This was the first parliament in the colony that proposed acts, of which the proprietors approved, and which are on record in the colony.

It might have been expected that this parliament, composed of men embarked in the same vessel, and having a common interest, would be particularly zealous to maintain harmony and a friendly understanding among themselves. They had the same interests to promote and the same enemies to fear. Unhappily, such was not the case. The most numerous party in the country, were dissenters, of various denominations, from the established church of England. Affecting, always, a superior sanctity, these people have been seldom found the most docile and subordinate members of the community. A large share of self-esteem distinguished their intellectual organization, and occasioned constant discontents with the existing authorities, and a restless impatience of control.

The cavaliers, who had also received grants in Carolina, were regarded by the proprietors, who were chiefly noblemen, with a more favoring eye. Though lively, impetuous, and given to excesses of various kinds, a taste for which had been engendered by the civil wars, in the time of the first Charles, and the Protectorate, they were yet regarded as men of loyalty, honor, and fidelity.

The puritans, who remembered them only as deadly enemies,

42. Where did Sir John Yeamans die ? 43. By whom was he succeeded ? 44. What is said of his administration ? 45. What was the conduct of the parliament, under West ? 46. What was the most numerous party in the colony ? 47. What is said of the cavaliers ? 48. What of the puritans ?

in England, were vexed to see them lifted into places of honor, in Carolina. The odious terms and ungracious epithets, of the old world, were soon revived in the new, among both parties; and, but for the prudence of Governor West, who, in the business of legislation, studiously discouraged every discussion of religious subjects, the bitter fruits of such dislikes and differences would have been renewed in a region, to the government of which the utmost tolerance had been decreed by the proprietors, from the beginning of their enterprise.

The differing manners and habits of the colonists, furnished another cause for the absence of harmony among them. The puritans were a sober, inflexible, morose people; hostile to amusements, without carefully discriminating between them — rigid in form — resolute to make no concessions, and tenacious, to the last degree, of those leveling opinions, which were held in particular dislike by the cavaliers. They denounced the vices and debaucheries of the latter, censured their freedom of deportment, their ill-timed levities; and, exasperated by their licentiousness, and unconcealed scorn of themselves, labored, with equal industry and malevolence, to keep them out of power, and abridge their influence and authority.

The cavaliers were not less active in their hostility, nor less careful to display their dislike. They ridiculed the puritans with a wit as reckless as it was unsparing, and employed all their influence in exposing them to public derision and contempt. Their contentious dispositions, and leveling notions, were denounced as deserving of the abhorrence of all men of honor — as having served to produce, in England, that race of sly, deceitful, and hypocritical wretches, which had been the scourge of the nation.

This war increased the animosity of both parties, daily; and, though the governor endeavored to arrest its violence, and subdue its virulence, the pernicious effects were soon perceptible, in the difficulty that arose in framing laws, distributing justice, and maintaining public tranquillity. His council being composed entirely of cavaliers, was a check upon his own ability.

49. Which party was most favored by the proprietors? 50. Which predominated in government?

In spite of his authority, the puritans were treated with neglect and injustice; and, the colony, distracted with domestic evils, not only failed to make that progress in fortune which its natural advantages promised, but became ill-prepared to protect itself against those enemies which threatened it from without. Briefly, all the struggles of parties in England were renewed in Carolina; the one, tenacious of prerogative; the other, restless and feverish, with vague desires for more liberty, and a more equable government.

The Stonos, at this unfavorable juncture, appeared along the settlements, and, in detached bodies, assailed the plantations, from which they carried the grain as soon as it ripened. The savages, everywhere, have deemed it the less laborious policy to rob the civilized, than to encounter the labor and risk of planting for themselves. The stock of the Carolinians shared the fate of their grain crops, and the apprehensions of famine, from which they suffered in the time of Yeamans, were renewed, under the government of West.

That gentleman, however, employed a new branch of policy in revenging and repairing the sufferings of his people. The planters were armed in defence of their possessions, and, in the war that ensued, which was waged, by the Stonos, with singular hate and perseverance, it was found necessary to fix a price upon every Indian brought in as a captive.

The savages, thus taken, were shipped to the West Indies, and sold as slaves. This mode of getting rid of cruel and treacherous enemies, however justified by ancient practice, has, latterly, been deemed more barbarous than taking their lives.

The planters, of that day, did not even see the necessity of vindicating themselves against such a charge, and their descendants seem to have grown up in the same faith. Without discussing the propriety of the policy which they pursued, it may be enough to say, that it was attended with the desired results. The Stonos were defeated, after a long and obstinate conflict. Their name, alone, remains to distinguish the site of their former habitations.

50. What effect had the distractions of party upon the prosperity of the colony? 51. What enemy appeared at this time? 52. What policy was adopted in the war with the Stonos? 53. What became of the Stonos?

# CHAPTER III.

## FROM 1682 TO 1696.

A PARLIAMENT was held, in Charlestown, at the close of 1682, when laws were enacted for establishing a militia system ; for making high roads through the forest ; for repressing drunkenness and profanity ; and, for otherwise promoting a proper morality among the people.  In the year following, Governor West was removed from office, and Joseph Morton, who had just before been created a landgrave of Carolina, succeeded to his place.

West had displeased the proprietaries, by introducing the traffic in Indians — a traffic which, because of its profitable results, seemed likely to be perpetuated among the planters ; and by curbing the excesses of the cavaliers, who formed the proprietary party, in opposition to the less loyal, or more turbulent members of the puritan faction.

With his removal, commenced a course of rapid changes in the government of the colony.  Two parties had arisen, as far back as 1674, on the first creation of a parliament, the general direction of whose principles undoubtedly came from the social and religious bias which they had each received from their conflicting relations in England.  One of these endeavored to maintain the prerogative and authority of the proprietaries ; the other contended for the rights and liberties of the people.

The cavaliers, or court party, insisted upon implicit obedience to the laws received from England ; the puritans contended, and with perfect justice, for the right to adapt their laws to the existing circumstances of their condition.

In this state of things, no set of officers could maintain their

1. When was a parliament held in Charlestown ?  2. What laws were enacted ? 8. Who succeeded West as governor ?  4. Why was West removed ?  5. What did the cavaliers and puritans severally contend for ?

places long. Neither party could be quite satisfied with the administration of affairs. In the short space of four years, from 1682 to 1686, there were no less than five governors: Morton succeeding West; West again displacing Morton; and being followed, in turn, by Sir Richard Kyrle, an Irishman, by Robert Quarry, and James Colleton.

Morton assembled a parliament, which established a variety of regulations, some of which were displeasing to the proprietaries. It enacted a law for raising the value of foreign coins, by which the currency of Carolina was first regulated; and suspended all prosecutions for foreign debts; a measure which was negatived by the proprietaries, whose own interests might have suffered from such an enactment, and which they declared contrary to the king's honor, as obstructing the proper course of justice.

Another cause of dispute, between the proprietors and the people, arose from the manner in which the parliament was constituted. The province, at this time, was divided between the three counties of Berkeley, Craven, and Colleton. Berkeley filled the space around the capital; Craven (including the district lately called Clarendon), lay to the northward; and Colleton contained Port Royal, and the islands in its vicinity, to the distance of thirty miles.

Of the twenty members, of whom the parliament was to be composed, the proprietaries desired that ten should be elected by each of the counties of Berkeley and Colleton. Craven was still deemed too inconsiderable to merit any representation.

Berkeley, which contained the metropolis, was the only county which, as yet, possessed a county court; and, the provincial government having appointed the election to be held at Charlestown, the inhabitants, by reason of their greater numbers, succeeded in excluding Colleton from all representation, and in returning the whole twenty members.

6. How many governors filled the office in the space of four years? 7. What laws were passed by the new parliament? 8. Did these laws, or any of them, displease the proprietaries? 9. How was the province divided? 10. Describe these localities, severally. 11. Of how many representatives was the parliament? 12. From what counties chosen? 13. Why none from Craven? 14. Which contained the metropolis? 15. What was the result of holding the election in Charlestown?

This enraged the proprietors, who dissolved the parliament, but without effecting any present remedy against the injustice of numbers.   Governor Morton, harassed by the strifes among the people, resigned his office.   His authority was conferred on West, whose policy, favoring the traffic in Indians, rendered him a very popular person among the colonists.   But he was not suffered to continue long in office.   Sir Richard Kyrle, was then intrusted with the government, by the proprietaries; but he died soon after his arrival in the province.

West, thereupon, was again chosen, but was soon superseded by Colonel Quarry, who kept the capricious station but a year. He was found, or suspected, to have afforded some countenance to piracy; was removed, in consequence, and the landgrave Morton once more reinstated in the government.

In the offence imputed to Quarry, the community had its share.   Indeed, it was one of the excesses of the time; a seeming sanction for which was to be found in particular circumstances.   Pirates were licensed by Great Britain, to cruise against the Spanish fleets, in the American waters; there being, in the phrase of the day, "no peace beyond the line." The king of England had even conferred the honors of knighthood upon one of the worst villains of the class.

The enormities, committed by the Spaniards, in all quarters of the new world, and upon all people, Christian and savage, seemed, in the eyes of other nations, to justify a corresponding treatment of themselves in turn.

But the pirates did not confine themselves to Spanish vessels; else, it is probable, that they might still have pursued their excesses with impunity, in the waters of Carolina.   There, the ports were freely opened to them, provisions supplied, and they were received as the favored guests of the planters.   The hostility entertained by these reckless rovers against the Spaniards, the mortal foes of the Carolinians, was, perhaps, the true reason of the countenance which they found among

16. What effect had this on the proprietors?   17. Why did Governor Morton resign?   18. Who succeeded to Morton?   19. Who succeeded West?   20. Who succeeded Kyrle?   21. Who succeeded Quarry?   22. What was the offence imputed to Quarry?   23. Why were pirates licensed by England?   24. What seemed to justify this practice?   25. Why were the pirates tolerated in Carolina?

the latter. It suggests the only reason which may serve, in some degree, to justify the colonists for the favor which they showed them. The governor, the proprietary deputies, and the principal inhabitants, are said to have equally stained themselves with this unbecoming intercourse; and the obloquy, which they thus incurred, was only obliterated in the manly warfare, in which they subsequently drove them from their waters. Their feebleness may have made them sanction the presence of those whom they did not dare to offend; and the fact, that the pirates chiefly warred against their inveterate enemies, the Spaniards, constituted them, in one respect, very useful, if not worthy allies, whom it was their policy to encourage.

It is certain, in support of this view of the subject, that the Spaniards themselves, regarded, in this light, the countenance which the Carolinians showed the pirates. They beheld the enemies who had infested their shores, and destroyed their shipping, sheltered and received as friends in Ashley river; and, if no such policy influenced the Carolinians, they were, at least, required to atone, as allies, for the excesses of those whom they received with the kindness due to allies only.

Other circumstances contributed to this conviction, and strengthened the hostility of the people of St. Augustine. They had always beheld the settlements of the English with jealousy, and the establishment of a new colony, under Lord Cardross, a Scotch nobleman, at Port Royal, served to renew the ancient grudge, and furnished a new provocation to hostility. They invaded the southern frontiers of the colony, and descended, suddenly, upon the Scotch, at Port Royal, whom they expelled. Laying the settlements waste as they went, they as suddenly retired, ere men could be mustered to encounter them, or resent the inroad.

The spirit of the Carolinians, whom continued wars had made a martial people, was at once aroused by this aggression, and they resolved, with one mind, to carry their arms into the enemy's territory. An expedition was determined upon, and preparations begun for an invasion of Florida. But the pro-

26. What was the effect upon the Spaniards? 27. What did they achieve? 28. What was the effect of Spanish invasion upon the Carolinians?

prietaries hastened to arrest this purpose. They succeeded, for the time; but the angry feelings, which were brought into activity, on this occasion, were never suffered entirely to sleep; and they found their utterance but a few seasons after this event, when, under the government of a man fond of warlike enterprises, the colonists prepared to "feed fat the ancient grudge," which they bore against their hereditary foes.

James Colleton, a landgrave of Carolina, and brother of one of the lord-proprietors, succeeded to Morton. For a time, his administration gave universal satisfaction; but, an endeavor to carry out his instructions, renewed the old conflicts between the people and their lords, in all their original virulence and vigor. The progress of discontent in the colony soon assumed a mutinous aspect, and the first leading measure of the new governor resulted in the utter forfeiture of his power. He endeavored to make the people pay up their quit-rents, which had been suffered to accumulate, without liquidation, for several years. The amount was trifling; but other feelings than those of interest mingled in with the consideration of the subject. It was the display of authority, at a time when that authority was already under censure, for trespasses upon the public liberties; and, taught in the severe school of self-succor and self-providence, from the beginning, the great body of the Carolinians were disposed to resistance. This spirit became more turbulent with every show of rigor, on the part of the indiscreet landgrave; riots and commotions succeeded; the parliament was assembled, and, in 1690, in consequence of Colleton's proclamation of martial law, and the dispersion of his mutinous house of commons, the contest was brought to an issue. This resulted in the partial triumph of the people, the formal deposition of the governor, and his solemn banishment beyond the limits of the province.

The government was then usurped by one Seth Sothel, a factious person, who had been driven from the Albemarle (N. C.) settlement. Availing himself of the general hostility

29. Who arrested them in their plans of retaliation? 30. Who next became governor of Carolina? 31. How did Colleton displease the people? 32. What was the result of his quarrel with the people? 33. When was Colleton expelled the country? 34. Who usurped the government?

to Colleton, he found but little difficulty in securing the favor of the Carolinians, in the first moments of their anger. They used him, for a season, as a screen between themselves and government; and, having sucked the juice from the orange, readily threw away the skin. He claimed the government in the double right of a proprietor himself, and a champion of the popular liberties. But his pretences were soon set aside, and the excessive tyranny of his mis-rule effectually rebuked and punished the folly of those who so readily yielded to his arguments. He is said to have trampled under foot every restraint of equity and the laws; to have been as much without moderation as justice; and to have ruled the colonists with a rod of iron, far more heavy than that of Colleton. His whole course was one of rapine, and his coffers were filled by every species of plunder and exaction. The fair traders, from Barbadoes and Bermuda, were seized, by his orders, under pretended charges of piracy, and either incurred a forfeiture of their goods, or were compelled to purchase their ransom from prison by enormous fines. Felons bought themselves free from justice by heavy bribes, and the property of individuals was seized and confiscated on the most frivolous pretences. Fortunately, the career of Sothel was short. Proprietaries and people, alike, joined in his expulsion; and, pursued by the laws which he had offended, and the hate which he had provoked, he soon followed Colleton into banishment.

Philip Ludwell was now sent out by the proprietaries, to fill the vacated chair of the governor. He was accompanied by Sir Nathaniel Johnson, who had been governor of the leeward islands, and who, having determined to retire to Carolina, was appointed a cassique of the province, and a member of council.

Ludwell, who was a man of sense and humanity, commenced his administration in a manner that appeared to promise well for its continuance; but this promising appearance was of short duration. There was a continual warfare going on between the supposed interests of the proprietors and people; and the measures of any governor, or council, supposed to be favorably inclined to the one, were sure to give offence to, and excite the jealous opposition of, the other party. Ludwell had been instructed, by the proprietaries, to admit the French Huguenots, settled in Craven county, to the same political privileges with the English colonists.

Unhappily, these elder colonists were far from regarding their new associates with good will or friendly feeling. The number of the strangers, and the wealth which was possessed by some among them, excited their personal jealousies, and these soon awakened all the ancient antipathies of the nation. When Ludwell proposed to admit the refugees to a participation in the privileges of the other planters, the English refused to acquiesce. They insisted that it was contrary to the laws of England; that no power but that of the British parliament could dispense with the legal disability of aliens to purchase lands within the empire, incorporate them into the British community, or make them partakers of the rights of native-born Englishmen. They even maintained that the marriages of the refugees, performed by their own clergymen, were unlawful, as not being celebrated by men who had obtained Episcopal ordination. For themselves, they declared a determination not to sit in the same assembly with the hereditary rivals of their nation; or of receiving laws from those who were the pupils of a system of slavery and arbitrary government. The unfortunate refugees, alarmed at these resolutions, turned to the proprietaries to confirm their original assurances.

Ludwell was compelled to suspend the contemplated measure until he could hear from Europe; and, in the meantime, Craven county, in which the French refugees lived, was not allowed a single representative in the provincial parliament.

To the application of these unfortunate and truly worthy exiles, from whom we derive many of the first families of our state, and some of the first names of our republic, the proprietaries returned an indecisive but a friendly answer. They

40. What were Ludwell's instructions?　41. What prevented him from carrying out these instructions?　42. What was the determination of the English colonists?　43. What was the effect upon the French refugees?　44. How did Ludwell act?　45. In what county chiefly had the French refugees settled?

continued in a condition of the most painful solicitude, and an entire privation of their rights for several years after, when their patient and humane behavior prevailed equally over the political and personal antipathies of the English. Their former adversaries, won over by their praiseworthy gentleness of demeanor, advocated the pretensions they had hitherto opposed; and a law of naturalization was at length passed in favor of the aliens.

But the dispute that had arisen in the province on this subject was productive of excessive irritation against Ludwell, which was farther increased by his decisive proceedings against the pirates. The arrival of a crew of these wretches in Charlestown, where, relying on ancient privileges, they still hoped to be secure, afforded him an opportunity to endeavor, by the infliction of a tardy justice, to relieve the colony of some of the obloquy which rested upon its name. He apprehended the marauders, and brought them to trial for their crimes.

The people exclaimed against this proceeding, and interested themselves so effectually, that the criminals were not only acquitted, but the government was even compelled to grant them an indemnity. It was not till twenty years had elapsed, and a hecatomb of victims had been offered up to the laws which they had offended, that Carolina was at length fairly freed from these wretches, and the stain of their communion washed from her hands and garments. Farther conflicts followed between the people and their rulers, in which Ludwell seemed to yield to the wishes of the former. This awakened the anxiety of the proprietaries, who at length deprived him of his office, and conferred it, with the dignity of landgrave, upon Thomas Smith.

The administration of Smith, if more peaceable, was not more successful than that of his predecessor. A popular man — wealthy — himself a planter, and long a resident among the people, he commenced his government with the most favorable auspices; but the province still remained in a confused and turbulent condition. Discontent prevailed in the land; and, in

46. What was their conduct?   47. What law was passed in their favor?   48. What was Ludwell's treatment of the pirates?   49. Who succeeded Ludwell as governor? 50. Who was Landgrave Smith?

utter despair at last, he wrote to the proprietors, praying to be released from a charge which brought him nothing but annoyance, and in which he could hope to do no good. He declared, in his letter, that he despaired ever to unite the people in affection and interest; and that, weary of the perpetual warfare among them, he, and many others, were resolved upon leaving the province, unless they sent out one of their own number, with full power to redress grievances and amend the laws. Nothing else, it was his conviction, would bring the settlers to a condition of tranquillity.

The proprietors adopted the suggestion of Smith, and he was succeeded by John Archdale, a Quaker, and one of their number. The Fundamental Constitutions were surrendered to the dislike of the people, and were formally abolished after an experiment of twenty-three years had shown them to be utterly impracticable in the condition of the colony. The government of the people was now severed from the powers conferred by the charter. Archdale entered upon his work, therefore, with a judgment entirely untrammelled. His administration seems to have been a wise one. It was not distinguished by any incident of importance; it was peaceable, and received, as it merited, at its termination, the thanks of the colony, for the first time given to any of its governors. He improved the militia system, opened friendly communications with the Indians and Spaniards, discouraged the inhumanities of the former so effectually, as to induce them utterly to renounce the inhuman practice of plundering shipwrecked vessels and murdering their crews; and combined, with singular felicity, the firm requisites of the governor, with the gentle and simple benevolence of the Quaker. "Yet," says the historian Grahame, "how inferior the worldly renown of Archdale, the instrument of so much good, to the more cherished fame of his less efficient and far less disinterested contemporary and fellow secretary, William Penn!"

51. What did he advise the proprietors, and what was his opinion of the colony? 52. Who succeeded Smith? 53. What was the fate of the fundamental constitutions? 54. What was the character of Archdale's administration? 54. What is said of Archdale?

It may be added that, for the first time during his govern-ment, a regular administration of the ordinances of religion was introduced among the English of the colony. The Hugue-nots brought with them their holy men ; and hence, perhaps, the more gentle habits, and the wise forbearance, which distin-guished their conduct toward their opponents, in the long strifes and bitter enmities which encountered their claims to an equal participation of the few pleasant fruits of exile.

56. What was done for religion during his administration ? 57. What is said of the religious habits of the Huguenots ?

4

# CHAPTER IV.

## BLAKE'S AND JOHNSON'S ADMINISTRATIONS, 1696—1719.

AMONG other extraordinary privileges, the power had been granted to Archdale of appointing his successor in office. He chose Joseph Blake, a nephew of the celebrated British admiral, a man of great prudence and popularity. Blake governed the colony wisely and happily. Shortly after his elevation to office, a new code of Fundamental Constitutions was transmitted to Carolina from the proprietors; but this code commanded far less consideration than the first. It does not seem to have been even recognised by the provincial assembly.

Blake's administration, which lasted from 1696 to his death, in 1700, was a season of political calm. Yet it was only in consequence of a succession of calamities that the strifes of party were suspended. The pirates, whom a more severe application of the laws had driven from their old haunts in Carolina, now, 1696, turned their arms against the settlement and harassed its commerce. Several ships, belonging to Charlestown, were taken by them as they left the port, the crews sent on shore, and the vessels kept as prizes.

During the autumn of the same year, a dreadful hurricane inundated the town and threatened its destruction. The swollen sea was driven in upon the shores with such impetuosity, that several persons were overtaken by the waves and drowned. Much property and many lives were swallowed up by the ocean. This inundation was followed by a fire, which nearly reduced the town to ashes. The small-pox succeeded this last disaster,

1. What extraordinary privilege had been granted to Archdale? 2. Whom did he choose as governor? 3. How did Blake govern the colony? 4. How long did Blake's administration last? 5. What arrested the strife of party? 6. What of the pirates? 7. What disaster happened to the colony in 1696? 8. What followed the inundation?

and spread death and desolation through the colony.  Professional ignorance proved no less fatal than the disease.

Scarcely had the colonists begun to breathe from these evils, when a pestilence (so called, but no doubt yellow fever) broke out among them, and swept off, among numerous other victims, nearly all of the public officers and one-half of the legislature.  Few families escaped a share in these calamities.  Despair sat upon every countenance, and many among the survivors began to think of abandoning a colony which Providence seemed to distinguish by every sort of calamity.

But even these afflictions did not quiet the turbulence of party.  The Carolinians appear to have possessed a stubborn character and a restless impatience of authority, which soon prompted a forgetfulness of sorrow, and of the causes of sorrow.  In the political strifes of the colony, fire, flood, and pestilence were forgotten.  The old conflicts between the people and the proprietors, on the subject of their respective rights, were revived with all the ancient acrimony ; and the acquisition of Nicholas Trott, a lawyer and an able man, by the party of the former, contributed to their audacity in a degree corresponding to the addition which his intellect had given to their strength.

It is not necessary that we should dwell upon the thousand little causes of provocation on the one hand or the other, which helped hourly to widen the breach between the parties.  There was a native incoherency in the union of their fortunes — a mutual distrust, arising from a real or supposed difference of interests ; and the proprietary lords were soon taught a lesson, which was afterwards bestowed in like manner upon their monarch, that a people, removed three thousand miles from the presence of their rulers, can neither be protected by their care nor long enfeebled by their exactions.

With the administration of Blake, who died in the year 1700, ended the short term of tranquillity which had originated with Archdale's government.  The conflicts between the people and

9. What the fire ?  10. What was the effect of these calamities upon the colonists ?  11. What was the social evil among the colonists ?  12. What was the character of the colonists ?  13 Who was Trott, and how did he affect the people ?  14. When did Blake die ?

their feudal lords waxed wármer daily, with the growth of population, the developments of new interests, and the growing evidence of the inadequacy or invalidity of the foreign rule. Blake was succeeded by James Moore, a man of considerable talent and military enterprise, ambitious in a high degree, and an industrious seeker after popularity. He renewed the traffic in Indians, begun in the time of West, and prepared to avenge upon the Spaniards at St. Augustine the frequent attacks which they had made upon the Carolinians. A rupture between England and Spain at this time made that a legitimate enterprise, which, a few years before, had been arrested by the proprietors as wholly unjustifiable.

Moore checked the domestic quarrels of the Carolinians by the suggestion of this favorite expedition. Florida, he assured the people, would be an easy conquest. Her treasures of gold and silver were proposed as the rewards of valor. The wrongs which they had sustained from the Spaniards, were such as, when dwelt upon, were sufficient to warm them to the desire of vengeance.

His eloquence was successful, as well in the assembly as among the people. His proposition was adopted by a great majority, and, in spite of the earnest opposition of a prudent few, who could not be deceived by the brilliant picture of success which had been held up to the imaginations of all. Two thousand pounds sterling were voted for the service; six hundred provincial militia raised, out of a population of about six thousand persons; an equal number of red men were incorporated in arms with the whites; schooners and merchant vessels were impressed as transports to carry the forces; and, in the month of September, 1702, Governor Moore sailed from Port Royal, the place appointed for the rendezvous, upon an enterprise conceived in rashness and conducted without caution.

The Spaniards were suffered to know all that was going on, and were preparing for defence with quite as much industry as

15. How did his death affect the colony? 16. Who succeeded Blake? 17. What did he do as regards the red men and the Spaniards? 18. What were the relations of England and Spain? 19. What lures did he hold out to the colonists for embarking in war? 20. How did he prepare for war? 21. Of what materials was his army composed? 22. What was the character of his enterprise?

their foes were preparing for attack. They had laid up four months' provisions in the castle at St. Augustine, which was also strongly fortified, and had sent timely despatches to the West India islands for the succor of the Spanish fleets.

Colonel Daniel, a Carolinian officer of great spirit, with a party of militia and Indians, made a descent upon the town of St. Augustine by land, while the commander-in-chief pursued his way by sea. Daniel's arrangements were made with equal secrecy and promptitude; and he attacked, took the town, and plundered it, before the fleet of Moore appeared in sight.

Upon Moore's arrival, the castle was closely invested, but without success. The cannon of the invaders made no impression, and Colonel Daniel was despatched in a sloop to Jamaica for supplies of bombs and mortars of the necessary calibre.

But, during his absence, the Spanish fleet appeared at the mouth of the harbor, and Governor Moore was compelled to raise the siege. Abandoning his ships, he retreated by land to Charlestown, having, according to the historians, fled with a rapidity as unbecoming as his rashness had been unwise and improvident. Daniel, on his return, to his great surprise found the siege raised, and narrowly escaped being made captive by the enemy. This fruitless expedition entailed a debt of six thousand pounds upon the colony.

Notwithstanding the unhappy result of his first military enterprise, Moore, fond of warlike exploits, soon resolved upon another. The Apalachian Indians, who had been stimulated by the Spaniards to hostilities against the colony, now commanded his attention. Determined to chastise them, he raised a force of Carolinians and Indians, and penetrated into the very heart of their settlements. Wherever he went, he carried fire and sword, and struck a salutary terror into the souls of the savages. The Apalachian towns, between the Savannah and Altamaha, were laid in ashes, the country was ravaged, the people made captives, eight hundred of them slain, and the most hidden settlements of the enemy laid open to the devastation which followed at his heels.

This exhibition of power was productive of immense moral good to the Carolinians, in that quarter. It taught the savages a new lesson of respect for their arms, and prepared the way for the English settlements that were afterward planted along the rivers of the interior. The benefit was almost equally great to the commander of the expedition. His courage and conduct removed the discredit which his previous rashness had incurred, and he received the thanks of the proprietors and the people, for the important conquests which he had made. Apalachia, the country thus won by the arms of Carolina, became, afterward, successively, the colony and state of Georgia.

Moore was succeeded, in the government, by Sir Nathaniel Johnson. This gentleman had been a soldier from his youth. He had, also, been a member of the House of Commons, in England. He was, therefore, esteemed to be well qualified for his trust. So, in some respects. he was; but he was, at the same time, strongly opposed to the dissenting party, and a docile agent of Lord Granville, then the lord-palatine of Carolina, whose hostility to the same class of religionists was equally bitter and inveterate.

Under the instructions of this nobleman, Governor Johnson, by a variety of measures, succeeded in establishing ecclesiastical worship and government in the colony. He enacted two laws, by one of which the dissenters were deprived of all civil rights. By the other, he erected an arbitrary court of high commission, for the trial of ecclesiastical causes, and the preservation of religious uniformity in Carolina.

These laws drove the dissenters to desperation. They sent a special messenger to London, and their petition for redress was laid before the House of Lords, who were filled with surprise and indignation at the high-handed despotism of the proprietors. The queen (Anne), by recommendation of the lords, issued an order, declaring the laws, complained of, to be null and void; and promised to institute a process of *quo warranto* against the provincial charter; but this promise was never fulfilled.

An idea of the impolitic assumptions of the bigoted palatine may be formed, by a reference to the opinion which the House of Lords expressed, in their address to the queen. The law for enforcing conformity to the church of England, in the colony, they describe as "an encouragement to atheism and irreligion, destructive to trade, and tending to the ruin and depopulation of the province."

It was in the year 1706, that the intolerant policy of Lord Granville received this check; and, from that period, the dissenters were permitted to enjoy, not, indeed, the equality which they had been encouraged to expect, but simple toleration.

In the year following, an act of assembly was passed in South Carolina, for establishing religious worship, according to the forms of the church of England. The province was divided into ten parishes, and provision made for building a church in each, and for the endowment of its minister. Before this period, neither the proprietors nor the people seem to have done much, if anything, worthy of notice, in behalf either of education or religion among themselves. The lords-proprietors had given little heed to a subject which constituted one of the pious pretexts in the application for their liberal charter. On behalf of the Indians, whose moral culture had, also, been one of the avowed purposes of their benevolence, in the establishment of the colony, at first, nothing was attempted. For bread they had received a stone. The only European instructions that the savages received, were communicated by a French dancing master, who acquired a large estate by teaching them to dance, and play on the flute or fiddle.

But, just then, the minds of the Carolinians were somewhat

38. What opinion did the House of Lords express touching these proceedings? 39. What act, in respect to religion, was passed in 1707? 40. How was the province divided? 41. What had the lords-proprietors done for education and religion among the people? 42. What for the education and religion of the red men? 43. What was the character of the instructions which they received? 44. What, at this time, were the relations of England, France, and Spain?

diverted from their domestic, by the approach of foreign, troubles. A war, at this time, waging between the great European powers of England, France, and Spain, necessarily involved the fortunes and interests of their separate colonies. A plan was set on foot, by the joint forces of France and Spain, to invade Charlestown, and the Carolinians were summoned to their arms. Governor Johnson was a military man, and the several expeditions of a warlike character, in which the Carolinians had been engaged, had infused into them a very martial spirit. Fortifications were pushed forward with rapidity, ammunition procured, provisions stored; and industry, stimulated by zeal and valor, soon put the settlements, at Ashley river, in a tolerable state of defence. Fort Johnson was erected on James' island, to meet this exigency; redoubts raised at White Point, now the site of a charming promenade — the battery — no less beautiful than appropriately named; and, having completed their preparations, the Carolinians calmly awaited the appearance of the foe.

The invasion took place in August, 1706, and while the yellow fever was raging in Charlestown, and when its principal inhabitants had left the place for their plantations. A French fleet, under Monsieur Le Feboure, having procured succors from Cuba and St. Augustine, appeared before the harbor. Five separate smokes, which were raised by a corps of observation, at Sullivan's island, announced the number of vessels in the invading armament.

The inhabitants of the town were at once put under arms, by William Rhett, the colonel in command. Despatches were sent to the captains of militia, in the country, and Governor Johnson, arriving from his plantation, proclaimed martial law at the head of the militia.

His presence, as a military man, of known capacity and valor, inspired the citizens with confidence. His measures were calculated to confirm it. He summoned the friendly Indians, stationed his troops judiciously, gave his commands

45. How did these relations threaten the colony? 46. What was the conduct of Governor Johnson? 47. What was done for defence against invasion? 48. What fleet appeared, and who commanded it? 49. Who took command in Charlestown? 50. What did the governor?

with calmness and resolve, and, as the troops came in from the country, assigned them their places and duties with the composure of one who had long before adjusted his plan of resistance.

The neighboring troops came to the defence of the city, in numbers, and with alacrity. That same evening, a troop of horse, under Captain George Logan, and two companies of foot, commanded by Major Broughton, reached the capital. The next morning, a company from James' island, under Captain Drake, another from Wando, under Captain Fenwicke, and five more, commanded by Captains Davis, Cantey, Lynch, Hearne, Longbois, and Seabrook, from other parts of the province, made their appearance in the city, and, with the resident militia, comprised, at that time, the chief military force of Carolina. At this period, the whole population of the colony was estimated at about nine thousand souls; of whom five thousand were negro and Indian slaves. The militia was about nine hundred. Some great guns were put on board such ships as happened to be in the harbor, and the sailors were thus employed, in their own way, to assist in the defence of the city. The command of this little fleet was given to Colonel William Rhett, a man of resolution and address.

Meanwhile, the enemy having passed the bar, came to anchor a little above Sullivan's island, and sent up a flag to the governor, demanding his surrender. The messenger was received blindfold, and conducted into the forts, where Johnson had drawn up his forces so as to display them to the best advantage.

By transferring his troops from fort to fort, by short routes, the Frenchman was led to quadruple, in his estimate, the real numbers of the defenders. Having demanded the surrender of the town and country to the arms of France, the messenger concluded, by declaring, that his orders allowed him but a single hour in which to receive an answer.

Johnson answered, promptly, that it did not need a minute.

51. Who were the captains in arms for the colony? 52. What was the population and military force of the colony, at this period? 53. Who commanded the fleet? 54. What was the progress of the enemy? 55. What their demand? 56. What the reply of Johnson?

"I hold this country for the queen of England," said he; "I am ready to die, but not to deliver up my trust. My men will shed the last drop of their blood, to defend the country from the invader."

This answer, with the report of his messenger, seems to have lessened the spirit of Le Feboure. His fleet remained stationary; and, instead of attacking the city, he contented himself with setting on foot some predatory incursions into the contiguous islands.

The day following this interview, a party went ashore, at James' island, from which the militia had been withdrawn for the defence of the city. They committed some petty trespasses, and burnt the houses upon one or more plantations, but were soon driven to their boats by a detachment, under Captain Drake, who had been sent over to encounter them.

Another party, of near two hundred men, landed on Wando neck, and commenced similar depredations. While in a state of fancied security, they were surprised, before the break of day, by a detachment of one hundred men, under Captain Cantey. A sharp fire, from several quarters aroused them, in the same moment, to equal consciousness and confusion. Many were killed, some drowned, and more wounded. Those who escaped the attack became prisoners of war.

Meanwhile, Colonel Rhett, having got his little fleet in readiness, weighed his anchors, and moved down the river to where the enemy lay. But the French did not wait his assault. They escaped by superior sailing, and put to sea without suffering an exchange of shots.

After they had disappeared from the coast, a ship of force, with two hundred men, arrived to their assistance, and was seen in Sewee bay, where she landed a number of troops. This intelligence induced the governor to send Captain Fenwicke against them by land, while Rhett, with two vessels, sailed round by sea, with the view to prevent their escape by that quarter.

Fenwicke, though he found the enemy well posted, charged them gallantly, and drove them, after a spirited conflict, to their vessels. They fled from one foe only to encounter another. The movements of Rhett and Fenwicke had been so well concerted, that the ships of the former encountered the enemy in the bay, where she struck without firing a shot.

Thus ended this expedition of Monsieur Le Feboure, against Carolina, as much to his own discredit as to the honor of the Carolinians. Of eight hundred men, who came against the colony, nearly three hundred were killed and taken prisoners. Among the latter, was their chief land officer, Monsieur Arbouset, and several other officers.

Governor Johnson was a man of courage and spirit; the militia were men hardened to danger, by frequent encounters with the Spaniards, the pirates, and the Indians. They executed their commands with the promptitude and valor of men who fought for, and in sight of, their homes, their wives, and children; and realized those results which seldom fail to reward the warrior who bares his sword under the same sacred auspices.

63. What ship was captured? 64. How ended the invasion? 65. What was the secret of Johnson's success against the invader?

# CHAPTER V.

## 1708 TO 1719.—CIVIL STRIFES.—WARS WITH THE RED MEN.

COLONEL EDWARD TYNTE succeeded Sir Nathaniel Johnson in office, under commission from Lord Craven, successor, as palatine, to Lord Grenville, in 1708. Craven's policy favored the dissenters, as much as that of Grenville had discouraged them; but Tynte had scarcely time to learn the real state of the country, and to establish proper regulations in it, before he died.

At his death, a controversy arose, in the provincial council, about the succession, which had almost produced civil war, and did, for a brief period, array two strong parties in arms against each other. One of these declared for Robert Gibbs, the other for Thomas Broughton.

Broughton drew together an armed force at his plantation, with which he marched upon the town. There, he encountered a similar array, under the command of Gibbs, who manned the walls with the militia, and closed the gates against him. Aided by some of the inhabitants, who let down the drawbridge, Broughton, however, forced a passage and entered the city. After blows were exchanged, and wounds given, the party of Broughton prevailed, and marched toward the watchhouse, in Broad street. There, two companies of militia were posted. The prudence of some of the leaders interposed to prevent the bloody consequences of an issue; and, after vainly endeavoring to make himself heard, in the clamor of drum and trumpet which prevailed, Broughton led his men off in another quarter.

Some farther excesses were committed, but the results were

1. Who succeeded Johnson, as governor, and when? 2. Who succeeded Grenville, as palatine? 3. What was Craven's policy? 4. Who were the competitors for the local authority when Tynte died? 5. What was the strife between them?

less fatal than was to have been feared from such a conflict. Broughton was persuaded to withdraw his party, and it was agreed, between himself and Gibbs, that their several claims should be left to the proprietors for arbitrament. Their determination was in favor of neither. The office of governor was conferred upon Charles Craven, a brother of the lord-palatine, who was immediately proclaimed in form, and took upon him the administration.

Craven was a man of good judgment, prudence, courage, and integrity; and, mutual esteem in council, and harmony in the colony, followed his appointment. He improved the defences of the colony, cultivated the friendship of the neighboring Indians and Spaniards, and took especial heed to the equitable and prompt administration of justice. Under his direction, the harbor of Port Royal was sounded and examined, and the spot selected for the future erection of the town of Beaufort — so called, in honor of Henry, duke of Beaufort, afterward lord-palatine of the colony.

In the year 1712, the Indians of the northern province, the Corees, Tuscaroras, and other tribes, rose in arms, and united to destroy the colonists. They murdered John Lawson, surveyor-general of the colony, and large numbers of other settlers. Aid was implored from South Carolina, and Craven despatched six hundred men, under the command of Colonel Barnwell, to their relief.

·Hideous and wild, indeed, was the wilderness, at this time, through which Barnwell was compelled to march. Unbroken forests, unopened swamps, deep waters, and tangled thickets, lay in his path. Without roads, he could employ neither carriages nor horses, and yet, the utmost despatch was necessary, in order to save the North Carolinians from their bloody enemies. In spite of every difficulty, Barnwell rapidly made his way until he came up with the savages. He attacked them

6. How did they compromise? 7. Who was made governor? 8. Who was Craven, and what his character? 9. What was done in respect to Port Royal harbor? 10. Whence the name of Beaufort? 11. What Indians rose in arms, in North Carolina, in 1712? 12. What crimes did they commit? 13. Who was sent to their relief? 14. What were Barnwell's difficulties? 15. How did he surmount them?

with boldness and success, slew three hundred men, and made captives of one hundred.

The Tuscaroras he found, to the number of six hundred more, in one of their towns, on the Neuse river. They were sheltered by a wooden breastwork. Having surrounded them, and slain a considerable number, he compelled the rest to sue for peace. This was granted; but, the faithless savages, as soon as he had returned to South Carolina, renewed their massacres. Barnwell's conduct in the war was complained of, by some of the persons in authority, in North Carolina, but without just reason. The people of the colony gave him their warmest approbation, and called the fort, which he had taken, by his name.

A second demand was made upon Governor Craven, and a second force, under the command of Colonel Moore, the son of the former governor, was despatched to meet the enemy. Moore found the Indians on the Tau river, about fifty miles from its mouth, where they had thrown up entrenchments. They were well provided with small arms, but were soon taught the folly of standing a siege. Moore defeated them, entered their works, and made eight hundred prisoners. The military strength of the Tuscaroras was annihilated in these conflicts.

This Indian war was succeeded by another, which, for a time, threatened the very existence of the colony. The numerous and powerful tribe, or nation, of the Yemassees, possessing a large territory, in the neighborhood of Port Royal, had long been friendly to the Carolinians. They had engaged, as allies, in most of the wars against the Spaniards, the French, and Indian tribes; had done good service, and always proved faithful. But, with the usual caprice of the red men, they suddenly became hostile. Instigated by the Spaniards, at St. Augustine — the hereditary enemies of the Carolinians — who

16. What were his successes against the Indians? 17. What was the conduct of the savages after they had been received to mercy? 18. What is said of Barnwell's conduct? 19. Who was next sent against the Indians from South Carolina? 20. What were Moore's successes against the Indians? 21. What enemies rose against the colony, in 1715? 22. Where dwelt the Yemassees? 23. What had been their previous bearing toward the whites? 24. By whom were they excited to war?

had united the Cherokees, the Muscoghees, and other Indian nations, in a league, for the destruction of the colony — the Yemassees also appeared in arms, in 1715. With so much secrecy had their proceedings been conducted, that, at their first foray, above ninety persons fell, under their hatchets, on the plantations, near Pocotaligo. Joined with the Muscoghees and Apalachians, they advanced along the southern frontier, spreading desolation and slaughter where they came. Dividing into parties, they attacked Port Royal and St. Bartholomew.

Their numbers were increased by the Congarees, the Catawbas, and the Cherokees; and the Carolinians, taken by surprise, were soon taught to apprehend the very worst consequences from the presence of a foe no less numerous than savage. The Indians, of the southern division, mustered more than six thousand warriors; those of the northern, were near a thousand more. From Florida to Cape Fear, they were banded together, and marching forward, from several quarters, to the destruction of the colony, at Ashley river.

But Craven proved himself equal to the emergency. He proclaimed martial law, laid an embargo on all ships, to prevent either men or provisions from leaving the colony, seized upon arms and ammunition wherever they were to be found, and armed a force of trusty negroes, to co-operate with the white militia. With two hundred and fifty men, at first, and, subsequently, twelve hundred, he marched to meet the enemy.

The Indians, meanwhile, continued to advance, plundering and murdering, without mercy, as they came. Thomas Barker, a captain of militia, with a small force, encountered them, and was slain, with many of his men. At Goose Creek, a force of four hundred savages surrounded a little stockade, which contained seventy white men and forty negroes. These maintained themselves, stoutly, for a while, but, listening imprudently to overtures of peace, they admitted the savages within their defences, and were all butchered.

25. What allies had they among other Indian tribes? 26. What was their first success? 27. How were their numbers increased? 28. What their entire force in arms? 29. From what different points did they march? 30. How did Governor Craven prepare for them? 31. What was his force? 32. What befell Captain Barker? 33. What happened at the stockade of Goose Creek?

In this manner, in a desultory march, the enemy overrun the country around the capital, until the approach of Governor Craven compelled their scattered bands to fall back upon their great camp, upon the Salke-hatchie.

Craven advanced with cautious but undeviating footsteps. The fate of the whole province depended on the success of his arms, and conquest, or death, were the only alternatives before him. Fortunately, for the Carolinians, they had long been accustomed to the Indian modes of warfare. Its strange cries, and sudden terrors, did not appal them. The war-whoop had become a familiar sound, which they had learned to echo back with defiance; and, when the battle joined, adopting the partisan warfare, which the deep thickets and interminable swamps of the country seem to suggest as the most likely to prove successful, they encountered their more numerous foes with confidence and success.

The Indians fought with desperation and fury, but were defeated. Driven from their camp, they maintained a flying warfare, but found the Carolinians as inveterate in the pursuit as they had been valiant in the conflict. Craven kept his men close at the heels of the enemy, until, step by step, in a succession of conflicts, in which Colonel Mackay, Captain Chicken, and other leaders of the Carolinians, followed the gallant example of Craven, they were finally expelled from the country, and escaped only by throwing the Savannah between themselves and their foes.

They found shelter in the walls of St. Augustine, and, for a time, until they grew troublesome, were treated there with sympathy and indulgence. Expelled from the allies, whom they could no longer serve, their future abodes were found in the everglades of the Seminoles, of which people they are conjectured, with sufficient plausibility, to be the ancestors. In

84. Where was their great camp established? 85. How did Craven approach them? 86. What was the result of the battle at Salke-hatchie? 87. What other captains distinguished themselves, after the example of Craven? 88. How did the red men finally escape? 89. Where did they find refuge? 40. Whither did they subsequently retire, and of what recent race of red men are they supposed to have been the ancestors?

this insurrection, Carolina gained a vast accession of valuable territory, but lost no fewer than four hundred inhabitants.

Craven was succeeded in his short but brilliant administration, by Robert Johnson, a son of Sir Nathaniel Johnson, who had formerly held the same office.

He found the Carolinians suffering from the vast debts accumulated by their recent wars, the invasion of the province by the Indians and Spaniards, and the destruction of their commerce by the pirates. To relieve them from this last annoyance, having no vessels-of-war of their own, application was made to the king of England, now George, of Hanover, who issued a proclamation, offering pardon to all pirates who should surrender themselves within twelve months. At the same time, a force was ordered to sea, for their suppression.

As the island of Providence had long been their harboring place, Captain Woods Rogers, with a few ships-of-war, took possession of it for the crown. All the pirates on the island, with the exception of one Vane, and about ninety men, who escaped in a sloop, surrendered themselves, under the proclamation of the king. Vane fled to North Carolina, and distinguished himself, soon after, by the capture of two merchant ships of Charlestown. Two pirate sloops, commanded by Steed Bonnett and Richard Worley, found refuge in Cape Fear river, whence they issued on their depredations.

Against these, Colonel William Rhett, the same gentleman who had distinguished himself in the French invasion, was sent, in a single ship. Rhett soon discovered Bonnett, pursued and, after a sharp action, captured him. Governor Johnson himself embarked soon after this achievement, and captured the sloop of Worley, after a desperate conflict. The pirates fought with the fury of doomed men, and were all killed or wounded. The wounded men were tried, and instantly exe-

41. What were the peculiar losses and gains of the colony, by this war? 42. Who succeeded Craven? 43. In what condition did he find the colony? 44. Where did the colony obtain vessels of war against the pirates? 45. What proclamation was issued? 46. Where did the pirates usually harbor? 47. Who captured it from them? 48. What pirate refused to surrender? 49. Whither did Vane fly, with what force, and what did he subsequently do? 50. What other pirates found refuge in Cape Fear river? 51. Who was sent against them? 52. Who did Rhett capture? 53. Who did Governor Johnson capture?

cuted, to anticipate the more honorable death which was threatened by their wounds. Bonnett and his crew were also tried, and all, except one man, were hung, and buried on White Point, below high-water mark.

Johnson increased his popularity by this display of valor. Other achievements, of the same kind, followed these, and the coast of Carolina was, at length, cleared of those robbers of the sea, who had fastened themselves upon the infant colony, almost from its commencement.

It was during the administration of Johnson (1719), that a revolution was effected in the colony, by which the people threw off the proprietary government, and placed themselves under that of the crown. It is needless to go into details, to show the causes which moved them to this change. They have, already, been summed up, in former pages, and it is enough, in this place, to say, that the interests of the two parties, not, perhaps, well understood by either, were never found to assimilate. It would be a miracle, indeed, if a colony, governed from a distance, should be well governed; and the natural evils, incident to such a state of things, were necessarily increased by those peculiar troubles which had harassed the fortunes of the Carolinians. Repeated wars, frequent invasions, robberies by pirates, and the heavy debts which accrued from these events, had made them ready to ascribe—either to political influence abroad, and to the operation of laws in which neither their wishes nor their interests had been consulted by the proprietors, the oppressive circumstances against which they had so long struggled. Briefly, the contest was for popular rights, and republican principles; for freedom of opinion in society, church, and state; all of which had been virtually denied by the government, which had usurped, wholly, the attributes of the representative assembly. These being the fruitful topics of quarrel, the conflict between the

54. How were the captured pirates dealt with? 55. What revolution followed in the affairs of the colony, in 1719, and during the governorship of Johnson? 56. Why did the people seek to throw off the proprietary government? 57. What were the various troubles of the Carolinians? 58. Briefly, what was the cause of conflict, at all times, between the people and the proprietors? 59. Of what usurpation had the government been guilty?

lords and the actual possessors of the soil, grew, daily, more serious; and, availing themselves of the presence of the provincial assembly, then in session, in Charlestown, the leaders of the people prepared, in secret, the scheme of a revolution, which proved perfectly successful.

To these proceedings, Governor Johnson, who was a faithful adherent of the proprietors, was an entire stranger, until he received a letter, dated November 28th, 1719, and signed by Alexander Skene, George Logan, and William Blakeway, in which they informed him of the general association to throw off the proprietary rule. Against these attempts, Johnson struggled earnestly, but vainly. A proclamation, for dissolving an assembly which he found himself unabled to manage, was torn from the hands of the marshal, he himself was deposed, and Colonel James Moore, already known for his military achievements, was made governor in his stead.

A day, which had been appointed by Johnson, for reviewing the militia, was that chosen by the convention which elected Moore, for the purpose of publicly proclaiming him.

The governor, having intelligence of this design, ordered Colonel Parris, the commander of the militia, to postpone the review. Parris, however, was one of the popular party, and Johnson was surprised, on the day appointed, to find the militia drawn up in the market-place, drums beating, and colors flying on forts and shipping. Exasperated beyond prudence, at this defiance of his authority, he advanced upon Parris, as if to assault him; but the colonel ordered his men to present, and fire, if he advanced a step nearer. Johnson found himself utterly unsupported. Moore was, temporarily, declared governor of the province, in the king's name; and, the acclamations of the populace, and the unanimity which prevailed among them, sufficiently declared to Johnson his own, and the downfall of the proprietary government.

60. How did the leaders of the people proceed? 61. What was the first communication which Governor Johnson had of their proceedings, and when? 62. How did he attempt to arrest the revolution? 63. What was the result, to himself, of his efforts? 64. Who was appointed in his stead? 65. What day was chosen for proclaiming Moore? 66. What order did Johnson issue to the commander of the militia? 67. How was he obeyed? 68. What was Johnson's conduct on the occasion, and how met? 69. In whose name was Moore proclaimed governor?

One circumstance, alone, revived his hopes. Having-received certain advice that a· Spanish fleet, of fourteen ships and twelve hundred men, had left the Havana, destined against South Carolina and the island of Providence, Johnson conceived it a proper time to endeavor to recall the people to a sense of their duty. He wrote to the convention, and strove to reclaim them, by showing the danger of military operations under illegal authority; but, the stubborn citizens remained firm in their defection, laughed at his warnings, and, in concert with the governor of their own creation, proceeded to make preparations for their defence. The militia was soon under arms, but escaped, this time, any trial of their strength. The Spanish expedition proved abortive. Repulsed from Providence, and dismantled in a storm, the hostile armament was incapable of injury to Carolina.

The arrival of several English armed vessels, in the port of Charlestown, suggested other plans to the deposed representative of the lord-proprietors. Their commanders having declared for him, as the magistrate invested with legal authority, he brought up the ships-of-war in front of the town, and threatened its immediate destruction, if the inhabitants any longer withheld their obedience to his authority.

But, with arms in their hands, and forts in their possession, accustomed to conflict, and, perhaps, rather pleased with its excitements, the Carolinians were not to be terrified by the threats of one whose persuasions had failed to pacify them. Their answer of scornful defiance, accompanied by a couple of shot from the forts, convinced Johnson of the hopelessness of his cause; and, finding the people so determined, he drew off his forces, and forbore all farther attempts to recover his lost authority.

The lords-proprietors, at length, made aware of the impolicy of any farther struggles in behalf of a plantation, which they had managed with reference to their own pride and love of

70. Did Johnson make any farther attempts to regain his lost authority? 71. What foreign danger, threatening the colony, encouraged his attempts? 72. Did he succeed? 73. What other event encouraged him in still another effort? 74. What were his threats, and how answered? 75. What persuaded him to submit, and satisfied him of the hopelessness of farther effort? 76. What did the lords-proprietors?

power, rather than to its real wants and the particular circumstances of its condition ; and, perhaps, wearied with the continual opposition of a fiery and headstrong people, were easily persuaded to dispose of their pecuniary interests to the crown of England. Their political rights, under the charter, had been already declared forfeited. The complaints of the people were, at length, heard by the crown, among whose councillors they aroused the liveliest indignation. The proprietors made a merit of necessity, and subsequently for a consideration, yielded up the province which they could no longer keep. It was about this time that the province was divided into the colonies of South and North Carolina. With the appointment of General Francis Nicholson, as governor of the former colony, begins the royal government of England over it.

77. How was the province divided ?  78. Who became the first royal governor of South Carolina ?

# BOOK III.

## ROYAL GOVERNMENT.——1719 TO 1736.

## CHAPTER I.

### 1719 TO 1736.

THE change from the proprietary to the royal government produced its natural effects, in temporarily harmonizing the several parties in the colony. These had all substantially arisen from the popular impatience of a foreign control, which did not recognise their claims, as men or citizens, having proper competence for the management of their own affairs. The people had imbibed too many ideas of their own rights to submit placidly to the revival, in the new world, of that feudal domination which was rapidly dying out in the old.

The government, now conferred on South Carolina, was modelled on that of the British constitution. It consisted of a governor, a council, and an assembly, with the power of making their own laws. The king appointed the governor, and delegated to him his constitutional authority. The council, also appointed by the king, was to advise with the governor, and assist in legislation — representing a House of Lords; while the assembly, like the English House of Commons, was elected by the people, and constituted the guardian of their rights, liberties, lives, and property. The governor could convene, prorogue, or dissolve the assembly, and had a negative on the bills of both houses, with other powers. But, even after bills had received his assent, they were yet required to

1. How did the change, from proprietary to royal government, affect South Carolina? 2. What kind of government was bestowed on the province? 3. What powers were confided to the governor?

be transmitted to Great Britain, for the king's approval, though still obligatory as laws until his decision was made known.

This establishment was a vast improvement upon the old, which it superseded. The people were satisfied with it. They were not yet prepared for anything more liberal; not yet ready to quarrel with a government which, though still foreign, had proved so satisfactory to their ancestors and brethren in Great Britain.

That government had been settled by usage and acceptance. It was no longer a speculative plan of rule, emanating from closet or mercurial politicians, theorists or dreamers, but a constitution which had been tried, tested, and matured by successive ages of experience.

For a time, accordingly, the political discontents of the colony were at an end; and, for a long while after, the royal government performed its duties with a vigor and wisdom which justified all the hopes of the colonists.

Its first object, after the transfer of the colony from the lord-proprietors to the crown, was to re-establish peace and harmony upon the most equitable foundation. Laws were passed, relieving the people from many of the evils of which they had complained. The treaties of alliance and amity with the red men were confirmed, and, during the administration of Nicholson, the fortunes of the people might be said to prosper surprisingly.

The population of white inhabitants numbered fourteen thousand, in 1724, and the importation of negro slaves, in this one year, is reported at more than four hundred. The imports, the same year, into the province, including the slaves and foreign goods, were estimated to amount to between fifty and sixty thousand pounds; in return for which, the exports were eighteen thousand barrels of rice, fifty-two thousand of pitch, tar, and turpentine, untold quantities of deer, bear, and beaver

4. What check upon the provincial government was secured by the crown? 5. What commended the new government to the people? 6. What is said of the British constitution? 7. Did the new government satisfy the expectations of the people? 8. What was the first object of government? 9. What laws were passed with this object—what treaties renewed? 10. What, at this period, was the white population of the province? 11. What number of negro slaves were imported this year? 12. What was the gross value of imports this year? 13. What were the exports?

skins and furs, together with a considerable quantity of raw silk, lumber, and other articles.

In the brief space of five years, under the new administration, the improvement had been astonishing. At the time of the change from the proprietary to the royal government, the colony was still a very feeble one. Kept under the former rule, it would, perhaps, never have emerged from a state of infancy, unless into one of greater decrepitude and final decay. St. Stephen's parish was its frontier, in 1719. There, at Dorchester, Wiltown, and other places, along the coast and country, forts were maintained — either stockades, blockhouses, or earthworks, each enclosing a barrack, for security from the red men. The settlers, Indian traders excepted, rarely ventured, unless in large bodies, and in marching order, with arms in hand, fifty miles from the seaboard. The middle and upper country was wholly in possession of the red men, who were rarely quiet, were restless, capricious, jealous, keen after blood and spoils, and ever meditating their incursions, for plunder, in some direction. They prowled about the settlements perpetually, and within twenty miles of Charlestown, with impunity.

The town, itself, relied upon very doubtful securities. The fortifications did not now (1720) include all the settled portions. They simply compassed that portion of the town, which lay between the central market and Water street, in one direction, the bay and Meeting street, in the opposite. The town had outgrown these limits without any corresponding growth of its securities, and a considerable, though somewhat scattered suburb, west and north of the old walls, was left wholly unfortified. Pirates and Spaniards, French and Indians, were ever on the watch to assail; yet the military organization was wretchedly imperfect; the frontier police feeble and inefficient;

14. What was the progress of the colony in the five first years of the royal government? 15. How did it compare with that of the proprietors? 16. What parish was the frontier, in 1719? 17. Where were forts maintained, at that period? 18. How far into the interior did settlers venture to go, and how prepared? 19. What then of the middle and upper country? 20. How near to Charlestown did the red men venture with impunity? 21. What were the securities of the town, itself? 22. What tract did its fortifications include? 23. What of its suburbs? 24. From whom had it most to fear? 25. What was the military organization — the frontier police — the means for bringing the militia to a rendezvous?

and the means for bringing the militia together so tardy and ineffective, that a fleet and vigorous foe might make his swoop, like a hawk, upon the quarry, and be gone before the alarm-gun could rouse the settlement. The royal government addressed itself, with prompt wisdom and energy, to the work of curing all these disabilities and deficiencies.

In 1725, Arthur Middleton succeeded Nicholson, as governor. Middleton had long before distinguished himself, as president of the council, and in other capacities, by his prudence, moderation, activity, and general intelligence. He had led the popular revolution, by which the proprietary government was overthrown.

The troubles of his administration, now, were chiefly with the Spaniards, the red men, and the emissaries of the French among the latter. Reprisals were made against the Spaniards and Indians, within the Spanish province of Florida, when argument and entreaty failed. The French, who, from the Mississippi had penetrated to the Alabama, and were in occupation of fortresses on that river, gave great trouble, also, in stirring up the Creek and Cherokee Indians to hostility. And this period of struggle between the rival races, inaugurates that terrible and protracted conflict, called the "Old French War," in which England and France so fiercely contended for the exclusive power and influence over the various nations of red men in the vast interior.

The summer of 1728 was marked by great disasters in the growing metropolis of South Carolina. The season had been one of extreme drouth, and was followed by a dreadful hurricane, in August, which threatened, for a time, the destruction of the town. The streets were inundated; the inhabitants found refuge in their upper stories. Twenty-three ships were driven ashore, most of which were destroyed. The storm was followed by the pestilence. The yellow fever swept off multi-

26. Under these circumstances, how did the royal government act? 27. Who succeeded to Nicholson as governor, in 1725? 28. How was Middleton previously known? 29. What were the troubles of his administration? 30. What were the approaches of the French? 31. What struggle was inaugurated, at this period? 32. What of the summer of 1728? 33. What happened in August of that year? 34. What followed the hurricane?

tudes — *both white and black.* All fled who could. The planters sent no supplies to town, and there was imminent danger
of death from famine, as well as from the disease. So great
was the mortality, and such the condition of those who remained, that it was not always found easy to procure the ordinary assistance for the burial of the dead.

Disasters so terrible and frequent, might well have discouraged the hope and enterprise of the infant city ; but the people of those days were possessed of an admirable elasticity of
character ; and, after each momentary shock, they shook themselves free of its terrors, and resumed their toils with the vigor
which had so often saved them from even harder fortunes.
Under the old rule, they might have been paralyzed, or continued only a feeble struggle for existence.

It was during this year that, by an act of parliament, the
title of the lords-proprietors in the soil of the colonies, was
finally extinguished by purchase. Hitherto, the government,
only, had been surrendered ; now, the soil was sold to the
crown. But, one of the lord-proprietors (Lord Carteret), refused to dispose of his share, and this was, accordingly, reserved
to him from the sale.

It will suggest matter of curious reflection to the Carolinian
of the present day, when told that *seven-eighths of the whole
territory of the present state of South Carolina, was bought, by
the crown of England, for seventeen thousand five hundred
pounds!— with the arrears of quit rents* (five thousand pounds),
due from the people to the proprietors, and which the crown
also assumed, but twenty-two thousand five hundred pounds,—
less than one hundred and twenty thousand dollars in all.

In 1730, with a proper regard to domestic security, and to
the increasing embarrassments with the red men, occasioned by
the machinations of French and Spaniard, an interesting em-
bassage was undertaken to the mountain-country of the Cherokees. At the head of this expedition was Sir Alexander Cum-

85. What was the condition of the city ? 86. How did the people behave, under
their calamities ? 87. What act of parliament, this year, was of peculiar interest to
South Carolina? 88. Who, among the proprietaries, refused to sell his share ?
89. For what was the territory of South Carolina sold to the crown? 40. What em-
bassage was sent, in 1730, to what people, and by what ambassador?

ming. Three hundred miles from Charlestown, in their chief town of Keowee, he met their principal warriors and head men; was well received, and assisted at the installation of some of their chiefs. Six of these wild inhabitants of the forest accompanied him, in the end, to England, where they proved to be objects of the most curious interest to both court and people. The king told them that "he took it kindly that the great nation of Cherokee had sent them so far to brighten the chain of friendship between his and theirs. That chain," he said, "is now like the sun, which shines as well in Britain as upon the great mountains where they live. It equally warms the hearts of Indians and of Englishmen; and, as there is no blackness on the sun, so neither is there any rust upon the chain. He had fastened one end of it to his breast, and he desired them to carry the other end and fasten it to the breast of Moytoy, of Telliquo, the great chief, and to the breasts of all their wise men, their captains, and the people — never more to be broken or unloosed."

The treaty which followed this interview was pronounced, by both parties, to be one which should endure while the rivers continued to run, the mountains to stand, and the sun to shine. Skiajagustah, the Cherokee orator, made a reply in the figurative language of his people.

"We are come hither," he said, "from a mountainous place, where all is darkness; we are now in a place where all is light. There was one in our country who gave us a yellow token of warlike honor, which is with Moytoy of Telliquo. He came to us like a warrior from you. As warriors we received him. He is a man — his talk was good — his memory is among us. We love the great king; we look upon him as the sun. He is our father; we are his children. Though you are white and we are red, our hearts and hands are joined together. We shall die in this way of thinking; we shall tell our people what we have seen — our children, from generation to generation, will remember it. In war we shall be one with you. Your ene-

41. By whom was Sir Alexander Cumming accompanied to Europe? 42. How were the Cherokee chiefs addressed by the king? 43. What answer was made by the Cherokee orator?

mies shall be ours; your people and ours shall be one, and shall live together; your white people may build their houses beside us. We shall not do them hurt, for we are children of one father."

He laid down a bunch of eagles' feathers as he added: " These stand for our words; they are the same to us as letters in a book to you. To your beloved men we deliver these feathers to stand for all that we have said."

For twenty years this peace was religiously observed by both parties; but we must not anticipate for so long a period.

In 1730, Robert Johnson, who, it will be remembered, was the last of the governors under the *régime* of the proprietors, was invested with the royal commission for the executive office of the colony. He had been faithfully tenacious of the rights and claims of the proprietors, and in opposition to the people; but these latter found no fault with him now for his fidelity to his employers then. He was honorably welcomed to the colony and his office. He brought back with him the Cherokee chiefs who had been carried to England.

The new governor was highly competent to his duties. His council was well chosen; he knew the wants of the colony, the character of the people, the resources of the country, and the influences which might endanger its peace. His measures were all taken accordingly, with moderation and wisdom. New privileges were conferred upon the colonists, calculated to encourage agriculture and enlarge the fields of trade; old restraints upon rice were taken off; a discount was allowed on hemp; the arrears of quit-rents were remitted by the crown; bills of credit were issued to the amount of £77,000; and seventy pieces of cannon were sent by the king for several fortresses. An independent company of foot was allowed for the defence of the province, and ships-of-war were stationed along the coast. These benefits and privileges wonderfully sweetened the popular mind,

44. How was the treaty then made observed by the parties, and how long? 45. Who became governor in 1731? 46. How was Governor Johnson received by the people, and whom did he bring with him? 47. In what degree was he capable of his duties? 48. What was the policy pursued, and what favor did it find with the people? 49. What help in men, arms, and ships-of-war, was accorded by the crown to the province?

and increased the general prosperity. The wealth, and consequently the credit, of the province grew rapidly, and especially in the trading and manufacturing towns of England. London, Bristol, and Liverpool, looked lovingly on the brisk and flourishing settlements between the Ashley and the Cooper. They poured in floods of African slaves for cultivating the fields, and cargoes of manufactures for supplying the plantations; and, in those days, these were thought very virtuous proceedings. Planters and merchants, equally, were happy in the conviction that they were blessings and beneficial, pleasant and profitable, as well as virtuous. Exports increased in proportion with the imports; wealth spread; lands rose in value; and, in a few years, the produce of the province was more than doubled.

The vast increase of negro slaves opened boundless plains of virgin fertility and freshness to the sun — regions, hitherto inaccessible to European labor, as antagonist to European life and health. In 1731, forty thousand barrels of rice were exported, besides great quantities of furs, skins, naval stores, and provisions. Charlestown soon numbered six hundred dwellings. The improvement was incessant. Art and labor reported daily progress. The accessions of population and property from abroad were such as very soon to distinguish the Ashley river settlement as one of the most flourishing of all the English colonies in America.

Nor was this progress confined wholly to the metropolis. Its influence naturally spread to the interior. A large accession of Indian lands won the more adventurous to the borders of the Cherokee country, and opened new tributaries to trade and enterprise.

Meanwhile, the territory beyond the Savannah was separated from the government of South Carolina, and, under the name of Georgia, was formed into a new colony, and settled, in 1733,

50. How did the government policy affect the interests of South Carolina in respect to profits, land, trade, negro slavery, and exports? 51. What was the effect of negro slavery upon the prosperity of South Carolina? 52. What were the exports in 1731? 53. What number of dwellings had Charlestown that year? 54. How was the settlement of Ashley river regarded abroad? 55. What was the effect upon the interior? 56. What new colony was created in 1788?

under the government of the celebrated General Oglethorpe. South Carolina was to be no longer a frontier. The auspices promised everything for both colonies. Emigrants were distributed between them, and both colonies became objects of desire and contemplation in the world of Europe, from which thousands were, every year, preparing to depart, seeking new fields of labor, or new securities for liberty.

There soon came one colony, and then another, of Swiss, who, settling on the Savannah, established the town of Purysburg, after the name of their leader, Pury. In 1734, a colony of Irish settled the precinct, in South Carolina, since called Williamsburg, and, by 1736, the settlement had spread westward some eighty or ninety miles from the seaboard. But these were mostly confined to two classes of persons — Indian traders, who were generally Scotch, and graziers, who sought wild pastures for large herds of cattle. The presence of their "cow-pens," as they were popularly called, necessarily implied a sparse population. The traders frequently dwelt with the red men, and took wives among them. One of these, in 1758, reported that he, with many others, had abandoned the homes of civilization more than twenty years before. He himself had then more than seventy children and grand-children among the red men. To this class of wanderers, and their descendants, the British were largely indebted for military service in the subsequent struggle with the colony in 1776. They were naturally a hardy, bold, half-savage people, who as naturally acquired singular influence over the Indians. Their sympathies were rather with the crown than with the mixed peoples of the colony, which they had abandoned; and toward whom they entertained the jealousies natural to a large self-esteem, when blended with a conscious deficiency in civilization.

Population was still, however, the great object of the British government. The increase, though large and rapid in South

57. Under whom? 58. What were the auspices in respect to both colonies? 59. By whom was the town of Purysburg established? 60. By whom Williamsburg? 61. How far, in 1736, had population spread westward? 62. By what classes of settlers? 63. What is said of the graziers? 64. What of the traders? 65. What did one of these report? 66. What is said of their relations with the crown, colony, and red men?

Carolina, was yet only relatively so. The settlements were still very small and far between. The plan adopted by the king's advisers for more speedily filling up the vacant places in the province, was to establish townships, each of twenty thousand acres, in square plats, along the banks of rivers — the lands being divided into shares of fifty acres for each several colonist, man, woman, or child. Eleven of these townships, on this plan, were thus established by Governor Johnson — two on the Altamaha, two on the Savannah, two on the Santee, and one on each of the rivers Pedee, Black, Waccamaw, and Wateree.

Under the new impulse given to trade, agriculture, and emigration, lands, which had hitherto lain everywhere derelect, were now eagerly sought, and soon became the subject of grievous strifes and heart-burnings. Everybody vied with his neighbor in the struggle for the acquisition of territory. The colony was finally vexed and troubled with the litigation which grew out of this struggle. But, though thus stimulative to cupidity and productive of strife, this evil had its benefits. Gradually, the roads were opened into the interior; choice spots were planted; hamlets grew as plantations spread, and religion soon began to rear her temples in the remote thickets which hitherto had heard no sweeter music than the long howl of the wolf and the more terrific yell of the savage. The wilderness, in a thousand places, was beginning to blossom with the rose; but it was the wild rose still. Education was wanting. Society was a rare possession. The life of the country was solitary — nursing self-esteem, it is true, and courage and independence, but lacking in all those softer influences which only art and civilization, education and religion, can duly nurture for humanity.

67. What is said touching the increase of population? 68. What plan did government adopt for inviting emigration? 69. How were the townships divided? 70. How many were established, and where? 71. What was the effect of the new impulse in the province upon lands and settlers? 72. What is said of religion, education, and society?

# CHAPTER II

### NEGRO INSURRECTION — WAR WITH THE SPANIARDS, 1740.

THE royal governors of South Carolina, from 1721 to 1743, were five in number. Francis Nicholson was in the executive chair from 1721 to 1725; Arthur Middleton, from 1725 to 1730; Robert Johnson, from 1730 to 1735; Thomas Broughton, from 1735 to 1737; and William Bull, from 1737 to 1743, when he was succeeded by J mes Glenn. The contents of the present chapter involve the events occurring under Bull's administration.

In the death of Johnson, Carolina was deprived of one of the most able, efficient, and popular of all her governors. He was succeeded by Thomas Broughton, a gentleman who had distinguished himself for a long time in her councils. We have seen, in previous pages, the progress of events under his administration. The next royal appointment was that of Samuel Horsley; but he died soon after his appointment, and without having left England.

The government then devolved on William Bull, a native of the province, in 1737. Bull was also well known to the people as an efficient counselor. He had their preferences as a native; was thoroughly acquainted with the affairs of the country; a man of high character, considerable abilities, and large popularity.

His government was not, however, a bed of roses. It did not commence under pleasant auspices, though welcomed by the people. His attention was soon called to the dangers from his neighbors, the Spaniards and French, and their influence among

1. How many royal governors of the colony from 1721 to 1743? 2. Name them, and their periods of office. 3. What is said of Governor Johnson? 4. What of Governor Broughton? 5. What governor died before reaching Carolina? 6. What is said of Governor Bull? 7. What of his government?

the red men.   He advised the home government of the growing power of the Spaniards in Florida; of formidable preparations on foot, threatening hostility, and of the weakness of Carolina for defence.   Georgia was still more feeble.   Both provinces needed European help.

A regiment of foot was accordingly ordered out from England, in response to this appeal, and the command was confided
to General Oglethorpe, who had great military reputation.   He
was entrusted with the military government of both colonies.
The early arrival of this regiment in Georgia, and the active
preparations made by Oglethorpe for defence, discouraged the
more open demonstrations of the Spaniards, but did not lessen
their desire to do something mischievously.   Their hostility
was unabated; they substituted an insidious for a warlike policy; they succeeded in corrupting some of the foreign soldiers
of Oglethorpe, so that his assassination was absolutely attempted; but the assassins were slain, and the conspiracy was discovered and defeated.

But this disappointment did not put an end to the schemes, or
lessen the hostility, of the Spaniards.   They worked in secret
as malignantly as ever, in the hope to destroy a people whom
they still continued to regard as trespassers on the territories
of Spain.   Their emissaries (black, red, and white) penetrated
the settlements equally of Georgia and Carolina.   In the latter
province, the field was more accessible, in consequence of the
large proportion of negro slaves to the white population.   The
numbers of this people had now grown, in Carolina, to forty
thousand; while the whites were but a third of that number.
Most of the negroes were raw Africans, just emerging from the
savage state.   It is not hard, when appealing to the appetites
and passions of such a race, to lead them astray; and, tampering equally with these and the red men, the Spaniards beguiled

8. What is said of the preparation of the Spaniards?   9. What was the condition
of Georgia and Carolina for defence?   10. What succor came from England?   11.
Who was made commander?   12. What was the effect of these succors upon the
Spaniards?   13. What their subsequent policy?   14. Whom did they corrupt, and
what followed?   15. Where did their emissaries operate?   16. What was the negro
population in South Carolina in 1740.   17. What was the proportion of whites?   18.
What classes did the Spaniards incorporate in their armies?
5*

hundreds of both people from Carolina to St. Augustine, where they found employment in the ranks of the Spanish army.

The Indians were employed as scouts and forayers. The negroes were formed into a regiment of their own, but with white officers. This fact, alone, was well calculated, when known in Carolina, to exercise a powerful effect on the imaginations of the negroes still remaining in slavery; and, the emissaries of the Spaniards, still at work in the province, at length, succeeded in stimulating the blacks to insurrection. The negro can not long resist temptations which appeal to appetite; his passions are too strong; his intellect too mean and feeble, to suffer him to reason, even from his own experience; and the cunning enemy soon used the semi-barbarians at his pleasure. The negroes, at first in small squads, and afterward, in large bodies, rose in revolt among the settlements along the Stono (1740), and, having plundered certain storehouses of arms and ammunition, proceeded to elect their captain — a fellow who was called, and whom his owner, probably, had christened, by the name of Cato, after the great Roman of the commonwealth.

Cato proceeded, with drums and colors, on his march, toward the southwest. On this march, the work of massacre was urged without remorse and without discrimination. They slaughtered the whites, mercilessly, without regard to sex or age; and compelled the negroes, however reluctant, to fall into their ranks, at all the plantations in their way.

It happened that Governor Bull, himself, was one of the first to discover their progress, without falling a victim to their rage. Returning to Charlestown, from the southward, he actually met them, but without being seen himself. He had sufficient time, and presence of mind, to ride into the thickets; and, by a wide circuit, to elude them altogether. He spread the alarm as he went, and hastened to muster his forces.

The report reached the Willtown church (Presbyterian),

19. What use did they make of the Indians? 20. How did they incorporate the negroes? 21. What was the effect of this upon the slaves of Carolina? 22. What is the negro character? 23. Where did the slaves rise in insurrection? 24. Who was their captain? 25. Whither did they march, and what performing? 26. Who first met them, and escaped? 27. What congregation was assembled at Willtown church?

where a numerous congregation was even then assembled for public worship. It was, fortunately, the custom of the planters — a custom counselled by experience, and enforced by law — to carry their arms with them, on all such occasions; a terrible experience had made the weapons of the Carolinians their invariable companions, for the whole seventy years of the existence of the province, whether the objects of the gathering were sport, or labor, or devotion.

The congregation, accordingly, was easily organized from a troop of pilgrims, into a stout band of rangers and riflemen. Leaving their women and children, filled with terror, in the church, the men sallied forth, under the conduct of Captain Bee, and took the direct route for the revolted slaves. They found no difficulty in tracking them to their camp; and came upon the miserable negroes while at their revels — carousing over the liquors which they had found by the way. They had halted in an open field, singing and dancing in all the barbarous exultation of success.

In this condition, to overcome them was an easy task. Dividing his force into two squads, Bee attacked with one, while the other closed the avenues of escape. Cato, the leader, and a number more were killed outright; the rest, dispersed in the woods, endeavored to steal back to the plantations which they had deserted. The surviving ringleaders suffered death, while the greater number were received to mercy.

A war which followed, between Spain and England, afforded the Carolinians an opportunity for commencing a series of reprisals upon the Spaniards, for the long train of evils which they had suffered at their hands (1740). The great foreign military reputation of General Oglethorpe, of the Georgia colony, indicated that gentleman as the proper person to lead the joint forces of the two provinces of Carolina and Georgia against their common enemy. A small European force was sent from Great Britain; companies were furnished by Virginia and North Carolina; the rest of the army was composed of the Georgia militia, and a strong regiment from South Carolina, under the command of Colonel Vanderdussen.

After various delays, which have been charged against General Oglethorpe as the true causes of the failure of the expedition, and which certainly enabled the Spaniards to provide against the invaders, Oglethorpe reached St. Augustine; having, on his way, captured two small forts, called Moosa and Diego. His force amounted to two thousand men. But, during his stay at Fort Diego, the garrison, at St. Augustine, had received an accession of strength from six Spanish galleys, armed with long brass nine-pounders, and two sloops, loaded with provisions. When he summoned the fortress, he was answered with defiance. The haughty Don, secure in his stronghold, sent him for answer, that he would be happy to shake hands with him within the castle. A bombardment followed this reply, but without effecting any change in the spirit of the defenders. The fire was returned from the castle and galleys, but little injury was done, on either side, and the besiegers found it wiser to consult than to cannonade.

The only hope of Oglethorpe had been to effect his object by surprise. Failing in this, the light weight of his metal, and the ample preparations of the Spaniards against blockade, left him but little prospect of achieving the conquest of so strong a fortress in any other manner. Meantime, the Spanish commander, perceiving that the operations of the besiegers were relaxed, and, suspecting their embarrassment, sent out a detachment of three hundred men against a small party, of Highlanders, under Colonel Palmer, which lay at Fort Moosa. Palmer suffered himself to be surprised, and his men, who were sleeping, at the time, were most of them cut in pieces.

This disaster, in connection with the desertion of the allied Indians, added to the already sufficient reasons which existed, for abandoning the expedition. These people, who are not calculated for tedious enterprises, that demand patience, and afford no opportunities for action, were offended with the haughty humanity of the general. When they brought him the scalp of an enemy, he called them barbarous dogs, rejected the trophy, and bade them begone from his sight. They compared this reception with that to which they had hitherto been accustomed, and, soon after, deserted him.

The siege was raised (August, 1740), and its failure was ascribed, by the Carolinians, to the too deliberate and measured advance of their commander, and to his subsequent timidity in making no bold attempt upon the town. He, on the other hand, declared that he had no confidence in the firmness of the provincials. There was, probably, some good ground for both complaints; but, the truth is, the place was so strongly fortified, well provided, and numerously manned, that, in all probability, such an attempt must have failed, under the circumstances, though conducted by the ablest officers, and executed by the best disciplined troops.

The mutual recrimination, between the allied provinces, which followed this failure, led to many injurious dislikes and misunderstandings. To so great a degree was this dislike carried, on the part of the Carolinians, that, in a subsequent period, when Georgia was invaded by a Spanish force, they at first declined sending help to the sister colony; alledging that they could not trust their troops to a commander in whom they had no confidence. At a late hour, indeed, and when it was certain that Carolina, herself, was not the object of invasion, they resolved differently, and despatched three ships to the assistance of the Georgians. It would, perhaps, have been unwise to do so before it was well known which colony was the object of attack. The appearance of this force upon the coast, gave a spur to the flight of the invaders. Oglethorpe had, already, beaten them — acquitting himself like a good captain

42. Why had the red men deserted? 43. To what was the failure of the enterprise ascribed? 44. What seems to have been the truth, in this respect? 45. What evil results followed this failure? 46. How was it supposed to influence the conduct of Carolina, subsequently? 47. What was, probably, the true reason and the justification of the Carolinians for withholding their succor, at first? 48. What the effect of their final action? 49. What had been Oglethorpe's previous successes?

and a brave man, and fully redeeming the errors, if any, which he had made in the expedition to St. Augustine.

To add to the disasters sustained by Carolina in the unsuccessful invasion of Florida — her losses of men, money and reputation — a desolating fire broke out, in Charlestown, on the eighteenth of November, 1740, in which fully one half of the city was destroyed. Three hundred houses were burnt; several lives were lost, and numerous families utterly ruined. The loss was immense in foreign goods, and provincial commodities. The British parliament voted twenty thousand pounds for the relief of the suffering city.

And here, it may be well to say that, thus far, the mother-country had showed herself a nobly nursing mother of the province. Under the two first Georges, indeed, the colonists had little of which to complain — much for which to be grateful. Lands were granted at cheap rates; there were no tithes to be paid, and taxation was nominal. England was sufficiently compensated by the colonial trade and produce. British manufactures were obtained at moderate rates; drawbacks were allowed on all manufactures of foreign production; arms and ammunition, men and money, were provided for the public defence; and, in all respects, no contrast could be more complete, no difference more grateful, to the people, themselves, than that between the government of the proprietary lords, and that of the English crown. And this feeling and conviction was still strong with thousands, when, under a changed dispensation, the people were required to array themselves against the royal authority. It is not a subject for surprise, that so many should be found unwilling to forego their loyalty in their republican patriotism.

50. What terrible event happened to Charlestown, at the close of this year? 51. What assistance was given by the British parliament? 52. What is said of the conduct of the mother-country, under the two first Georges? 53. What of lands— tithes—taxation? 54. How was England compensated? 55. How the colony benefitted by indulgences and succors? 56. What the contrast between the old proprietary and the royal government? 57. What effect, upon many, had this paternal government of the crown, in the subsequent struggles of the Republic?

# CHAPTER III.

## FROM 1740 TO 1743.

WHILE the war continued between Great Britain and Spain, a bill was brought into parliament, to prevent the exportation, among other provisions, of rice, into France or Spain. Against this measure, the Carolinians remonstrated with the House of Commons, alleging that rice was the commodity of most importance raised in Carolina, and if any stop be put to its exportation, it will render them unable to pay their debts. Their memorial states that, from 1720 to 1729 — ten years — their export of rice was two hundred and sixty-four thousand four hundred and eighty-eight barrels; or, forty-four thousand and eighty-one tons; from 1730 to 1739 — another ten years — the export was four hundred and ninety-nine thousand five hundred and twenty-five barrels; or, ninety-nine thousand nine hundred and five tons; and that, of this vast quantity, scarcely one fifteenth part is consumed in Great Britain, or in the British dominions; so that the fourteen parts are clear gain to the nation; making the national gain, from rice, several times greater than that arising from sugar and tobacco; since, of these articles, the greater quantity, made in the colonies, is consumed in the British dominions. The exports of rice, alone, in that very year (1740), are estimated at ninety thousand barrels, at twenty-five shillings sterling per barrel, making a value, in sterling money, of one hundred and ten thousand pounds, at home prices, and not including cost of freight, insurance, and commissions; but, at final sale, in Europe, being

1. What bill was brought into parliament, affecting the colony? 2. What was the remonstrance of the Carolinians? 3. What did they say of rice? 4. What of its export, at sundry periods? 5. What proportion of this was consumed in Great Britain? 6. What was the value of this export, in sterling money?

worth to the nation two hundred and twenty thousand pounds; besides employing, annually, more than one hundred and sixty British ships, of one hundred tons each.    From 1739 to 1740, the number of British vessels employed in the transportation of Carolina produce, had increased to two hundred and fifty-seven, showing a tonnage of sixteen thousand, and employing fifteen hundred British seamen.    There was little trade with any foreign plantations, and none with any part of Europe, but Britain.

This *exposé* gives an interesting idea of the degree of prosperity to which the colony had arrived at this time, and of what importance she was to the British empire.

Unhappily, there was no corresponding growth in the more important respects of morals, and education, and religion.    For the first twenty-eight years of the settlement, divine service was rarely performed beyond the limits of Charlestown; and, even there, in 1704, the Episcopalians had but one church, and the Dissenters three; yet the former succeeded in obtaining a legal establishment of the Anglican church.    The Dissenters struggled in vain, for years, to obtain the removal of their disabilities. In 1706, the colony was divided into ten parishes, and, subsequently, into twenty-four, most of which were in the maritime districts, and none more than ninety miles from the sea-coast. At first, the Dissenters were excluded from the legislature; but this law was soon repealed by the provincial assembly.    In a minority of the people, the Episcopalians were compelled to be modest  and if they, themselves, enjoyed a peculiar preference of government, they soon found it politic to accord toleration to all other sects.    The people were always jealous of ecclesiastical domination.    The laity had ecclesiastical jurisdiction, and could deprive ministers of their livings at pleasure.    Governor

7. What was the value to the nation ?    8. What shipping did it employ, and what number of sailors ?    9. What was the degree of trade done with other parts of Europe, and other plantations ?    10. Did education and religion prosper in the same degree with agriculture and trade, in the province ?    11. What of the Episcopal church ?    12. How was the province divided, in 1706—and subsequently ?    13. Where were these parishes located ?    14. What was the exclusion of the dissenters, at first ? 15. What was the effect upon the Episcopalians, of their numerical inferiority ? 16. What was the peculiar jealousy of the people ?    17. What jurisdiction was allowed the laity ?

Bull exercised the power of excommunication, equivalent to a sentence of outlawry, in a single instance, as late as 1765.

In 1733, Alexander Garden was appointed, by the bishop of London, his commissary; and, as such, to exercise spiritual and ecclesiastical jurisdiction, in North and South Carolina, Georgia, and New Providence. Garden, himself an able pulpit preacher, and eminent man, came in collision with the celebrated Whitfield, who, about this time, appeared in Carolina, gathering multitudes wherever he went. The aberrations of the latter, from the canons, were such that he was finally suspended, in 1740, from his office; but Whitfield was not to be suspended. For thirty years after he continued to preach, and always with the power to move the multitudes, even as the tempest sways the forest.

The Dissenters increased in Carolina, by emigration from Scotland and Ireland — chiefly from the latter country; though they came, besides, from Germany and Holland, in considerable numbers. In 1685, the Baptists had formed a church, in Charlestown; the Independents, in conjunction with Presbyterians, in 1690; and, by themselves, other churches, in several other parishes. There were few or no Roman Catholics, before the Revolution, most of the Irish being Presbyterian. They were not organized as a church, until 1791. The Methodists first appeared in 1785, and camp-meetings began in 1800. The revocation of the edict of Nantz, in 1685, brought great numbers of French protestants to Carolina. The German protestants began to build in Charlestown, in 1759. The Jews, with fresh privileges, had a synagogue in Charlestown, somewhere about 1750, with several hundred members. With this diversity of population, toleration was inevitable; and, with few and brief exceptions, the government of South Carolina

18. What ecclesiastical power did Governor Bull exercise? 19. What appointment was made, in 1733? 20. What of Alexander Garden? 21. What of Whitfield? 22. When was he suspended? 23. What was his popularity? 24. From what sources did dissenters increase? 25. When did the Baptists first form a church? 26. When the Independents and Presbyterians? 27. What of the Roman Catholics, and Irish? 28. When did the former organize a church? 29. When did the Methodists first appear? 30. When were camp-meetings first held? 31. What was the effect of the revocation of the edict of Nantz? 32. When did the German Protestants begin to build? 33. What of the Jews? 34. What was the effect of this diversity of sects?

has accorded to all, of whatever denomination, equal privileges, equal securities for life, liberty, and property.

For the first ninety-nine years of provincial Carolina, Charlestown was the source and centre of all judicial proceedings. No courts were held beyond its limits, and as population spread into the interior, justice became impossible. We shall see, hereafter, what was the result of this state of things, in the back country. Enough, that the absence of courts not only abridged the means, and baffled the hopes of justice, but cut off most of the means for popular education. This led to the wild justice which ensued, from the extempore courts of the regulators, who, necessarily, sprang into existence, as population expanded beyond the centres of civilization. But, of these, things the details belong to future pages.

We have shown that religion and law were not easily available to the people. We may reasonably conclude that education, and the opportunities for it, were quite as impossible of attainment. Of the arts, there were but two in exercise — the military and the agricultural; and, in these, the Carolinians could report progress. In the military, perhaps, all that may be said, will simply recognise the courage and the capacity of the provincials to fight in their own defence. Military science was unknown. The arts of fortification were not requisite in high degree, and any backwoodsman could conceive the plan of an adequate fortress against the red men; as riflemen and cavalry, the people were capable of becoming the best soldiers. They were accustomed to the constant use of weapons, to the horse, and their chief amusement was hunting. In the sports of the field, they acquired dexterity, vigilance, keenness, a quick sight, and a wiry muscle. Out of the towns, all were hunters and riflemen. In simple forest strategy, the rangers had become fully equal to the red men; could practise all their arts, and, as if by instinct, resort to their use. In almost all cases, when fighting with British regulars, against the Indians, they had

85. For how long was Charlestown the only seat of justice? 86. What was the effect of this limitation of justice to the one precinct? 87. What the progress of religion and law? 88. What were the arts which were in exercise and progress? 89. What of the military? 40. In what respects were the people of the country good soldiers?

taught the former, and, probably, saved them, scores of times, as they finally rescued the remains of Braddock's army. Their training, in these fields, was the secret of their wonderful successes, when, as partisans, under native leaders, they baffled, in the Revolution, all the generalship and regular forces of Britain.

In agriculture, they had done wonders, though confining their enterprise and industry to favorite spots. But these were in unfavorable situations. The culture of rice they had, already, carried to a degree of perfection, beyond that of the eastern nations, whence its seed had been borrowed. A little bag of rice, brought from Madagascar, in 1693, by a vessel, in distress, had been planted in the city garden of one of the landgraves. It grew well, and the little crop, when matured, was distributed among his friends. In fifty years from this seedling beginning, it had become the prime staple of the province, yielding an income of two hundred thousand pounds. And, about this period, the people were beginning the cultivation of another commodity — indigo — which was destined, for a time, to become a staple, also. Silk, the mulberry, the native grape, the olive, the orange, hemp, flax, tobacco, madder — all had received more or less of the agricultural care of the provincials. The princess-dowager of Wales, and the earl of Chesterfield, wore, in 1756, garments made of the silk of Carolina. In regard to maize, or Indian corn, the colonists had improved so largely upon the first proprietors — the red men — that the latter but too commonly looked to the cornfields of the whites, planting none of their own. There were many experiments in progress, even as far back as 1745, in numerous objects of culture, which only did not mature, as superseded by successive staples, rice, indigo, tobacco, and, lastly, and more potent conqueror than all — cotton.

A few paragraphs may be given to the fiscal history and the financial condition of the province, from the beginning to our present date. For the first twelve years of the colony, there were no taxes. In 1682, an act of the legislature raised

41. What had the people done in agriculture?  42. What productions had shared their attention?  43. What were the successive staples?  44. What was the taxation for the first twelve years?

four hundred pounds, by taxation, for defraying public charges. In the first thirty-two years of the colony, the highest sum raised was eight hundred pounds; and, during all this period, the sum total of taxation did not exceed two thousand four hundred pounds. In 1691, a duty was laid on skins and furs, then the principal exports, and, for ten years, this duty sufficed for the public exigencies. In 1702, to prepare for the expedition against St. Augustine, two thousand pounds were levied; and, as this proved inadequate, two thousand pounds more was raised in each of the years following. In 1708, an act was passed for raising five thousand pounds; in 1710, for three thousand pounds; in 1713, for four thousand pounds. In 1714, a duty was laid on all negro slaves imported. In 1715, there was an act for raising thirty thousand pounds from real and personal property. In 1716, an act for raising fifty-five thousand pounds, and thirty thousand for each of the years following. Of these taxes, one thousand six hundred pounds were apportioned among the merchants and inhabitants of Charlestown — the first tax to which they were expressly subjected. In 1719, the sum of seventy thousand pounds was raised on lands and negroes. This augmentation of taxation was due, not to the increasing prosperity of the province, nor to the increased value of its territory and property, but, rather, to the reverse. It was the result of its disasters; to its various military expeditions; the invasions by French and Spaniard; expedition against the Tuscaroras; war with the Yemassees, and with the pirates; all of which events occurred between 1701 and 1719. In 1712, the enormous sum of fifty-two thousand pounds was issued in bills of credit, and loaned out to the inhabitants, increasing their extravagances, raising the value of property, and depreciating the currency. As a British province, Carolina nominally employed a British currency; but very little British money was in circulation in any of the colonies. Most of their gold or silver coin was foreign — Spanish,

French, Portuguese, etc. British laws, regulating the value of the coin, were little regarded, where the demand for coin was so urgent. In Carolina, finally, paper had so depreciated, in process of time, that ten dollars currency were required to meet the demand for one sterling. The royal government unwisely repeated the error of the proprietary, in this respect; bills of credit continued to be issued. Governor Nicholson, in 1722, gave his assent to an emission of forty thousand pounds; and the people clamored for more. Parties for and against the measure, struggling so fiercely, as, between the years 1727 and 1731, almost to defeat legislation — the king's council refusing farther emissions, while the House of Commons refused their concurrence in all other measures.

The latter prevailed, in 1736, so as to issue two hundred and ten thousand pounds more, to be loaned out at 8 per cent. It was in vain that Arthur Middleton, president, and Kinloch and Wragg, members of council, vehemently opposed it. They have left their protest, with the arguments influencing them, upon the records. The consequences of these wild emissions of paper, without the proper money basis, were its unsteadiness of value, its ultimate loss of value; and, the various injuries to capital, credit, and social stability, which usually follow upon the expansions of a bank in a speculative temper of the community.

The commerce of South Carolina had a noble origin. Its first merchants were the lords-proprietors themselves. They established lines of shipping between Great Britain and Charlestown, and between the latter and the several provinces of Virginia, and the British West India islands, and, especially, Barbadoes. And this, without contemplating mercantile profit, but to encourage emigration and provide supplies to the colonists. We have, elsewhere, shown what were the exports and imports of the province to the date of the present chapter. In 1740, ship-building was begun, and five ship-yards were erected;

51. What was the result, finally, of the excess of paper money? 52. What act received Nicholson's assent, in 1722? 53. Who protested against it? 54. What was the origin of commerce, in South Carolina, and who were its first merchants? 55. When was ship-building begun, and where?

one in Charlestown, three in its vicinity, and one at Beaufort; and, from these, between 1740 and 1776, twenty-four square rigged vessels, besides sloops and schooners, were launched successfully. The Revolution reduced all enterprises, for a time, to ruins.

But, we must not anticipate. Enough, perhaps, has been shown, in this summary, to indicate the progress, the condition, and the resources of the province, down to a certain and turning period in its fortunes. Events are now maturing for more important struggles, and a career of more imposing state, as well as dangers, for our infant province.

56. What number of ships, sloops, and schooners, were built, between 1740 and 1776?

## CHAPTER IV.

### FROM 1743 TO 1756 — WAR WITH THE CHEROKEES.

GOVERNOR GLENN assumed the chair of state in 1743. This gentleman has left us a useful narrative and statistical report of the colony to the close of his administration, which continued till 1756, and from which the historian derives many of his most important facts during this interval. It was during his career that Charlestown, twelve years after the great fire, was nearly destroyed by a hurricane (1752). The devoted city was only saved from being utterly swallowed up in the seas by a providential change of wind. The waters of the gulf-stream, which had been driven by the blast upon the shores, were permitted rapidly to retire into their accustomed channels. Within ten minutes after the wind had shifted, the water fell five feet. But for this merciful dispensation, every inhabitant of Charlestown might have perished. As the event-was, many were drowned—many more hurt or endangered ; the wharves and fortifications were demolished ; the crops growing in the fields were destroyed ; vast numbers of cattle perished, and the trees and gardens of the town were ruined. The city emerged from the waters a universal wreck, which it required a long time of prosperity to repair.

This event, as a matter of course, seriously retarded the growth of the city. Meanwhile, however, population had been gradually extending itself into the interior, from the commencement of Bull's administration in 1737, so as to plant settlements in numerous places, though still remote from each other in that belt, near the seaboard, which is called the middle country, from seventy to one hundred miles westward from the coast. At an earlier period there was a fort upon the Congaree, and this

1. When did James Glenn assume the reins of government ?  2. What has he left us ?  3. What happened in Charlestown during his administration ?  4. What saved the city ?  5. What was the injury to the city ?  6. How was population extending ?

implied the germ of a settlement. In 1737, Orangeburg had a few settlers, and, gradually, the farmers and graziers, passing still farther upward, planted seeds of colonies along the margin of the upper belt of the province. In 1750, there were small settlements two hundred miles from Charlestown, chiefly of emigrants from Virginia and Pennsylvania, who had crossed the barriers of the Blue Ridge or Apalachian mountains. Colonel Clarke, with a party of Virginians, settled in that year on the Pacolet. Other parties subsequently joined him, dotting with civilization the forests along the Fair Forest and Tiger rivers. A few other parties, here and there, with these constituted the only white settlements of the back country until 1755, the year when Braddock was defeated. This lamentable event, by which the frontiers of Pennsylvania, Virginia, and Maryland, were laid open to the war parties of the red men and the French, impelled the terrified borderers of the colonies to turn their eyes in the direction of South Carolina; and in this year Governor Glenn, having succeeded in effecting a treaty with the Cherokees which ceded to Great Britain a large portion of the upper country, served greatly to allure settlers to the western parts of the province. In 1756, Patrick Calhoun, with four families, planted himself in Abbeville, in the southwestern extremity of this region. Here he found that two other settlers had preceded him. Until 1756, however, the progress of colonization was so very slow in this remote quarter, that the whole number of families scarcely exceeded twenty-five. But, for the two years which followed, the influx of inhabitants, especially from the provinces mentioned, was very considerable.

While war raged in these provinces, Carolina, from her timely treaty with the Cherokees, remained at peace. The Cherokees were the allies of the British, and had sent their warriors to fight with those of Britain against the French

7. How did population spread in 1750? 8. Whence did the new settlers come? 9. Where did they settle? 10. What was the effect upon South Carolina of Braddock's defeat? 11. What treaty did Governor Glenn make in 1755? — and what cession did he obtain? 12. In 1756, who were the settlers, and where? 13. What condition did Carolina enjoy during this period? 14. With whom were the Cherokees in alliance? — where and against whom?

invaders on the Ohio. But this was all to change in 1758, when Fort Duquesne was reduced.

Meanwhile, according to Glenn, indigo had been a profitable staple production in the low and middle country, sharing the public favor with rice. In 1747, the *white* population of these two sections had grown to twenty-five thousand, of which five thousand were capable of bearing arms. The negroes, however, had diminished to thirty-nine thousand. The increase of the whites was chiefly from Germany and the British colonies. The diminution of the negroes was due to removals of slaves into Georgia, which had adopted negro slavery, and had only begun to flourish after it did so, and to the fact that the heavy duties on the importation of slaves amounted, at this period, to a prohibition.

In the same year (1747), a terrible frost destroyed all the orange and olive trees along the seaboard. The former had been found greatly to flourish in previous seasons; the latter had so prospered that a single tree was found to yield several bushels of fruit, and this originally from a single stick, lopped at both ends, brought from Fayal, and stuck in a garden-spot in Carolina. So severe was the winter, that the very birds perished of the cold.

Britain and British shipping still enjoyed a monopoly of the trade and commerce of the province. Charlestown, Port Royal and Winyah, or Georgetown, had each its collector now; the former, for some years before. There was little or no illegal trading — by sea, at least. The trade, with the red men of the interior, was large enough and loose enough, perhaps, to cover a thousand illegal practices. The Indian traders of Carolina carried their packs — nay, the arms of the colony — to the Mississippi, and strove in battle with the French, while they traded with the red men, with whom they not unfrequently lost scalps as well as packs. The French had subsidized the Choctaws.

15. What is said of Indigo? 16. What were the white and negro populations of South Carolina in 1747? 17. To what were the increase of the one and decrease of the other respectively due? 18. What injurious event occurred in 1747? 19. What is said of the orange and the olive? 20. What of the commerce of South Carolina? 21. Where were the ports of entry? 22. What is said of the trade? 23. What of the Indian traders? 24. What of the French and Choctaws?

But in 1748, and for several years after, the administration of Governor Glenn remained undisturbed from any quarter. Some predatory parties of red men, generally fugitives or outlaws from scattered tribes, found their way into the settlements of the the lower country, and committed horrid depredations. In 1751, flying parties of these marauders plundered the plantations along the Santee and at the head of Cooper river. A party, in the same year, was dispersed with loss, near the seaside, in Christ church parish ; and a successful foray into Beaufort, from which some women and children were carried off, was ascribed to the Cherokees, but was more probably due to the Spanish Indians. In 1753, some of this same fugitive class of red men, mere marauders, committed their depredations within forty miles of the city. But for such parties the nation no more held itself responsible than do those more civilized states, from whence flibustering parties go forth on adventures of their own.

With these insignificant exceptions, South Carolina was suffered for several years, and during the greater part of Glenn's administration, the enjoyment of repose. The red men, as peoples, had receded farther from the settlements. As already mentioned, in part, the Cherokees, in 1755, renewed their treaty of peace with the Carolinians, and accompanied this act by the cession of a large territory, including what are now the districts of Greenville, Pendleton, and portions of other districts. In the general state of security, following this condition of the province, the measures of war were relaxed. The armed galleys and scout-boats of the seaboard were abandoned ; even the rangers of the frontier were disbanded, and an immense cost in money was saved to the province. There were no taxes on real or personal property ; all the expenses of the government were amply met by duties raised upon exports or imports.

In respect to agriculture, the results of peace were wonderful. In 1745, the exports of indigo, which had grown to be a staple, reached £200,000. In 1757, of raw silk, ten thousand

25. What of Glenn's administration in 1748, and subsequently ? 26. From what disturbances did the colony suffer, and in what quarter ? 27. What happened in 1753 ? 28. What was the condition of South Carolina ? 29. What districts were formed out of the ceded territories ? 30. From what was the revenue derived ? 31. What were the exports of indigo in 1745 ?

pounds weight were exported through Savannah from the Swiss settlement at Purysburg, on that river. In 1754, the exports of the province had risen to the enormous sum of £242,529. But a more important item still, as illustrated by a subsequent history, may be found in the fact that, in the same year (1754), *cotton*, now the pacificator of states and nations, was also exported, though in very small quantities. It continued to be grown and used for domestic purposes, and, mixed with wool, constituted a frequent article of clothing in the state during the war of the Revolution.

Governor Glenn, soon after the cession of lands from the Cherokees, proceeded to fortify in several places in the ceded territory. He built, among other forts, one upon the banks of the Savannah, and within gunshot of the Indian town of Keowee. It contained barracks for a hundred men, was built in the form of a square, had an earthen rampart six feet high, on which stockades were fixed, with a ditch, a natural glacis on two sides, and bastions at the angles, on each of which four small cannon were mounted.

On the banks of the same river, about one hundred and seventy miles below, another fort was raised, called Fort Moore, in a beautiful and commanding situation.

Another, called Loudon, was built on the Tennessee, upward of five hundred miles from Charlestown. These strong holds were garrisoned by regular troops from Britain; and the establishment of these defences in the interior led to the rapid accumulation of settlers in all the choice places in their neighborhood. They were each to be distinguished by a tragic history.

In the year 1756, William H. Lyttleton, afterward Lord Westcott, was made governor of Carolina. The year after this event, a large party of Cherokee Indians, who had been serving in the armies of great Britain against the French in the west, and had assisted in the conquest of the famous Fort Du-

82. What of raw silk in 1757? 33. What of the total exports of the province in 1754? 84. When was cotton first exported from South Carolina? 85. How was it used at home? 86. Where did Governor Glenn fortify? 87. Where was Fort Prince George, and how described? 88. What other forts upon the same river? 89. What upon the Tennessee? 40. How were these forts garrisoned? 41. Who became governor in 1756?

quesne, returning from the wars to their homes, took possession of a number of horses belonging to the whites as they passed through the back parts of Virginia.

The Virginians rashly resented the robbery by violence; they killed a number of the warriors, and took several prisoners.

This aggression kindled the flames of war among the injured people, who commenced the work of reprisal by scalping the whites wherever they were found.  Parties of the young warriors rushed down upon the frontier settlements, and the work of massacre became general along the borders of Carolina.

The Carolinians gathered in arms, and, when the chiefs of the Cherokees became aware of the fact, they sent a deputation to Charlestown to disarm the anger of the people by a timely reconciliation.

Unhappily, Governor Lyttleton, who was an ostentatious and not a wise governor, treated these messengers with indignity, and finally made them prisoners.  Having resolved upon a military expedition, he refused to listen to their orator, but proceeded with all his force — the chiefs being under guard — to his rendezvous on Congaree river, where he mustered fourteen hundred men.

The Cherokees, burning with indignation at this treatment, were yet subtle enough to suppress the show of it.  They agreed to such terms as Lyttleton proposed — gave up twenty-two out of twenty-four hostages which he demanded, to be kept till the young warriors who had committed the murders upon the Carolinians should be secured and delivered — and renewed their pledges of peace and alliance.

But he had scarcely returned to the capital when he received the news of the murder of fourteen whites within a mile of Fort George.  A Lieutenant or Captain Cotymore — colonel, possibly, as in an independent command — had been left in charge of that fortress.  To this officer the Indians had taken

42. What about the Cherokees in 1757?  43. What did the Virginians?  44. How did their violence affect the Cherokees?  45. What was their action?  46. What did the Carolinians?  47. How did the Cherokees endeavor to disarm their anger?  48. What was the error of Governor Lyttleton?  49. What were his subsequent movements?  50. What policy did the Cherokees adopt?  51. What treaty was made?  52. How kept?  53. Who had charge of Fort George?

an unconquerable aversion. Occonostota, a chief of great influence, had also, for reasons not now known, become a most implacable enemy of the Carolinians, and proposed to himself the task of taking Prince George.

Having gathered a strong force of Cherokees, he surrounded it; but finding that he could make no impression on the works, nor alarm the commander, he had recourse to stratagem to effect his object. He placed a select body of savages in a dark thicket by the river side, and sent an Indian woman, who was always received with favor at the garrison, to tell Cotymore that he wished to see him at the river, where he had something of consequence to communicate.

Cotymore, accompanied by his two lieutenants, Bell and Foster, imprudently consented. When he reached the river, Occonostota appeared on the opposite side, having in his hand a bridle. He told Cotymore that he was on his way to Charlestown to procure a release of the prisoners, and would be glad of a white man to go with him as a safeguard, adding that he was about to hunt for a horse for the journey.

Cotymore told him that he should have a guard; and, while they parleyed, Occonostota thrice waved the bridle over his head. This signal to the savages in ambush, for such it was, proved fatal to the three officers, who were instantly shot down. Cotymore was mortally wounded, and soon after died.

In consequence of this deed, the garrison proceeded to put in irons the twenty hostages that had been left with them. They resisted the attempt, and stabbed three of the men who endeavored to put the manacles on them. The garrison, in the highest degree exasperated, fell upon them in a fury, and butchered them to a man. The whole affair was wretchedly unfortunate. Some excuses have been found, or fancied, for this massacre; but these are mostly after-thoughts, and valueless. It was a massacre at once brutal and impolitic.

The catastrophe maddened the whole nation. There were few Cherokee families that did not lose a friend or relative in

54. Who was Occonostota? 55. What did he undertake? 56. To what stratagem did he resort? 57. What error did Cotymore commit? 58. What was his fate? 59. What did the garrison do? 60. How is the affair described? 61. What was the effect upon the nation?

this massacre, and with one voice they declared for battle. They seized the hatchet, and singing their songs of war, and burning with indignation for revenge, they rushed down — a reckless and countless horde — upon the frontiers of Carolina.

Men, women, and children, without discrimination, fell victims to their merciless fury; and, to add to the misfortunes of the borderers, Charlestown, laboring under the presence of that dreadful scourge, the small-pox, was too feeble to send them succor.

What could be done, however, was done. Seven troops of rangers were furnished by Virginia and North Carolina; and a British force under the command of Colonel Montgomery, afterward earl of Eglintoun, was sent by General Amherst, the commander-in-chief in America at that time, to the relief of the province.

Montgomery chastised the Cherokees in several severe engagements, in which they lost large numbers of their warriors; but without humbling them to submission. He was compelled to return to New York, leaving his work unfinished.

In the meantime, the distant garrison of Fort Loudon, on the Tennessee river, consisting of two hundred men, was reduced by famine. The Virginians had undertaken to relieve it, but failed to do so; and the miserable occupants were reduced to the necessity of submitting to the mercy of the Cherokees.

Captain Stuart, an officer of great sagacity and address, to whom the post had been entrusted, succeeded in obtaining good terms of safety, upon which he capitulated. By these terms the garrison were permitted to march out with their arms and drums, as much ammunition as was necessary on their march, and such baggage as they might choose to carry. The Indians were to take the lame and wounded soldiers into their towns, provide as many horses as they could for the garrison, furnish guides, and an escort which was to protect them; for all of which they were to be paid according to certain estimates, which were understood among them. The fort, cannon, powder, and ball, were delivered up to the Indians.

The capitulation took effect, and the garrison had proceeded fifteen miles upon their march, when they were deserted by their guides and escort, beset by a large body of savages, and, though fighting gallantly, were overcome. Twenty-six men fell at the first fire — a few escaped by flight — while Stuart, the commander, with many others, was carried into captivity.

Stuart, through the friendship of one of their chiefs, finally escaped, after many hardships, into Virginia; but the rest of the prisoners were kept in a miserable captivity for some time, and redeemed at last only at great expense.

Though the Cherokees had suffered severely from the measures of Montgomery, they were not yet disposed for peace. The French maintained emissaries among them, who continually fomented the appetite for war. "I am for war!" cried Salooe, a young warrior of Estatoe, in a council where an agent of France had been busy to make them discountenance the efforts of some of their own chiefs, who labored in the cause of peace: "I am still for war! The spirits of our brothers call upon us to avenge their death. He is a woman who will not follow me!"

The savages, moved by his wild eloquence, seized the tomahawk again, and the war was renewed in all its former fury.

66. What was the fate of its garrison? 67. What became of Stuart? 68. Were the Cherokees humbled? 69. How was their hostility fomented? 70. What was the language of Salooe, the young warrior of Estatoe? 71. What was the effect of his wild eloquence?

# CHAPTER V.

### FROM 1756 TO 1764.

THE terrors of an Indian war roused the Carolinians to the most strenuous efforts to meet the emergency on the threshold, and to anticipate the forays of the red men, by carrying their arms into the enemy's country. But this was no easy matter. It involved the sacrifice of vast sums of money; the loss of time consequent upon the embodiment of troops to be brought from remote distances; the passage through great wildernesses, which, as yet, offered no openings for transportation of provisions, or artillery, and in every fastness of which might lurk an overpowering ambush. And, in the meantime, what massacres were to dye the frontier settlements in blood, and lay waste their habitations. But, facing these dangers and discouragements boldly, the authorities of South Carolina proceeded to work with the vigor which became a martial people. A provincial regiment was raised, the command of which was given to Colonel Middleton. He was admirably seconded by lieutenants, who were destined, in this campaign, to lay the foundations of great reputations, which were to rise during another war, at a much later period, to which this contest of the red men was, comparatively, a play at soldiers, rather than a sanguinary conflict. Among the field officers, in this provincial regiment, we find the names of Henry Laurens, William Moultrie, Francis Marion, Isaac Huger, and Andrew Pickens; all of whom subsequently became greatly distinguished, at once, in the annals of the state, and of the confederacy. It was during this expedition that they commenced that admirable course of

1. How did the prospect of the Cherokee war affect the Carolinians? 2. What preparations did they make? 3. What were their embarrassments? 4. What force did they raise, and by whom commanded? 5. What field-officers accompanied Middleton?

training which prepared them for the more arduous trials, and the prolonged conflicts of the Revolution, the thunders of which were already muttering in the sky, though audible, perhaps, only to the keener senses of the sagacious few.

But, the war with the Cherokees was not allowed to fall wholly upon provincial shoulders. The British government, since it had taken the place of the proprietary, had never withheld from the colony that nursing care and protection which its infancy demanded. Whatever the offences of Great Britain, under either of the Georges, in respect to their usurpation or abuse of power, it is to their credit that they rarely showed remissness or indifference, when the safety of the province was threatened by the enemy, or when it needed succor for its absolute maintenance. On this occasion, the native regiment was supported by a large body of regular troops, under Colonel James Grant, who reached Charlestown early in 1761, and proceeded to the rendezvous with the provincials. With a small auxiliary force of red warriors, from the friendly tribes, the little army numbered in all some twenty-six hundred men, all of whom were under the general authority of Colonel Grant.

It was soon put under marching orders, and, on the twenty-seventh of May, 1761, had reached Fort Prince George, the scene of Cotymore's massacre. Here, the long-tried friend of the Carolinians, Attakullakulla, hastened to the camp of the whites, filled with grief, and sought, by prayers and promises, to avert the blow from his nation. But, as Grant and Middleton well knew that however much the old chief might be a favorite with his people, he had no influence sufficient to arrest the young ones—the red sticks—in their vindictive moods and sanguinary appetites. Attakullakulla received no encouragement, and the army steadily marched on; a scouting party being sent forward, under Captain Kennedy, of ninety Indians, with thirty white men, painted and habited like the red warriors. Another body of two hundred, rangers and light in-

6. What did the British government to assist the Carolinians? 7. By whom were the British regulars commanded? 8. When did the forces reach Charlestown? 9. When did they reach Prince George? 10. By what chief were they met? 11. With what precautions did Grant and Middleton proceed? 12. Who led their advanced scouting party?

fantry, followed in support; and these scoured the thickets and defiles, in regions which might well have been chosen for fatal ambuscades. As they advanced, in this order, and with becoming circumspection, "the Indian sign" became abundant, and it was soon apparent that the conflict was at hand. At length, about the twelfth of June, the Cherokees encountered the English and Carolinians, near the town of Etchoe, very near the spot which had been signalized in the previous campaign, by their conflict with Montgomery. They were posted in force along a hill, on the right flank of the army, and beside which it was compelled to pass. The Cherokees, with great fury, rushed down upon the advanced guard, pouring in the most destructive fire as they came, and fearlessly, and with wild shouts, darting forward to the close combat of knife and tomahawk. The advance guard held its ground firmly, and, being promptly supported, succeeded in repelling the assailants. They recovered their heights as rapidly as they had descended, and the conflict became general in the effort to dislodge them. This was necessary, indeed, to the progress of the army — the only route lying directly beneath the heights of which they were in possession; while, on the other hand, lay the course of a river, from the banks and thickets of which another body of the Indians maintained an incessant fire, as the army continued to advance. To escape either of these fires, it was necessary to silence one of them; and, while the party, covering the bill, were assailed by one division of the Carolinians, in front, another division maintained the conflict with the river party. The engagement, thus begun, constituted two actions, separate in their progress, though mutual in object and result. It was waged by the Cherokees with the greatest obstinacy. They were advantageously posted, in both situations, well covered by the forest thickets, which, along the river, were dense, and almost impervious; they were familiar with the ground, and all its covers, and all its defiles; could recede, without difficulty, from pressure, and re-advance to the conflict as soon as the pressure was withdrawn. Under these circumstances, the issue,

13. Where, and when, did they meet the Cherokees? 14. How were the Cherokees posted? 15. In what order were they assailed? 16. How did they fight?

for three hours of mortal struggle, was doubtful, in high degree.
The whites were not in the best condition for such a combat.
They had suddenly come upon the foe, and though guarded
against surprise, they could use no military skill in the choice
of ground. The battle had been forced upon them, in a position
chosen by the savage. They were fatigued by a dreary and
long march, in wet weather, and totally ignorant of the scene
of action; so completely surrounded by the forests, that sight
could penetrate in no direction, and galled, on every side, by
fires from an invisible enemy, against whom they could only
oppose perpetual charges and a random fire; and these charges
usually found a flying foe, whose alertness, in his native thickets
baffled pursuit, and found a ready and contiguous shelter, from
which he could emerge, at any moment, and promptly renew
the exhausting conflict. But, the stout rangers had fearless
hearts, and knew the merits of bush-fighting, in general; the
British regulars held their ground with bull-dog tenacity, and
plied their bayonets with a rapidity which admirably seconded
the irregular warfare of the provincials. The auxiliary Indians
of the army, were brave experts, who answered the yells of the
Cherokees in their own style, and met them with like stratagem; and, the result was the victory of the Carolinians, after
one of the fiercest battles with the red men on the records of
America. At the end of three hours, the Cherokees were
driven from the field; from their hill and river fastnesses,
equally, and, though dropping shots continually encountered
their advance, for three hours longer, yet the battle array, the
hope and spirit of the enemy were broken. The persevering
valor of the whites, their better weapons, and science — such
as might be displayed in such a field — triumphed, finally and
entirely, over the fierce, wild warriors of the forest. But, they
fled fighting — grimly delivering their fires from every shelter
in their retreat. They were not again suffered to re-unite in
force; were pressed, in the flight, with an energy that never
gave them leisure to make a stand, or renew the conflict.

17. In what condition were the whites? 18. How did the provincials and British
respectively behave themselves? 19. The red auxiliaries of the whites? 20. What
was the result of the battle?

Their loss in the action is unknown; that of the Carolinian army was fifty or sixty killed and wounded. The slain were not buried, but sunk in the river, that their bodies might not be exposed to the mutilations of the savage.

This victory opened the way to the nation. The Cherokees were broken in spirit, and did not seek to re-organize. The army advanced upon Etchoe, one of their largest towns, which was reduced to ashes. The towns, in their middle settlements, shared the same fate. Their granaries and cornfields, the corn still growing, were likewise destroyed; the necessity being evident that to bring them to subjection, and curb their ferocious spirit, it was necessary to drive them to the refuge of deeper forests, and deprive them of the means of support in their settlements. This terrible measure, the fruit of a paramount necessity, was of fatal consequences to the feebler portions of their tribes. Their miserable families were driven to the dismal shelter of barren mountains, which could yield them nothing but a shelter. They are said to have perished in large numbers. The name of Grant, who was the leader of this army, grew, in time, to be a proverbial word, signifying "devastation," among the red men. For years after, when they discovered the cattle in their corn-fields, they drove them out with wild yells of "Grant! Grant!"

But, while the whites remained among them, they offered no farther defense of corn-field or habitation. They had fought a pitched battle, on their own ground, with determined valor. It is conjectured that they had been posted and counselled by certain experienced French officers, who were among them. But, even these failed to rouse them to a renewal of the struggle. They were completely overcome; the native-spirit was subdued; they looked down from their hill-tops, with the supineness of despair, upon the flames which swallowed up their hamlets, and the devastation which laid waste their fields. They

21. How many of the whites were slain or wounded? 22. Upon what town did the whites then advance, and burn? 23. What was their farther progress, and what their performance? 24. What was the effect upon the families of the Cherokees? 25. How did they use the name of Grant? 26. Did the Cherokees continue the war? 27. By what European officers are they supposed to have been led?

humbly sued for peace. The good old, friendly chief, Attakullakulla, was now permitted to seek and make terms with the Carolinians. He proceeded to Charlestown, and, addressing Governor Bull, he asked once more for mercy, on indulgent terms.

" I am come," said the venerable chief, " to see what can be done for my people. They are in great distress. As to what has taken place, forgive us. I believe it has been decreed by the Great Master, who is above. He is father of red men and white. We all live in one land — let us live as one people."

Governor Bull, a prudent, and moderate statesman, was disposed to be indulgent. He satisfied himself that the spirit of the Cherokees was sufficiently humbled. The prayer of the aged chief was granted; a peace was made between the parties, and the end of this savage war, which was supposed to have had its origin in the machinations of French emissaries, was among the last humbling blows given by the joint valor of the provincials and Britain, to the power of France in North America.

The Cherokees, though humbled, were not subdued. They harbored, in their hearts, spite of the influence of their chief, spite of their seeming submission, an eager spirit of revenge, which, not many years afterward, found its fierce expression against the Carolinians, when Britain, in her anger with the colonies, adopted the old expedients of French and Spaniard, and set the savage warriors to work, with fire and tomahawk, upon the frontier settlements. The Cherokees could still bring two thousand warriors into the field. The machinations of Britain soon found them willing. But this belongs to future pages.

This campaign of Grant and Middleton, so creditable to the valor of all concerned in it, was followed by an unhappy difference between the commanders of the regular and provincial forces. Colonel Grant seems to have been a person of haughty and arrogant temper. He is, we believe, the same Colonel Grant, who, in the British parliament, affirmed that, with three

28. Did they entreat peace, and by whom? 29. Were they forgiven, and by whom? 30. Were they really subdued, or secretly resentful? 31. What force could they still bring into the field? 32 What is said of Colonel Grant?

regiments, he could march through all America. He was distinguished by all that insolent spirit of superiority, which was so apt to distinguish the conduct of officers of the mother-country in their treatment of the provincials; a signal instance of which exhibited itself, not long before, in a neighboring colony, in the deportment of the depraved and arrogant Braddock toward the modest provincial, Washington. This mood of assumption is, probably, characteristic everywhere, in the deportment of the regular toward the militia service.

In its indulgence, Grant, after he reached Charlestown, gave offence to Colonel Middleton, his associate in the command of the forces. Middleton was one of the first persons in the colony. His family had always been distinguished by its conduct, and by its influence. He was a gentleman as tenacious of the honor of the province as of his own position. Grant, it seems, had, during the Cherokee expedition, displayed a most offensive indifference to all the suggestions of the provincial officers; enacting, in brief, the character of Braddock, so far as this ignored the proper consideration of the provincials. They were not held to be authority in military operations, even though these were conducted in their own country, and in a war so anomalous as that with the red men.

To this offence he added by claiming the chief credit for himself and regulars, of having subdued the Cherokees. There may have been some direct, as there was certainly much tacit disparagement of the provincials, in this assumption.

The claim was resisted and resented by Middleton, with promptitude and spirit. A controversy ensued, the result of which was, according to one of our authorities, that Middleton caned Grant, on Vendue Range, in Charlestown. A duel followed, and shots were ineffectually exchanged. Here, the affair was arrested — how, we know not — and Grant left the country. But the affair occasioned an intense excitement, and bitter feelings of animosity in the community. The native Carolinians generally sided with their champion; but, the Scotch

83. Who resented his conduct, and how? 84. Who was Middleton, and how did he behave? 85. Was their duel harmless? 86. How did the affair affect the community?

merchants, in the city, who constituted the largest portion of the trading population, as naturally took sides with Grant. The bitter animosities which followed, it is not improbable, contributed considerably to awaken, in the provincials, a more keen conviction of the arrogant and usurping spirit of the mother-country, which then, or soon after, began to display itself in various ways, a spirit no less impudent than usurpative, and which, finally, by its exactions and its insolence, led the colonies into a defiance of British power and authority, which, though inevitable in the end, might otherwise have been delayed for, possibly, a hundred years.

From this period, and from these and other events, we may date the true beginning, not only of the prosperity, but of the independence of Carolina. Hitherto, she had been straitened by deficient resources of wealth and population — had been hemmed in on all her borders, by Spaniards, French, and savages. Now, all external pressure was withdrawn, and she was left free to expand, according to the degree of her natural energies, and the resources of her soil and climate. The red men, upon the frontier, had succumbed. The " peace of Paris " had relieved her from the secret machinations and the open hostilities of France. Florida, with Fort Augustine, and the bay of Pensacola, with all that Spain possessed, on the continent of North America, east or southeast of the Mississippi, had been ceded to Great Britain, and though in the hands of Great Britain, Florida was destined to be as much a thorn in the side of Carolina as she had ever been while in possession of the Spaniards; yet, as no human foresight could conjecture this, the Carolinians held themselves to be now secure against danger, from this, as from any other quarter, and exultingly devoted themselves to the building up of the republic, with a zeal and confidence wholly free from distrust and doubt. Security from all enemies left her free for self-development; it left her free, also, to the analysis of her own relations with Great Britain — a study which now began to force itself upon all of the

87. What had been the condition of Carolina before the conquest of the Cherokees? 88. How did this conquest, and the " peace of Paris," affect the province? 89. How did this peace affect the relations of Great Britain with the provinces?

American colonies, about the same time. Then, and not till then, and under such conditions of security from foreign pressure, could the spirit of political and social inquiry show itself active or confident. Once alive, and free to work, this spirit, passing from fact to fact, and from principle to principle, with amazing rapidity, soon arrived at those convictions of political truth, law, and equity, which learned to question the tenure of foreign authority, and the legitimacy of these relations with the mother-country, which placed the provincials wholly at her mercy. The summits of republican freedom were not far from sight, in the new spirit of political inquiry, thus made bold, active, and intelligent. But, of all this, hereafter.

Never did any colony flourish in more surprising degree than South Carolina, as soon as the Cherokees were overcome, and the French and Spaniards driven from her borders. Her back country began to fill up. Hitherto, the settlements, two hundred miles from the sea, did not include twenty families. Now, multitudes of emigrants, from all parts of Europe, flocked to the interior, and perusing the devious courses of fertilizing streams, sought out their sources, sought out favorite spots for culture, and planted their little colonies along the side of sloping hills, or in the bosoms of lovely valleys. Six hundred poor German settlers arrived in one body. But Ireland, probably, gave to the province its most principal elementary population. She poured forth such numbers, from her northern counties, as almost to threaten, in that portion, the depopulation of the Green Island. Scarce a ship sailed for any of the plantations, that was not crowded with men, women, and children, destined for the warm and fertile region of Carolina, of which such glowing tidings had reached their ears, and where the land was proffered in bounties to all comers.

. Nor did the province receive these accessions from Europe only. Pennsylvania, Virginia, and Maryland, all made their contributions. In the space of a single year, more than a thousand families, with their effects, their cattle, hogs, and horses,

---

40. What was its prosperity? 41. What the progress of settlement? 42. From what regions did settlers come?

crossed the Apalachian ridges, from the eastern settlements, and pitched their tents along the Carolina frontier.

These accessions *made* the country, till then a wilderness. They brought strength and security. In proportion, as the settlements grew and spread, and with the increase of numbers, the terrors of savage warfare were diminished. The Cherokees, who still held that portion of the country, which now forms the districts of Greenville, Pickens, and Anderson, looked on the rapid approach of civilization with the natural apprehension of the savage. Their instincts taught them to feel the coercion of a power, which was to dispossess them of the soil, but it needed years for their recuperation from the paralysis into which they were thrown by their late defeats. We shall see them, hereafter, again in the field, and again paying for the rashness of revolt, by the usual penalties of subjugation and privation. Another war will dispossess them of all that remains of the national inheritance within the limits of South Carolina.

But with the increase of population in the backwoods of South Carolina, there was a considerable diminution of numbers in the lower country. The acquisition of Florida, by Britain, the security of the frontier against the savages, and the admission of African slavery into Georgia, wonderfully accelerated the growth of this latter province. Many of the more wealthy inhabitants of Carolina bought lands, and removed their property to Georgia. The result of this was a vast increase of wealth and prosperity in this province. In 1763, her exports were but twenty-eight thousand pounds sterling; but, in less than ten years from that period, they had reached one hundred and twenty-one thousand six hundred and seventy-seven pounds sterling.

And still this prosperity of the more southern colony, though drawing somewhat from the resources of Carolina, did not seem to diminish them. She, too, was prosperous in high degree. In 1762, Thomas Boone had succeeded as governor to William

43. What was the effect of this rapid increase of population? 44. Of what districts did the Cherokees still keep possession? 45. What was the effect of increased security upon the low country? 46. How did Georgia thrive? 47. What were its exports in 1763? — in ten years after? 48. Who succeeded Bull as governor of South Carolina?

Bull, to be succeeded by Bull again, in 1763. During all this period, the province flourished, grew, prospered, and extended its domain and cultivation to large increase of profits. In 1764, the German palatines, six hundred in number, settled upon the Santee, in a township given to them, called Londonderry. The assembly voted them an appropriation of five hundred pounds sterling. They addressed themselves to the culture of silk and the vine. England and Scotland sent subsidies of population, though in far less degree than Ireland; and now, the British government, with, perhaps, a proper policy, interposed a check to the progress of settlement in the back country, by limiting the colonists to the sources of the great rivers that fall into the Atlantic; having, in this, a three-fold object — to protect the red men from encroachment, to keep the frontier-men from sudden dangers, and to condense, within accessible boundaries, the whole strength of the province. The subject was prohibited from purchasing lands from the red men. Traders were required to take out licenses for trading among the tribes, and a general superintendent, Captain John Stuart, an able man, was installed, having control of all the intercourse between the two races. All this tended to the amelioration of the condition of the red men, and the comparative security of the white.

In 1765, William Bull, being still the governor, the province may be stated to be one hundred years old. But a very few years were needed to make it so. Yet, with all the rapid progress we have reported, the increase seems wretchedly insignificant in modern times. In this year (1765), the number of white inhabitants, in Charlestown, was between five and six thousand; of negroes, between seven and eight thousand. The population of the province was but forty thousand whites; the whole number capable of bearing arms between seven and eight thousand. The negro population was between eighty and

49. Who Boone? 50. How did the province flourish, meanwhile? 51. What European emigrants came to it in 1764? 52. Where did they settle, and what raise? 53. What regulation did the British government make, touching the Indian country? 54. Who did they appoint Indian superintendent? 55. What were their objects in this policy? 56. How old was the province in 1765? 57. What, then, was the population of Charlestown? 58. What of the whole province? 59. What the negro population?

ninety thousand. The harbor of Charlestown was feebly fortified. On the Cooper river line there were several batteries.
Fort Johnson, on James' island, was a slight fabric, with barracks for fifty men. The guns were mounted, in tolerable
numbers, on all these forts; but, there had been but little science shown in the erection, and neither fort nor town could
have long stood the conflict with a couple of ships-of-war, using
very heavy metal. Outside of Charlestown, the towns were
mere hamlets of the smallest size. Beaufort, Purysburg, Jack-
sonburg, Dorchester, Camden, and Georgetown, were inconsiderable villages, not one exceeding forty dwellings, and most of
them within twenty or thirty. But, Charlestown, in that day,
took rank, second to none, with the largest and most prosperous cities of North America. The people within, and in its
precincts, were opulent, gay, showy, and hospitable; their sons
had been sent to England, for education. They brought back
taste and refinement, as well as habits of expenditure. Fashions
in dress and ornament were rapidly transferred from Europe.
Luxury had found its way into the wilderness. Nearly every
Charlestown family kept single-horse chaises, and most of the principal planters, their carriages, drawn by teams of four, and the
horses were imported from Europe, and of good blooded stocks.
They drank fine wines of Madeira, and used freely, also, the
French, Spanish, and Portuguese wines. These were commonly
displayed at dinner parties. Tea, coffee, chocolate, were among
the breakfast and evening beverages, and the drink, in ordinary, through the day, was punch. But, though thus living,
the *gentlemen*, in general, were temperate. "In short," says
the old Scotch Presbyterian, Hewatt, "the people were not only
blessed with plenty, but with a disposition to share it among
friends and neighbors; and, many will bear me witness, when
I say, that travellers could scarcely go into any city where
they could meet with a society of people more agreeable, intelligent, and hospitable, than that at Charlestown."

60. How was Charlestown fortified? 61. What towns, or villages, are mentioned
outside of Charlestown? 62. What their size? 63. What was the rank of Charlestown? 64. What is said of the people, their habits, mode of life, education, fashions,
luxuries, wines, beverages? 65. Were they temperate? 66. What does Hewatt say
of their character?

The same writer tells us —."They, the Carolinians, discover
no bad taste for the polite arts, such as music, drawing, fencing,
and dancing; and, that the women outshine the men.   .   .   .
They are not only discreet and virtuous, but adorned with most
of the accomplishments which become the sex.   .   .   .   The
Carolinians, in general, are affable and easy in their manners,
and exceedingly hospitable and kind to strangers.   .   .   .   As
every person, by diligence and application, may earn a com-
fortable livelihood, there are few *poor* people in the province,
except the idle and unfortunate." He adds — " There are more
persons possessed of between five and ten thousand pounds sterling, in the province, than are to be found anywhere among
the same number of people.   In respect of rank, all men regard
their neighbor as their equal, and a noble spirit of benevolence
pervades the society.   In point of industry, the town [Charles-
town] is like a bee-hive, and there are none that reap not advantage, more or less, from the flourishing trade and commerce.
Pride and ambition had not, as yet, crept into this community ;
but the province is fast advancing to that state of power and
opulence, when some distinctions among men necessarily take
place."

From 1732, the Carolinians had possessed a newspaper; they
had, also, a good bookstore, and had formed a society and library, which was furnished with all new British publications
of value.   Their sports, in the city, were balls and assemblies,
which "were attended by companies almost equally brilliant
as those of any town in Europe, of the same size."   In the
country, the sports of the field were enjoyed on a bolder and
more adventurous scale than in Great Britain.   The planters
had the best dogs and horses; were greater riders, and good
riflemen; and there were foxes to be hunted, and deer and
bear formed the ordinary objects of pursuit.

Such were Charlestown and Carolina at the close of the
Cherokee war, and when, all enemies withdrawn from their

67. What of their capacities — of their women?   68. What of their hospitality, industry, wealth, their social standards, and the progress of the colony?   69. When
did the Carolinians first possess a newspaper?   70. What of their bookstore and
books?   71. What of society, at their assemblies?   72. What of their field-sports?

borders, they were suffered to pursue their occupations in peace. But peace was not yet secure. Even in the moment of assured prosperity, the seeds were in rapid progress of cultivation which were to produce intestine war, separation from the mother-country, and all the pride and all the perils of independence.

78. What seeds of future trouble were sown at this period of prosperity ?

# CHAPTER VI.

### REGULATORS — SCOVILITES — SEEDS OF REVOLUTION.

WE have, in previous chapters, shown the origin and end of the Cherokee war, and the advantages, especially in the back or mountain country, which followed their overthrow and the " peace of Paris." While the Cherokees could be stimulated by the machinations of the French, strengthened by their weapons, and cajoled by their arts, it was impossible that a white population could exist in the great forests of the interior.

The growth of the upper country was, of course, retarded by this sinister and hostile influence. We have shown, however, that, with the peace, population began to flow in as a spring-tide. But, as there is no mortal good utterly unmixed with evil, so it happened that an increase of population in these wild regions brought with it some of the seeds of mischief.

It was one of the evils of this population that it was heterogeneous. There were ancient antipathies, nursed in older countries, that accompanied the new settlers. These founded their settlements, not together, but in colonies. Here, in one place, were Scotch, loyal, intense in their loyalty, and stubborn in their prejudices.

There were Irish in another, more eager, enthusiastic, impulsive, somewhat reckless, and never remarkable for their loyalty to the English domination. There were settlements of Quakers, rigid of habit, unaccommodating in regard to the habits of others ; not warlike, yet little desirous of any social union, except among themselves.

There were Germans, and Swiss, and French, in small bodies,

1. What is said of the growth of the upper or back country ?  2. How was it retarded ?  3. How after the " peace of Paris ?"  4. What was the evil in the population ?  5. From what foreign nations did the colonists come ?

but mostly living to themselves — a series of camps, as we may describe them all — regarding each other with no friendly eye, and holding so little communion with one another that they wrought out but few of the common purposes of society together. Even the common necessity of all, good roads for the maintenance of trade and communion were not to be found; and the country, from settlement to settlement, was only to be traversed along the ancient narrow footpaths of the red man.

Most of these people, for many years, preserved their foreign mode of speech. The Germans continued to speak German; there were settlements of the Scotch that spoke in Gaelic to the time of the Revolution.

The French, and Irish especially, were the first to amalgamate with society, and to show themselves flexible enough to promote, in some sort, the common objects of all social organizations.

In this condition of things, society naturally remained feeble; a foray of the Indians would find their several communities unprepared. They had few motives prompting them to seek each other; and the lack of established facilities and a regular intercourse subjected them to great embarrassments and a tardy progress whenever any necessity arose for conveying intelligence essential to the common safety. A large portion of these early settlers, the Scotch and Germans especially, were graziers, and kept great herds of cattle. They took up large bodies of wild land, sometimes many miles remote from their own settlements, which they established as pastures. Here the herbage was plentiful, and the cattle bred in vast numbers, needing but occasional tendance and a little salt for keeping them docile.

These large pastures, which were technically known as "cowpens," occupied immense tracts; and a selfish policy naturally made their owners unwilling to witness the approach of civilization. Every additional colony abridged the resources of the grazier in his cattle-pasture.

To such a region, remote from society, unrestrained by law,

6. What communion did these hold together? 7. What languages were spoken? 8. Who were most ready to amalgamate? 9. What was the chief occupation of the colonists? 10. What were there pastures?

there naturally came numbers of reckless adventurers: rude, savage, lean, and hungry men, who preferred the life of the hunter or squatter, and who were just as likely to prey upon the possessions of the good citizens as upon the wild denizens of the forest. Our backwoods settlers very soon found themselves infested by tribes of ruffianly wanderers, who could give no proper account of their lives, conduct, and means of subsistence. Cattle stalking, hog and horse stealing, became legitimate occupations with all this class of people. They recognised the good old rule of the Highlander, as laid down by Rob Roy, that—

" They should *take* who have the power,
And they should keep *who can*."

They recognised no control of any other law. These outlaws grew bold from impunity and numbers. Burglaries and murders naturally followed horse-stealing, and there was no redress in society. There were no courts, no officers of justice, to enforce the law and protect the peaceful. The only court of justice in the state was in Charlestown, two hundred miles distant. Were the offender to be taken in the act, and carried to the seaboard for justice, he had ninety-nine chances in the hundred of being rescued from the officer before he could reach Charlestown by his comrades in iniquity. It was an expensive thing to carry him thither, and still more costly to bring witnesses for the prosecution from such a distance. In brief, there were no laws in operation, and society, following its usual practices, was too feeble for its own defence.

Extraordinary remedies were to be sought in such a condition of things, and, in sheer despair of any other means of security, the peaceable settlers put on their armor and took, with the weapons of war, the business of doing justice into their own hands. Under the lead of Thomas Woodward, Joseph Kirkland, Barnaby Pope, and a few others, they organized a band of rangers, giving themselves the style of Regulators.

This is said to be the first beginning of a practice which we

11. What disorderly people came among them? 12. What was their rule of conduct? 13. What was the effect upon society? 14. What remedies did the laws afford? 15. Who were the first " Regulators ?"

suspect is the natural resource of all new settlers in wild forest countries. It was soon generally known as *"Regulation."*

Our Regulators went to work with equal ardor and resolution. They proceeded, also, with great deliberation and system. An instrument of writing was drawn up, which stated their grievances and the necessity of the case. In this they bound themselves to make common cause in the pursuit and punishment of all public offenders.

They prosecuted their purpose with an energy which soon filled the country with commotion. Their processes were very summary. They hunted up, or hunted down, the horse-thief and the burglar. He was generally quite too notorious to need any array of witnesses for his conviction. When caught, he was tied to a tree and subjected to the usual sentence — "forty stripes, save one, on the naked leather." This was generally administered with a will, and the tally was not too closely counted. It is probable that many gratuitous strokes were given. When discharged, the criminal was warned to disappear from the precinct within a given time. If again caught, he was subjected to severer punishments, among which were tarring and feathering, carting, and riding the rail. Such was Regulation.

The Regulators, no doubt, began their work with an honest desire to protect society. But, when men take the law into their own hands, it is usually very difficult to keep themselves within the bounds of justice. The hands will be heavy, or light, in proportion to their sympathies and antipathies. It is probable that our Regulators were not always scrupulous as to their victims. A personal grudge will readily assert itself in the name of justice and the public welfare.

The Regulators, accordingly, soon roused a serious excitement and a spirit of resistance throughout the country which it was not easy to allay. The horse-thieves and cattle-reivers themselves were quite too numerous and too hardy to submit peaceably to the wild justice which took their outlawries in hands. They, too, made common cause in defence, and were sustained

16. What was "Regulation?" 17. How did the Regulators proceed? 18. What were their punishments? 19. What the abuses of Regulation? 20. What opposition did they create?

by many, not like themselves, offenders, who felt indignant at the usurpation of authority, and, perhaps, abuse of justice. The issue between the two parties became one of arms, and threatened a civil war. In this exigency, the civil authority of the province was required to interpose.

The governor of South Carolina, at this period (1766), was Lord Charles Greville Montague. With the view to the suppression of these strifes, he conferred a high commission on a man named Scovil — a name frequently written Scophil, and so pronounced by the common people.

The governor was particularly unfortunate in the choice of his agent. Scovil was himself a suspected and offensive person among the Regulators. He was a truculent, noisy ruffian, who, swelling with his appointment, made his commission ridiculous as well as mischievous. As if the country had been in actual rebellion, Scovil raised the royal standard, collected a force of rude men about him, probably drawn from the ranks of the worst offenders, and summoned the Regulators to answer before him for their usurpation of authority. He proceeded with a bold hand to seize upon some of the more eminent among them, and to send them to Charlestown for trial. He sided with the outlaws; and, as a matter of course, the Regulators took up arms against the government, as it was represented in the authority of Scovil.

The camps of Regulators and Scovilites confronted each other. Both parties were armed — embittered by frequent collisions, reproach, and mutual antipathies — and a bloody civil war threatened, the extent of which could scarcely be conjectured, when, by the interposition of some cooler heads, an armistice was agreed upon between them. The decision was rather that of the people themselves than their leaders. Both parties shrank from the odium of firing the first shot. It was agreed to separate, to break up their camps, and submit their mutual grievances to the governor. The danger thus passed away. Subsequently, in 1769, courts of justice were established at

21. What danger impended ? 22. What was done by the governor ? 23. Who did he commission to harmonize the country ? 24. Who was Scovil, and what did he ? 25. What was the result of his proceedings ? 26. How were the parties reconciled ?

Ninety-Six, Cambridge, Orangeburg, and Camden, supposed to be sufficiently convenient for the several precincts, the population of which was large enough to sustain them. The pretext for regulation was thus taken away from the Regulators; the specious plea of the wrongdoers that they were only resisting usurpation was set at rest, and, for the time, both parties appeared to submit with cheerfulness to the authorities of the land.

But the parties did not cease to exist. The Regulators exulted in having brought so many criminals to justice, and in having forced the establishment of their local courts; and they continued to point to the followers of Scovil as an outlawed and roguish population. Regulators and Scovilites became the party names of the back country, and the several terms of reproach, freely employed, kept up the grudges and the animosities between them until these found their free exercise and ferocious expression in the war of the Revolution, when the name of Scovilites became changed to that of tories, and the Regulators became the whigs.

The first conflicts of the civil war (1775) in South Carolina were really between these old parties under their new names.

The pacification of these parties, however temporary, enabled the back country to continue the progress in settlement which had been so actively begun at the close of the Cherokee war. The civil power in the province judiciously addressed its attention to this object. Emigration from Europe and from the American colonies was encouraged, and the auspices were generally favorable for the growth and prosperity of a province which had scarcely, at any time before, been suffered the opportunity of free development.

And now, when everything seemed auspicious, the seeds of war and revolution of strife, intestine division, and every form of social trouble, were ripening fast, to arrest that growth which seemed so promising. George the Third had succeeded to the

27. What courts of justice were established? 28. What effect had this upon the parties? 29. Into what subsequent parties did Scovilites and Regulators resolve themselves? 30. Between whom, in South Carolina, were the first conflicts of the civil war in the Revolution? 31. Did the back country prosper after these quarrels? 32. What seeds of war were sown in this time of peace?

throne of Great Britain. Under his predecessor, South Carolina had found favor, encouragement, and protection. Things were about to change, and in due degree with the exactions and usurpations of the British crown was the revolution, in feeling and opinion, in active progress among the people of Carolina, in common with all Americans.

With the gradual growth of numbers in the province, the freedom from external danger, the increase of prosperity, came the exercise of mind and inquiry. This soon induced a natural pride in their own strength, a questioning of the legitimacy of foreign authority, and a proper jealousy of those liberties in behalf of which they had encountered so many perils. They had hitherto endured, rather than obeyed, a foreign government. They had resisted its usurpations from the beginning. They had thrown off the yoke of the lord-proprietors as soon as they grew strong enough to do so; and the assertion of the same principles which were then involved in the struggle brought them into fierce collision with the British crown.

George the Second had been rather a patron than a sovereign. The Carolinians had known his authority rather by favor and protection than dominion ; to these they were largely indebted. The ascent of George the Third to the throne brought with it a change of policy in Britain, and with regard to the province, which awakened the anxieties of the intelligent and aroused the fears of the vigilant and jealous.

Great Britain, covered with debt, and at a loss for pretexts for taxation at home, conceived the idea of fastening some portions of her burdens upon her American colonies. Her pretext for this was sufficiently plausible. She claimed that, as her debt was largely due to her efforts to expel the French from America, and as this expulsion must enure principally to the benefit of the colonies, so, properly, it was rather their debt than hers, and in justice they should be required to bear its burdens. But the war was that of Great Britain herself, and it was a struggle for power with an hereditary rival, and these parties had simply used America as their battle-ground; thus removing from themselves and transferring to the colonies all the miseries, losses, privations, massacres, and burnings, which belong to a merciless and protracted conflict.

Great Britain, meanwhile, had used the colonies as children who should have no voice in the administration of their own affairs. She had appropriated all their offices, civil and military, to her favorites, and monopolized their trade, which, left free to the enjoyment of all nations, would, in all probability, have put them in perfect security from war.

It was enough, thought the colonies, that Great Britain should derive her profits from the enjoyment of their trade and commerce exclusively, without charging them with the cost of a war which had been prosecuted chiefly for her own ambition. But power is not easily persuaded by plea or petition, or convinced by arguments, however rational and just. And, perhaps, it was in the providence of God that Great Britain should turn a deaf ear to the prayers and pleadings of her colonies. We are not prepared to say that the American colonies were prepared to go alone, and were quite equal to the exigencies of self-government. The Revolution was, perhaps, premature, in its development, in the case of such feeble and scattered populations as those of South Carolina and Georgia. But even in these there was a consciousness of strength and growth that led to a surprising self-esteem. Their rapid increase of numbers, their rich territories, the variety of their productions, the value of their staples, the wealth which these necessarily procured, had the effect of inflating the popular idea in regard to its power; and it was by a sort of instinct, by which, in the national imagination, they were led to a gradual lessening of the overweening estimate which they had, in their infancy, put upon British power, its genius and resources; they had fought side by side with the British regulars, and not unfrequently

89. How answered? 40. How did Great Britain treat the colonies? 41. What thought the colonies? 42. What is said of the Revolution here? 43. What was the consciousness, growth, and strength of the colonies? 44. What their opinion of British power?

saved them from defeat; they began daily to feel less and less the importance of a British connection, and this connection was but too frequently accompanied by a treatment which mortified self-esteem, and goaded provincialism into the assertion of independence. The royal government in the colonies was but too commonly represented by imbecility, which suffered, even in the vulgar eye, by contrast with the gifts and acquisitions of the natives. Favorites of court, younger sons, were sent out to rule a people who could produce from their own ranks a far superior moral and intellect. And these favorites of court, royal governors, judges, counsellors, and commanders, solicitous of place and power, were not only apt to abuse it, but found or thought it their policy, to keep the crown ignorant of the facts in the case of the colonies, or who grossly misrepresented them.

Whatever the sympathies of the colonists for the mother-country, these things, and the great stretch of sea which divided them from the foreign power, naturally led to their alienation from it. The people saw few of its pomps, enjoyed few of its favors, were daily vexed by the abuses of its creatures, and, when the arrogance of parliament sought only to make them sensible of its power, by reason of its exactions, it is easy to conceive how, in process of time, they should come to regard it only as an enemy.

From the moment when the peace of Europe led to the withdrawal of all pressure from an external enemy, the people had been receiving these impressions, and acquiring that strength which prepared them to perceive, and enabled them to resist, all such laws as they deemed hostile to their interests or dangerous to their liberties. The hardships they had endured, in the establishment of the colony, had made them singularly jealous from the beginning. Many of them had inherited a natural aversion to monarchy from their ancestors, the puritans; and the removal of the cavaliers from the sources and shows of royalty, had gradually weaned them, also, from that faith in its saving virtues by which they had been so ready of old to swear.

45. How was the royal power in the colonies commonly represented? 46. What influences naturally weaned the colonies from Britain? 47. From what period did this *free* opinion begin to be active?

After nearly a hundred years' abode in the same regions, there had been, in most cases, an utter overthrow of those social and political barriers which had made these parties hostile to one another. They had measurably amalgamated; and freedom of religion, and an equal share of power, had taken from both parties the ancient sting of prejudice, and they now worked together amicably for the common good. There was no longer any rivalry between them. This was true of the lower and middle country of South Carolina, in 1770. And, in these regions especially, the progress of education and intelligence had been such, that they were not only prepared to assert independence, but were equal in intellect and courage, to the argument, in any court in christendom. But even here, and with this unanimity generally existing among such as were *old* inhabitants, and their descendants, there were classes who were tenacious of the crown and of its rights in defiance of all considerations. These were mostly British subjects. A large portion of the mercantile community were Scotch and English. In the first blush of the popular discontents they took little part — trade being always reluctant to peril capital upon the caprices of politics. Subsequently, however, they showed themselves in their true colors, as bigoted loyalists, hostile to all popular proceedings, a danger in the very heart of the commonwealth.

This was particularly the element of mischief in the back country. When the first steps were taken in the Revolution, a large portion of the people were foreigners, born British subjects, had been only eight or ten years in the country, had no intercourse, no sympathies, with the people of the seaboard, and were particularly jealous and resentful of the superiority which they asserted in arts, refinements, wealth, and education. It is well to keep these facts in mind, as furnishing the clues to that bloody civil war, of whigs and tories, by which the country was subsequently torn and ravaged from one extreme to the other.

But we should greatly err were we to convey the idea that

---

48. What is said of the blending of old parties in South Carolina? 49. Of what regions was this true? 50. What was their intellectual capacity? 51. What classes in Charlestown were loyal? 52. How did these show themselves hereafter?

any portion of the province was ripe for revolution, or contemplated, at the outset, an utter severance from the British nation. There were, no doubt, a few daring spirits, such as Christopher Gadsden, who saw, from afar, the absolute result, and regarded it with satisfaction. But the greater number were drawn gradually, step by step — by degrees, almost insensible to themselves — into the maelstrom of revolution, into a bloody war, when they contemplated at the beginning simply a redress of grievances and a reform of abuses in government. The province, as we have said, was not ripe for anything further; and, though there can be little doubt that, as soon as the infant could throw off its swaddling clothes, it would seek to walk alone, yet there is as little question that South Carolina was in no such advanced condition. Her population was quite too sparsely settled, and too much wanting in homogeneousness. She was goaded prematurely to the precipice, when it became a point of honor and pride that she should take the leap, regardless of all consequences.

But, down to the period of which we have been speaking, 1765, the period of the stamp act, South Carolina, had no sufficient reason for a quarrel with Great Britain. She had, on the contrary, many good reasons for loving her with undeviating loyalty. Her government was closely modelled on that of the British constitution. The mother-country gave her warm and prompt succors in all her emergencies, and not an enemy to the Hanoverian succession to the British Constitution, or to the regal system, could be found within her limits prior to 1765. The people were especially fond of British tastes, manners, and opinions; their children had a British education, and they spoke of the mother-country invariably under the endearing appellation of " home." The institutions of civil and religious liberty which they brought from Britain were tenaciously preserved and enthusiastically insisted on. They had flourished under these, loved them, and cared for no other. They cheerfully obeyed the laws under the crown, though these contem-

54. What was the element of mischief in the back country, and why? 55. Was any portion of the province prepared at first for separation? 56. Was there an exception? and who? 57. Why not prepared for separation? 58. What were the relations of South Carolina to the mother-country in 1765?

plated a monopoly for the benefit of the parent-state. The grievances arising from British law, which bore hard upon some of the northern colonies, such as were engaged in the fisheries, manufactures, and shipping, did not affect their interests; and, looking to the array of evils, wrongs, and abuses, as set forth by the Declaration of Independence, and as furnishing adequate cause of quarrel and a justification of revolution, there will not be found one, not purely constructive and abstract, as an evil of which they had reason to complain.

But the assertion of a right of colonial taxation by parliament, without representation accorded, was a sufficient cause of jealousy and suspicion, in keeping with the natural spirit of liberty and right which fills the bosom of an English stock. Let us proceed now to trace the several steps by which a loving and loyal people became the determined enemies of the crown and British government.

59. Did the grievances of the northern colonies affect her? 60. What was the first sufficient cause of disaffection on the part of the province to the crown?

7*

# BOOK IV.

## PROGRESS TO REVOLUTION.

## CHAPTER I.

### FROM 1765 TO 1775.

THE whole progress of the province of South Carolina had been calculated to nourish a spirit of independence among the people. Planted under the auspices of the English constitution, they had been nursed in danger, and made vigorous by years of strife and suffering. They had grown prosperous in spite of trial. In most cases cultivators of the soil, agriculture had taught them simplicity, hardihood, and a frank, bold, free speech and thought; and, wealth had not yet so grown as to introduce luxury. There were few families so far raised above the rest, by opulence or education, as to constitute an aristocracy. The very fact that their settlements were scattered, contributed to individual self-esteem. Negro slavery had the farther effect of making them jealous of their own liberties, while elevating them to a high sense of their own dignity and character. Most of the white inhabitants were freeholders, having no superiors; their own grounds yielding them all the necessaries of life. There were no religious restraints; there was nothing to fetter the spirit of free inquiry, and the whole tendency of the popular education was to independence. Nothing was wanting to its assertion but a continued and unembarrassed growth to adequate power and dimensions, or such provocation as should precipitate events, and anticipate such as were inevitably grow-

1. What effects had the progress of the province of South Carolina upon the people? 2. What had agriculture taught? 3. What sparseness of settlement and negro slavery? 4. What was the whole tendency of the popular education?

ing in the womb of Time. The recklessness of British authority, the selfishness of its officials, the lack of wisdom in all, soon gave the required provocation, and forced the crisis upon the country, which, under different auspices, might have continued to acknowledge the sovereign of Britain fifty years longer.

The first British statute that awakened the general opposition of the colonies, was one entitled the " Stamp act." It was passed in the year 1765. By this it was enacted, that all instruments of writing, which are in use among a commercial people, should be void in law, unless executed upon stamped paper or parchment, charged with a duty imposed by parliament.

South Carolina declared her opposition to this assumption of arbitrary power, without waiting to consult with any other colony. Her example had considerable effect in recommending measures of like opposition to many others, who were more tardy in their concurrence. The assembly of Carolina embodied the sentiments of the greater number of the people, in the principles contained in the following resolution :—

"*Resolved,* That his majesty's subjects in Carolina, owe the same allegiance to the crown of Great Britain, that is due from its subjects born there. That his majesty's liege subjects of this province, are entitled to all the inherent rights and liberties of his natural born subjects, within the kingdom of Great Britain. That the inhabitants of this province appear, also, to be confirmed in all the rights aforementioned, not only by their charter, but by an act of parliament, 13th, George II. That it is inseparably essential to the freedom of a people, and the undoubted right of Englishmen, that no taxes be imposed on them, but with their own consent. That the people of this province are not, and from their local circumstances can not be, represented in the house of commons in Great Britain ; and, farther, that, in the opinion of this house, the several powers of legislation in America, were constituted, in some measure, upon the apprehension of this impracticability. That the only

5. How was independence precipitated ? 6. What was the first British statute that aroused this spirit ? 7. What did it enact ? 8. What did South Carolina declare ? 9. What effect had her declaration upon other colonies ?

representatives of the people of this province, are persons chosen by themselves, and that no taxes ever have been, or can be, constitutionally imposed on them, but by the legislature of this province. That all supplies to the crown being free gifts of the people, it is unreasonable and inconsistent with the principles and spirit of the British constitution, for the people of Great Britain to grant to his majesty the property of the people of this province. That trial by jury is the inherent and invaluable right of every British subject, in this province. That the act of parliament, entitled, an act for granting and applying certain stamp-duties, and other duties, on the British colonies and plantations, in America, etc., by imposing taxes on the inhabitants of this province; and, the said act and several other acts, by extending the jurisdiction of the courts of admiralty beyond its ancient limits; have a manifest tendency to subvert the rights and liberties of this province. That the duties imposed by several late acts of parliament, on the people of this province, will be extremely burdensome and grievous; and, from the scarcity of gold and silver, the payment of them absolutely impracticable. That, as the profits of the trade of the people of this province ultimately centre in Great Britain, to pay for the manufactures which they are obliged to take from thence, they eventually contribute, very largely, to all the supplies granted to the crown; and, besides, as every individual, in this province, is as advantageous, at least, to Great Britain, as if he were in Great Britain, as they pay their full proportion of taxes for the support of his majesty's government here (which taxes are equal, or more, in proportion to our estates, than those paid by our fellow-subjects, in Great Britain, upon theirs), it is unreasonable for them to be called upon to pay any further part of the charges of government there. That the assemblies of this province have, from time to time, whenever requisitions have been made to them by his majesty, for carrying on military operations, either for the defence of themselves, or America in general, most cheerfully and liberally contributed their

10. By whom alone did this resolution declare that taxes could be imposed?
11. What did they declare to be the tendency of the stamp act and other acts?
12. How had the assemblies met the British requisitions upon them?

full proportion of men and money for these services. That, though the representatives of the people of this province had equal assurances and reasons with those of the other provinces, to expect a proportional reimbursement of those immense charges they had been at for his majesty's service, in the late war, out of the several parliamentary grants for the use of America; yet, they have obtained only their proportion of the first of those grants, and the small sum of two hundred and eighty-five pounds sterling received since. That, notwithstanding, whenever his majesty's service shall, for the future, require the aid of the inhabitants of this province, and they shall be called upon for this purpose, in a constitutional way, it shall be their indispensable duty most cheerfully and liberally to grant to his majesty their proportion, according to their ability, of men and money, for the defence, security, and other public services, of the British-American colonies. That the restrictions on the trade of the people of this province, together with the late duties and taxes imposed on them by act of parliament, must necessarily greatly lessen the consumption of British manufactures among them. That the increase, prosperity, and happiness of the people of this province, depend on the full and free enjoyment of their rights and liberties, and on an affectionate intercourse with Great Britain. That the readiness of the colonists to comply with his majesty's requisitions, as well as their inability to bear any additional taxes, beyond what is laid on them by their respective legislatures, is apparent from several grants of parliament, to reimburse them part of the heavy expenses they were at in the late war in America. That it is the right of the British subjects of this province to petition the king, or either house of parliament.

*Ordered,* That these votes be printed, and made public, that a just sense of the liberty, and the firm sentiments of loyalty of the representatives of the people of this province, may be known to their constituents, and transmitted to posterity."

The people of South Carolina did not confine themselves to

13. What reimbursement had been made by parliament? 14. How did they pledge themselves to meet constitutional demands in future? 15. What did they declare themselves unable to do? 16. With what order did the resolution conclude?

these declarations.   On the arrival of the stamped paper in the harbor of Charlestown, the lieutenant-governor, Bull, perceiving the temper of the people, did not venture to bring the stamps into the city.   He found himself too feeble to coerce obedience. The stamps were, accordingly, stored at Fort Johnson, on James' island.   This ascertained, a body of volunteers, one hundred and fifty in number, were organized and armed, proceeded, at midnight, to the fort, surprised it, secured the garrison, and seized the stamp-paper.   Then, arming the batteries, and making all preparations for the defence of the fort against the British sloop-of-war which had brought the stamps, and which lay directly under their guns, they hung out a flag at daylight, showing a blue field with three crescents.   The sight of this flag brought about a parley with the commanding officer of the sloop.   He was invited into the fort, and shown the preparations for its defence — was told that they were prepared to resist any assault ; but, that they would re-deliver to him the stamped paper, on his solemn pledge to depart with it to Europe, and sail immediately.   The officer, upon reflection, complied with the requisition, and, receiving the paper, weighed anchor, and went to sea that very day.

Thus was the Revolution begun in South Carolina (October, 1765).   The governor was powerless, and confounded by the audacity of the proceeding.   Nor did the popular spirit content itself with so bold a demonstration.   Suspicions were entertained that a portion of the stamped paper had been smuggled into the city, and was secreted in certain houses. At this suspicion, the populace rose in tumult, paraded the streets with arms, searched the suspected houses, threatened as well the persons as the property of the king's officers, and made them drink " Damnation to the stamp act !"

The assembly, spite of the law and governor, proceeded to do business, as usual, without recognising the necessity of

17. Did the people of South Carolina confine themselves to these resolutions? 18. What course did Governor Bull pursue? 19.-Where were the stamps secured? 20. What party surprised Fort Johnson, and with what object? 21. How did they act? 22. What was their flag? 23. What was the result of the interview with the captain of the sloop-of-war? 24. What was the effect upon the governor of these bold proceedings? 25. What was the action of the populace? 26. How did the assembly proceed?

stamped paper; but, there was a protracted struggle between them and the crown officers on the subject. This struggle led to frequent prorogations of the assembly, and to the as frequent defeats of all legislation — the commons house representing the republican tendencies of the people, in opposition to the governor and his council.

The proceedings of the assembly, the declarations and resolutions, were all duly reported to the home government. So, also, was the popular violence, as illustrated in the mobs of the city, and the seizure of Fort Johnson, and of the stamped paper. The intelligence produced its effect in Great Britain. The crisis was alarming; it effected a favorable change in the ministry, and the stamp act was repealed (1766).

It is in proof of the fact that the South Carolinians had sought only a redress of grievances, and the assertion of their rights as British subjects, and not the separation of the province from the mother-country, that they received the tidings of this repeal with great rejoicings. In their gladness of heart, they proceeded to erect a marble statue in Charlestown, of William Pitt, in recognition of his great and patriotic endeavors to bring about this repeal, and in urging the rights and claims of the Americans. This statue is preserved to the present hour.

But the exultations of the Carolinians were short-lived. Great Britain lacked the magnanimity to do full justice. The crown was jealous of its prerogative, and the right to impose taxes upon the colonies, at pleasure, was not yielded. It was re-asserted, in a like measure of arbitrary authority, in the year following. Duties were imposed on glass, paper, tea, and painters' colors. The opposition of the colonies was renewed with partial success; the duties, with the exception of that upon tea, were all withdrawn; and, the Americans determined to defeat the effect of this reservation, by refusing to consume a commodity which was made the medium of unjust taxation.

This resolution was rendered inoperative by a scheme of the

27. What was the effect of their proceedings in Great Britain? 28. What was the effect of the repeal of the stamp act, in South Carolina? 29. What of William Pitt? 30. What did Great Britain lack? 31. What was its next enactment?

West Indian company. It sent to the colonies large shipments of tea, to be sold on account of the company.

This measure increased the anger of the colonists. They promptly entered into combinations to obstruct or prevent its sale. In some places, the landing of it was forbidden. The cargoes first sent to Charlestown were stored, and rotted in the storehouses, the consignees being denied to expose it in the market. A second supply was thrown overboard, both at Charlestown and Georgetown. At the latter place, this summary process was resorted to in the first instance as at Boston, where a few persons, disguised and painted as Indians, entered the vessels, and thus disposed of their cargoes. The Bostonians were the first in this achievement. The Carolina leaders, however, executed the same process without resorting to disguises.

This violence brought down upon the colonies the legislative vengeance of the British parliament. Boston was the first to feel its indignation. Acts were passed which virtually put that city in a state of blockade. Other acts followed rapidly, by which the whole executive government was taken out of the hands of the people, the nominations to all offices vested in the king or his special representative, and the privileges secured by the colony charter, were usurped in some of its most vital and important features.

Great was the sympathy for the people of Boston expressed and felt in all the colonies. In none more passionately than South Carolina. These proceedings of crown and parliament had the effect of producing a general confederacy of the colonies, sustaining Massachusetts against the measures which not only threatened her ruin, but held out to all of them the prospect of utter subjugation to a wholly arbitrary and irresponsible authority. South Carolina, in an assembly of the people, declared that " the late act for shutting up the port of Boston, and the other late acts relative to Boston and the province of Massachusetts, are calculated to deprive many thou-

32. What measure increased the anger of the colonists? 33. What did they do about the tea? 34. What with a second supply? 35. What action did Parliament take in regard to these proceedings? 36. What acts did they pass? 37. How did the treatment of Boston affect South Carolina? 38. What was the act of all the colonies?

sand Americans of their rights, properties, and privileges, in a most cruel, oppressive, and unconstitutional manner — are most dangerous precedents, and, though levelled immediately at the people of Boston, very manifestly and plainly show, if the inhabitants of that town are intimidated into a mean submission to said acts, that the like are designed for all the colonies, when not even the shadow of liberty to his person, or of security to his property, will be left to any of his majesty's subjects residing on the American continent."

On the sixth day of July, 1774, one hundred and four deputies from all parts of the province, a few small precincts only excepted, assembled in Charlestown to take into consideration the relations of crown and colonies, and for the better assertion and protection of the rights of the latter. Their resolutions declared, among other things, that " the king's subjects in America are entitled to all the inherent rights and liberties enjoyed by natural born subjects within the kingdom;" that " taxes should not be imposed on the people without their own consent;" that " an act (35 Henry viii.) for the trial of treasons committed out of the king's dominions " does not and can not extend to any crimes committed in any of his majesty's American colonies ;" that the three late acts of parliament, relative to Boston, are of the most alarming nature to all his majesty's subjects in America," &c. They resolved that every justifiable means ought to be tried to procure a repeal of those acts, and of all others affecting the constitutional rights and liberties of America. To effect these objects, they resolved farther to adopt a vote of non-importation, a refusal to use the articles taxed, and to send deputies to a general congress of representatives from all the disaffected colonies, to assemble at Philadelphia. The deputies chosen were five, viz.: Henry Middleton, John Rutledge, Thomas Lynch, Christopher Gadsden, and Edward Rutledge. These were authorized "*to concert, agree to, and effectually prosecute such legal measures as, in the opinion of these deputies, and of the deputies of the other colonies, shall*

39. What were the declarations of South Carolina？ 40. What assembly met in South Carolina in 1774? 41. With what object? 42. What were their resolves? 43. Who did they choose as deputies to Congress?

*be most likely to obtain a repeal of the late acts of parliament
and a redress of grievances."*

This duty done, upon a reassemblage of this body (8th July,
1774), they resolved that a committee of ninety-nine persons —
fifteen merchants and fifteen mechanics representing Charlestown, and sixty-nine planters representing the rest of the province, should constitute a general committee to continue to act in
authority until the next general meeting of the representatives.   It will be seen from this and previous chapters that the
usurpation of civil power by the people was almost complete;
that the authority of the crown was almost nominal, and its
officers reduced to ciphers.   But the forms of legislation were
observed, as usual, though measurably inoperative.

While these events were in progress, there were new riots
about tea, in consequence of new importations.   A Captain
Maitland, who had brought out some in his vessel, was compelled
to fly and put himself under the protection of a vessel of war,
lying in the harbor.   The vessel, with the tea, was only saved
by being hauled out into the stream, and under the guns of the
man-of-war, by armed barges despatched from her for this purpose.

About this time a new act of parliament, which quartered the
troops of his majesty upon the inhabitants of the colonies, deep-
ened the discontents of the people, and increased the violence of
their passions.   The general assembly of South Carolina, which
had been repeatedly prorogued by the governor, assembled at
an earlier hour than usual, anticipated his message, and passed
their resolutions — among others, one for paying the expenses
of their delegation in the general congress out of the funds of
the province.   They also applied for arms for the defence of
the back country against the Indians.   This was no doubt, a
mere pretext to supply the country with munitions of war.

The feeling waxed warmer daily.   On Sunday, August 14,
1774, the Rev. John Bullman, assistant minister of St. Michael's, preached a sermon which was supposed to reflect on

44. How instructed?  45. What committee did the assembly appoint?  46. With
whom now lay the civil power in South Carolina?  47. What of Captain Maitland?
48. What new act of parliament increased the popular anger?  49. What was the
action of the general assembly?

the popular proceedings. His audience could scarcely hear him out, and he was subsequently dismissed the church. When, in the vestry, the vote for his dismission was put, there was a cry, " Now shall we see who are the enemies of the country." The vote against him was welcomed with a shout that shook pulpit and altar, as a proof of the strength of the American cause.

In the meantime, the congress representing twelve of the colonies assembled at Philadelphia (1774). Their proceedings must be sought for in the general history of the confederacy. We may mention, however, that, on the retirement (from sickness) of their first president, Peyton Randolph, Henry Middleton, of South Carolina, was chosen to supply his place. We may add, briefly, as these proceedings were subsequently the subject of warm discussion in South Carolina, that the congress adopted the acts of non-importation and non-consumption, which had been previously agreed upon by several colonies. These agreements contained a clause to discontinue the slave-trade, to which the southern members offered no opposition, and a provision to except rice as an article of export from the list of non-exportations.

While the congress of the colonies were thus busy, William Henry Drayton, one of the leading minds of South Carolina, and one of the assistant judges of the crown, published a series of papers, entitled " Letters of Freeman," addressed to the Philadelphia Congress. These letters reflected upon the British judges, and gave great offence to those of the crown in South Carolina. Drayton was removed by *supersedeas ;* but the triumph of the crown-judges was short. He soon after became chief justice of South Carolina, an independent republic.

On the 9th November, 1774, the general committee of South Carolina issued a call for a general meeting of the inhabitants of the province by representation. Thirty representatives were allowed to Charlestown ; ten to each of the four large districts, Ninety-six ; between Broad and Saluda rivers ; between Broad

50. What took place Sunday, August 14, 1774 ?   51. When did the congress meet in Philadelphia ?   52. What resolutions did they pass ?   53. Upon what exception did the southern members insist ?   54. Who was William Henry Drayton ?   55. What did he publish ?   56. What was done with him ?   57. What did he afterward become ?   58. What general meeting was called ?

and Catawba; and for the territory east of Wateree. Such were then the divisions. Six representatives were allowed for each of the parishes. The representation was thus increased from forty-eight, which composed the commons house, to one hundred and eighty-four members. The assembly was appointed to meet in Charlestown, January 11, 1775.

59. How was the representation distributed?  60. What was the number of the old, and what of the new assembly?

# CHAPTER II.

## FROM 1775 TO 1776.

THE delegates, chosen under this call, assembled, at the appointed time (eleventh of January, 1775), at the Exchange, in Charlestown; subsequently adjourning to the commons house of assembly, in the statehouse. The proceedings of the Philadelphia congress were submitted, and their own delegates appeared to make their reports. These were considered, and the proceedings of the congress were fully approved; rather, because of an unwillingness to show dissent, at such a time, than because the action of the congress was entirely satisfactory. There was, indeed, not a little discussion, and much disapprobation, in respect to certain of the proceedings.

Charles Pinckney was chosen president, and Peter Timothy, secretary, of this convention of the people of South Carolina. Meanwhile, Lieutenant-governor Bull still acted as governor, under the crown. His position was an awkward one; he was a native of the province, and closely allied with some of the popular leaders; was a favorite of the people, and greatly beloved by all; was moderate in his own opinions, and indulgent to those of others; and, no doubt, deeply regretted the rash counsels by which the crown was precipitating upon the country the evils of civil war, and perilling its own possessions. There is little question that Bull's sympathies, and connection with the people of the province, were among the secrets of the local weakness of the British government. A more stern and decisive executive, with fewer sympathies, and more devotion

1. When and where did the delegates of South Carolina assemble? 2. What report was made by their deputies, and what action had upon it? 3. Was the assembly unanimous equally in their action and opinion? 4. Who was president, and who secretary, of the assembly? 5. Who was acting as royal governor at this time? 6. What was Bull's position, and how did it affect the government?

to the crown, might have arrested for a longer period, the popular tendencies to revolution. So, perhaps, thought the royal government, for we see, shortly after this, that Bull was superseded in the executive office.

It was among the subjects of discussion, in this revolutionary assemblage, why, when American grievances were the topics of consideration in the congress, that body had limited its researches to the year 1763? — why they had not gone farther back, and reported the many aggressions of Great Britain upon her infant colonies, from a far earlier period ; aggressions shown in jealousies, monopolies, and prohibitions, for the express purpose of arresting their growth to power; abridging their trade and manufactures, and crippling those energies which must otherwise have made them all great and prosperous states.

Something of the spirit which dictated these inquiries may be shown by the action of one in especial among their delegates. Christopher Gadsden, in the first Philadelphia congress, counselled boldly, that General Gage should be attacked and overcome in Boston, before the reinforcements should arrive from Britain. It was a subject of great subsequent regret, that these counsels, and the vigorous action which they urged, had been overruled — congress being then of opinion that the action would be premature. We may here mention that Gadsden was one of the first of the American patriots to counsel bold measures ; to insist upon determined action ; to assert the fullest independence for America. There were few other leaders in the country, at this period, who did not prefer to temporize.

The delegates replied to all this, that the representatives of Virginia opposed any more remote retrospect of the relations between the crown and the colonies, being desirous of flinging all the reproach of misgovernment upon the reign of George the Third.

The next subject of discussion in the revolutionary assembly related to the non-exportation act, which, pledging the country

7. What was the first subject of discussion ? 8. What did Gadsden propose in the congress, at Philadelphia ? 9. What is said of Gadsden ? 10. What was the reply of the delegates ? 11. What special exception was made in the non-exportation act ?

to export no merchandise, or commodity, whatsoever, to Great Britain, Ireland, or the West Indies, made a special exception in favor of *rice*.

This exception gave great offence, as it seemed to sacrifice all other descriptions of labor and produce, for the benefit of the rice-planters. The exception had been opposed in congress by Christopher Gadsden, who proposed and urged that the clause "except rice to Europe," should be struck out of the instrument. The arguments against the clause were, undoubtedly, plausible enough; but, John Rutledge answered for himself and his associates, and showed clearly that the case was properly an exceptional one, and the clause perfectly justified by the existing condition of things.

Rutledge, subsequently, even more highly distinguished by South Carolina and in the confederacy, was a profound and sagacious politician, an acute lawyer, and an admirable orator; one of the ablest, in that day, in all the confederacy.

He said, in reply, " that, at an early period, he and the other delegates from South Carolina, had warmly pressed an immediate non-importation, and total non-exportation act; that, as a non-exportation to Great Britain and Ireland was to withhold from thence the advantages their people might derive from the receipt of American commodities; so, the end would be more surely effected, by retaining these commodities altogether in America. Such measures, however, could not be effected; *the northern colonies resolving to remit to England, as usual, to pay their debts by the circuitous mode of their flour and fish trade* TO THE REST OF EUROPE. In short, *the commodities they usually sent to the* MOTHER-COUNTRY *were but trifling; and their* REAL TRADE *would be but little affected by the association* [for non-exportation to Great Britain]. For instance, Philadelphia carried on a trade of export, to the amount of *seven hundred thousand pounds sterling; yet scarce fifty thousand pounds of that amount went to the markets of the mother-country.* It was evident that *those colonies were less intent to annoy the mother-country than to preserve their own trade.* He

12. Who of the delegates had opposed it? 18. Who answered for the delegates? 14. What is said of Rutledge? 15. What did he say in reply?

thought, accordingly, that *justice to his constituents required that their trade should also be preserved as entire as possible.* The northern trade," said he, " will be *little affected* by the association. *He saw no reason why ours should be ruined.* For *nearly all our indigo, and two-thirds of our rice, went to the mother-country.* And these were our chief exports. If we must bear burdens," he said, " let them be as equal as possible. Upon the whole," he added, " *the whole affair seemed a great commercial scheme, among the flour colonies, to find a better vent for their flour, through the British channel, by taking the place of Southern rice. He was not willing that we should be dupes of the North.* He would not yield to their exactions. The exceptions claimed were necessary to supplying ourselves with the necessaries which we absolutely require."

The argument was one of many ramifications. Indigo, hemp, lumber, corn, pork, butter, all had claims for exemption, as vehemently urged as rice; but, after protracted and continued sessions, and long debates, the parliament, without a dissenting voice, approved of what had been done by the congress.

They passed, in addition, a number of resolutions, suited to the times. They resolved the parish committees into a local magistracy, etc.; briefly, they superseded the royal government in most of its details. They concluded, finally, by a mixed recommendation to all the inhabitants, which savors of the old leaven of puritanism, to practise the use of fire-arms, and set aside a day for prayer, fasting, and humiliation. These recommendations for arming and praying, were carried into effect with equal zeal, and Charlestown resumed the appearance, which it had so frequently worn before, of a garrisoned town. Volunteers formed themselves into separate bands; and the very boys of the city, emulating their seniors, were soon busy in the use of mimic weapons, and in the practice of the manual.

The revolutionary parliament proceeded to establish a system of government for the colony. They now assumed the

16. What other interests claimed exemption, also? 17. What was the final action upon the exception? 18. What the other proceedings of the assembly? 19. What appearance did Charlestown assume? 20. What did this parliament establish?

style of provincial congress, by which we hereafter know the body, and, to all intents and purposes, became a legislature, to be convened when necessary. An independent government then arose, which effectually superseded the royal authority. This retained only a show of government without power; officers, without the ability to exercise office; the name of rule, without any essentials of government or state.

*Rice* became the standard of value. The late delegates to the general congress were re-elected. On the seventeenth of January, 1775, the provincial congress waited on Lieutenant-Governor Bull, with an address. He refused to recognise them. The next day, the general committee met, under the authority of the *provincial congress*, and resolved, among other things, to have no dealings with the colony of Georgia; holding it "as inimical to the liberties of the country." This was in consequence of the reluctance of that colony to join the associated colonies. The parish of St. John's, Georgia, one of the richest and most populous of that colony, finally, sent deputies to the Charlestown committee, and prayed to be admitted to their alliance; in fact, setting up for themselves. Georgia soon put herself right with the other colonies.

In South Carolina, the terms of the association were rigidly complied with. Ships, arriving from England, were emptied of their cargoes, which were thrown into the sea, at Hog-island creek. Even a cargo of three hundred slaves was interdicted, and sent elsewhere. The private carriage and horses of a citizen, from England, were not suffered to be landed. Non-conformists were hung in effigy; and, the public mind, at least, in the seaboard parishes, and at Charlestown, took an attitude of defiance, that overawed all opposition, and triumphed for a season, at least, in measures of the most decided character.

21. What style did it assume? 22. What sort of government arose from this? 23. What became of the royal government? 24. What did rice become? 25. Who were elected to the general congress? 26. How did Governor Bull receive the provincial congress? 27. What did the provincial congress, resolve in respect to Georgia? — and why? 28. What parish, in Georgia, sent deputies to the provincial congress of South Carolina? 29. Did Georgia finally associate? 30. How were the terms of association observed in South Carolina? 31. What was done with British cargoes, and imported slaves, etc.? 32. What was the condition of the public mind in Charlestown?

The general assembly met the sixth of September, 1774, but satisfied that nothing favorable to the crown could come of their legislation, the governor (Bull), commenced a series of prorogations, which continued till January 24, 1775, when they were allowed to meet. They proceeded to compliment their popular delegates to the continental congress, and to approve of what had been done. They re-nominated and appointed them again to the congress at Philadelphia. It was during this session, that William Henry Drayton was suspended, as a member of the royal council; a proceeding which only rendered him more popular with the community. The session was closed without reconciling the parties or doing much for the country.

Meanwhile, the measures in the British parliament amounted to a declaration of war. There was an augmentation of the national forces, and regiments of foot and horse, and ships-of-war, were despatched to America.

The general committee of South Carolina met again on the 19th April, 1775. The startling news, recently received from Great Britain, was quietly discussed, and the conclusion reached was that war was inevitable, and that every preparation must be made for it. It was silently and secretly resolved that the public military stores should be seized into the hands of the people.

Charles Pinckney, William Henry Drayton, Arthur Middleton, Charles Cotesworth Pinckney, William Gibbes, and Edward Weyman, were the committee chosen for this purpose. To them was confided substantially the charge of placing the colony in a proper posture for defence.

They proceeded to their duties with rare energy and decision. On the night of the 21st April, 1775, one party seized all the powder at the Hobcau magazine; another possessed themselves of that at Cochran's, on the neck; a third party broke open the armory in the state-house, and carried off eight hun-

33. When did the general assembly meet? 34. What was Governor Bull's policy? and why? 35. When were they at length suffered to do business? 36. What did they do? 37. Who was suspended from the king's council, and with what effect? 38. What were the measures of the British parliament? 39. How was this news received and acted on by the general committee of South Carolina? 40. What did that body secretly resolve? 41. Who did they appoint as a committee for this purpose? 42. How did this special committee proceed? 43. What did they on the 21st April, 1775? 44. What arms did they secure?

dred stands of arms, two hundred cutlasses, and all the cartouches, flints, and matches that could be found; in short, emptied the arsenal! The affair took place, in each instance, by night and without commotion, but without disguises. Sentinels were posted throughout the town, order was maintained, and the contents of all the arsenals carried off without loss, and secreted safely. The governor offered the usual reward; but there was none found to betray the secret.

The same parties proceeded to borrow money on account of the revolutionists. On the first day they procured a thousand guineas. They also sent liberal supplies to the suffering poor of Boston to the amount, in rice and cash, of nearly £3,500 sterling. These contributions were continued liberally from time to time. And, while the committees were secretly and sternly incurring the doom of treason if not its penalties, the popular humor, in Charlestown, amused itself by exhibitions calculated to ridicule the British ministry and the more odious office-holders of the place under the crown. In caricature, Lord North, Lord Grenville, the pope, and the devil, were exhibited in the streets on scaffolds with wheels, which moved to and fro in all populous quarters. These effigies were ingeniously framed, so as to bob the head, or wave the hands, or bend the knee; and these evolutions were severally performed on the approach of all placemen, crown-officers, or suspected persons. The mob seized the machine with delight, and whirled it about in all quarters. The boys modelled their own machines after it. ·It became one of those symbols, appealing to the senses, which served to enforce and illustrate the abstract questions which it was otherwise not so easy to explain. We may mention that the pope was lugged in because one of the charges against George the Third was, that he sought to force the Roman Catholic religion upon the country. That the devil should be a party in such an arrangement, was, with many, but a natural agency in such a design. The machine, and all its *dramatis personæ*, was afterward solemnly committed to the flames.

In May, 1775, a letter from Arthur Lee, in London, advised that a plan had been laid before government to instigate the slaves to insurrection. The negroes had already begun to entertain the idea that the quarrel between crown and colonies had originated in the desire of the latter to procure their enfranchisement. This subject was then under discussion in the assembly, when news came of the battle of Lexington. The seizure of the king's mail a month before had amply assured the Carolinians that the king had resolved to coerce America by arms.

The news from Lexington showed that the experiment was already begun. This event, though not known for long after, happened only two days before the sacking of the arsenals of Charlestown. The effect of the intelligence was conclusive and stimulating to the last degree. The excitement among politicians and people became intense. The feelings of indignation — the passions of revenge — stirred in every patriot bosom. Blood had been shed. This extremity reached in the issue, the time for argument — the hope of reconciliation — the desire for it — were at an end! A fierce spirit, swelling for freedom, was burning in every heart. All allegiance was considered as repealed — all ties sundered — as men reflected on the bloody plains of Lexington!

52. What letter came from Arthur Lee? 53. What was the notion among the negroes? 54. What was the effect in Charlestown of the battle of Lexington? 55. What was supposed to be repealed — what sundered — by the blood spilled at Lexington?

# CHAPTER III.

### PROGRESS — FROM 1775 TO 1776.

THE news of the battle of Lexington was received in Charlestown, the eighth of May, 1775. The provincial congress was at once called to meet on the first of June. The trial of arms was approaching, and it was necessary to prepare for it. There was no escape now, from the usual tests of revolution. Parties were compelled to declare themselves without evasion. There were timid councillors to be stimulated; there were suspicious citizens to be overawed. There were numerous foreigners — residents — who could not be otherwise than hostile.

The provincial congress met on the first of June, and Henry Laurens was made president. This body prepared resolutions which declared the relations of the province, and all of the provinces, with Great Britain. They published articles of association, pledging themselves, "under every tie of religion and honor, to associate as a band in defence of the country, against every foe,"—"solemnly engaging that, whenever our continental or provincial councils shall deem it necessary, we will go forth, and be ready to sacrifice our lives and fortunes to secure the freedom and safety of the state." They added, "we will hold all those persons inimical to the liberties of the colonies who shall refuse to subscribe to this association."

They passed a prohibition against the exportation of rice and corn, except with the consent of the secret association, who might need such exports in order to procure arms and ammunition from abroad. They resolved to raise two regiments of

1. When was the news of the battle of Lexington received in Charlestown? 2. What was the conviction it produced? 3. What duties lay before the patriots? 4. When did the provincial congress meet? 5. What did they declare and publish? 6. To what did they pledge themselves? 7. What prohibition did they pass? 8. What did they resolve to raise?

infantry, fifteen hundred men; a regiment of cavalry rangers, four hundred and fifty men; and, these were to be enrolled under the articles of war, and subjected to the discipline of British troops. They voted a million of money; commissioners of a treasury were resolved upon, and a council of safety was elected, consisting of Henry Laurens, Charles Pinckney, Rawlins Lowndes, Thomas Ferguson, Miles Brewton, Arthur Middleton, Thomas Heywood, jr., Thomas Bee, John Huger, James Parsons, William Henry Drayton, Benjamin Elliott, and William Williamson. These were vested with supreme power — the executive power of the province.

On the eighteenth of June, Lord William Campbell arrived, superseding William Bull as the governor of the province, under the crown. He was received with a sullen sort of civility. The provincial congress made him an address, stating their causes of complaint, and justifying their proceedings. He refused to recognise their existence as a legal body, and declared himself unable to decide the dispute between the colonies and the crown. The legality of his own official position was, however, no guaranty of authority. He was powerless.

The provincial congress continued to raise their regiments. They elected Christopher Gadsden and William Moultrie, colonels; Isaac Huger, Isaac Motte, and William Thompson, lieutenant-colonels; Owen Roberts, Alexander McIntosh and James Mayson, majors; Charles Cotesworth Pinckney, Barnard Elliott, Francis Marion, William Cattell, Peter Horry, Daniel Horry, Adam McDonald, Thomas Lynch, William Scott, John Barnwell, Nicholas Eveleigh, James McDonald, Isaac Harleston, Thomas Pinckney, Francis Huger, William Mason, Edmund Hyrne, Roger P. Saunders, Charles Motte, and Benjamin Cattell, captains, of the regimental companies.

The captains of cavalry-rangers were Samuel Wise, Eli Kershaw, Edward Richardson, Ezekiel Polk, Robert Goodwin, Thomas Woodward, John Caldwell, Moses Kirkland, and John

9. What did they vote? 10. Who did they elect as council of safety? 11. What power did they confer on this council? 12. Who arrived on the eighteenth of June? 13. How was Lord Campbell received? 14. How did congress address him, and how did he reply? 15. What election did they make? 16. Who were elected colonels? 17. Who majors? 18. Who captains? 19. Who were captains of rangers?

Purvis. They also appointed, about the same time, all the lieutenants and subalterns. The congress pledged itself, and the public faith, to provide the means for maintaining the troops, carrying on the affairs of state, and satisfying the public creditors. The recruiting was urged; fifty men being allotted to each foot company, and thirty for the horse companies.

Meanwhile, the governor, through his Indian agents, Stuart, Cameron, and others, was operating against the patriots, by exciting the settlers and red men of the interior, and seeking to organize them in behalf of the crown. The facts were ascertained by intercepted letters.

A British ship-of-war was expected on the coast with several tons of powder, designed for the savages. The secret committee issued instructions to Captains Barnwell and Joyner, of Beaufort, to seize the vessel. A schooner was fitted out, accordingly, and commissioned by the Georgia congress. A joint force of Carolinians and Georgians manned her, put to sea, captured the British vessel, and appropriated all her ammunition. A portion of the powder thus taken enabled Washington to continue the siege of Boston.

The secret committee, about this time, found it necessary to put their powers into active operation, in Charlestown, in silencing foreign incendiaries. Some of these were tarred and feathered (an ancient British punishment), carted through the streets, and shipped to England.

The leading members of the secret committee were William Henry Drayton, Arthur Middleton, and Charles C. Pinckney. They were prompt, vigilant, and resolute; hence, they led public opinion, overawed opposition, encouraged the timid, and silenced discontent, for the time. Henry Middleton, Thomas Lynch, Christopher Gadsden, John Rutledge, and George Rutledge, were then in Philadelphia, serving in the continental congress.

Hearing that British powder and arms might be seized at

20. To what did the congress pledge the province? 21. What did the governor, meanwhile? 22. What sea-enterprise was undertaken? 23. Was it successful? 24. What help was the powder to Washington? 25. What ancient British punishment was used in Charlestown? 26. Who were the leading members of the secret committee? 27. How did they behave? 28. Who were delegates, at this time, from South Carolina, to the continental congress? 29. What other enterprise was undertaken under Captain Lempriere?

New Providence, and upon the high seas, the council of safety fitted out a sloop for this purpose, under Captain Lempriere. Cruising off St. Augustine, he captured one of the expected vessels — an armed brig, of which he had been in search. From her he procured a large supply of military stores and the desired gunpowder. He succeeded, though pursued by a superior force, in making the port of Beaufort, and safely storing his spoils on shore.

On the second of July, the British mail was seized by Drayton, of the secret committee, by which was obtained the correspondence designed for the governors of North and South Carolina, and Georgia, and for Stuart, superintendent of Indian affairs. These despatches were important, as revealing the policy of the British ministry. Other letters, from some of the southern governors to Admiral Graves and General Gage, calling for sloops-of-war and British troops, to maintain their authority, were also intercepted at the same time. These were cunningly counterfeited by the committee, and the despatches made to say that no succor was needed. This *ruse* probably gained some respite for the South from the assaults of the enemy, and delayed her day of trial.

While the committee in Charlestown were thus energetically working, the Germans in the interior were showing themselves disaffected to the revolutionists. George Wagner and Felix Long, two of their countrymen, were sent out to them from the city, with the hope that they might be pacified; but, it was not easy to explain the case to them, and there were already among them certain influential persons, who were busily working for the crown, under the auspices of the governor. We shall see, hereafter, that these active emissaries precipitated a brief but threatening civil war, in the interior, which, but for other and fortunate events, might have resulted in disaster of the most distressing character.

Twenty-two leading persons of Charlestown, meanwhile, had

declined to sign the articles of association. The most of these were, or had been, officers of the crown. It was, finally, proposed to them to take an oath of neutrality, during the quarrel; and, such as refused this oath, either left the province, or, disarmed, were confined to the limits of Charlestown.

The rangers, meanwhile, under Major Mayson, seized upon Fort Charlotte, on the Savannah river, where they possessed themselves of a considerable armament; great guns, powder, shot, and lead. This spoil was borne away to the post of Ninety-six, where it was deposited, under the charge of Captain Kirkland, with one company of rangers; another company was left in garrison at Fort Charlotte.

At this time, twentieth of June, 1775, the popular authorities were in possession of every fort or arsenal of the crown, in the province, except the single one of Fort Johnson, in the harbor of Charlestown. This fortress had been, as we remember, captured before, as far back as 1765, when it became necessary to seize upon the stamped paper. This obtained, and the sloop-of-war which brought the stamps being made to depart with them, under a threat of cannonade, the fort was re-surrendered to the garrison. It was held, at this time, by a small command, and only needed a similar enterprise to secure its possession. But this measure was to be delayed a while longer, and in accordance with the gradual ripening of events.

We require to resume our narrative of the affairs of the interior, where, under most artful treacheries, and the conflict of opinion, the excitement had been growing with mischievous influence over the affairs of the country, and, especially, to the hopes of the revolutionary party. We have seen that the powder, arms, and munitions of war, taken at Fort Charlotte, had been carried to Ninety-six, and there deposited with a company of rangers, under Captain Moses Kirkland.

Kirkland betrayed his trust. This man was a Scotchman, who had been, probably, less than nine years in the country.

He was busy, restless, and ambitious, and had acquired not a little influence over his section.

It seems, that the council of safety, though making him captain in his regiment, had rated his claims somewhat below his own standard. There was an old rivalry between himself and Major Mayson, who had received the very commission which he desired. He did not forgive the offence; betrayed his charge into the hands of one Major Robinson, another Scotchman, and recent settler, who had been actively stirring up the loyalists of his section, and had framed articles of counter-association to those of the patriots. Robinson's proceedings were winked at by the colonel of his regiment, Fletchall, who, a determined loyalist at heart, was simply temporizing, during a transition period, and feeling his way, rather than choosing it.

Mayson was lodged, by Robinson, in jail, charged with plundering the royal fortress; he was, subsequently, suffered to go free, on bail, to answer at the approaching session. In a few days, Kirkland openly joined with Fletchall, Robinson, and others, in raising the king's standard. He carried off with him a troop of the regiment of rangers.

Fletchall was soon at the head of fifteen hundred men, and was capable of overawing the country from the Broad to the Savannah rivers; he did so, and greatly increased the disaffection of the people in those precincts, the larger number of whom were foreigners and settlers within the preceding ten years.

The loyalists, thus embodied, maintained a close correspondence with the royal governor; and, had he been an enterprising leader — had he stolen out of the city, and made his way into the interior — used money, collected weapons, armed the red men, as well as the foreigners, by whom he would have found himself surrounded — Scotch, English, German — it would have been scarce possible for the patriotic party to have maintained the standard of revolution for a single campaign.

44. What did he resent? 45. Into whose hands did he betray Mayson? 46. Who was Robinson? 47. What of Fletchall's conduct? 48. What was done with Mayson? 49. Who raised the king's standard? 50. What might the governor have done had he been a man of enterprise?

With a British fleet in the harbor, and along the coast, and thousands of loyalists in the interior, the revolutionists along the seaboard would have been crushed as between the upper and the lower millstone.

Fortunately, Lord Campbell, though brave enough, was deficient in the necessary enterprise.

But the affairs of the interior were sufficiently critical. His influence was exercised, if he did not give his presence; and, it became necessary that the council of safety should take those steps, which ought to have been taken at an earlier period — should proceed to conciliate the new settlements and settlers of the upper country.

William Henry Drayton and the Reverend William Tennent were appointed to make a progress through the disaffected region, and explain to the people the causes of the dispute between the crown and colonies; to settle disturbances, and produce a pacification and reaction, if possible. Drayton had, besides, secret powers to call upon the rangers and militia, where these could be found faithful, and had full discretion to employ force whenever necessary.

We have already shown, in repeated instances, why the people of South Carolina were not homogeneous; why they could not be one in popular sentiment; why the motives and reasons for the quarrel should be found, in some sections, unintelligible to the masses. We may add that, at this period, there was very little sympathy between the people of the upper and lower country; a fact not merely to be ascribed to the European character of so large a portion of the province, but to the natural jealousies of poor and insulated settlements toward an affluent people, already in possession of wealth and importance. The common appeal of the loyalist leaders was to the vulgar prejudices against rank and wealth, the haughty assumptions of the citizens and planters of the seaboard, and their free expenditure of the public money. The upper settlements had been little considered by the popular leaders, in the whole progress of the revolutionary proceedings; had been, until a recent period, un-

51. Who were sent to pacificate the upper country? 52. What secret powers had Drayton? 53. What were the differences between the lower and the back country?

represented in their congresses and public meetings; and, but few efforts had been made to conciliate the more talented and influential of their leading men. These were hurt and jealous. Such neglect had offended the self-esteem of many, and rendered others indifferent to the result.

As yet, they were, as settlements, almost wholly unaffected by the oppressions of the crown, which were felt to be so onerous in the regions which cultivated large and valuable staples, and built and held shipping, and were engaged in manufactures and commerce; and, when the leaders in the low country decided in favor of one class of public men in the disaffected region, they naturally forced all the rivals of these preferred parties into active opposition.

The loyalists possessed numerous citizens of talents and real worth, who might have been conciliated, at least, to acquiesce in the movement which they might yet refuse to lead. Such were Fletchall, the Cunninghams, Robinson, Kirkland, and many others: and these people had strong arguments for their neutrality, and even their hostile action. They were, mostly, born subjects of the British sovereign; born in Europe, naturally of loyal races, and had only been a few years in that country which now called upon them to throw off British rule.

The British government, until a recent period, had been known to South Carolina chiefly by its benefactions; and at no period had the latter any such causes of complaint as formed the staple of grievances of the northern colonies, who were already known as manufacturers, and engaged in commerce and the fisheries, and so rivals of Britain herself in the industrial arts.

The causes of quarrel, on the part of South Carolina, might almost wholly be summed up in the denial of a few abstract popular principles. The duties on tea and stamped paper were not felt, regarding the amount; but as the assertion of an authority adverse to the rights of the people and the province.

54. What did the leading men of the back country resent? 55. What able men had the loyalists? 56. What arguments had they against revolution? 57. How had the British government been known to South Carolina? 58. How are the causes of quarrel summed up between the crown and colony?

British treasures, meanwhile, had helped them in their feebleness; British power had protected them from savage and other foes; its men, money, and munitions, had been yielded promptly to supply their need, or meet their emergencies.

All these were arguments, appealing strongly to the new colonists of the interior, which no subtle reasoning, however excellent, dealing only with abstract principles, could meet or overcome. They were wholly inefficient, in the ears of a simple people, satisfied with present securities, in opposition to the substantial advantages which had accrued to them from the connection with a powerful nation, and one which had, generally, throughout the colony, been distinguished by the endearing terms of relationship — "the mother-country."

South Carolina had, indeed, been a favorite plantation of the crown, and the reluctance of thousands to sever the friendly bands which had linked them together, was not less honorable to their principles, than natural to their affections. In respect to a large section of the province, the revolutionary movement was, undoubtedly, premature. The lack of adequate population, the lack of homogeneousness in that population; their deficiencies in the *materiel* as well as the *personnel* of war; the feebleness of the frontier colony of Georgia; the near neighborhood of the province of Florida, still faithful to the crown, and already filling fast with refugee loyalists, driven from all the southern colonies; these were all sufficient to prove the revolutionary movement premature, in the case of South Carolina. The argument, from policy, was clearly against the movement.

No doubt that many of the loyalists were persons of little principle, and much more governed by their passion and prejudice, than by any right reasoning; but, that the people who were subsequently degraded, under the general and opprobrious term of "tories," were, in many instances, moved only by an honest and loyal, if not a wise and just sense of duty, can not well be questioned. That they were behind the time — had made no such advances in the knowledge of the popular rights as had the popular leaders — and were too slow to recognise

59. Why was it difficult to make these clear to the people? 60. Was the revolution premature? — and why? 61. What is said of the loyalists generally?

the necessities of the country, its interests as well as rights, is equally undeniable. If the patriots might be reproached as being too warm, it is equally certain they were too cold; if to the one party the shadows of coming events were beheld at too great a distance, to the other, the substance itself appeared little more than a shadow. Unhappily, the indiscretion of individuals of both parties increased the differences between them, and the gulf through which they had to wade, to sympathy and union in the end, was one that dyed their garments in blood, the stains of which, to this day, are scarcely obliterated.

The prompt and decisive measures of the seaboard, had, as we have shown, soon placed that section of the colony in a tolerable state of defence. This done, the popular leaders had extended — but a little too slowly — their precautionary labors to the interior; but it was not now so easy, in many parts of the country, to persuade the people that such measures were necessary; and the manner of proceeding, on the part of some of the agents intrusted with these measures, led to a suspicion among the people of the country, that their adversaries intended to dragoon them into compliance.

This suspicion, artfully encouraged by certain emissaries of the royal cause, whom the forethought of Lord William Campbell had sent into the interior, aroused all that fierce spirit of independence, which repeated strifes and trials had made no less suspicious than active; and, instead of signing the document by which the leaders of the lower country had pledged their lives and fortunes to each other, in a joint opposition to the royal authorities, they entered into counter-resolutions, just as resolute in expression, to oppose the patriots, to whom they ascribed motives and designs as dishonorable as they were unfounded. To remove these imputations, disabuse the ignorant, arouse the patriotic, teach the argument of the people against the usurpations of the crown, and conciliate or coerce, as circumstances required, was the difficult duty of the commissioners.

The first efforts of Drayton and Tennent, to soothe the dis-

62. Into what equal extremes did loyalists and patriots fall? 63. What suspicions were entertained by the people of the interior, and by whom fomented? 64. What did they resolve? 65. How, and whither did Drayton and Tennent proceed?

contents of the interior, led them to the Dutch settlements of Saxe Gotta, on the Congaree. But the Dutch refused to meet them; they had been tampered with, and taught to believe that, to take part against the king would result in the forfeiture of all the grants of land which they had received in his name; they were told, also, that the rangers were to be let loose upon them. These things terrified them. The rangers, by the way, were already collecting, and in camp, along with the commissioners. Some of the Dutch companies of Colonel Thompson's regiment were brought together; but, a portion of them behaved mutinously, though subsequently quieted.

But little was done in this quarter, in regard to the object had in view. The Dutch were simply soothed, for a while, not reconciled.

Changing their scene of operations a few miles, the commissioners were more successful with another body of the same people, most of whom signed the articles of association.

They were less successful at another Dutch settlement, on the Saluda, where they obtained but one signature. The enemy had been before them.

A Scotch trader, named McLaurin, influenced another settlement unfavorably, and the commissioners made no converts; and so, of many other places.

On the Enoree, at a great gathering, Robert Cunningham, one of the leading loyalists, was present; and Brown, another, who had been subjected, for his insolent toryism in Georgia, to the penalty of tar and feathers.

Here, the commissioners obtained some advantages with the people, in debate with the loyalist leaders. They then proceeded to Colonel Fletchall's residence, at Fair Forest. He was found to be closely watched by Cunningham, Brown, and Robinson, who had him in keeping.

But little was done here; though the success of the commissioners was much greater everywhere, after they had left the Congaree. They formed volunteer corps of horse-rangers, wher-

66. With what success, upon the Congaree, and among the Dutch? 67. On the Salnda? 68. On the Enoree? 69. Who met and argued with them? 70. To whose residence did they go? 71. With what result?

ever they found themselves strong enough to do so. Fletchall was indecisive — too wanting in character to resolve openly, yet too popular to be contemned. He was a tool in the hands of others. Robinson, Cunningham, Brown, were all decisive and daring men; the former openly avowed himself as armed with a commission to raise troops for the king. Their passions were growing beyond restraint, and the commissioners themselves were becoming irritable. The latter, feeling the temper of the loyalists, found it necessary to reinforce Fort Charlotte, making it a garrison of seventy men. They went on forming volunteer companies.

The loyalist leaders were equally busy, but more secretly, in the same office.

The progress of the commissioners carried them through all that portion of country which spreads from the Wateree and Catawba rivers, westwardly, to the Savannah; and extends northwardly, from the Saluda to the Cherokee nation, and to the boundary between North and South Carolina. They had done much, perhaps, in all these regions, but not all that was necessary or hoped for. It was too late for full success.

On the 23d of August, 1775, they again met the people — the loyalist leaders all present — at Ford's, on the Enoree. Here, the parties had nearly come into collision. They were all armed, and angry. Some of Fletchall's captains were won over by the commissioners; but they got few fresh signatures.

Their farther progress brought them next to the Savannah river, on their way to Ninety-six; when the tidings suddenly reached them that the loyalists were already in arms, and marching on Fort Charlotte, and Augusta. This put an end to their farther efforts at pacification. Conciliation now was required to give way to coercion.

Drayton at once asserted his secret powers, and called out the militia. Major Williamson, with three hundred men, were

72. What was Fletchall? 78. What is said of Robinson, Cunningham, and Brown? 74. What place did Drayton reinforce? 75. Whither did the progress of the commissioners carry them? 76. What had they done? 77. What is said of the meeting at Ford's, on the Enoree? 78. What tidings reached the commissioners on their way to Ninety-six? 79. What did Drayton? 80. What officers took the field, and with what forces?

put in motion; Colonel Thompson, with his rangers, and three hundred foot soldiers, and Colonel Richardson, with another force of three hundred men. These were ordered to march in such directions as were indicated by the course of the loyalists. A proclamation was made, at the same time, denouncing Moses Kirkland, who had assembled the insurgents, and calling upon all good citizens to put him down with the sword.

The effect was good. Kirkland was paralyzed, disbanded his men, and fled to Charlestown, in disguise. Here he succeeded in making his way on board the British sloop-of-war, Tamar. For the moment, the loyalists kept quiet, while the revolutionists grew more active. Volunteer companies increased, and we find, among their captains, for the first time, the name of Andrew Pickens, afterward the famous general of militia.

But the paralysis of the loyalists was for the moment only. The flight of Kirkland did not discourage Cunningham and Brown; they continued to collect troops. Drayton prepared to anticipate them, and advanced, with one hundred and twenty men and four swivels, upon Fletchall's quarters. He despatched a party to seize Robert Cunningham, the ablest of the loyalist leaders; but he had quitted his house the day before.

Drayton's force, increased by eighty volunteers, from Georgia, was now two hundred and twenty-five men. He was warned that the loyalists were about to march upon him, in strength. He prepared, after advising with Majors Mayson and Williamson, and Captain Hammond, to prepare for the enemy, however strong, and lay an ambush for his approach.

But their preparations were made in vain. The loyalists were not yet prepared for the issue. Hearing of a camp of Fletchall, Drayton marched toward it. Both parties, meanwhile, had been growing; the loyalists already mustered twelve hundred; the revolutionists were not quite a thousand. But, Fletchall's camp receded as Drayton's advanced; this encouraged Drayton, who thought it a good sign, and the time proper,

81. What proclamation was made? 82. What was the effect on Kirkland, and what became of him? 83. What did Cunningham and Brown? 84. What did Drayton resolve? 85. Upon whom did Drayton march? 86. What proclamation did he now issue?

to issue another proclamation, denouncing the arts by which the people had been misled, and inviting the repentant to make terms with a power which proffered them safety and the security of their rights.

Fletchall, and other malcontent leaders, were not unwilling to escape the extremities of war; they presented themselves at Drayton's camp to treat of peace. Articles were signed between them, which said, among other things, that the loyalists had no unfriendly designs against the congress or the colony; that they never did mean to aid or assist the British, and promised never, directly or indirectly, to do so; in brief, that they only desired to be let alone, and, in this event, they would harm nobody.

This pacification, though it bound only themselves, in a great measure, restored the quiet of the upper country, for a time at least. But Fletchell's proceedure did not bind the Cunninghams, and others, who had not signed it, and did not meet their approbation. This was unfortunate. But one great effect was reached; the faction was divided — broken; there was dissention and distrust among them.

Drayton proceeded next to pacificate the Cherokees; made them presents, and promises of presents; and got their promises, also; but with these, too, the enemy had been before him, and the British Indian agents, Stuart, Cameron, and others, were quite as able, with British presents, to undo all that the commissioners could do, or had done. We shall see, hereafter, that all these pacifications were of brief duration.

87. With what effect? 88. What was the substance of the treaty? 89. Did it bind all the loyalists? 90. Whither did Drayton then go, and with what object? 91. Did he treat with the Cherokees? 92. What is said of all these pacifications?

# CHAPTER IV.

## SEABOARD STRUGGLES — CIVIL WAR IN THE BACK COUNTRY — THE SNOW-CAMP.

THE active proceedings of our commissioners in the interior, will equally show the spirit of the revolutionary party and the difficulties with which they had to contend.   Their labors having reached the object contemplated, they returned to Charlestown, leaving the affairs of the country in better order thán before, in consequence of that rallying of the whigs which had awed the loyalists into temporary submission.

On the 10th of July, 1775, the general assembly was convened by Governor Campbell.   This, it must be remembered, was under the regal authority, the shows of which were still maintained, though the real power of the province had been absorbed by the provincial or revolutionary congress ; but no business was done.   The several houses and the governor were at cross-purposes — the greater part of the royal commons house being members either of the provincial congress, the council of safety, or the committee ; and all these were revolutionary bodies.   This period was chosen for requiring all persons in the colony to sign the provincial association.   Arthur Middleton, in general committee, moved to attach estates in case of the flight of the owners, and to *excommunicate* from all social privileges all persons who should refuse to sign the association.

The popular commotions continued, with an occasional spectacle of tarring and feathering.   The mob was active and angry.

1. When did Governor Campbell convene the general assembly ?  2. Where was the real power of the province ?  8. What business was done ?  4. What were the people required to subscribe ?  5. What resolutions were submitted by Arthur Middleton ?  6. What of the popular commotion ?

Governor Lord Campbell became angry, too, and a little apprehensive. Dr. Milligan, chief surgeon of the British for his majesty's forces in South Carolina, fled, when no one pursued. Middleton writes, at this time, of Charlestown: "The plebeians are for war — the *noblesse* perfectly pacific." A temporary discontent among the volunteer companies of Charlestown filled the governor with new hopes; but they were pacified.

The governor, meanwhile, continued his secret correspondence with the loyalists of the back country. By a clever *ruse*, his scheming was discovered. Arthur Middleton moved that he should be taken into custody. But for this decided measure the general committee were not quite prepared. They preferred to temporize as long as they were permitted to do so. But they demanded of Campbell his late correspondence with the back country, his late despatches from England, and the surrender of the body of Moses Kirkland, then on board the Tamar.

He refused to comply with any of their demands.

The revolutionary committees, satisfied now that British troops were on their way to the province, determined upon more decisive action. They resolved to take possession of Fort Johnson. The bastions of the town were manned (15th September, 1775) by detachments of artillery, and the appearance of the city began to be that of a camp of vigilance.

Meanwhile, Lord Campbell, with his secretary Jarvis, and a detachment from the crew of the sloop Tamar, under the cover of the night, took possession of Fort Johnson, dismounted the cannon from the platform, and thus sought to render them incapable of immediate service. But he had not spiked them, nor did they break off their trunnions. He and his party were fortunate in escaping — the governor to the city, and the crew of the British sloop to their vessel, before the night was over. An hour later, and they would have been all sacrificed. Moultrie had already made his preparations for manning the fort, and

7. Who fled? 8. What did Middleton write of the people? 9. What practices did the governor continue? 10. What did Arthur Middleton move to do in respect to him? 11. What did the committee demand of the governor? 12. How did he reply? 13. What did the revolutionary committees resolve and propose? 14. What secret achievement was executed by Lord Campbell?

putting it in fighting order; and, under his instructions, a detachment led by Colonel Motte, consisting of Captains Pinckney's, Elliott's, and Marion's companies, left the city for this purpose. They reached the fort, but too late to find an enemy in sufficient force for combat. They were allowed to take quiet possession, to disarm the small garrison that remained, and, at leisure, to restore the cannon to their places upon the platforms.

This was done by daylight, and the guns promptly trained to bear upon the British armed vessels lying in the harbor — the Cherokee and Tamar.

The next day, Lord Campbell prorogued the assembly; and that very day fled to the shelter of the Tamar, in Rebellion roads, carrying with him the great seal of the province. His occupation was gone! The province was irretrievable. No laws had been passed by the present assembly during his administration; and though his influence, in the interior, had been sufficiently mischievous, he had not proved himself the man to turn it to profitable account for his sovereign.

Fort Johnson was soon recruited with troops from the city, and put in fighting order. Moultrie devised for it a flag — a blue ground with a single silver crescent in one corner. This was devised from the uniforms of the first and second regiments, which were of blue cloth, with a silver crescent in their caps.

At sight of this flag, waving proudly from the walls, Lord Campbell despatched an officer from the ship-of-war, to demand its meaning — to know by what authority the fort had been seized, and what authority held it.

He was answered briefly — "By authority of the council of safety."

The Cherokee and Tamar then made a demonstration of attack, and presented themselves within point-blank shot before the fort; but withdrew without giving fire. They found them-

15. What was done by the detachment of Moultrie the same night? 16. Who led this detachment? 17. In what condition did they place the fort? 18. What was done next day by Lord Campbell? 19. What was done during his administration? 20. What is said of his influence? 21. What flag did Moultrie devise for Fort Johnson? and why the design? 22. What was Campbell's demand on seeing this flag? and how answered?

selves fully prepared for, and retired peaceably to their former anchorage.

Fort Johnson was strengthened. It was determined to fortify Sullivan's island also, and to sink hulks in the channel, preventing the ingress of an assailing fleet.

But, to do this, it was first necessary to dislodge and drive out the British sloops-of-war. A new water-battery was made on James's island, and bastions and fortifications rapidly followed in other quarters — the resolve being taken to fortify all the approaches to the city.

This brings us to September, 1775. William Henry Drayton succeeded Henry Laurens as president of Congress, and about the same time the disquiets of the upper country had been renewed. Robert Cunningham for seditious language, had been arrested by Major Williamson, and, with others, sent to Charlestown jail for safe-keeping.

This proceeding aroused his brother, Patrick Cunningham, and he, with some sixty followers, pursued, in the hope to rescue Robert from the sheriff. They failed to do this, but succeeded in another performance, in which they hurt the province much more seriously.

When Drayton made a treaty with the Cherokees, he agreed to send them powder. This had been done. Patrick Cunningham, failing to rescue his brother, encountered the guard with the powder, seized the guard, and carried off the powder.

This, however small in itself, was a serious evil. The engagement with the Cherokees had not been kept. Powder was in great requisition, and this supply armed the upper-country insurgents for a season.

It became necessary that the disaffected whites and the red men should be equally kept quiet, in prospect of that assault that was threatened from Britain. The rangers, under Richardson, Williamson, and others, were set in motion against Cunningham.

23. What did the Cherokee and Tamar? 24. What measures were taken against these British vessels? 25. To what period have these events brought us? 26. Who succeeded Laurens as president of congress? 27. What discontents were renewed, where, and why? 28. Who was made prisoner? 29. What did Patrick Cunningham? 30. What mischiefs were likely to follow his proceeding? 31. What became necessary?

Meanwhile, the council of safety was endeavoring to increase the securities of Charlestown. It was resolved, as we have seen, to sink hulks to obstruct the passages of Marsh channel and Hog-island creek. Schooners were purchased for the purpose. But, before this could be done, it was necessary to provide a naval force sufficient for the encounter with the British sloops-of-war, and to prevent them from interfering with the work of closing the channels. A schooner, called the Defence, Captain Tuffts, armed with ten guns, and a complement of seventy men, was prepared for this purpose. Drayton, president of the council, went on board as chief in command. The Tamar and Cherokee sloops-of-war — the one of sixteen guns, the other six — endeavored to arrest the performance of the work ; but the hulks were sunk. The British sloops and the " Defence " exchanged frequent shots with some effect. After awhile, the British drew off. Fort Johnson took a part in the affair, and the troops of Charlestown assembled at their several posts in expectation of worse trials.

The war was thus begun (11th November, 1775), and the affair was quite spirited. The next day was Sunday, but did not prevent the patriots from doing business. They met in council, and resolved to take the merchant ship Prosper into the service of the colony, and man her, also, against the British sloops.

Other resolves were made for the erection of batteries. A regiment of artillery was voted, to consist of three hundred men. Dictatorial powers were conferred on a council consisting of the president (Drayton), Colonel Pinckney, and Thomas Heyward, jr. On the 16th November, 1775, the congress elected a new council of safety, consisting of Charles Pinckney, Henry Laurens, Henry Middleton, Thomas Ferguson, Arthur Middleton, Thomas Heyward, jr., William H. Drayton, Rawlins Lowndes, Thomas Bee, Benjamin Elliott, James Par-

32. What steps were taken by the council of safety in the harbor? 33. What schooner was employed ? — how manned and commanded ? 34. What was the result of the attempt to sink the hulks ? 35. Who drew off? 36. When did this battle take place ? 37. What did the council do on Sunday ? 38. What resolves were passed ? 39. What powers were conferred on Drayton, Pinckney, and Heyward ? 40. When was the new council of safety elected ? 41. Of what persons did it consist ?

sons, D. Olyphant, and Thomas Savage.   Henry Laurens was chosen president.   At this time, and with the immediate prospect of a war with Britain, there was not a single piece of gold or silver in the treasury.   It had a *paper currency* to the amount of £126,500.

The insurrection in the back country was increasing.   The whole militia of Charlestown was embodied.   The ship Prosper was manned, and Drayton took the command.   The forces under Colonels Powell, Rothmaler, Bull, Roberts, and Colonel Richardson, all under the latter, were ordered to repair to the scene of disaffection.   Major Williamson, and the loyalist insurgents respectively, had been for some time gathering their forces.   The insurgents were greatly helped by the accession of Colonel Richard Pearis, an influential man, who, having been overlooked by the revolutionists, had joined the discontents.   He inculcated the slander that the powder seized by Cunningham was meant to subsidize the red men against the loyalists.

Williamson seems to have been dilatory, and was only roused up when the insurgents were on the march to attack him.   He then proposed to meet them on the march, and attack them in the night, but was overruled by a council of war.   He then took ground at Savage's plantation, near Ninety-Six.   Here he enforted himself, hurriedly and imperfectly with fence-rails chiefly, and was soon after besieged — his force consisting of less than six hundred ; that of the insurgents nineteen hundred.

There was some sharp fighting between the parties ; subsequently they treated — Williamson agreeing to surrender the fort, but not his people ; and both sides consenting to refer their disputes to Lord William Campbell, who was in no condition to decide anything.

Williamson and his patriots were fortunate in such an ar-

42. What was the state of the treasury ?   43. What was the condition of the back country ?   44. What officers and troops, and under whose command, were ordered to the scene of trouble ?   45. What parties had been respectively gathering their forces ?   46. What acquisition had the insurgents made ?   47. Who was Colonel Pearis ? and how influenced ?   48. Where did Williamson enfort himself, and how ?   49. What was his force, and by what numbers was he besieged ?   50. What fighting followed, and what treaty ?

rangement, considering their want of provisions and the inequality of numbers. But Robinson, who commanded the other side, had an unmanageable and disorderly body; hence his readiness to treat and his favorable terms. He was, perhaps, unable to render his troops effective. A few were killed on both sides, and some twenty or thirty wounded.

But the affair did not end here. The insurgents were in exultation and insolent, because of their success, and continued embodied. Richardson marched against them. His force soon reached three thousand men. Their approach overawed the insurgents, who gradually began to disband. Several of their chief men were made prisoners — Fletchall, Pearis, and others. Fletchall, who was no hero, was caught in a cave; the others, in similar hiding-places. These were all sent to the Charlestown jail.

The junction of Richardson with Williamson and others, including a few Georgians, made the army four thousand strong. A detachment, under Colonel Thompson, proceeded against Patrick Cunningham, and had nearly surrounded his camp, when they were discovered. The insurgents were overcome at a blow. Cunningham made his escape on a fleet horse. A few of the loyalists were killed, and it was with difficulty that Thompson prevented a general massacre.

This campaign, which had for the present achieved all its objects, was a terribly severe one. The troops were without tents or covering — almost without shoes. Provisions were scarce, and they found themselves in a snow-storm of three days. The campaign was ever afterward known as the *snow-camp*.

Richardson disbanded his troops on Christmas day. Their holidays were gloomy; but the insurrection was again *scotched*; but only scotched! Except Robinson, Cunningham, and M'Laurin, no considerable leader escaped apprehension.

<hr />

51. What caused Robinson to grant Williamson such terms? 52. What were the casualties? 53. Did the insurrection end then? 54. Who next marched against the insurgents, and with what force? 55. What leaders were taken? 56. How many men did the patriots finally number? 57. Who next did they proceed against? — with what success? 58. What was the character of this campaign, and what was it called? 59. When were the patriots disbanded? 60. What loyalists leaders of note escaped?

In this campaign, we find the names of Pickens and Sumter
—the latter acting as adjutant-general.

In February, 1776, the measure for disarming the insurgents was suspended, as they appeared to be subdued; and in
March a declaration of amnesty and pardon was made, with a
few exceptions.

The object was now to conciliate the people who had been
pardoned. Pains were taken to this end. Many of the loyalists subscribed to the terms proposed by the congress. Some,
who did not among the leaders, abandoned the colony and fled
to Florida. There they remained, brooding over their wrongs,
until a strong British army penetrated Georgia and Carolina,
when they emerged from their hiding-places, and formed an
auxiliary portion of the invading army, ranking rather with its
red allies than its white.

61. What distinguished names of revolutionary heroes do we find in this campaign ?
62. What was done February, 1776 ?  63. What now was the object of the revolutionary party?  64. With what success pursued ?  65. Who fled to Florida ?  66. When
did they return ?

# CHAPTER V.

### THE PROVINCE BECOMES THE REPUBLIC.

THE revolutionists of Carolina had thus, to all appearances, quieted their domestic dissentions.  It was now necessary that they should resume their preparations against the approaches of the more formidable external enemy.  The seaboard was now the scene of danger and excitement.  That the province should escape, without fierce handling, was next to impossible ; the provocation had been too great for pardon.  Already had the British sloops-of-war, in Charlestown harbor, received an accession to their force in the arrival of the Scorpion ship, Captain Tollemache.  He was for attacking Fort Johnson and the city at once ; but, his colleagues declined the experiment ; they all knew of larger forces on the way, and did not despise their enemies, as Captain Tollemache avowedly did.  But they harassed the trade of the place, and were a perpetual threat and danger, seizing upon vessels arriving, appropriating their contents, and giving refuge to runaway negroes.

To rid the harbor of these guests was the eager desire of the patriots.  The ship Prosper was put in charge of Drayton ; a battery was raised on Haddrell's point, in a single night, and, guns were mounted by the dawn.  A few shot from the eighteen-pounders, thus put in position, soon compelled the men-of-war to fall down to Sullivan's island.  The harbor grew too hot to hold them ; they were allowed neither food nor water ; and they put to sea a few days after.

The provincials then proceeded to erect a fort on Sullivan's

1. Where was now the scene of danger ?  2. What accessions of force had the British made ?  3. What did Captain Tollemache propose ?  4. How did the British ships trouble the harbor ?  5. What measures were taken by the provincials ?  6. What was the effect of their eighteen-pound shot ?  7. Where did the provincials proceed to erect a fort ?

island, which they continued, though slowly, to work on at intervals.

They had much to do. The civil affairs of the province required the nicest management. Colonel Gadsden introduced into the council chamber a flag, such as was to be used in the American navy, with a yellow field, and a rattlesnake, livelily represented in coil, and ready to strike, with these words beneath,—" Don't tread on me!" He also introduced Paine's pamphlet called " Common Sense," which declared, as he did, for the absolute independence of the colonies. The congress was not quite prepared for this, and the speech produced a sensation.

But, nevertheless, the spirit of independence was active. On the 11th of February, 1776, a committee of eleven was chosen to report a plan of government; this committee, consisting of Charles C. Pinckney, John Rutledge, Charles Pinckney, Henry Laurens, Christopher Gadsden, Rawlins Lowndes, Arthur Middleton, Henry Middleton, Thomas Bee, Thomas Lynch, jr., and Thomas Heyward, jr., decidedly among the ablest men in the province. But, we see that the upper country still lacks representation; it might have been better policy to assign to that and to the middle country a position in the popular councils, even though the controlling vote was still reserved to the seaboard.

On the 19th of February, apprehending, and with good reason, early invasion, ten hundred and fifty of the country militia were ordered to be drafted, for the defence of the city. A few days after, the military establishment was decreed to be increased by two rifle regiments, one of seven, the other of five hundred men. Of one of these, Isaac Huger was made colonel, the other was given to Thomas Sumter, lieutenant-colonel commandant, with William Henderson as major; and these regiments were ranked as fifth and sixth of the provincials in the colony's service. Paul Trapier was made captain of a company of artillery, at Georgetown, and William Harden of the Beaufort

8. What flag did Colonel Gadsden introduce? 9. What pamphlet?—and with what effect? 10. For what purpose was a committee chosen, 11th of February, 1776? 11. Who were the committee? 12. What is said of the exclusion of the back country? 13. What decree was issued, 19th of February, and how was the military establishment increased? 14. Who were put in command of the new regiments?

artillery. A constitutional post, or mail, was established, in recognition of a recommendation of the continental congress. On the 6th of March, there remained in the treasury, but three hundred thousand pounds, *paper currency.* Seven hundred and fifty thousand pounds more were voted, in regard to the exigencies of the province.

While the provincial congress was debating the terms of a constitution for the state — preparing to shake off all the forms of dependency upon Britain, news were brought of the act of the British parliament (December 21, 1775), which authorized the capture of American ships and property — which, briefly, put all the rebellious colonies under the ban of war.

This act encouraged the independent members of the congress, and silenced the dubious and timid. The members proceeded to act with decision. A British ship in the harbor, laden with sugars, was seized and confiscated, and the amount, nearly fifty thousand pounds, placed in the colonial treasury.

On the 24th of March, 1776, John Rutledge, from the committee to prepare a plan of government, submitted a report or preamble, and constitution, which was adopted.

This constitution shook off substantially the rule of Britain, and converted the province into a republican state! Under this constitution, the provincial congress became the general assembly of South Carolina, with all the powers of sovereignty, as derived from the people. The representation recognised twenty parishes, and ten districts or counties. The executive and judicial officers were the president and commander-in-chief; the chief justice and assistant judges; the attorney-general; the ordinary, and three commissioners of the treasury.

John Rutledge was elected president and commander-in-chief; Henry Laurens, vice-president; William Henry Drayton, chief justice; Thomas Bee, John Mathews, and Henry Pendleton, assistant judges; Alexander Moultrie, attorney-gen-

15. What sum remained in the treasury on the 6th of March? — and what additional sum was voted? 16. What British act influenced the proceedings of the congress? 17. How did it affect all parties? 18. What was done with a British ship in the harbor? 19. What was done on the 24th of March? 20. What did the provincial congress become? 21. What was the allotted representation? 22. What officers were elected under the constitution?

eral, etc. The legislative council consisted of Charles Pinckney, Henry Middleton, *Richard Richardson*, Rawlins Lowndes, *Le Roy Hammond*, Henry Laurens, David Olyphant, Thomas Ferguson, George Gale Powell, Stephen Bull, Thomas Bee, *Joseph Kershaw*, and Thomas Shubrick. The names in *italics* were from the *middle* and *back* country.

The legislature proceeded to do business as if they had never known a king.

The officers of the regular government of South Carolina — *the first formed by any of the American colonies* — proved themselves wise and efficient. They resolved to communicate with Britain only through the continental congress; magistrates were appointed; the courts of law were re-opened; justice received her robes, and authority its sword; and William Henry Drayton, in his first charge to the grand jury, a famous production, anticipated the whole Declaration of Independence, as adopted subsequently by the continental congress.

We must not omit to notice, in passing, that, during these proceedings in South Carolina, succors were sent to Georgia, where hostilities had taken place, also. Colonel Bull, with five hundred Carolinians, Major Bourquin, with a smaller detachment, were active and useful participants in the first struggles of the Georgians, in throwing off the foreign government and meeting their assaults. In North Carolina, the intrigues of the governor (Martin), brought about a similar insurrection among the people of that colony, as had been produced in South Carolina, by the machinations of Campbell; and the insurgents there were defeated also.

The die of revolution was thus solemnly cast. We have seen what were the resources, in men and money, what the degree of harmony existing between the several sections of the state, and we may readily estimate for ourselves what were the prospects of her success in maintaining a conflict with Great Britain; single-handed, *none* of the colonies could have done it;

23. Who constituted the legislative council? 24. What colony of America formed the first independent constitution? 25. What did the new government resolve? 26. What first charge was made to the grand jury? 27. How did South Carolina help Georgia? 28. What is said of North Carolina? 29. What is said of the power of any single colony to resist Britain?

and South Carolina was, next to Georgia, one of the feeblest. *The hope of the colonies lay in their union, their faithful support of one another, prompt succor*, willing self-sacrifice; by which, alone, could they baffle the efforts of a power like Britain; compelling her to scatter her strength along a vast coast, and over a vast forest-country, and so extend her arms, as to leave them constantly liable to surprise and defeat.

The population of South Carolina, as well as most of the other colonies, was greatly exaggerated by the estimates of congress. The object of this estimate was to impress, equally upon friends and foes, the notion of their strength. Thus, the thirteen colonies, supposed to be three and a half millions, at the opening of the war, were found, at the close of it, by actual census, to be considerably less than three millions.

South Carolina was estimated to contain ninety-three thousand whites, when she could not possibly have had sixty thousand; when, in fact, her own writers rated her at forty thousand in 1775, and, during the five years preceding 1776, she had very little increase, and, most probably, a decrease. Take a single illustration: — In 1775, when, of course, every effort was made to make her numerical resources as great as possible, she could number but thirteen regiments of militia; allowing to each of these the usual complement in that day, of five hundred men, and we have seven thousand five hundred men; add to these the regulars, enlisted after the organization of the congress, say three regiments and a battalion, the former six hundred and the latter three hundred and fifty, and you have twenty-one hundred to add to the former sum; ten thousand men, in brief, was the whole disposable force in South Carolina, when she threw down the gauntlet to the power of Great Britain.

North Carolina, with twice the number of whites, and a far inferior negro population, might bring fifteen thousand into the field, and this is a liberal estimate; while the whole disposable force of Georgia, according to the representations of her chief

80. Which were the feeblest colonies? 81. In what lay the hope of all? 82. What of the estimated population of all the colonies? 83. What was the estimate of South Carolina? 84. What was probably the true estimate? 85. What was her militia force in 1775? 86. What is the estimate made of her strength in 1776? 87. What of North Carolina and Georgia?

men, was but *two* thousand soldiers.   It is clear that these feeble provinces could only hope for safety, in the full sense entertained by other communities, of the *common* necessity; their
unselfish co-operation, the promptness of their succor, the liberality of their appropriations, and the good conduct of her own,
and their chief men.   It was in this latter respect that South
Carolina was particularly strong, and it was *their* devotion, talents, and extraordinary exertions, that led to the subsequent
overrating of her resources for defence.

Having quieted their domestic difficulties, the popular leaders,
now under the sanction of a regular government, resumed their
preparations against their British assailants.   Batteries were
constructed at Georgetown, and other places; a fort and magazine were established at Dorchester, which became a rendezvous
for the country troops.   Charlestown was a garrison.   The palmetto fort, on Sullivan's island, was begun by Moultrie, which
continues to bear his name: even before completion it was
destined to be identified for ever with his military reputation.
Arms and the munitions of war were gleaned and gathered
from every possible source.   Lead was taken from the house-
tops and churches, to be run into bullets.   Vessels were impressed and manned as men of war.   For sailors, a bounty was
offered.   Negroes were haled from the plantations to help throw
up defences; and, without rashness or exultation, but sufficient
enthusiasm and firmness, the citizens of the new state looked
to the hour of bloody trial as one which they could not escape,
which they should not wish to escape, and which must, of necessity, be at hand.   The seeds of revolution had been sown
two years before; the fruits were now to be gathered, and with
crimson hands, as from the wine-press.   But we must reserve
the grand openings of the drama to another book and chapter.

38. In what was South Carolina strong?   89. Where were batteries, and forts, etc.,
erected?   40. What was Dorchester?   41. What Charlestown?   42. Where the Palmetto fort?   43. How were arms, men, and munitions, procured?   44. How were the
negroes employed?   45. What was the temper of the people at the approach of danger?

# BOOK V.

## THE REVOLUTION IN SOUTH CAROLINA.

## CHAPTER I.

### BATTLE OF FORT SULLIVAN.

THE prowess of the infant republic was shortly to be tried. She was required to go through the usual baptism of free states — that of fire and blood. Her people had been particularly forward in asserting their rights and liberties, and in provoking the anger of the mother-country. They had lacked prudence, no doubt; but they were full of spirit. In fact, the spirit of the province was far beyond her strength, and led her not only to the exaggeration of her strength, but to a partial disregard of her real resources. Of these she had not been sufficiently economical — had been neglectful — as we have seen in her too-late attention to the task of conciliating her new population of the back country.

These were only quieted upon the surface. For a time, there was a general quiet in the state, of which the president and privy council took advantage, to improve its strength and the preparations for its defence. It was fortunate, indeed, that the administration was now concentrated, and in a single hand. There was no dissenting voice — no confusion of council. John Rutledge, as president of the republic, in his best vigor, was adequate to its emergencies.

The interval of repose was not of long duration. Accounts were received, early in May, announcing a British fleet off the

1. What was the prospect before the Carolinians? 2. What had been their errors? 3. Were the discontents quieted? 4 What was fortunate in the administration of the government? 5. What accounts were received?

9*

coast of North Carolina.   Now, the very same reasons which
had arrayed a large portion of the Carolinians in opposition to
their countrymen, had provoked the especial indignation of the
British government.   The conduct of Carolina was regarded
as particularly ungracious.   She was selected, therefore, as
especially deserving of chastisement.   Her sympathy with the
wrongs of Massachusetts, rather than any injuries done to herself, had been the true cause of her taking part in the conflict.
She had few, if any, of those occasions for quarrel which
brought the people of the North into collision with those of
Europe.   She had no manufactories to maintain in opposition
to those of England — she had no shipping or seamen which
could enter into competition with that marine by means of which
Great Britain indulged a fond ambition to rule the waves.   She
provided the raw material which the other manufactured, and
she received the manufactured goods in exchange for her productions.   The intercourse was simple enough between them,
and the occasions for conflict were few and unimportant.

The overweening arrogance of British officers and officials,
by offending the self-esteem of her sons — a proud and ambitious race — may be enumerated among these occasions; and
the jealousies engendered between the troops of the province and
those of the mother-country, which led to the affair between
Colonels Grant and Middleton, recorded in a previous chapter,
were as keenly felt and remembered as they were warmly indulged at the time of their provocation.   These, no doubt, contributed much more effectually than the duties on stamps or tea,
to place South Carolina in that attitude of defiance which goaded
the mother-country to vengeance.   It was soon apparent that
the young republic would be required to put in exercise her
best energies and her utmost manhood.

The British fleet of Sir Peter Parker was a formidable one,
including a large body of land forces, under Major-General
Clinton.   To help South Carolina, the continental congress had

6. How was the conduct of South Carolina regarded by the British government?
7. What had been the influence prompting her to revolution?  8. What reasons were
there why she should not revolt?  9. What evil influence is ascribed to the conduct
of British officials?  10. What fleet and army now threatened her?

ordered a body of Virginians and North Carolinians to her aid, under the command of Major-General Charles Lee. Preceding him, came Brigadier-General Armstrong, a man of moderate abilities, who took temporary command of the troops in the vicinity of Charlestown.

Early in June, Major-General Charles Lee arrived — a man of unquestionable talents, but irregular, if not unprincipled; mercurial, selfish, vain, and desperately ambitious. As a colonel of cavalry, Lee might have done, and did, some brilliant things; as a commander of armies, he seems to have been incapable. But his career is to be looked for in other histories. On the 9th of June, Rutledge, the president of the colony, formally invested him with the chief military command of the threatened city and its precincts.

Lee was immediately busy with a feverish restlessness. He had thousands of projects, and covered the shores of the city with cannon and the streets with *flêches,* or small redoubts. In the little fortress on Sullivan's island, he had no faith, and would have abandoned it at once, but for the determined resistance of Rutledge. To Moultrie, the latter wrote — "I will sooner cut off my right arm than write you such an order." When Lee told Moultrie that the British fleet would knock his fort about his ears in half an hour. Moultrie replied, with great coolness, "Then we will fight them behind the ruins, and still prevent their landing."

There is no doubt that Lee was correct in his estimate of the value of Fort Sullivan as a place of defence; but he did not take into his estimate the blind insolence and self-sufficiency of the British commanders. Their error was in stopping deliberately to do battle with a little fortress which could not materially have impeded their progress, and which, if conquered, did not, in the slightest degree, help them to the conquest of the city. Their battles would then require to begin anew. They should have clapped on all sail and passed the fort, with favoring winds and tides, without exchanging a shot. They might

11. What help and generals were sent to South Carolina? 12. What is said of Lee? 13. What was Lee's opinion of Fort Sullivan? 14. What said Rutledge? 15. What Moultrie? 16. What was the error of the British commodore?

have suffered in sails and rigging, with possibly a few shot in their hulls, but the damage would have been comparatively slight and the danger soon over.

But the commodore, Sir Peter Parker, no doubt thought, with Lee, that the Americans would be driven from their guns at a single broadside, with their ruined battlements tumbling about their ears. He risked unnecessarily, through mere insolence of strength, the fleet and the whole expedition upon a little wooden and sand fortification, which presented the most insignificant mark for his cannon.

Fort Sullivan was a simple square, with a bastion at each angle, and was large enough, when finished, to contain one thousand men. It was built of palmetto logs, laid in sections, one upon the other, the parallel lines being sixteen feet apart. They were bound together at intervals with timber, dovetailed and bolted into the logs. The space between the parallel lines was filled with sand. The walls thus rudely raised were ten feet above the platform; and these were raised upon pillars of brick. Such was the plan of this fort; but it was unfinished when the hour of action arrived. It presented only a walled front to the enemy on the southeastern side, looking out upon the channel, and partly upon the southwestern side, looking to the city. The northeastern and northwestern sections were unfinished.

To close up the places thus exposed, some temporary structures of plank were employed, which would help the defence simply against escalade. Connected with the front angle of each rear bastion, these lines, which military men call cavaliers, were thrown up right and left of the fort for a certain, but small, distance. Each of these was mounted with three twelve-pounders. The fort itself was mounted with twenty-six cannon, consisting of nine French twenty-pounders, three English eighteen-pounders, and fourteen twelve-pounders; of all these only twenty guns could be brought to bear at one time upon the enemy. The flag waved from the southeast bastion.

East of Fort Sullivan, which occupied the most southerly

point of the island, directly covering the channel, there was a breastwork manned by a lieutenant and a quarter-guard, at a point where the island was most narrow.

At the northeastern extremity of the island, breastworks had been also erected, about two miles from Fort Sullivan. These were defended by one eighteen-pounder and a six-pounder brass field-piece. This position was maintained by Colonel William Thompson, of the third regiment of rangers, with seven hundred and eighty men in all, consisting of the third regiment of South Carolina rifles, three hundred men ; Colonel Horry, with two hundred South Carolinians ; the Raccoon (South Carolina) company of rifles; fifty militia men of South Carolina, a small detachment of artillery (city), and two hundred North Carolina regulars under Colonel Clark.

Thompson's position was among a cluster of barren sand-hills, overlooking " the breach," an arm of the sea, which the British, under Clinton, were preparing to cross, and facing the western extremity of Long island, of which they had taken full possession.

The whole of the British land-forces — three thousand men, under Major-General Clinton — were on Long island. Clinton had with him Earl Cornwallis and Brigadier-General Vaughan. Here he had thrown up works and mounted them ; had gathered boats and sloops and schooners, and was busied in the preparations to cross to Sullivan's, and take Fort Sullivan in the rear, as soon as Sir Peter Parker should begin the action in front.

Having shown what were the plans of the enemy, and what the immediate defences of the island, it may be well to state that, opposite to Long and Sullivan's, but in the rear, a force was posted, under Brigadier-General Armstrong, at Haddrell's and along the main, consisting of five hundred Virginia regulars; six hundred North Carolina regulars ; the fifth South Carolina rifles, two hundred and sixty-eight ; sixth South Carolina rifles,

19. What other fortifications east of Fort Sullivan ? 20. How was that on the eastern part of the island manned and defended ? 21. What force had Colonel Thompson ? 22. What was his position ? 23. Where were the British land-forces ? — and under whom ? 24. What troops occupied Haddrell's point and the contiguous shores ?

one hundred and sixty; and a militia artillery of forty men — in all a force of more than fifteen hundred troops.

The defence of the city proper, Major-General Lee reserved to his own command.   Here he concentrated most of his energies, never supposing that the petty fortress of Sullivan's could prove any obstacle in the way of a well-appointed and very powerful British fleet ; and most probably supposing that the ships would never stop deliberately to engage it, but content themselves with giving it a contemptuous shot in passing.

Meanwhile, Rutledge was present everywhere, at fort and city, stimulating and encouraging the troops and people, and hurrying the archives, the printing-presses, women and children, such as could and were willing to depart, into the country.

The city lay under arms.   All the stores along the wharves were levelled, and batteries of heavy cannon took their places. The opinions of Lee, heedlessly expressed, naturally affected all classes ; and they waited the moment when, Fort Sullivan silenced, they should require to brace themselves up to the final struggle.

Lee was so satisfied of the uselessness of Fort Sullivan, that he withdrew from it half the garrison and half the gunpowder, a most mischievous economy, which exposed the fortress to its worst danger, and deprived the defenders of the means of doing *wholly* what they did in part — destroying the assailing squadron.

The result of Lee's apprehension was to leave Moultrie, and his exclusively Carolina command, to a monopoly of all the glory of the event.   It was fortunate for the city that the British commodore and general were willing to expend their first fury on a point so remote and small.   Even if they succeeded in knocking the palmetto fortress about the ears of its defenders, it would, at least, break the first shock of the conflict for the citizens, and leave to them only the struggle with assailants already greatly breathed in the fight.   The whole force left under Moultrie in Fort Sullivan was four hundred and thirty-five of all ranks.   Of these, four hundred and thirteen were of

25. Where did Lee take command ?   26. What was Rutledge doing ?   27. What did Lee withdraw from Fort Sullivan ?

the second South Carolina regiment of infantry, and twenty-two of the fourth regiment (South Carolina) of artillery.

The larger vessels of the British were three days in getting over the bar. It was something of a surprise to the Carolinians to find them successful in getting over their fifty-gun ships. The enemy taught them the capacities of their bar, which they had hitherto underrated.

The enemy began civilly with a proclamation, which was sent in to Moultrie under a flag, denouncing the rebellion of the colony, and calling upon the magistrates and the loyal people of South Carolina to lay down their arms and receive pardon. The proclamation produced no effect ; and Clinton and Sir Peter Parker prepared themselves for the last method of enforcing submission. '

On the 28th day of June — a day which should be famous to all succeeding time in the annals of Carolina — this fleet, under the command of Sir Peter Parker, consisting of two fifty-gun ships, four frigates, and a number of smaller vessels, advanced to the attack.

The first object which drew their attention was the little fort of Moultrie, a mere speck upon Sullivan's island, which, it was not supposed, could maintain any protracted conflict. Such was the opinion, not of the British merely, but, as we have seen, of General Lee, who commanded in Charlestown. He had called it a mere slaughter-house, and asserted that a couple of British frigates would knock it about the ears of its defenders in half an hour. It was built of palmetto logs, as we have already described it. The palmetto is a tree peculiar to the southern states, the wood of which, being remarkably soft and spongy, is singularly suited to the purposes of defence against cannon. A bullet, entering it, makes no splinters nor extended fractures, but buries itself in the wood, without doing hurt to the parts adjacent. Within the fort was a morass, which favored the defenders, as it extinguished the matches of such shells as fell within the enclosure. Some of the shells thrown

28. What number of men were left to Moultrie ? 29. What proclamation was sent by the British, and with what effect ? 80. What day should be famous in the annals of Carolina ? 81. What was the fleet of Sir Peter Parker ? 82. Of what tree was the fort built ?

on this occasion were found fifty years after, unexploded, with the fuse unconsumed, and the missiles with which they were charged, still in their original integrity — harmless memorials of the direst purposes of harm.

While the British fleet was preparing to attack the fort, Colonel Thompson, at the head of the third Carolina regiment, kept the land-forces of the enemy, under Clinton in check, at the eastern extremity of the island. His excellency tried to get across, but Thompson's rifles and two pieces of artillery effectually defeated his efforts.

The main attack was upon Fort Sullivan. Between ten and eleven o'clock, the Thunder bomb-vessel began to throw its shells upon the fort. Four of the ships — the Actæon of twenty-eight guns, the Bristol and Experiment each of fifty, and the Solebay of twenty-eight — came boldly on to the attack. A little before eleven o'clock, the garrison fired four or five shot at the Actæon while under sail, but without doing hurt. When she came near the fort, she anchored, with springs on her cables, and commenced the battle with a broadside.

Her example was followed by the other vessels, and a storm of iron was rained upon the little fortress with the most unremitting fury. The bomb-vessel continued to throw shells until she was disabled; and, amidst the roar of three hundred heavy cannon, the courage of the defenders, who were almost wholly natives of Carolina, was summoned to its most fearful trial.

But their conduct did not belie their well-earned reputation, nor leave it doubtful what would be their course in the war which was to ensue. They stood as coolly at their posts as if they had been trained veterans. With a limited supply of ammunition, which forbade the constant exercise of their guns, they were enabled to time their discharges with regularity, and direct them with a singular precision of aim which told fearfully upon the enemy.

At one time, the commodore's ship, her stays shot away, swung round with her stern upon the fort, inviting, in that un-

83. What did Colonel Thompson while the fleet was approaching to the attack? 84. What vessel commenced the action? 85. How was her example followed? 86. How did the Carolinians behave? 87. What is said of the commodore's ship?

favorable situation, the fire of all its guns.   For a moment, every cannon that could be made to bear, belched forth its iron upon her.

"Mind the commodore — the fifty-gun ship!" was the cry, echoed by men and officers, along the whole range of the little battery.

Dreadfully did she suffer from this attention.   Her scuppers ran with blood ; her quarter-deck was twice swept of every man but her commander, and he himself narrowly escaped with two wounds, which disabled him.   With a loss in killed and wounded of more than one hundred men, she was at length, but with some difficulty, withdrawn from the action.

Nor was the loss of the other vessels, comparatively speaking, much less.   That of the Experiment, in slain, was greater. Her captain was maimed, fifty-seven of her men killed, and thirty wounded.

The battle lasted till near nine o'clock in the evening, and the ammunition of the little fortress was exhausted during its continuance.   The guns were almost hushed, firing only at stated intervals.   This led to the belief, on the part of the assailants, that the defence had ceased, and they sent up three vigorous cheers in token of their satisfaction.   But a fresh supply of powder from the city soon undeceived them.   And Marion obtained another supply from the schooner Defence, at the island cove, which renewed and increased the warmth of the conflict. The battle was renewed with ten-fold fury, and, though the imperfect structure which sheltered the Carolinians reeled and trembled to its base at every broadside which they fired, they kept to their guns, prepared to meet the invaders behind the crumbling ruins — such was Moultrie's resolve — rather than yield in a conflict upon which were equally staked the pride and the possession of their country.

By a mishap of the invaders, which was of the most providential good to the garrison, they were deprived, almost in the beginning of the conflict, of one of their most formidable means

38. How did she suffer ?  89. How the Experiment ?  40. How long did the battle last ?  41. What did the fort lack ?  42. How was powder procured ?  48. What mishap of the invaders helped the fort ?

of annoyance. Three vessels — the Sphinx, the Actæon, and
the Syren — were sent round to attack the western extremity
of the fort, which was so unfinished as to afford a very imperfect cover to the men at the guns, not only in that, but in almost
every other part of the structure. This exposed region had
been one of Lee's terrors. These vessels, in aiming to effect
their object, got entangled with a shoal called the Middle
Ground, and ran foul of each other. The Actæon stuck fast,
and was finally abandoned by her crew and destroyed; but not
before a detachment of the Carolinians had boarded her, and
discharged her loaded cannon at her retreating consorts. The
Syren and Sphinx got off and escaped; but not until they had
suffered too many injuries to enable them to take any farther
share in the battle.

The fire of the fort was chiefly directed against the Bristol
and Experiment, both of which suffered severely and equally in
hull, masts, and rigging. The Bristol had forty men killed and
seventy-one wounded. She was hulled in several places, and
but for the smoothness of the water must have filled and sunk.

Lord William Campbell, late royal governor of the province,
acting as a volunteer on board, received a wound which ultimately proved fatal. The loss of the garrison was but ten men
killed, and twice that number wounded. The shot of the British flew over the fort, or buried themselves in the soft wood of
the palmetto.

One of its defenders distinguished himself by an instance of
daring which alone has made him famous. In the beginning of
the action, the flag-staff was shot away. The flag of Carolina,
in this her first battle for independence, was a simple stripe of
blue cloth, bearing a silver crescent — the very flag which
Moultrie had waved from the walls of Fort Johnson. Sergeant
Jasper, of the grenadiers, a gallant fellow of Irish descent, immediately leaped over upon the beach, and, amid the hottest
fire of the foe, recovered the ensign, ascended the merlon, and
deliberately restored it to its place. Another brave man, Ser-

44. What was the fate of the Actæon? 45. What of Syren and Sphinx? 46. What
vessels suffered worst? 47. What befel Lord William Campbell? 48. What was the
loss of the garrison? 49. What is said of Sergeant Jasper? 50. What of Sergeant
Macdaniel?

geant Macdaniel, mortally wounded by a cannon-ball, still continued to cry aloud to his comrades to maintain the liberties of his country. His words of patriotic exhortation, coupled with his name, have survived his own sufferings and the thunders of that fearful day. "I die, my comrades; but do not let the cause of liberty die with me!"

President Rutledge gave Jasper his sword, and would have given him a commission, but the modest fellow declined it, on the score of his illiteracy. He had been uneducated, and a commission implied the necessity for some degree of education. We shall hear more of him hereafter. While the half-wrecked shipping of the British were drifting out to sea, Mrs. Barnard Elliott, one of the finest women of Charlestown, presented Moultrie's regiment with a pair of richly-embroidered colors of blue and red silk. Moultrie pledged himself for his men that they never should be dishonored. They were not. But they were saved at Savannah only by the blood of the brave Jasper and of *three* gallant officers — Lieutenants Bush, Hume, and Gray.

51. What were his dying words? 52. What did Rutledge give to Jasper? 53. What did Jasper decline? 54. What did Mrs. Barnard Elliott present the regiment? 54. Who perished in defence of these colors?

# CHAPTER II.

1776 TO 1778 — WAR WITH LOYALISTS AND CHEROKEES —
INVASION OF FLORIDA — CAPTURE OF SAVANNAH.

WHEN the engagement began with the fort, General Clinton
made his dispositions for attacking Colonel Thompson, at the
east end of the island. But the fire from Thompson's eighteen-
pounder, and the sharp shooting of his rifles, very soon discouraged the attempt. Clinton, after some loss in the effort to land,
was compelled to remain a quiet spectator. He was very much
censured, and pleaded that "the breach," was impassable; the
ocean being angry, and the water deep.

When Moultrie commenced the action, he had less than five
thousand pounds of powder; equal to twenty-six rounds for his
cannon; five hundred pounds more were subsequently obtained
from Charlestown, and three hundred from the schooner Defence,
during the action: in all, five thousand four hundred pounds.
The British ship Bristol, alone, expended fifteen thousand
pounds; the Experiment seven thousand five hundred. The
amount total expended, of all the assailing ships, was thirty-
four thousand pounds. The fort, with so small a quantity, was
compelled to economize; to throw away nothing at random, and
Moultrie, Marion, and the other officers, *sighted* every gun that
was fired, and every gun told, accordingly. The two fifty-gun
ships, as the best marks, were fairly riddled; had the sea been
rough, they could scarcely have been kept from filling.

Lee visited the fort during the action. A bridge of boats,
providing for the retreat of the garrison, was established from
the island to Haddrell's, to facilitate Moultrie's retreat. But,

1. What passage-of-arms took place between Clinton and Thompson? 2. What was
said of Clinton? 8. What was the consumption of powder, on both sides, in the battle of Fort Sullivan? 4. What was the effect of their deficiency of powder in the gun-
nery of the fort? 5. With what effect on the fifty-gun ships? 6. Who visited the fort
during the action?

had Moultrie retreated, as Lee counselled, Thompson would have been sacrificed; had Clinton forced Thompson, Moultrie must have been overcome on the landside; had the smaller British vessels been able to have taken position west of the fort, its batteries would have been enfiladed and useless; and, but for Lee's economical withdrawal of five thousand pounds of powder from the fort, his majesty's ships would have been sunk; for the artillerists at Fort Sullivan, fired like riflemen, as they pretty generally were.

The victory was, however, complete, though the results might have been greater. The British disappeared. Fort Sullivan changed its name for Fort Moultrie, which it now bears. Lee, Moultrie, and Thompson, received the thanks of the continental congress, July 20, 1776.

The British gone, the militia was discharged. Moultrie had gained the honors of the day; yet, had the British not attacked on the very day when they did, Lee had resolved to supersede him, and put General Nash in his place, thinking Moultrie quite too lymphatic, and lacking in energy for the exigency.

Six days after this battle, the continental congress declared the United Colonies free and independent States!

The disappearance of the British fleet from Charlestown, enabled other and trading vessels to run into port. These brought gunpowder, munitions of war, and dry goods, in barter for rice and indigo, replenishing the magazines and supplying the people. The victory, and all the recent events, had exhilarated the Carolinians. General Lee, though he shared the triumph, with very little propriety, was yet willing "to partake the gale." Governor (British) Tonyn, of Florida, had been very troublesome to Georgia and South Carolina; and Lee was persuaded, in midsummer, to undertake an expedition against Florida. He, accordingly, marched the Virginian and North Carolina troops to the Ogechee, whither the South Carolina troops followed them. He marched headlong, without clothing, medicine chest, or provisions, and at a season of the year when mere fatigue must prove fatal to European life.  At Sunbury, the average mortality in his camp, was fifteen deaths per day; and, at the moment when everybody saw that the expedition must be abandoned, Lee, luckily for himself, was called off to the northward, where the British, having taken New York, were becoming very formidable.  He left immediately, ordering the troops of Virginia and North Carolina to follow him.  His miserable management left the South in greater distress than ever; having lost them more men than all the assaults of the enemy.

When Lee again got to Charlestown, he was persuaded by the president, to leave the North Carolina troops there; those of South Carolina having been left in Georgia.  Major-General Moore was left in command of the southern troops in Carolina.

On the 17th of September, Gadsden and Moultrie were made brigadiers by the continental congress; but they ranked lower than the brigadiers of the North who had not yet smelt gunpowder, but who were timelily put on the establishment.

A few words on the new condition of affairs in South Carolina, consequent upon the changed relation of the state and its invaders.

The result of the ill-conducted expedition against South Carolina contributed greatly to establish the popular government in the affections of the people.  It quieted the fears of the many and overcame the opposition of the few; the revolutionists exulted and the royalists were silenced.  The doubtful grew confident in the success of a cause thus prosperously begun, while the patriotic appealed to it for the confirmation of everything which had been predicted.

Experience had now shown that a British fleet might be successfully resisted; and this conviction, alone, was of the most beneficial importance to the cause of the revolution.  It emboldened the popular spirit, and drew forth, in aid of the col-

14. Why did it fail?  15. Whither was Lee called?— and why?  16. Who succeeded him in command?  17. Who were made brigadiers?  18. What was the effect of the battle of Fort Moultrie upon the people of South Carolina?  19. What had experience proved?

ony, many who had hitherto withheld themselves because of the exaggerated estimate which they had made of the power of Great Britain to quell the rebellion at a blow.    It brought money forth from its hiding-places; and a general feeling of confidence began to arise in the public mind, as the prospect became stronger of a permanent condition of independence. Perhaps it had its disadvantages, also, as it inspired presumption instead of confidence; leading the Carolinians into a false security, and making them neglectful of those precautions, which, in a state of war, are the only just guaranties of complete success.

Among the fruits which this battle produced, was a liberal concession of favor to the loyalists at home, by the leaders of the revolutionary party.    Victory, which inspires generosity in all noble foes, prompted the Carolinians to set free the leaders of the opposition, whom they had taken into custody.    There was, of course, some policy in this.    The state wished to conciliate their friendship rather than provoke their hostility, and restored them to the rights and privileges of citizens.    But the venom was not withdrawn with the weapon.    Their minds rankled under a sense of injury, which was increased rather than diminished by the defeat of the British arms; and, though pledging themselves to good behavior, they remembered, in bitterness and blood, in long succeeding years of strife, the mortifications to which they had been exposed, and the wrongs which they believed themselves to have suffered.

The successful defence of Fort Moultrie gave a respite of two years to South Carolina, from the calamities of foreign war. But there were internal strifes not less difficult to be overcome. The loyalists were busy, and they had brought the red men of Cherokee into the field.    The back country was again the scene of strife and insurrection.    There, the active machinations of John Stuart, an officer of the crown, had succeeded in exasperating the Indians against the Carolinians, and in rousing them to arms.    A plan had been arranged by Stuart, in concert with

20. What were among the fruits of victory?   21. What respite followed to the Carolinians?   22. What mischief from internal strifes were in preparation?   23. What was the plan of Stuart, and others?

the royal governors, to land a British army in Florida; which, uniting with the Indians on the western frontiers of Carolina, and the tories in Florida, and elsewhere, would fall upon the back parts of the state, at the same time that a fleet and army should invade it on the seacoast.

The plan was fortunately discovered by the Carolinians, and timely preparations led to its partial defeat; but, so active had been the royal emissaries among the Cherokees, that, simultaneously with the battle of Fort Moultrie, they commenced their massacres upon the frontiers. This invasion was marked by the usual barbarities of Indian warfare.

Poorly provided with arms, the borderers betook themselves to stockade forts, in which they were shut up. Colonel Williamson, meanwhile, who was charged with the defence of the back country, succeeded in raising a force of five hundred men. A small affair with the Indians, in which they were defeated, led to a discovery which opened a new and bloody page in southern history. Thirteen of their number, who were taken, proved to be white men, disfigured, disguised, and painted so as to resemble Indians.

Henceforth, a warfare between the civilized was to ensue, so savage in its atrocities as to justify the subsequent description given of it by General Greene, who asserts that the "parties pursued each other like wild beasts." Other states knew nothing of the horrors which were the consequence of the domestic feuds of the South.

The news of the defeat of the British fleet produced the best effects when it reached the theatre of this bloody warfare. The patriots were encouraged, the tories dispirited. The former turned out with alacrity, and Williamson soon found himself at the head of twelve hundred men. With a detachment of three hundred horse, he advanced upon a tory and Indian force at Occnoree creek. His approach was known, an ambuscade laid

24. What event occurred simultaneously with the battle of Fort Moultrie? 25. Who was charged with the defence of the upper country? 26. Who were discovered among the red men? 27. How was the subsequent warfare described by Greene? 28. What effect upon the insurgents had the defeat of the British? 29. What was Williamson's force? 30. Against what force did he advance, and with how many horse? 31. What disaster followed?

for him, and he found himself in the thick of a desperate conflict for which he was only partially prepared. His horse was shot under him, an officer slain at his side, and, under a dreadful fire, his army was thrown into disorder.

It was rallied by Colonel Samuel Hammond — the thicket was charged, and the day retrieved. Marching through the Indian settlements, Williamson proceeded to lay them waste. With an army of two thousand men, he penetrated their country where the people were most numerous.

Entering the narrow defile of Noewee, enclosed on each side by mountains, a second ambuscade awaited him. Twelve hundred warriors, from the surrounding heights, poured in a constant fire upon his troops, from which they were only saved by the charge of the bayonet. The Indians fled after a severe conflict, in which they lost ground rather than men. The Carolinians suffered severely from their fire.

Williamson proceeded on his task of destruction, which, in a short time, was made complete. Penetrating their planted and beautiful vallies, he destroyed their crops and villages. But there was much hard fighting and several severe engagements. The savages, assisted by tory leaders, were with difficulty overcome. All their settlements eastward of the Apalachian mountains were laid waste; and, to avoid starvation, five hundred of their warriors fled to join the royalists in Florida. The conquest of the country was complete, and the Cherokees sued for peace. They were compelled to cede to South Carolina all their lands beyond the mountains of Unacaya. These lands form, at this moment, the flourishing districts of Greenville, Anderson, and Pickens. The narrative of this war forms a vivid episode in the history of the revolutionary struggle in South Carolina.

As we have seen, the declaration of American Independence, by the congress at Philadelphia, followed hard upon the battle

32. Who rallied the army? — and how was the fight retrieved? 33. With what force did Williamson penetrate the Cherokee settlements? 34. What ensued in the defile of Noewee? 35. What sort of fighting followed, and with what result? 36. How did Williamson treat the crops and settlements of the Cherokee? 37. What became of their warriors? 38. What lands were ceded to the Carolinians? 39. What districts now cover these lands? 40. What is said of this war? 41. What event followed the battle of Fort Sullivan in the American congress? — and on what day?

of Fort Moultrie.   The latter event took place on the 28th of
June; the former, on the 4th of July following, 1776.   The
representatives of South Carolina in the continental congress,
at this exciting period, were Edward Rutledge, Thomas Heyward, Thomas Lynch, and Arthur Middleton.   They were the
signers for South Carolina.

For this event, South Carolina had been long prepared.
She had, in fact, herself maintained an independent government for two years before; and the solemn declarations of her
own, and of the liberties of her sister states, while it gave a
more imposing aspect to the revolution, lifting it out of the reproach of mere insurrection and rebellion, could not add a whit
to the firmness of her resolves, or the determined aspect of
her opposition to the royal authority.   The news of the Declaration of Independence was received in Charlestown with the ring-
ing of bells, the beating of drums, discharge of cannon — all the
jubilation which belongs to a great and welcome popular event.

The device for the great seal and arms of the state was made
after the battle of Fort Sullivan, and thus the palmetto became
conspicuous, bearing a pair of shields; while an oak-tree — the
British ships — lay prostrate at its base and lopped.   The arms
were designed, in part, by Drayton; the reverse by Arthur
Middleton; and this, too, refers to the battle of Fort Moultrie.
This was the first free baptism of blood, in pitched battle, which
was essential before the champion could carry shield at all.

Rutledge assembled the general assembly and legislative
council in Charlestown, September 17.   His speech, and the
answer to it, make the battle of Fort Sullivan, and the Cherokee war, the leading topics.   From both these dangers the
state was now relieved.   But Rutledge urged laws for the
improvement of the militia system, and every preparation
against a renewal of British aggression.

Hitherto, the troops of South Carolina had been on the state
establishment.   The house resolved that the two regiments of

42. Who were the delegates of South Carolina in congress, and signed for her the
Declaration? 43. How was the Declaration received in South Carolina? 44. What
is the device for the great seal and arms of South Carolina? — by whom designed,
and when? 45. When did Rutledge assemble the legislature? 46. What chief subjects were considered? 47. What change was made in the military establishment?

infantry, one regiment of rangers, one of artillery, and two of riflemen, should henceforth be placed upon the continental establishments.

During this session of the legislature, one hundred and thirty thousand pounds were issued in dollar bills; and, subsequently, an act was passed for issuing five hundred thousand pounds more for the public service. The courts were again in operation. On the 15th of November, 1776, thirteen persons were convicted of sedition at Ninety-Six, and sentenced to be hanged. But Rutledge pardoned them, after frequent respites. In the temporary peace and security of the state, mercy was, perhaps, the proper policy.

For more than two years after the battle of Fort Moultrie, the arms of the British were chiefly employed at the northward. Britain, at no time, had in the colonies more than forty thousand men; and, to scatter these over so extensive a surface, as that embraced in the thirteen colonies, was to render them useless. It was necessary that she should first possess herself of the chief cities and colonies of the North, before she could spare the necessary forces for the conquest of the South. During this interval, South Carolina escaped most of the sufferings of war, beyond those which followed from the capricious red men of her borders, and the sullen discontents of her loyalist frontier population. In the meanwhile, Charlestown enjoyed a lucrative commerce, and her people grew prosperous and fortunate. In 1777 and 1778, she was the mart which supplied with goods most of the states south of New Jersey. An extensive inland traffic sprang into existence between her and the northern towns, in consequence of the presence of the British fleets along the coasts of Virginia and New York. In this traffic, more than a thousand wagons were incessantly employed.

The prosperity which followed from this trade was, with the selfish, an additional argument in favor of the revolution. But

48. What money was issued by the legislature? 49. What convictions took place in Ninety-Six precinct? 50 What did Rutledge? 51. Where, for the next two years, were the arms of Britain employed? 52. What was her largest complement of troops? 53. What was her necessity? 54. What advantages did Charlestown employ during this interval? 55. What were the effects of this prosperity?

it tended somewhat to emasculate the popular will, and to supersede patriotism by reasons drawn from profit wholly.　There was another argument, however, more legitimate, which had very great weight in South Carolina, as it had, no doubt, in all the colonies.　This was the alliance with France.　Her recognition, alliance, and arms, lifted the revolution into European dignity, and thus naturally reflected back, with greater brilliancy and force, upon the rising republic.　Lafayette, Steuben, De Kalb, and other foreign chiefs and nobles, had thrown themselves into the lists, and entreated to wear the virgin colors of America.

These influences were nowhere felt more strongly than in South Carolina, whose people are singularly ambitious of foreign recognition.　Add to this, that, in 1779, the united forces of the colonies had sustained three campaigns against the arms of the mother-country, and though sorely stricken, beaten, wounded, famished, they were not crushed ; had not succumbed, and had endured with firmness, where they had not been enabled to escape defeat.　The British lion might be taken by the mane with impunity ; the South Carolinians had done so ; they had heard him roar his loudest, and were not terrified.　Briefly, the events of three years had not affected the temper, the courage, or the confidence of the South Carolinians, or lessened their resolution to continue their own masters.　From this resolution, amid many falterings, and frequent overthrow, they never shrank ; and, though victory for a while fled their banner, and disaster upon disaster mortified their hopes, yet their faith was steadfast, and the brave men who represented the fortunes of the state, never despaired of them.　They mostly remained firm, when most fiercely assailed and terribly threatened.　A flag, sent into the port of Charlestown, from the commissioners of Great Britain, denounced them with the last and worst extremities of war, if they continued to prefer the alliance with France

56. What the effect of the American alliance with France ? 57. What European persons of distinction fought under the American banner? 58. What encouragement was drawn from the fact that the colonies had sustained the war for three years? 59. Was there any change in the temper or feeling of the Carolinians? 60. How did their chief men bear themselves? 61. How was the British flag treated that came into Charlestown to demand submission?

to a re-union with the mother-country. The answer was prompt defiance, and the flag-vessel was commanded instantly to depart from the waters of the state. Rawlins Lowndes was, at this time, the president of South Carolina. The reader will remember that, in all these overtures from Great Britain, she demanded unconditional submission. Such a demand it was an indignity to make, and would have been the extremity of baseness to comply with.

But, though South Carolina had enjoyed peace and prosperity for more than two years within her borders, she had not been inactive, nor wanting to any enterprises which might contribute to the common cause. Fifty men of her first regiment volunteered, as marines, on board the frigate Randolph; and there went forth with this unfortunate frigate, on a cruise, the Polly, of sixteen guns; the General Moultrie, of eighteen; the Fair American, of fourteen; and the Notre-Dame, of sixteen. The Randolph was of thirty-six guns; after a few weeks at sea, she encountered, at night, the British ship Yarmouth, of sixty-four guns; and, in the short but bloody conflict between them, blew up; losing all her crew save three men. A few days after this event, which lost South Carolina a fine company, a dreadful fire broke out in Charlestown (15th January, 1778), which destroyed two hundred and fifty-two dwelling-houses, not including stores and kitchens, valued at five hundred and seven thousand eight hundred and thirty-five pounds currency. This conflagration was imputed to incendiary tories, and to some of the crews of British ships, on the coast, whom the former received at night into the city.

But these misfortunes did not lessen the public spirit, nor prevent the government from assisting her sister colony of Georgia, against the common enemy.

We have somewhat rapidly sketched her campaigns against the Cherokees, led on, as they were, by tories and British emis-

62. Who was president of the state, at this period? 63. Had the Carolinians been inactive during her two years' respite from invasion? 64. What fleet went to sea from Charlestown? 65. What was the fate of the Randolph? 66. What was the special loss of South Carolina in that ship? 67. What dreadful event happened in Charlestown?—and when? 68. To whom was the fire ascribed? 69. How did these misfortunes affect the Carolinians? 70. What state did they assist?

saries from Florida. Florida was still destined to prove a thorn in the side of South Carolina as in that of Georgia. We have seen that, under the vexatious goading of this thorn, General Lee attempted a hasty incursion into Florida at the head of the troops of Georgia and South Carolina. But he only reached Ogechee, when the sufferings of his troops, at the worst season of the year for such an expedition, led to the abandonment of the enterprise. But, as Florida still continued troublesome, another expedition was planned in 1778, under General Robert Howe (of North Carolina), who was in military command of the forces of the two states of South Carolina and Georgia. His army was made up, the greater portion, of the regular troops of South Carolina, and a considerable force, besides, of South Carolina and Georgia militia. Howe was a man of patriotism and talents, but, as a general, of very moderate military abilities; at all events, fortune seldom gave him an opportunity of proving to the contrary. He, too, suffered failure from various causes, but chiefly through the pestilential character of the climate, in the dreary wastes through which he had to pass. His means and appliances were very small; horses, wagons, boats, stores, were wanted. His army sickened, and without meeting an enemy in any sharp conflict, he lost more than five hundred of his troops; a terrible loss to the two feeble states, and to be seriously felt hereafter.

The expedition was abandoned, like the preceding; and the two colonies, though relieved awhile from annoyances on the part of Florida, and because of this enterprise, was yet only respited for a season. But a little while, and the predatory game was renewed; Georgia, especially, suffered by water, from Florida *privateers*, and from the incursions, by land, of a predatory body of cavalry loyalists, called the " Florida rangers," whose movements were rapid, and could not be foreseen.

It was not long before these incursions assumed a more dar-

71. What was Florida in the side of Georgia and South Carolina? 72. What expedition was planned in 1778?—and under whom? 78. What troops had Howe? 74. What is said of Howe's abilities, and his fortunes? 75. What was the result of the expedition? 76. What losses were sustained, and how felt? 77. What predatory forces assailed Georgia? 78. How were these forays increased in mischief?

ing and dangerous character. General Provost, who commanded in Florida, led a large foraying expedition, in turn, into Georgia, and, dividing his forces, they covered a large tract, committing the most atrocious and brutal excesses; they penetrated as far as Sunbury, burning and plundering; but, in small bodies, which, when encountered, were usually defeated, or compelled to retreat, in haste. These expeditions were so many overtures to the more serious drama, which was now at hand.

An expedition from New York, under Lieutenant-Colonel Campbell, an able officer, reached Tybee, and effected a landing near Savannah, in December, 1778. Campbell was opposed by General Howe, who rashly resolved to fight him without preparation, and with an inferior force. Campbell made the discovery of a secret passage through a swamp, by which he found means to get into the rear of Howe, with a large portion of his choice troops, while with a sufficient body, he was amusing the American general in front. Howe, taken by surprise, was defeated. Campbell, in a short time, obtained a complete victory. The capital of Georgia, with all its stores, fell into the hands of the British general. That portion of the American army which escaped, crossed the Savannah, and found refuge in South Carolina. General Provost, meanwhile, crossing the country with all his forces, from Florida, united them safely in Savannah with those of Campbell.

General Howe was ruined for ever by this event; and General Lincoln, of the regular army, succeeded to him, in the command of the army in South Carolina.

Lincoln had considerable reputation as a military man. He was amiable and sensible, but not intellectual; was simply a respectable soldier, of prudence, courage, firmness, but without any traits of decided military ability. It is due to him to say that, under many disadvantages, and with deficient resources, he maintained the state for fifteen months without suffering serious

79. What expedition succeeded the foray of Provost? 80. Where, and when did Campbell land? 81. By what force was he encountered? 82. How did he baffle and defeat Howe? 83. What were the fruits of his victory? 84. Where did Howe's army find refuge? 85. What force united with that of Campbell? 86. What was the fate of Howe? 87. Who succeeded him in command? 88. What is said of Lincoln?

disaster. His worst was his last ! Still, it may be permitted us to wish, henceforward, that the commanders of our troops may be always found among our own people. There might have been found many, at this very period, who, probably, would have been much more fortunate than Lincoln, having a better knowledge of the temper, character, and interests of those whom they would lead, and a proper knowledge of the soil, the situation and circumstances of the country which they undertook to defend.

Wanting in this sort of knowledge, commanders, otherwise brave and skilful, have led thousands of gallant men to defeat, whom a better judgment and a native genius might have led to victory. The delegates of South Carolina, in congress, seem to have attached quite too much importance to the fact that there was a grand *national* army from which they might select.

89. What ought to be our wish in the event of future war ? 90. What sort of officers are desirable for a people ?

# CHAPTER III.

PROGRESS OF THE ENEMY — LINCOLN MARCHES INTO THE INTERIOR OF GEORGIA — PROVOST MAKES AN ATTEMPT ON CHARLESTOWN.

THE loss of Savannah opened the avenues to South Carolina. The troops of Georgia — few at first, and thinned by the recent expedition of Howe to Florida — were now reduced to a merely nominal force. The arms and munitions of the state were all lost. The tories and *Scovilites*, as bands of them were still called, who had gathered from Florida like vultures in the wake of the British army, were now scattering themselves over middle and upper Georgia, and devastating the settlements of that state, from whence they were beginning to look greedily into Carolina. There, too, the loyalists were beginning to grow restive. Such was the prospect at the opening of 1779.

The prisoners taken at Savannah were crowded into prison-ships, where they perished in great numbers. Many of the best citizens of Georgia, though not taken in arms, shared their fate. Neither age nor worth served to mitigate their treatment when they showed themselves faithful to the country.

Lieutenant-Colonel Campbell, when the discretion lay with him, acted with a judicious policy, and, by timely forbearance, secured the submission of numerous citizens. He established civil government, and the lower portions of the state were left comparatively in peace. But the peace was subjection, under superior force. Not so with the upper country; that was yet to be subdued, and the British light-troops penetrated the inte-

1. What avenues were opened by the fall of Savannah? 2. What evils and loss ensued from this event? 3. How were the Georgia prisoners treated? 4. What was Campbell's policy?

rior, and the loyalists from Florida, under their cover, were cruelly busy. The times were such as to favor outlawry, and all the scattered settlements of the Georgians were overrun.

The anxieties of the two Carolinas were greatly aroused. The continental or regular force of North Carolina was at the North, in the grand army of Washington. That state (North Carolina) now raised two thousand new troops for five months, and put them under Generals Ashe and Rutherford. These were sent, without delay, to the South, but they had to look to South Carolina for arms and munitions of war. The North Carolinians were delayed, and only joined the remnant of the army after its retreat across the Savannah. Their timely arrival might have saved Howe.

President Lowndes, of South Carolina, put forth all his energies. An embargo was laid upon all vessels sailing from the state. The cattle from the sea-islands were removed ; the militia of the state were drafted in large numbers, put under the command of Colonel Richardson, and marched down to headquarters. They were yet to be drilled, and knew little of subordination. The continentals in South Carolina, put under Lincoln, did not now exceed six hundred men. The rest of his force consisted wholly of militia men, whose term of service changed every second or third month. This miserable system was, perhaps, forced upon the authorities in consequence of their total inability to maintain a regular army of any dimensions. They were without money, or the materials of war. South Carolina had to provide the necessary funds, as well as arms and ammunition.

Lincoln found his militiamen insubordinate. How could it be otherwise with men enlisted for brief periods of three or five months only? He established his first post at Purysburg, on the Savannah river, for the purpose of maintaining close watch upon the movements of the British in Georgia, and labored with proper diligence to recruit his continentals and discipline his militia.

5. What efforts did North Carolina make ?   6. What President Lowndes ?   7. What is said of the militia and their term of service ?   8. Why this system of short service ? 9. What its evils ?

Meanwhile, the British began to feel their way into South Carolina. An advanced corps of some two hundred men was detached, under Colonel Gardner, to take possession of Beaufort. But Gardner was encountered promptly by Moultrie with a similar force, wholly of Charlestown and Beaufort militia. A very sharp passage of arms followed, in which Captains Heyward, Rutledge, and Barnwell, greatly distinguished themselves;—the Charlestown artillery proving singularly efficient in producing the result. Gardner was defeated, losing nearly all his officers and many of his men, and was driven from the island.

This little success had its beneficial effects in delaying the contemplated invasion of the British into South Carolina. Their emissaries, however, were still busily at work among the tories of the interior. Very soon, there were hundreds of these embodied upon the western frontier of the state ; many of those who had hitherto kept quiet, and numbers who had been expelled, on a previous occasion, from the country, along with numbers of refugees from other states.

They were embodied under a Colonel Boyd ; but they, too, had but a brief career of fortune. They were encountered by Colonel Pickens, at the head of three hundred men, near Kettle creek, and severely handled. After a vigorous conflict of an hour, the loyalists were dispersed, and with great slaughter — Boyd, their commander being among the slain. More than forty fell with him. The prisoners taken were treated as insurgents — were tried as traitors to the laws — tried regularly by a jury, under an enactment of the state legislature passed subsequently to the abolition of the royal government. Seventy of them were condemned to death ; but the sentence was only carried into effect upon five of the ringleaders of revolt. The rest were pardoned.

The failure of this second insurrection of the tories, and the prompt severity of the punishment in the case of those taken,

10. What British force appeared in South Carolina, and where ? 11. By whom was Gardner met ? 12. What officers distinguished themselves ? — and what corps ? 13. What was the result ? 14. What bodies were arming in the interior of South Carolina, and under whom ? 15. Who encountered Boyd, and where ? 16. What the result ? 17. How were the prisoners treated ?

filled other discontents with panic. They felt that there was still a danger, though the British army was at hand. The event defeated the plans of the loyalists, curbed their passions for a time, and temporarily deprived them of their vigor. Unsupported by the British, they fled and dispersed themselves over the country, while a few sent in their adhesion to the new government, and cast themselves upon its mercy.

As the British extended their posts on the south side of the Savannah, Lincoln made encampments at Black Swamp and opposite Savannah. From these points, he crossed the river in two divisions, with the view of limiting the operations of the enemy to the seacoasts of Georgia only. In the execution of this design, he sent general Ashe, with fifteen hundred North Carolinians and a few Georgians, across the river at a point a little above the British army. Ashe proceeded to Briar creek, where he suffered himself to be surprised, by the most miserable neglect of ordinary watch and vigilance, by Lieutenant-Colonel Provost; the militia, taken in front and rear, were thrown into confusion and fled at the first fire. Several were killed — many were drowned in attempting to cross the river—and a large number were made captive. Sixty men, the few continentals under Colonel Elbert, attached to Ashe's army, fought with the greatest bravery, but were forced to surrender. Ashe was tried and cashiered.

This unhappy event deprived Lincoln of one-fourth of his army, and opened a communication between the British, the tories and Indians of the states of North and South Carolina. It also emboldened Provost to undertake an expedition of considerable daring, which, had he been more of the adventurer, might have been successful. He hesitated in the moment when audacity would have been wisdom. Availing himself of the critical moment when Lincoln, with the main force of the southern army, was one hundred and fifty miles up the Savannah river, he crossed with four thousand chosen troops, flanked by several hundred Indians and loyalists, and pressed on with all despatch for the conquest of Charlestown.

General Lincoln does not seem to have apprehended this event. But it was the obvious result of his withdrawal of all the regular soldiers from the precinct. Charlestown was accessible equally by land and water. There was an inland route, by bay and river, for schooners and small vessels into Ashley river and the very harbor of Charlestown. The land route, it is true, was exceedingly wild and broken, intersected by swamp and marsh, where there were numerous defiles and places in which resistance might be made, and Moultrie had been left in command at Purysburg, a contiguous point, with a thousand militiamen. He did all that he could. He threw himself across the path of the invading enemy, slowly retiring and offering resistance where he might do so with propriety. His main object was to regain the city without disaster, impede the British where he could, and thus gain time for the citizens to improve their fortifications.

In this effort, he several times crossed weapons with the assailants. Several sharp skirmishes marked the mutual progress of the combatants. There was a smart passage at arms at Tulifinnee, and another at Coosawhatchie bridge, where Lieutenant-Colonel Laurens, with a small force, disputed the march of the enemy. But his troops were mostly militiamen, who had never seen the smoke of an enemy's fire, and who were overawed by the superior strength of the British. That they should offer impediment at all, and compel any delay in the enemy's march, was probably all that could be expected of them. The British, besides, were covered by the houses on the opposite bank. Laurens was wounded, and lost half of the eighteen continentals who were with him. He was forced to retreat, which he did; the troops being led over a long causeway, by Captain Shubrick, and in the face of the enemy, without much loss.

Meanwhile, despatches had been sent to Lincoln. But he

25. What is said of the accessibleness of Charlestown? 26. Who threw himself across the path of Provost? 27. What was Moultrie's object? 28. Were there any skirmishes?—and where? 29. What took place at Coosawhatchie bridge? 30. Who was wounded and forced to retreat?

could not be persuaded that Provost's march was any thing but a feint, designed to divert him from his operations in upper Georgia.   And yet he should have known, that, with Moultrie's small force of militiamen, he could not for an hour have withstood the march of such a force as Provost commanded.   And why a feint, when Charlestown lay open to him, and Lincoln was not in any way pressing upon Savannah, where the British had their base of operations?   The employment of such a force of continentals as Lincoln had, in the upper parts of Georgia, which were thinly inhabited, was immeasurably beyond the objects to be gained and the necessities of the region.   The country through which Provost had to pass, from Savannah to Charlestown, was singularly defenceless.   The white population was few and far between ; the negroes numerous.   The army of Provost was reported to be six thousand men.   It reached two thirds of this number, and had with it, besides, a large number of tories and red men, and these were soon put to their legitimate uses ; they were let loose upon the country, while the regular army of Provost marched forward in unbroken column, and with a force quite too powerful to suffer much impediment, or for any length of time, from the ill-regulated militia under Moultrie.

The red men and the tories, meanwhile, were doing their predatory work.   They scattered themselves along the route, searching all the plantations which were known to belong to the opulent, and not always discriminating between those who favored them and those who were hostile.   They sacked, burned, ravaged, robbed, committed all manner of excesses.   The seat of the Bull family at Sheldon, the church at Sheldon, were put to the flames.   Houses were plundered of their plate, slaves carried off, and women brutally treated.   Their fathers, sons, brothers, were in Moultrie's army.   As soon as they apprehended the danger to their families, each man set forth for his homestead — nothing could stay them ; and before Moultrie could reach Ashley river, half of his army had thus abandoned him.

31. What was Lincoln's opinion ? — and what ought he to have seen?   32. What is said of the country through which Provost had to pass ?   33. What use was made of his tories and red men ?   34. What did they on the route ?

With the remainder he still maintained a bold front to his enemy while receding with proper industry. But for his steadiness and the zeal of the citizens during his progress, he would have come too late. Provost was a dashing general, clever at a *coup de main;* and anything like a fugitive retreat on the part of Moultrie would have enabled him to attain his object.

When this object was fully made known to Lincoln by despatches, and he could be made to see that Provost would be a blockhead to aim at less than the conquest of the defenceless city, he wheeled about and made every possible effort to recover lost ground and return in season. And yet he would have been too late, had not Moultrie been steady in the retreat, had not the citizens been properly on the alert, and had not policy swayed subtilely the counsels of Rutledge and the authorities. When Provost crossed the Savannah, Charlestown was almost defenceless. No provisions for defence had been made on the land-side. No attempt had been apprehended in this quarter. Lincoln, it was thought, and Moultrie, must both be defeated before the danger could come home to them. So there were no works, no batteries, no bastions, no boats covering the Ashley with artillery and men. But zeal compensated for past remissness. A brief delay of Provost in his march lost him *one* opportunity; and when he had reached the city, he was persuaded to negotiate, when a proper military wisdom would have prompted him to storm. But of this hereafter.

His delays enabled the citizens to fortify Charlestown neck with lines and an abbatis. The militia in the vicinity were hurriedly collected. The whole country was in commotion. Five several bodies of men, at the same moment, were marching at full speed for the capital. Moultrie, with the remnant of his thousand militiamen —say six hundred — was hurrying in, having but the one object, the defence of the city. But for this paramount object, he might have taken bloody harvest at hundreds of defiles and dismal passages along the route. Lincoln, with some three or four thousand troops, seeking to recover

85. What was the effect on Moultrie's militia? 86. How did Moultrie? 87. What combined influences tended to save the city? 88. What was its condition at Provost's first marching? 89. How did he err? 40. How did his errors avail the Charlestownians? 41. How many several bodies of men were at once marching for the city?

lost ground, was pressing as fast as possible on the tracks of Provost. Rutledge, governor of the state, who had been a short time before, formally invested with dictatorial powers, was pressing down with six hundred men, whom he had collected at the rendezvous at Orangeburg ; and Colonel Harris, with a detachment of two hundred and fifty light-troops, had been despatched by Lincoln, in advance of his own march, to the assistance of the threatened city. These last three bodies reached Charlestown before the British had yet crossed the Ashley ; and the troops were drilled, and the mattock and spade were plied by a thousand hands, in order properly to prepare against the coming of the enemy.

They crossed the river — one body, nine hundred strong — on the 11th of May. Almost in the moment of their appearance, the citizens had been cheered by the arrival of the gallant Pole, Brigadier-General Count Pulaski, with his legion of mixed cavalry and foot. The cavalry of the British were encountered by Pulaski's infantry soon after their arrival, and a sharp action ensued. After a brave struggle, the Americans were forced to retire within the walls of the city ; but not before they had shown to the enemy, and to the citizens, that the contest for the ascendancy must be a bloody one, and that the city was not destined to fall an easy prey to the daring invader.

This little affair may have had some effect in producing a pause in the mind and progress of the British general. His whole army had crossed the Ashley during the day and night, and had taken position about a mile above the lines of the city. His true policy was instant action. This was expected. Unprovided for a regular seige, the only hope of Provost lay in prompt assault. Looking for no less, the garrison stood to their arms all night. They were unfortunately but too vigilant. Patrols had been sent forth, under cover of the night, to scour the space between. By a neglect of proper precaution, a false alarm, during the night, led to a general discharge of mus-

42. What force did Rutledge bring with him, and whence? 43. What Colonel Harris, and whence? 44. Did they arrive in season? 45. When did Provost cross the Ashley? 46. What other celebrated man arrived at the same time? 47. By whom were the British first encountered? 48. With what effect? 49. Where did Provost take position? 50. What was his policy? — in what lay his hope?

ketry along the lines, by which unfortunate procedure, Major Benjamin Huger, at the head of one of these patrols, a gallant officer, was killed, with twelve of his men, by his own people. The fact shows that, however mournful the mistake, the watchers of the garrison were vigilant, and their fire singularly effective.

Provost waited till the next day before he demanded the surrender of the town. Some hours had been thus gained ; but more time was still required, and Rutledge proposed to negotiate. He knew that Lincoln was urging his progress, and that Provost had no means of besieging or blockading — that he must take the city by storm, or forego his prey.

Under the circumstances, to gain time was of the utmost consequence. A day was consumed in tendering and returning flags. Provost was deluded. The better to beguile him, a large hope was held out as a lure to expectation. The commissioners were instructed to propose the neutrality of South Carolina during the war, and that the future of the state should be determined by the event of the war.

It has been assumed, by certain writers, that this offer was made in good faith ; and it was the policy of Rutledge that it should appear so. There were hundreds of loyalists in the city who found means to communicate by night with the enemy. It was necessary that people and army should equally believe that the governor and his council were in earnest, in order that Provost should believe it also. Meantime, the end was gained.

Provost discovered, after a while, that the negotiations did not include the army ; that, even if the city were surrendered, the troops in it might all cross to the east side of the Cooper and escape, and that he should only possess the shell of the oyster. He demanded to treat with the military commandant, who was Moultrie. When Rutledge referred the matter finally to him, he exclaimed, " I will save the city !" and his exclamation encouraged the people to enthusiasm. They had heard of the negotiations. They were roused to mutiny, people and army, and, had the governor and council persisted, which we have no

51. What disaster happened to the garrison that night? — and who was slain ? 52. What were Provost's delays? 53. What the policy of Rutledge ? 54. What grand lure did he hold out to the British general? 55. Was the object gained by these negotiations? 56. What did Provost finally demand ? 57. What was Moultrie's resolve ?

reason to suppose that they designed to do, they would have been torn in pieces.

Meanwhile, an intercepted letter of Lincoln taught Provost that a formidable enemy was marching fast upon his rear. He had lost the golden opportunity, the precious moment, when, confusion and panic, and lack of all preparation, might have won for him, though in bloody fight, the prey which he had so eagerly sought! The defiance of Moultrie — the tidings of Lincoln's approach — were sufficient. He did not attempt the assault. He decamped that very night, recrossed the Ashley, and hastened down toward the sea-islands, in the creeks and inlets of which his boats were expected. The delay of that night would have compromised his whole army — brought them between two fires : the militia from the city — the continentals in his rear. When the garrison looked forth next morning, there was not an enemy to be seen !

58. What was the temper of the troops and people hearing of the negotiations?
59. What the result on Provost ? — and what did he do?

# CHAPTER IV.

BATTLE OF STONO — DEFEAT AT SAVANNAH — REDUCTION
OF CHARLESTOWN — 1779 TO 1780.

THUS was baffled the second attempt of the British upon the city of Charlestown. Provost filed off from the main to the islands along the seacoast, taking possession of James island; from whence, on the 20th of May, a detachment crossed to John's island, where the British surprised a party of seventy or eighty of the Americans, who were posted nearly opposite, at Mathews's plantations.

Robert Barnwell, in this affair, received seventeen bayonet stabs; but afterward recovered. Many of the Americans were bayoneted. The surprise had been complete: first of a sentinel, from whom the enemy extorted the countersign, and then of the whole party. Surprise is the great danger of militiamen, who have yet to learn the various stratagems of the regular army; and two thirds of the misfortunes of the Americans, everywhere, are attributable to want of proper vigilance and watch. The British burned the house of Mathews, but continued on the island, and finally entrenched themselves on Stono river. James island, being within easy reach of the city, they soon abandoned. Fort Johnson, by the way, had been previously destroyed by the Carolinians, as not defensible from the rear — being easy of access, and likely to be a danger to the harbor, if once in possession of the British. Besides, its garrison was wanted in the city. We are not sure that the arguments were valid for its destruction. But, in all probability, with small resources, of men, money, and munitions, it was not easy to maintain an ex-

1. What course was taken by Provost? 2. What surprise did he effect, and where? 3. What of Robert Barnwell? 4. What is said of the danger of militiamen? 5. Where did the British entrench themselves? 6. What of Fort Johnson?

posed position, the uses of which were not obvious at the moment, nor conceived to be necessary at any time, since Fort Sullivan, after its successful defence against the British fleet, was held to be quite adequate for the defence of the harbor.

The British, as we have said, threw up entrenchments at Stono, within thirty miles of the city. Here Lincoln determined to attack them. He made his dispositions accordingly, agreeably to a concerted plan. A feint was to have been made from James island by the militia from Charlestown ; but, by delay and mismanagement in procuring and providing boats, the troops from Charlestown, under Moultrie, did not reach their destination till some hours after the action. The action took place on the 20th of June, 1779. The force engaged in the fight was, on the part of the Americans, about twelve hundred men — of whom one-half were militia. The militia of North and South Carolina were on the right ; the continentals or regulars, on the left. Colonel Malmedy led a corps of light-infantry on the right, and Lieutenant-Colonel Henderson another on the left. The militia and cavalry of Virginia formed a corps of reserve. The British numbered at first from seven to eight hundred men ; but they were entrenched, and they were subsequently re-enforced. They had three redoubts, with lines of communication, and their field-pieces were judiciously posted in the intervals, the whole front being secured by an abbatis.

That they might be harassed, and at the same time deceived, their quarters were beaten up by alarm-parties for several nights preceding the attempt which was designed to be made in earnest. When the real attack was made, two companies of the seventy-first regiment sallied out to support the pickets. They were charged triumphantly by the light-infantry of Henderson, and were discomfited. But nine men of their number escaped ; and every man at the field-pieces, between the redoubts, was killed or wounded. The retiring parties were, however, re-enforced promptly. The battle became general, and was waged fiercely for one hour and twenty minutes, during which time the Americans had the advantage. But the British were strengthened by new reinforcements; to prevent which the feint from James' island had been designed. Had the force under Moultrie been in season, the enemy could not have received this succor. Their coming finally changed the state of affairs, and a retreat became necessary on the part of the Americans. As soon as they began to retire, the British made a sally with their whole garrison. But the American light-troops, under Malmedy and Henderson, so completely masked the retreat and retarded the pursuit that Lincoln was enabled to draw off with regularity, and to bring away all his wounded.

The loss of the Americans, killed and wounded, was above one hundred and fifty. The South Carolina officers especially suffered. Colonel Roberts, a very brave and accomplished gentleman, was among the slain. The loss of the British was equally or more severe; but the absolute number of casualties was never ascertained.

This battle took place at a season when the weather was quite too hot for military operations, and both parties needed respite and shelter from heat and sun. The British soon after abandoned the position and all the adjacent islands, retreating from one to another, until they reached Beaufort, and finally Savannah. They were provided with boats, in which the Americans were deficient. This enabled them to expedite their retreat with little loss. The American militia, after the battle, generally retired to their homes. Lincoln, with his regulars, took a position at Sheldon. For a brief season, both armies were glad of the respite of " summer " quarters, in which they might rest and repair their losses.

This invasion of General Provost was creditable neither to the valor nor the honor of British soldiers. His troops distinguished themselves by predatory depredations only. Private houses were robbed of their plate; persons of their jewels. The very

13. How long did the battle last? 14. Who had the advantage? 15. How were the British relieved? 16. How was the retreat conducted, covered, and by whom? 17. What was the loss of the Americans? 18. What course did the British afterward pursue? 19. Where did Lincoln take post?

vaults of the dead were broken into for concealed treasures, and three thousand slaves were carried off and sold to the planters of the West Indies.   Numbers of these unfortunate people, following the camp of the British, fell victims to disease, being left to perish without medicine or attendance, wherever they sank down.   Hundreds of them expired of camp-fever on Otter island, their unburied carcasses being surrendered to the beasts of the forest.   For years after, the island was strewed with bleaching bones — a miserable memorial of their own folly, and of the inhumanity of those who first seduced them from their homes, and then left them to perish.

A brief calm succeeded the action of Stono in the affairs of Carolina.   The Americans and British kept close in their respective encampments, until the arrival of a French fleet on the coast aroused them to immediate activity.

This fleet, commanded by Count D'Estaing, consisted of twenty sail-of-the-line.   Its arrival at once led to the adoption of a joint resolution of the allied troops to attack Savannah; and orders were issued to the militia of Carolina and Georgia to rendezvous in the neighborhood.   Flushed with the faith that the fall of Savannah was inevitable, the Americans turned out with alacrity, and, on the 16th of September, 1779, that city, beleaguered by the united forces of Lincoln and D'Estaing, was summonded to surrender.   It had been summoned by D'Estaing alone, in the name of the king of France, before Lincoln had reached the scene of operations.

The garrison requested four and twenty hours to consider !

Provost had taken a lesson from his recent experience at Charlestown.   He had failed there, because of his good nature, in allowing the garrison so much time in which to consider ; he now made use of a similar lure to obtain time himself; he was willing to entertain the demand to surrender, but he wished to consider the terms, and  negotiation was again employed to baffle enterprise.

20. What excesses were committed by the British ?   21. What became of the fugitive slaves ?   22. What aroused the two armies to activity ?   23. What force had the French ?   24. Who commanded ?   25. When did the allied troops appear before Savannah ?   26. By whom was it summoned ?   27. What lesson had Provost taken ? — and where ?

D'Estaing, having little time to spare, yet accorded the required hours to the garrison of Savannah, which, at the moment of the summons, was really at the mercy of the French; and, just as in the case of Provost at Charlestown, time gained was safety and victory. The delay granted, the fortunate moment was lost and could never be regained. An assault, an hour after the summons, must have been successful. Provost used the interval allowed him in strengthening his works. Meanwhile, the force of Colonel Maitland, of the British, who had been stationed at Beaufort, succeeded in eluding the besiegers, and throwing itself into the beleaguered city.

The arrival of such a reinforcement determined the garrison to risk an assault. The besiegers were reduced to the necessity either of storming or regularly besieging the place. The former measure was resolved upon. On the evening of the 23d, they broke ground, and on the 4th of October following, opened a fire upon the city from nine mortars and thirty-seven pieces of cannon, from the land-side, and sixteen from the river. These continued to play with little intermission for four days, but without making any serious impression on the defences of the place. Preparations were then made for an assault.

This measure was forced on D'Estaing, by the necessity of withdrawing his fleet, without delay, from a coast which is so dangerous to shipping at such a season of the year. The morning of the 9th of October was fixed upon for the attack. Two feints were made with the country militia, and a real attack on the Spring-Hill battery, with two thousand five hundred French troops, six hundred continentals, and three hundred and fifty of the Charlestown militia; the whole being led by D'Estaing and Lincoln. The assault was ordered to take place at four o'clock in the morning; but some miscalculations having been made, it was broad daylight when the troops advanced to the attack, when all their movements were perceptible to the enemy.

By the desertion of a grenadier, the night before the assault,

28. How did Provost employ the time allowed him? 29. What force came to his succor? 30. To what necessities were the besiegers reduced? 31. When did they begin the bombardment, and for how long was it continued? 32. What day was fixed for the assault? 33. What force employed, and how disposed? 34. From whom did the British learn these details?

the British were also apprized of the contemplated arrangements, and were enabled to strengthen themselves in the Spring-Hill battery by additional forces, which were withdrawn from those points against which the feints were to be made.   Under these disadvantages, the allied troops, nevertheless, marched forward with great boldness to the assault, but under a heavy and well-directed fire, not only from the batteries, but from several armed galleys, which lay in the river and threw their shot directly across their path.

This cross-fire did such fearful execution as to throw the front of the column into confusion.   A general retreat was commanded, after it had stood the enemy's fire for about fifty-five minutes; but not before the ramparts were carried by the South Carolina regiment.   Lieutenants Hume and Bush planted its colors upon the walls, but they were shot down a moment after.

These colors had been presented to the regiment for its gallant conduct at Fort Moultrie.   It was a point of honor that they should not be lost.   Lieutenant Gray endeavored to save them and received his mortal wound in the attempt.   Jasper, the brave man who replanted the crescent flag of Fort Moultrie on the merlon in the hottest fire of the foe, was more successful.   He bore them back from the bloody heights and delivered them in safety to his comrades; but he paid for his chivalry with his life; he, too, received a mortal wound in doing so, and died in a little time after.   Dearly did the little regiment pay for the preservation of this object of military pride.

In this unfortunate attempt upon Savannah, the combined armies sustained a heavy loss.   D'Estaing himself received two wounds, and nearly a thousand men were slain or wounded in the brief but sanguinary conflict which ensued.

After this repulse, the idea of taking the place by regular approaches was resumed, but soon discarded.   D'Estaing was uneasy at the exposed situation of his fleet; and the militia were no less anxious to return to their homes.   The leaguer

85. How were the assailants met?   86. What was the result?   87. What colors were planted on the walls, and by whom?   88. What their fate?   89. Who sought to save them and perished?   40. Who finally bore them off in safety?   41. What the fate of Jasper?   42. What was the loss of the combined armies in this affair?

was conducted without spirit and was soon discontinued. D'Estaing soon after re-embarked, and left the continent, while Lincoln returned to Charlestown.

With this affair, the campaign of 1779 ended in the South. The arrival of the French, if productive of no other good, served, for awhile, to confine the British to the ramparts of Savannah, to prevent them from overrunning the back settlements of Georgia and Carolina, and bringing into activity the malignant and discontented partisans of royalty, who were scattered in great numbers throughout the country.

But this respite was of brief duration. The failure of the attack upon Savannah, prepared the way for the fall of Charlestown. The departure of the French fleet removed the chief obstacle to this enterprise. There were several other concurring causes that invited the invasion of Charlestown. The unfortunate expedition against Florida had totally broken up the southern army. The Carolina regiments were thinned, by sickness, to mere skeletons; the Virginia and North Carolina forces were all melted away, chiefly by the expiration of their time of enlistment. The Georgia regiments filled the prisonships of the invaders. The possession of Georgia by the British disarmed the patriotic citizens, and gave strength and activity to the royalists and Indians. South Carolina was, in brief, a frontier, on three sides hemmed in by bitter and uncompromising enemies. The loyalists of North Carolina, Georgia, and Florida — the Indians always ready for war, which is a kindred life with that of the hunter — were gathering in restless and roving bands upon her borders.

The conquest of Charlestown thus promised to be easy, and with its possession, particularly if the southern army should fall with it, the British ascendancy in the South would be complete. The reduction of the whole state, and, probably, that of North Carolina, would ensue; and no obstacle would then remain in the way of an uninterrupted backward path of conquest through Virginia, from the Savannah to the Delaware.

43. Whither did D'Estaing and Lincoln retire? 44. What temporary good resulted from the arrival of the French? 45. For what catastrophe did this failure prepare the way? 46. What was the condition of South Carolina? 47. What would probably result from the British conquest of Charlestown?

The enemy were also well acquainted with the embarrassments of the state in procuring men and money.  Of the six regiments of South Carolina, but eight hundred men could be raised; and so miserably depreciated was the value of her paper, that the price of a pair of shoes was seven hundred dollars.  The invasion of Carolina was resolved upon.

On the 11th of February, 1780, the British army landed within thirty miles of Charlestown.  The approach of danger led to the immediate action of the people.  The assembly, then in session, dissolved, after having conferred upon John Rutledge the powers, with some limitation, of the dictator in ancient republics.  He was commissioned to see that the " republic sustained no harm."

With these powers, he issued a proclamation, commanding the militia to repair to the garrison; but this proclamation produced very little effect.  The people of the country were unwilling to leave their plantations unprotected, and have always been particularly averse to being cooped up in a besieged town, at a season of the year when the seaboard cities are particularly liable to disease.  They dreaded small-pox and yellow fever with a mortal apprehension.  Had Sir Henry Clinton, the commander-in-chief of the invading army, at once advanced against the city, it must have fallen in a few days.  But that cautious commander, a good soldier, but one not formed for brilliant or prompt achievements, adopted the slow mode of regular investiture.

At Wappoo, on James' island, he formed a depot and built fortifications.  More than a month elapsed, after his first landing, before he crossed Ashley river.  On the 1st of April, he broke ground at the distance of eleven hundred yards, and, at successive periods, erected five batteries on Charlestown neck.  His ships-of-war, about the same time, crossed the bar, and, passing Fort Moultrie with a fair wind, avoided a second regular combat with that fortress.

48. How were shoes sold?   49. When did the British army land? — and where? 50. Who was made dictator?   51. What proclamation did he make, and with what effect?   52. What is said of Sir Henry Clinton?   53. What were his proceedings at Wappoo, and subsequently?   54. Where, and when, did he first break ground against the city?   55. How did his shipping enter the harbor?

They were not, however, suffered to pass without a heavy penalty. Colonel Pinckney, who commanded at the fort, kept up a brisk and severe fire upon them, and did much execution. The ships generally sustained considerable damage. Twenty-seven seamen were killed or wounded. The fore-top-mast of the Richmond was shot away, and the Acetus ran aground near Haddrell's point, and was destroyed by her crew, under a heavy fire from two field-pieces, commanded by Colonel Gadsden; the crew escaped in boats. The royal fleet came to anchor within long shot of the town batteries.

Fort Moultrie being now of less use than the men who manned it, they were in great part withdrawn, and it soon fell into the hands of the enemy. Colonel Pinckney's force, together with that which had served to man the small fleet of the Americans, was transferred to the city, where they helped to swell the inconsiderable numbers of the garrison. This force, at no time, amounted to four thousand men; they were required to defend an extent of works which could not be well-manned by less than ten thousand; yet, even for this small army, a sufficient quantity of provisions had not been furnished, and, before the siege was over, the citizens were suffering from starvation.

But the garrison, though feeble, was neither idle nor dis-pirited. The field-works which had been thrown up against the invasion of Provost, were strengthened and extended. Lines of defence, and redoubts, were stretched across Charles-town neck, from Cooper to Ashley river. In front of the lines was a strong abbatis, and a wet ditch picketted on the nearest side. Deep holes were dug, at short distances, between the lines and the abbatis. The lines were made particularly strong on the right and left, and so constructed as to rake the wet ditch in its whole extent. In the centre was a strong citadel. On the sides of the town, and wherever the enemy could effect a landing, works were thrown up. The continentals, with the Charlestown artillery, manned the lines in front of the foe on

56. Did they suffer?—and how much? 57. What became of the garrison, at Fort Moultrie? 58. What force was had to man the city lines, and what was requisite? 59. How did the garrison do their duty? 60. What were the fortifications?—and how manned?

the neck.    The works on South bay and other parts of the
town, which were less exposed, were defended by the militia.

The marine force of the Charlestownians had been increased
by converting several schooners into galleys, and by two armed
ships which had been purchased from the French.    The inferior numbers of the garrison forbade any serious attempts to
oppose the descent of the British upon the main, but did not
prevent several little affairs, in which both officers and men
exhibited no less spirit than good conduct.    In one of these, a
corps of light-infantry, commanded by Lieutenant-Colonel John
Laurens, encountered the advance-guard of the British in a
skirmish of particular severity.

Though the lines of Charlestown were field-works only, Sir
Henry Clinton made his advances with great caution.    At the
completion of his first parallel, the town was summoned to surrender.    Its defiance was the signal for the batteries on both
sides to open, which they did with great animation on the 12th
of April.

The fire of the besiegers soon showed itself to be far superior to that of the besieged.    The former had the advantage of
twenty-one mortars and royals ; the latter possessed but two, and
their lines soon began to crumble under the weighty cannonade maintained against them.    The British lines of approach
continued to advance, and the second parallel was completed by
the twentieth, at the distance of three hundred yards from the
besieged.    The Americans soon perceived the hopelessness
of their situation.    Councils of war were called, and terms of
capitulation offered to the besiegers, which were instantly rejected and the conflict was resumed.

The weakness of the garrison prevented any sallies.    The
only one made during the siege, took place soon after the re-
jection of these offers.    Lieutenant-Colonel Henderson led out
two hundred men, attacked the advanced flanking party of the

61. What was the marine force of the city ?    62. What skirmishes took place ?
63. How were Clinton's approaches made ?    64. When did the batteries open ?
65. What was the difference of force and fire between them ?    66. When was the
second parallel completed ?    67. What did the Americans discover ? — and what offer ?
68. What answered the British ?    69. Was there any sally during  he siege ? — under
whom, and with what result ?

enemy, killed several, and brought in eleven prisoners. In this affair, Captain Moultrie, of the South Carolina line, was among the slain.

On the 26th of April, a plan of retreat by night was proposed in council, but rejected as impracticable. On the 6th of May, Clinton renewed his former terms for the surrender of the garrison. At this time, the flesh provisions of the city were not sufficient for a week's rations. There was no prospect either of supplies or reinforcements. The engineers admitted that the lines could not be maintained ten days longer, and might be carried by assault in ten minutes. General Lincoln was disposed to accept Clinton's offer, but he was opposed by the citizens, who were required by Clinton to be considered prisoners on parole. To their suggestion of other terms, they received for answer that hostilities should be renewed at eight o'clock.

When that hour arrived, the garrison looked for the most vigorous assault, and prepared, with a melancholy defiance, to meet the assailants at their ruined bulwarks. But an hour elapsed without a gun being fired. Both armies seemed to dread the consequences of an assault, and to wish for a continuance of the truce.

At nine in the evening, the batteries of the garrison were reopened, and being answered by those of the British, the fight was resumed with more vigor and execution than had been displayed at any time from the beginning of the siege. Ships and galleys, the forts on James' and John's islands, on Wappoo, and the main army on the neck, united in one voluminous discharge of iron upon the devoted garrison. Shells and carcasses were thrown incessantly into the town, in all quarters, and it was everywhere covered by the cannon of the assailants. The city was on fire in several places; and, by this time, the third parallel of the enemy being completed, the parties were within speaking distance of each other, and the rifles of the Hessian

70. Who was slain? 71. What plan was proposed in council?—and when? 72. What terms did Clinton offer?—and when? 73. What was the condition of the city? 74. What was Lincoln's desire, and by whom opposed? 75. At what hour were hostilities renewed? 76. With what spirit and effect? 77. To what condition were city and garrison reduced?

Yagers were fired at so short a distance, as never to be discharged without effect. The defenders could no longer show themselves above the lines with safety. A hat raised upon a cane, was instantly riddled with bullets.

On the 11th of May, the British crossed the wet ditch by sap, and advanced within twenty-five yards of the besieged. All farther defence was hopeless. Lincoln found himself obliged to capitulate. He had maintained his post with honor, if not with success; had shown himself steadfast and firm, if not brilliant. For nearly three months, with less than four thousand ill-fed, ill-clad, and undisciplined militiamen, he had maintained himself in walls, the lines of which required, at least, thrice that number to man them, and had thus long baffled fully twelve thousand of the best troops in the British service, headed by their best generals. The terms of surrender were not harsh in the case of a town reduced to extremity.

78. What was the approach of the British, on the 11th of May? 79. What was Lincoln now compelled to do? 80. What is said of his conduct?

# CHAPTER V.

### FROM THE FALL OF CHARLESTOWN TO THE DEFEAT OF GATES AT CAMDEN — 1780.

THE ill success of this first attempt, in the American war, to defend a city, approves of the general policy of Washington on this subject. The sterner wisdom, by which the city should have been sacrificed to the preservation of the army, would have produced far less evil to the state.

The conquest of the interior rapidly followed the loss of the city. The troops, which might have successfully baffled the march of the invader through the forests, were in his power; and his progress, for a while, was almost entirely uninterrupted through the country.

Lieutenant-Colonel Tarleton, of the British army, a soldier more remarkable for the rapidity of his movements than for his talents, and more notorious for the sanguinary warfare which he pursued in Carolina, than for any other better qualities, commenced a career of victory, as a cavalry leader, soon after the landing of the enemy, which was continued for a long period after with little interruption.

While Clinton was pressing the siege of the city, he achieved sundry small but complete successes, that deprived the garrison of most of those advantages which necessarily must have resulted from their keeping a body of troops in the field.

On the 18th of March, 1780, he surprised a party of eighty militiamen, at the Salkehatchie bridge, many of whom were slain and wounded, and the rest dispersed. He was equally successful, a few days after, against a second party which he surprised near Ponpon. On the 27th, he encountered Lieuten-

1. What followed the reduction of Charlestown? 2. What is said of Colonel Tarleton? 3. What did he while the siege was in progress? 4. Whom did he surprise at Salkehatchie? — and Ponpon?

ant-Colonel Washington, at the head of a regular corps of horse, between the Ashley river ferry and Rantowle's bridge on the Stono. Here his successes were temporarily arrested. The advantage lay with the Americans. The cavalry of the British legion was driven back, and lost several persons ; but, wanting infantry, Washington did not venture to pursue his advantages.

At the beginning of the siege, General Lincoln ordered the regular cavalry, three hundred in number, to keep the field, and the country militia were required to support them as infantry. The militia, on various pretences, refused to attach themselves to the cavalry ; and this important body of horse was surprised at Monk's Corner by a superior force under Lieutenant-Colonels Tarleton and Webster. About twenty-five of the Americans were killed or taken. The fugitives found shelter in the neighboring swamps, from whence they made their way across the Santee.

Under the conduct of Colonel White, they recrossed the Santee a few weeks after this event, captured a small British party, and carried them to Lenud's ferry. But the victors were followed closely by Tarleton, with a superior force, and charged before they could get over the ferry. Retreat was impracticable, and resistance proved unavailing. A total rout ensued. A party of the American force, under Major Call, cut their way through the British and escaped. Colonel White, with another party, saved themselves by swimming the Santee. Thirty were killed, wounded, or taken ; the residue found refuge in the swamps.

These repeated disasters were not the only consequences arising from the fall of Charlestown. That event was followed by a train of circumstances, which, while they disgraced the British soldiery, exhausted the spirits and resources of the country. The invasion of Provost, recorded in a previous chapter, had been followed by scenes of devastation and acts of pillage which would have shamed a Tartar banditti. But these acts were ascribed to the tories and Indians in his retinue.

The invasion of Charlestown was notorious from like causes ;

but the loyalists and Indians were no longer obnoxious to the charge. The royal troops were the robbers, and their commanders openly shared in the proceeds of the plunder. Thousands of slaves were shipped to a market in the West Indies. Mercantile stores, gold and silver plate, indigo, the produce of the country, became equally convertible to the purposes of these wholesale plunderers, with whom nothing went amiss. They plundered by system, forming a general stock, and designating commissaries of captures. Spoil, collected in this way, was sold for the benefit of the royal army; and some idea of the quantity brought to market may be formed from the fact, that though prices must have been necessarily low in so small a community, yet the division of a major-general was more than four thousand guineas. Apart from what was sold in Carolina, several vessels were sent abroad for a market, laden with the rich spoils taken from the inhabitants.

In the capitulation of Charlestown, Lincoln had surrendered all the forces within the city proper, including all the continental or regular troops within the state. Moultrie, Gadsden, all the field-officers of the low country, were prisoners on parole. This capitulation was supposed to include the people of the state at large, as well as the city; and it pledged the royal government to their protection, or was thought to do so, so long as they remained peaceful. The officer of highest rank within the state, not a prisoner, was General Andrew Williamson, of Cambridge. This person, as we remember, had behaved well in the wars of the frontiers, and in all the early conflicts with the loyalists. He was by birth a Scotchman, had been a cow-herd, or cow-driver, as he was called, and was singularly illiterate, scarcely able to write his own name. But, among the new settlers of the back country, he possessed great influence, was an admirable woodsman, and had acquired property. But, when the British began to make progress in Georgia, it was observed that he was tardy in taking the field. He failed, in several cases, to appear in season to be of service. While Charlestown was in danger, and wanting troops, he had some three hundred

10. What persons were included, and supposed to be included, in the capitulation of the city? 11. Who was General Williamson? 12. What were his services?

militiamen in arms, whom he never brought, or offered to bring, to the succor of the beleaguered city.    In the history of Georgia, he is distinctly denounced, as even then in the pay of the British, having been corrupted by Cameron, the Indian agent of the British, and as having a British commission in his pocket. But these suspicions, at that time, were confined to very few persons ; and when, at the fall of Charlestown, he summoned the officers of the militia of the interior to meet and consult with him at M'Lean's avenue, near Augusta, they did so, having the most perfect confidence in his fidelity, ability, and zeal.    There were numerous small parties of militia in South Carolina and Georgia, which were in the habit of co-operating, and, as rangers, were perpetually on the wing, in pursuit of the tories.    The captains and other officers of these parties assembled and met him at a special rendezvous, where he unfolded the condition of the country, showed its lack of resources, the absence of all continental troops, the difficulty of maintaining themselves, and then submitted the terms which had been agreed upon in the capitulation of Charlestown, and the privileges of which were supposed to be accorded to all the state.    He was circumspect, but his bias was obvious enough.    He discouraged many—discouraged all, in fact — and the result of his proceeding was to disband his militia, while he retired to his own residence, near Cambridge, where he seems to have awaited the period when he could render his submission to the enemy with decency and safety.    He finally took refuge with them in Charlestown, and was popularly branded with the epithet of the " Arnold of Carolina."    Subsequently, it is well known, he was again seduced into becoming a spy *for* the Americans in the British camp ; and Marion obtained for himself and Greene the greater part of his information in respect to the operations of the enemy from this doubly-polluted fountain.

But, disbanding the militia, giving up the conflict, and, perhaps, working in secret upon his officers, he influenced certain

18. What were the imputations against him ? 14. Who did he summon to meet him, and where ?  15. What parties were still at large in the country ?  16. How did Williamson depict the affairs of the state ?  17. What did he with his command ? — and whither did he retire ?  18. What epithet was subsequently given him ?  19. How was he doubly a traitor ?

of them to make terms with the enemy also. They were
ignorant men — wanting in mind, perhaps, rather than moral —
and Williamson's influence was paramount. It was easy to
persuade them that Congress could do nothing for the rescue of
the state, and it was very clear that the state, with its chief
men in captivity, and with neither money nor munitions, could
do but little for herself.

But there were some stout rangers, colonels and captains, who
felt differently, even though they may have thought despond-
ingly. Pickens, the Hammonds, M'Call, Hampton, Liddle, and
other South Carolinians, with Governor Hawley, of Georgia,
and the gallant Colonels Dooley and Clarke, of Georgia, resolved otherwise, and preferred a present flight to regions of security, from whence they might emerge in power, to a base, submission, which promised only security for life. They disappeared, and, with Williamson's submission and their flight, the
country appeared wholly prostrate at the feet of the invader.
But this was in seeming only, and during a brief period of paralysis, the natural consequence of the fall of the chief city and
the capture of the army which had been regularly organized.

The capital having surrendered, the next object of the British was to secure the general submission of the state. To this
end, the victors marched with a large body of troops over the
Santee, toward the populous settlements of North Carolina, and
planted garrisons at prominent points of the country during
their progress. Their advance caused the retreat of several
small bodies of Americans, which had approached with the
view to the relief of Charlestown.

One of these, commanded by Colonel Buford, consisting of
three or four hundred men, was pursued by Tarleton with a
force about double that number. Tarleton came upon Buford
near the Wexhaws. Buford neither promptly yielded nor
promptly prepared for battle. He behaved without decision.
A battle ensued, in which Buford was defeated. The cry of his
troops for quarter produced no effect upon the assailants. The

20. What was his influence upon the officers and militia? 21. Did he influence all?
— and who were most conspicuous in their withdrawal? 22. What was the apparent
condition of the state after this? 23. After the fall of the capital, what was the course
of the British?

battle was a mere massacre, in which, according to Tarleton's own account of the bloody business, five in six of the whole body of the Americans were either killed or so badly mangled as to be incapable of removal from the field of battle; and the British did not lose a dozen men.

To the errors of Buford may be ascribed the defeat of his party; but the effect of this wanton massacre was beneficial to the country. The Americans were taught to expect no indulgence from their foes. "Tarleton's quarter" became proverbial, and a spirit of revenge, in all subsequent battles, gave a keener edge to the military resentments of the people.

The British commander-in-chief followed up these severe and sanguinary lessons by proclamations, which denounced vengeance against all who still continued in arms; while offering "to the inhabitants, with a few exceptions, pardon for their past treasonable offences, and a reinstatement in the possession of all those rights and immunities which they had enjoyed under the British government, exempt from taxation, except by their own legislatures."

Suffering from the sword, their armies overthrown, the state everywhere in the hands of the foe, and no help apparent at the hands of Congress, the people numerously listened to these specious offers, and abandoned for a few weeks every hope of successful resistance. From several parts of the state, the citizens gave in their adhesion to the royal authority, and, believing his conquests to be complete, Sir Henry Clinton sailed from Charlestown to New York, leaving to Lord Cornwallis the chief command of the southern department.

The seeming general submission of the inhabitants was followed by a temporary calm. The British believed the state to be thoroughly conquered. With this conviction, they proposed to extend their arms to the conquest of the neighboring states; and their own force, now, of five thousand men, being inadequate to this object, they conceived a plan to carry out their operations, which had the effect of undoing much which had been done by

24. Describe the massacre of Buford's detachment. 25. What is said of Buford? 26. What was the effect of this massacre? 27. What proclamations were issued by the British general? 28. What effect had they? 29. Who succeeded to Clinton in command?

their arms and previous policy. They summoned the inhabitants to repair to the British standard. Paroles given to citizens, not actually taken in Charlestown, were declared null and void, and the holders of them were called upon to act the part of British subjects, by appearing in arms at a certain time, under pain of being treated as rebels to his majesty's government.

From this moment, the British popularity and power began to decline; and the seeming submission which followed this command was the disguise assumed by disaffection, under the pressure of necessity. The mask was thrown aside by the greater number at the first sound of the signal trumpet which rallied the patriots under the banner of Sumter, Marion, Pickens, and many other patriots, who were as chivalrous in the pursuit of glory as they were earnest in their attachment to their country.

But we must not anticipate. Governor Rutledge had, fortunately, left Charlestown before the unfortunate finish of the siege, the better to employ himself in other states for the benefit of his own. He personally sought the several authorities and people of North Carolina, Virginia, and, finally, Congress, and received liberal promises from all. With these, he returned to South Carolina, full of hope, to give vigor and concentrative energy to all the efforts that might be employed against the invader.

Meanwhile, General Rutherford had succeeded in raising fifteen hundred men, whom he brought together at Charlotte (N. C.), the well-known "Hornet's Nest," as this whig region was called by the British.

This force was sufficient to discourage the approach of Tarleton in that quarter; and Lord Rawdon, who had established a post at the Wexhaws, deemed it now prudent to abandon it.

But time was required to arouse the country; and, in the meanwhile, under British auspices, the loyalists grew active and audacious. A large body of these, embodied in North Carolina, had collected at Ramsour's on the 22d of June, 1780, under a Colonel Moore. A detachment of Rutherford's force, under Colonel Locke, attacked and defeated them. Other parties of loyalists were growing in both the states. But they did not grow alone. Their rising sufficed to give new spirit to the old-line whigs and patriots. They, too, soon showed themselves in the field, here and there, in North and South Carolina, in bodies more or less numerous, mostly small at first, and badly armed, but full of eagerness and, perhaps, vindictive passions. There was one small troop of South Carolinians which had retreated before the British, from the Swamp regions, as the latter advanced into the back country. This party was led by Colonel Sumter, a gentleman who had formerly commanded one of the continental regiments, and who had already distinguished himself by his fearless valor, great military talents, and unbending patriotism. Known to the British by these qualities, they had wreaked their fury upon his dwelling, which they had burned to the ground with all its contents, after expelling his wife and family from it.

A sense of personal injury was thus superadded to that which roused his hostility in behalf of his country ; and, rallying his little force, which he strengthened by volunteers from North Carolina, he returned to his own state at the very moment when the cause of its liberty seemed most hopeless to the inhabitants.

The attitude of this forlorn few was no less melancholy than gallant. The British were everywhere triumphant — the Americans desponding — the state without any domestic goverment, and utterly unable to furnish supplies to this little band, whether of arms, clothing, or provisions.

Never did patriotism take the field with so few encouragements or so many difficulties. The iron tools of the neighboring farms — the ploughshare and the saw — were worked up into rude weapons of war by ordinary blacksmiths. The partisans supplied themselves, in part, with bullets by melting the pewter which was given them by private housekeepers. Sometimes they came into battle with less than three rounds to a man ;

and one-half were obliged to keep at a distance until supplied by the fall of comrades or enemies with the arms which might enable them to engage in the conflict. When victorious, they relied upon the dead for the ammunition for their next campaign. The readiness with which these brave men resorted to the field under such circumstances, was the sufficient guaranty for their ultimate success.

The British commander was suddenly aroused to fury by the tidings of this new champion in that field which he had so lately overrun. At a moment when Carolina lay, as he thought, lifeless and nerveless beneath his feet, her sword was waving in triumph above the heads of his warriors. The little force led by Sumter, consisting of less than one hundred and fifty men, soon distinguished themselves by the defeat of a large detachment of British militia and tories, under the command of Colonel Ferguson of the former, and Captain Houck of the latter.

The affair took place on the 12th of July, 1780, at Williamson's plantation, in the upper part of the state. The British, not apprehending an enemy, were posted at disadvantage in a lane, both ends of which were entered at the same time by the Carolinians.

Ferguson and Houck were both killed, and their men completely routed and dispersed. At the fortunate moment in which the attack was made, a number of prisoners were on their knees, vainly soliciting mercy for themselves and families at the hands of the British officers. Houck had become notorious for his cruel atrocities, in the very performance of which the retributive Providence decreed that he should be slain. On this occasion, Colonel Bratton and Captain M'Clure especially distinguished themselves. These two gallant officers had already made their mark upon a large body of marauding British and tories, in an affair only a month before at Mobley's meetinghouse, in Fairfield district, where (June, 1780), and only a few weeks after the surrender of Charlestown, they had attacked the enemy, and, after a severe handling, succeeded in dispersing

39. What were the dependences of the patriots?   40. What was the affair at Williamson's plantation?   41. Who were surprised and slain?   42. Who particularly distinguished themselves in this affair?   43. What had been their achievement at Mobley's?

them.   One of the gallant young partisans, in the affair with Houck and Ferguson, became well known long afterward as the distinguished General Adair.

The success of Sumter, and of the officers acting under him, rallied around him the people of the neighborhood, and his little force soon amounted to six hundred men.   At the head of this force, on the 30th of the same month (July), he made a spirited, but unsuccessful, attack on the British post at Rocky Mount. Baffled in this attempt, he passed without delay to the attack of another post at the Hanging Rock, in which a large force of regulars and tories were stationed.   Here his assault was equally daring and more successful.   The Prince of Wales' regiment was annihilated at a blow; and the tories under Colonel Bryan, of North Carolina, after suffering severely, were totally routed and dispersed.

These successes of Sumter and others, equally spirited and well managed, tended greatly to encourage the Carolinians, and to abate the panic which had been occasioned by the fall of their chief city.   Little partisan squads rose in arms in every section of the state — falling upon British and tories whenever there was reasonable prospect of success, and pressing from point to point wherever they heard of the appearance of the loyalist or British party.   To the former, indeed, they principally addressed themselves.   The British generally marched in force, or occupied commanding and fortified positions.   The loyalists, with roving commissions, were scattered in small bodies, with whom the whig partisans could more hopefully match their strength; and against these outlawed and licentious people their passions had been roused to most vindictive extremities of hate, in consequence of their reckless, brutal, and sanguinary excesses, which were habitually urged, and with a degree of ferocity which seemed designed to obscure even the bloody massacres of Tarleton.   All that was wanted by these scattered bands of patriots were good weapons, ample munitions, and an able military leader — prompt, energetic, vigilant, versed in stratagem, capable of guiding large bodies, and having the

44. What young partisan was it here who became distinguished afterward? 45. What was the result of the attempt on Rocky Mount?   46. What at Hanging Rock?   47. How were the Americans encouraged?   48. Against whom did the whigs chiefly operate, and with what feeling?

proper courage to show the way.  The partisans chose their own leaders, severally ; and these were men better calculated for small commands of cavalry or riflemen than for the conduct of large bodies of men, in grand army.  Such, at least, was the supposition, and hence the continual call upon the main army of Washington for general officers.  But that our partisans were fully competent to the adroit management of the desultory warfare in which they engaged, the evidence is ample.  We proceed to details.

A collection of the scattered bodies, under Colonel E. Clarke, was made, which included the several commands of Clarke, with the Georgia volunteers — M'Call, Liddle, and Samuel Hammond, with the South Carolinians — in all some hundred and ninety men — proceeded to the neighborhood of Cedar Springs, Spartanburg (July, 1780).  Here they were suddenly warned by two women, Mrs. Dillard and Mrs. Thomas, both of whom acted without the knowledge of each other, that they were shortly to be attacked by an overwhelming force of British and tories, led by Colonel Dunlap.  They prepared themselves accordingly, and were all in readiness when the enemy came on, an hour before daylight.  It was almost too dark to distinguish friends from foes.  But the British, expecting to surprise the Americans, were, in some degree, themselves the subject of surprise.  They were met firmly, hand to hand, and a fierce conflict ensued, in which they were defeated, and were pursued for near a mile.  They lost twenty-eight of Dunlap's dragoons, and, perhaps, a score of loyalists.  Most of the wounds given were with the broad-sword.  On the retreat, Dunlap was joined by Colonel Ferguson, and their united forces were more than five hundred men. · The Americans retired without precipitation or pursuit, and with the loss of but five killed and thirty wounded.

Another of these little bands of patriots had been raised by Colonel James Williams, of Ninety-Six district — a gentleman who had previously made himself known by his valor, zeal, and

49. What did the patriots lack ?  50. What collection took place.of their several squads ?  51. What was the affair at Cedar Springs ?  52. What women advised the Americans of their danger ?  58. How did the fight terminate ?

excellent spirit. He took the field about the same time with Sumter, Bratton, and others, and was destined to become famous by his future exploits in guerilla warfare. He was indefatigable in collecting and animating the militia in and around the district of Ninety-Six, and with these he perpetually harassed the marauding squadrons of the British.

On the 18th of August, almost at the very moment when Gates found himself a fugitive at Camden, Williams, assisted by Bratton, Shelby, McDowel, Inman, and others, achieved one of his happiest successes at Musgrove's mill (Gordon's), with an inferior force of one hundred and fifty men, against a British and loyalist force of three hundred men, one half of whom were regulars, under the command of Colonel Innis, assisted by Major Fraser. Williams formed a very pretty little ambuscade along the river thickets, for his enemy, and, by adroit management, succeeded in drawing the British colonel into it. Innis was surrounded by a circular fire, at the moment he supposed himself to be riding down a band of fugitives. The sharp-shooters of Williams and his colleagues, then poured in their fires, and rushed upon the foe. Taken by surprise, confounded by assailants on every hand, Innis and Fraser fled, with their regulars, breaking through the fiery circle, but at great loss of life. His militia were left to their fate; and such of them as did not bite the dust, were made prisoners. They lost nearly ninety men slain, and one hundred prisoners.

Williams, from this and other adventures, became the hero of the popular ballad. We have fragments of rustic verse, which show how strongly he had impressed himself on the confidence of the people. We shall hear of him, in future pages, and behold him crowning a career of noble adventure with a heroic death!

The sudden appearance in the field of such men as Sumter, Marion, Williams, etc., almost simultaneously, in so many different parts of the state, at once dissipated all the fairy bright imaginations of the British, which had made them declare the

54. What of Colonel James Williams? 55. What was the affair at Musgrove's? 56. Who were defeated, and with what loss? 57. What is said of Williams? 58. What was the effect upon the British of this revival of the conflict?

country conquered. In less than six weeks after the fall of Charlestown, hundreds of bold and daring champions, had sprung up, like the dragon's teeth, from the soil, and each of them had achieved some notable successes. They lacked but arms and armor. The soul was there — the spirit — but they had to present the naked bosom to the foe; had to wait the death of comrades before they could find the weapons of war with which to rush into battle; had to strive, with the implements of the shepherd, against the mailed warriors of Christendom!

But they were suddenly encouraged by tidings of great joy. They were to be furnished with weapons, and armor, and munitions, and a regular army was marching to their relief; and there was sent to marshal them to victory, a great general, whose name, at this period, was music in every patriot ear, as the synonyme of victory! This was General Gates, the hero of Saratoga; the rival, for renown, of Washington himself; with a reputation gradually obscuring that of the commander-in-chief.

It was now known that a strong body of continentals, very much exaggerated in numbers by report, was on its way to the relief of the South, and Gates was ordered to take charge of the army. While the siege of Charlestown was impending, some fourteen hundred continentals, consisting of the Delaware and Maryland lines, had been ordered by congress to its relief. They were confided to the command of Major-General Baron De Kalb, a brave German, and an officer of European experience. But, lacking means of transportation, without cash or credit, and relying, for facilities of march, upon states so thinly settled and resourceless as Virginia and North Carolina, the progress of these troops had been too slow for the succor of the besieged city. They were still on the march when the tidings were received of the fall of Charlestown.

But the march was not arrested. De Kalb led his men with a proper care, and with due regard to their sufferings, which were great, through a wild and almost uninhabited region.

59. What is said of the Americans? 60. What was the promise at this season? 61. Who were on the march for the South? 62. What delayed them?

He had pushed his progress to the South by the direct route from Petersburg in Virginia for Camden in South Carolina. On the 6th of July, he reached Deep river, and halted at Cox's mills to collect provisions, and determine upon his future course.

Here, he was overtaken, and superseded in command, by General Gates. The arrival of Gates increased the activity of this little army, without improving its condition. Gates, unhappily, was one of those men whom success intoxicates and destroys. He had no sooner arrived than he issued orders to his troops to hold themselves in readiness for marching, and, on the 27th, the army was under way, over a barren country, to Monk's ferry, in direct opposition to the counsel of all his officers.

The troops were without provisions and clothes, many without arms, and suffering from fatigue, from a protracted journey, at every step of which they had been compelled to undergo the most severe privations. Still, the army was increased in its progress by accessions, from Virginia and the Carolinas, of lean detachments; and, with a little delay to permit of the coming in of the militia, and the procuring of arms and supplies, it might have been swollen to a very respectable force of four or five thousand men.

Sanguine of success, and pressing on with the despatch which was all that this unfortunate general seemed to think necessary to secure it, he reached Clermont, where he encamped on the 13th of August.

Here, he was informed, by Colonel Sumter, of the advance of a considerable convoy of British wagons, on the route from M'Cord's ferry to Camden, and solicited by that brave partisan for a small reinforcement to enable him to capture them. Four hundred men were detached on this service; while General Gates put the army under marching orders to Camden, where the British maintained a strong post, under the command of Lord Rawdon. On the night of the 15th, at ten o'clock, the Americans moved from Rugely's mills, little dreaming of the terrible fate which awaited them.

63. Who superseded De Kalb ? 64. What the condition of the army ? 65. When did Gates reach Clermont ? 66. What application was made by Sumter ? 67. When did Gates move from Rugely's ?

Gates was in ignorance of several facts which he might have known, but did not know, and which it was of infinite importance to his objects that he should have known. He was ignorant that, by forced marches, Lord Cornwallis had reached Camden from Charlestown, bringing with him a considerable detachment. With a picked force of more than two thousand men, Cornwallis, an enterprising commander, took up his line of march from Camden, to meet his enemy, at the very hour when Gates left Clermont. The latter had given himself little time to learn anything. He committed a variety of blunders. He undervalued cavalry, one of the most important portions of every army, and one particularly important in a level and sparsely settled country like that through which he had to march.

He hurried his men, when fatigued, without necessity, and commenced a night movement with untried militia, in the face of an enemy. In this march he showed none of that vigilance upon which the success of all military enterprises must mainly depend.

Lord Cornwallis, on the contrary, appears to have been accurately informed of every particular in relation to the Americans, which it was important for him to know. It is even said that an emissary of the British commander succeeded in passing himself upon Gates as a fugitive from Camden, and, having won his confidence, made his escape to his British employer.

In a fatal state of security, the result of his own self-delusion, the commander of the American army hurried his troops forward, blindly, to their doom. The armies felt each other at midnight. The fire of the British advance first announced to the Americans the presence of their foes. The cavalry of Armand's legion wheeled and fled at the first discharge; but the infantry, under Colonel Porterfield, which was advancing in files, on the right of the road, coolly returned the fire, and the march of the enemy was checked.

As if by tacit consent, the respective armies recoiled, and

68. What enemy was approaching him? 69. What were Gates' errors? 70. What of Cornwallis? 71. When did the two armies meet? 72. What happened at their first meeting?

prepared to await the daylight for the conclusion of the strife. The Americans were quickly formed for battle. The first Maryland division, including the Delawares, under De Kalb, was posted on the right; the Virginia militia, under Stevens, on the left; the North Carolinians, under Caswell, held the centre; the artillery, in battery, upon the road. Both wings rested on morasses, and the second Maryland brigade was posted a few hundred yards in the rear of the first, to act as the reserve. The British were formed in a single line, with the wings covered and supported by bodies in reserve.

The battle began with the dawn of day (August 16). It was brought on by the advance of the American left on the British right, which had the appearance of being in some confusion. The reception which the Virginians met proved this to have been an error; they were repulsed, and, the British charging, at this moment, with a cheer, the Virginians fled in the utmost confusion, many of them without even discharging their pieces.

This unworthy example was followed by the North Carolina militia, with the exception of a single corps, under Major Dixon. The cavalry of Armand, which had behaved with so little resolution in the encounter of the night, increased the panic by a second and irretrievable flight; and the continentals stood alone, abandoned by the militia, and maintaining their ground as they could, against the entire force of the British army.

The artillery was lost; the cavalry — a miserable apology for a legion, made up of the worthless outcasts of foreign service — were swallowed up in the woods; and the regular infantry, reduced to a mere point in the field, and numbering but nine hundred men, were now compelled to bear the undivided pressure of two thousand men.

But they resisted this pressure nobly, and, their bayonets locking with those of the foe, bore them back upon the field, in many places, yielding them prisoners from the very heart of the British line.

73. How did the Americans form for battle? 74. How the British? 75. When did the battle begin? 76. How did the Virginia militia behave? 77. Who followed their example? 78. What did Armand's cavalry? 79. Upon whom did the brunt of battle fall?

This triumph was momentary only — these gallant men were unsupported. De Kalb had already fallen under eleven wounds; Gates had fled, or was borne from the field by the flying militia; and Cornwallis, observing that there was no cavalry opposed to him, poured in his dragoons, now returning from pursuit of the fugitives, and ended the contest.

Never did men behave better than the continentals; but they were now compelled to fly. The only chance that remained to avoid a surrender on the field, and escape from the sabres of the dragoons, in whom the British were very strong, was to break away for the morass in their rear, into which they could not be pursued by cavalry.

This was done, and by this measure, alone, did any part of this devoted corps find safety. The Americans lost the whole of their artillery, upward of two hundred wagons, and all their baggage. The loss of the British, in killed and wounded, was about three hundred. Though the royal army fought with great bravery, they must have been beaten but for the flight of the militia. The terrible conflict which followed with the continentals, proves what must have been the event, had the former behaved like men.

80. What of De Kalb and Gates? 81. What did Cornwallis? 82. How did the continentals? 83. Where did they seek refuge? 84. What were the respective losses, British and American?

# CHAPTER VI.

### SUMTER — MARION — THE BATTLE OF KING'S MOUNTAIN.

·The militia composed so large a part of General Gates's army, that he lost all hopes of victory on seeing them leave the field. He does not seem to have used any generalship, and nothing can be said of his heroism. His flight was thence to Clermont and Charlotte, where he hoped to rally the fugitives. It was in the midst of the hurry of flight that he was overtaken by a courier, who brought him the consoling intelligence of the complete success of Sumter in his enterprise. He had succeeded in his attempt against Carey's fort on the Wateree, had captured the garrison, and intercepted the escort with the wagons and stores.

On hearing of the defeat of Gates, Sumter began his retreat up the south side of the Wateree. He was pursued by Tarleton with wonderful address and celerity, followed by his legion and a detachment of infantry.

The movements of Sumter were necessarily and greatly impeded by his captives. He had with him forty baggage-wagons, filled with booty of the very kind that the Americans were most in need of. He was encumbered, also, by three hundred prisoners.

Tarleton, never relaxing his pursuit a moment, succeeded in overtaking Sumter. He came suddenly upon the camp of the Americans, near Fishing creek, and a complete surprise was effected. The British cavalry burst upon the militiamen when there was not a man standing to his arms, and threw themselves between the men and the parade where their muskets were

1. What is said of Gates's flight and generalship? 2. What success did Sumter achieve on the Wateree? 3. By whom was he pursued, and with what force? 4. What impeded his retreat?

stacked. The videttes were probably sleeping on their posts, seduced into a false security by the belief that the foe was at a distance. Not a drum was beat to arms, and no alarm given which could apprize the Americans of the approach of danger. The rout was total. A few of the regulars maintained a fire from behind the wagons for a while, in hopes of rallying the militia, but without success. Their opposition only served to infuriate the dragoons. The carnage was dreadful, and the aggregate loss in killed, wounded, and prisoners, was very little short of that sustained by Gates in his defeat of the 16th.

Sumter himself had the good fortune to escape; but very few of his officers or men got off. Of the prisoners taken in these two battles by the British, several were selected, bound with cords, and carried to Camden, where they were hung without trial as rebels, under the express order of Lord Cornwallis.

Nor was this the only measure of severity adopted by the invaders. In almost every section of the state, their progress was marked with blood, and with other deeds of equal atrocity. Many of the militia were executed on various and worthless pretexts, and most frequently without even the form of trial. Private citizens were made close prisoners on board of prison-ships, where they perished of foul diseases and without attendance. From Charlestown alone, after the defeat of Gates, sixty of the principal inhabitants were transported to St. Augustine, where they were subjected equally to bondage and every form of indignity, and kept as so many hostages for the good behavior of the citizens. After André's execution, these hostages were frequently threatened with the halter, in retaliation for the fate of André. The determination of the British commander seemed to be to annihilate the spirit of independence by trampling upon the persons of its best asserters. This was a short-sighted policy. True manhood is never more resolute than when it feels itself wronged, and the Carolinians were

5. Where was he surprised, and by what neglect of duty? 6. What was the result of this affair? 7. What became of Sumter? 8. Of the prisoners in the British hands? 9. What was the general treatment of people and militia? 10. What inhabitants were transported to St. Augustine, and with what object? 11. With what fate were they threatened, and why? 12. What is said of the British policy in this proceeding?

never more determined for their liberties than in the moment of their greatest denial and disaster.

General Gates, after several ineffectual attempts to rally his men, finally retired to Hillsborough, in North Carolina, to solicit the support of the state legislature, then in session. Here, upon bringing together the remnant of his little army, it was found to number little more than one thousand men. In South Carolina, after the dispersion of Sumter's command, there did not remain a man in arms, except a small band embodied by Marion. The other partisans, after Williams's victory over Innis, had been compelled to take refuge in the mountains. Marion found his security in the swamps.

This able partisan maintained his ground below and along the Santee river, and managed, among the defiles and swamps of that region, to elude all the activity of his enemies. His force had been collected chiefly among his own neighbors, were practised in the swamps, and familiar with the country. Like Sumter, utterly unfurnished with the means of war at first, he procured them by similar means. He took possession of the saws from the mills, and converted them into sabres. So much was he distressed for ammunition, that he has engaged in battle when he had not three rounds of powder to each man of his party. At other times, without any, his men have been brought in sight of the foe simply that their number might be displayed. For weeks, however, his force did not exceed seventy-five; sometimes they were reduced to one-third that number — all volunteers from the militia.

Yet, even with this inconsiderable band, he maintained his ground, secure amidst hundreds of tory enemies, who hung around his footsteps with all that watchful hostility which the peculiar animosities of civil warfare is so likely to sharpen into personal hatred. Various were the means employed to draw off or drive away his followers. The houses on the banks of the Pedee, Lynch's creek, and Black river, from whence they

13. Whither did Gates retire ? — and what army had he ? 14. What band still remained embodied in South Carolina ? 15. How did Marion arm his men ? — and under what conditions did he employ them ? 16. How did the British treat the houses and plantations of his followers ?

MARION.                                                    **267**

were chiefly taken, were destroyed by fire, the plantations devastated, and the negroes carried away.

But the effect of this wantonness was far other than had been
intended. Revenge and despair confirmed the patriotism of
these ruined men, and strengthened their resolution; and the
indiscriminate fury of the foe only served equally to increase
their numbers and their zeal. For months, their only shelter
was the green wood and the swamp — their only cover the
broad forest and the arch of heaven. Hardened by exposure,
and stimulated by the strongest motives of patriotism and feeling, they sallied forth from these hiding-places when their presence was least expected; and the first tidings of their approach
were conveyed in the flashing sabre and the whizzing shot.
They were perpetually engaged in skirmishes which history
does not record, and which are only cherished in local tradition.

With a policy that nothing could distract — a caution that no
artifice could mislead — Marion led his followers from thicket
to thicket in safety, and was never more perfectly secure than
when he was in the neighborhood of his foe. He hung upon
his flanks along the march — he skirted his camp in the darkness of the night — he lay in wait for his foraging parties — he
shot down his sentries, and, flying or advancing, he never failed
to harass the invader, and extort from him a bloody toll at every
passage through swamp, thicket, or river, which his smaller parties made.

In this sort of warfare — which is peculiarly adapted to the
peculiarities of the country in Carolina, and consequently to the
genius of her people — he contrived almost wholly to break up
the British communications by one of the most eligible routes
between the seaboard and the interior; and a masterly enterprise, marked with the boldness and intelligence that distinguished all his movements, drew on him the anxious attention
of his enemy, and made it necessary for Cornwallis to dislodge
him.

Hearing that a body of prisoners taken at the defeat of Gates,

17. What effect had this treatment upon them? 18. How did they live? 19. What
is said of their frequent skirmishes. 20. What were his stratagems? 21. How does
this sort of warfare suit the region? — and why?

about one hundred and fifty in number, were under march to Charlestown, under a strong escort, Marion determined upon their rescue. Placing his mounted militia in ambush, in one of the swamps that skirt the wood from Nelson's ferry to Monk's Corner, he darted upon the escort, and succeeded in taking the whole party captive. Having put the arms of the British into the hands of the rescued Americans, he hurried across the Santee, and did not pause until his prisoners were safely disposed of within the limits of North Carolina. He was far upon his way beyond the arm of danger, before the parties detached by Cornwallis, to drive him from his covert, had reached the scene of his enterprise.

The temporary departure of Marion left South Carolina almost wholly abandoned to the enemy ; but the fruits of his daring and success were yet to be seen. Opposition to the British was never wholly extinct in the state, even when it may have most appeared so ; and soon after the defeat of Sumter, on the 18th of August, he began to recruit his force from among the people of York district — a section of the state which had never made any concessions to the invader.

Major Davie, another enterprising officer, had, about this time, equipped, as dragoons, some fifty or sixty men in the same neighborhood ; and these two bands were still in arms, though quiet, and only waiting for the occasion which was to call them into renewed activity. It is probable that the knowledge of the existence of these and other growing parties drew the attention of the British commander to this part of the country.

Colonel Ferguson, a brave and efficient leader of the seventy-first British regiment, appeared among these bold borderers with a strong and disorderly force, consisting of loyalists and British, nearly fifteen hundred in number. His march through the country was distinguished by every sort of atrocity and violence. The lively representations of those who had suffered at the hands of these marauders, awakened the mountaineers to a sense of their own danger. Hitherto, they had only heard of

22. What captives did Marion rescue ? — and where ? 23. Did opposition to the British general ever cease in South Carolina ? 24. Who raised a dragoon corps in York ? 25. Who was Colonel Ferguson ? — and what force did he lead ? 26. How was his march distinguished ?

war at a distance; and, in the peaceable possession of that independence for which their countrymen along the seaboard had been contending, they had probably been rather more indifferent to the issue than their own interests and sympathies could well have justified.

The approach of Ferguson aroused them from their apathy, and they determined to embody themselves for their own defence. Being all mounted men, and unincumbered with baggage, their movements were prompt and rapid. Each man set forth with his blanket and rifle, in the manner of a hunter, and as if in pursuit only of the wild beasts of the forest. The earth was his couch at night, and the skies his covering. The running stream quenched his thirst, and the wild game of the woods, or the cattle which he drove before him, supplied him with food. The several bands thus collected from remote tracts — from the waters of Cumberland, Virginia, or from the Saluda and Savannah in Carolina, and the wild valleys of Watauga in the West — rendezvoused, at length, among the passes of the mountains in South Carolina.

There was some fifteen hundred men thus collected, especially for the pursuit of Ferguson. He, meanwhile, was making his way, as was supposed, to unite with Cornwallis. It was important to overtake him before he could effect this junction. Accordingly, nine hundred and ten, of the best mounted of the army, was selected to urge the pursuit. They were all gunmen, and on the best horses; and they sped with the eagerness of hunters who have roused the prey.

Ferguson was one of the ablest of the British light-infantry officers. He was specially renowned as a leader of riflemen, and had himself made considerable improvements in the rifle, and its use. His force was mixed, of British regulars and loyalists. The latter, it was known, would fight. They fought with halters round their necks; they, too, were expert riflemen.

The Americans overtook Ferguson within five or six miles of King's Mountain proper. He occupied one of its lower

27. Whom did it arouse? — and how did they take the field? 28. From what remote tracts were they drawn? — and where did they rendezvous? 29. How many men did they detach in pursuit? 30. What is said of Colonel Ferguson? 31. Of his troops, regulars and loyalists? 32. Where was he overtaken?

ridges, and was, no doubt, surprised while speeding to the security of the mountain. Had he reached this eminence, he would probably have been secure, at least for a time, and against the sort of warfare under which he fell. But, when overtaken, he was in possession only of one of the lower steps of the mountain, a long narrow ridge, thinly covered with woods, and easy of ascent.

The fleet horses of the Americans afforded him little time for preparations. Not expecting them so soon, he had probably been stopped in his march by a heavy fall of rain which had taken place, or he had possibly paused for rest and refreshment, as a fine spring of water gushed from the side of a hill, near that upon which he had encamped. The road lay between these eminences. The Americans divided themselves naturally into four bodies, representing almost as many states. Each of these divisions was represented by its own colonel, and the authority of each was paramount over his own command. The colonels were Campbell, Shelby, Cleveland, Sevier, and Williams. It is said that Williams had Governor Rutledge's commission in his pocket, as a brigadier, at this very time, but that he magnanimously suppressed the fact, fearing, perhaps, that its assertion might cause jealousies and distrust; and, by common consent, the general command was confided to Colonel Campbell, of Virginia.

The mode of attack was simple, and suggested directly by the situation of the British; no other plan could be pursued. The elevation was attainable easily from several sides, and a simultaneous attack, from all quarters, was clearly the best method of distressing and for defeating the enemy. The several divisions, accordingly — the side of ascent being first allotted to each — prepared themselves to ascend the ridge, advancing under cover of the trees, and delivering their fire as they came. In this way, they all proceeded to ascend the hill, at nearly the same moment.

THE BATTLE OF KING'S MOUNTAIN.

It happened that the party of Cleveland was the first to ascend the ridge, and to encounter the enemy's pickets. History has preserved for us the simple but eloquent apostrophe of this gallant leader, when urging his men into action :—

"My brave fellows," he said, "we have beaten the tories already, and we can beat them again. They are all cowards; if they were not, they would support the independence of their country. When engaged with them, you will want no word of command from me. I will show you how to fight by my example. I can do no more. Every man must be his own officer, and act from his own judgment. Fire as fast you can, and stand your ground as long as you can. When you can do no better, run ; but do not run quite off. Get behind trees, and retreat. If repulsed, let us return and renew the fight. We may have better luck the second time than the first. If any of you are afraid, let them retire, and I beg they may take themselves off at once."

This was a good speech, which his men could understand. The effect of it was such as every commander must desire. The battle began. The British picket soon gave way, and was forced up the ridge to the main body. Here the pursuers were met by Ferguson. They recoiled before the charge of the British bayonet, to which they could oppose nothing but the American rifle. They fled down the hill ; but, obeying the directions of their commander, they availed themselves of every shelter, to stop, reload, and throw in their fire.

They were soon relieved by the appearance of the party under Shelby, who, by this time, had made the circuit of the height, and was rushing on with his rifles in like manner. Ferguson was compelled to turn and encounter a new foe. The fresh party, under Shelby, poured in a well-directed fire, but sunk back, like that of Cleveland, under the charge of the British.

The plans of the mountaineers, though simple, were singularly effective, and the party of Shelby was relieved by the ap-

41. How was it begun ?—and by whom ? 42. What speech was made by Cleveland ?—repeat it ? 43. How did Ferguson meet his assailants ? 44. How did the several parties relieve each other ? 45. How did Ferguson repel them, severally ? 46. Describe the several alternations in the battle ?

proach of another band, whose unerring fires compelled the
British commander once more to change his front.    While
busy with these, a fourth came upon the ground; and, as often
as one of the American divisions was driven down the height,
another rose in the rear or on the flank of the enemy.

Ferguson's valor was unavailing.    The ridge was encircled
by foes as bold and deliberate, as they were prompt, active,
and skilful.    His men were falling around him on every side;
the success of his bayonets gave him barren ground, which he
could only for a moment retain.    Still he refused to surrender.
His shrill silver whistle was heard over all the cries of the
combat; and he sped from side to side with invincible determination.    The conflict was ended only by his fall.    The sec-
ond-in-command, De Peyster, sued for quarter.

The havoc had been terrible on the side of the British.
Thirteen hundred men were killed, wounded, and prisoners.
But two hundred escaped.    Fifteen hundred stand of arms fell
into the hands of the Americans.    They lost but few men, but
among these was the brave Colonel Williams, of South Carolina.    The bloody conflict was marked by a crowning sacrifice
of vengeance; ten of the prisoners — loyalists — conspicuous
for their outlawries, and well-known, were tried, condemned,
and hung, by the victors, almost in the moment of victory!
Thirty were condemned, but twenty respited.    They are alledged to have been, all of them, notorious for their crimes, the
monstrous atrocity of which forbade the plea of pity in the ears
of their captors.    They had long been doomed, by a thousand
threats of vengeance, from as many outraged enemies!

Something, too, is alledged in behalf of this wild and summary justice, in the right and policy of retaliation, for the murders which Cornwallis had committed on his captives at Camden, Ninety-six, and Augusta.    The deed was supposed to be
justified by that code which requires eye for eye, tooth for
tooth, life for life!

47. By what instrument did Ferguson give his orders and rally his men?    48. In
what event did the battle cease?    49. Who was slain? — what the havoc and loss of
the British?    50. Who did the Americans lose?    51. What act of vengeance followed
the victory?    52. What is alledged in excuse for this act?

The tradition reports that Williams and Ferguson perished by each other's hands; that, after Ferguson had fallen by the pistol of Williams, and lay wounded on the ground, the latter approached and offered him mercy; and that his answer was a fatal bullet from the pistol of the dying man!

To this day, the traveller reads on a rude stone, at the foot of the scene of battle, and near the spring from which he quenches his thirst :—

" SACRED

*To the Memory of*

MAJOR WILLIAM CHRONICLE,

CAPTAIN JOHN MATTOCKS, WILLIAM ROBB, AND JOHN BOYD,

Who were killed at this place on the 7th day of October, 1780, fighting in defence of America."

On the opposite side you read :—

"COLONEL FERGUSON,

An Officer of His Britannic Majesty,

Was defeated and killed,

At this place,

On the 7th day of October,

1780."

53. What does the tradition report of Williams and Ferguson?   54. What does the traveller read near the scene of battle? — repeat the inscriptions.

12*

# CHAPTER VII.

## TO THE BATTLE OF COWPENS.

THE defeat and death of Ferguson, and the overthrow of a force so formidable as that which he led, reinspirited the Americans; it also served to baffle the plans of Lord Cornwallis; to whom it gave such serious alarm that he retreated from Charlotte, to which place he had pursued the fugitive army of Gates, and fixed himself at Winnsborough.

The boldness of the Americans increased daily. The panic which followed the defeat of the continentals began to dissipate. Small bodies of troops, under favorite leaders, began to show themselves even in the neighborhood of Cornwallis's encampment; cutting off his foragers and intercepting his convoys. The sharp-shooters of the Carolinas penetrated his very lines, and, under the shelter of shrub, tree, and hillock, picked off his sentries. Such was their audacity, that, on his march from Charlotte to Winnsborough, single riflemen often rode up within gunshot of his army, singled out their victims, and, having discharged their pieces, went off in safety.

Andrew Jackson, then a boy but fourteen years old, took the field on this occasion.

The approach of Ferguson and Cornwallis had summoned all classes to the field. The old sire, better fitted to grasp the crutch than the brand, as well as the boy whose sinews had not yet hardened into manhood; and, long after the storm of battle had subsided on the plains of Carolina, the boy of the Wexhaws still remembered its fury, while grappling with the same enemy on the field of New Orleans. Little was it imagined then, that the slight, obscure stripling, who was sabred by a British offi-

1. What were the events which re-inspirited the Americans and baffled Cornwallis? 2. What did the sharp-shooters of Carolina? 3. What is said of Andrew Jackson, at this period?

cer for refusing to clean his boots, should be honored, thirty-five years after, with the greatest victory ever obtained over a British army in America. Could the officer who smote the boy have foreseen the event, can it be doubted that the edge of the sabre, not its side, would have been employed, and that murder would have justified itself under the plea of patriotism?

The retreat of Cornwallis followed closely upon Ferguson's defeat, and the confession of weakness, betrayed by this retreat, gave new encouragement to the Americans. They everywhere began to repair in considerable numbers — the sparseness of population considered — to the camps of their respective commanders. Of these, there were large numbers, captains and colonels, in the field, of whom the historians say little. And they achieved, day by day, successes on a small scale, of which but little has been reported.

These parties, with their leaders, now began to acknowledge and to exercise a better discipline, and to become more efficient as soldiers. They had suffered too many disasters from the neglect of duty by the militia not to feel the necessity of vigilance, and a better observance of the duties of the regular service. The legislature of North Carolina put all the militia of the state under General Smallwood, of the continental army. Generals Sumner and Davidson had, also, large commands of militia, and were good officers. Major Davie was also an active and efficient partisan of that state; so were Shelby, Sevier, McDowal, and Locke, of the same state. Georgia contributed several able captains, in Colonels Clarke, McCall, Jackson, and Twiggs; and there was not a precinct in South Carolina that had not some body of troops in the field, under a favorite leader, Hammond, the Hamptons, Harden, Cleveland, as well as Marion, Sumter, and Pickens.

It was one of the mistakes of the British to suppose that the spirit of the country, thus excited and active, could be subdued by cruelty and terror. Cornwallis issued his orders to hang,

4. What followed closely on Ferguson's defeat? 5. What is said of the spirit and conduct of the Americans, at this period? 6. Who was appointed commander of the militia of the state? 7. What other officers are named as having command? 8. What officers did Georgia contribute? 9. What was one of the mistakes of the British?

and burn, and oppress, the rebels in every possible way; and his lieutenants, such as Tarleton, Wemyss, and others, were not unwilling to follow out his decrees to the fullest extent of privilege and persecution which they allowed.

Gates, still in command of the remnant of the defeated army, at Hillsborough, detached Brigadier-General Morgan, early in October, with three hundred Marylanders and Delawares, and some eighty dragoons, to assist the patriots of Mecklenburg and Rowan. From this force, Lieutenant-Colonel William Washington was detached, to the vicinity of Camden.

On the 4th of December, 1780, Washington showed himself before a British post, near Camden, which was held by a militia-colonel, one Rugely, whose genius for war was singularly undeveloped for one of his rank. The post was a stockade, and garrisoned by about one hundred men. Washington was without artillery; but eager to get possession, and stratagem was resorted to, in the absence of the proper materials of war. A pine log, ingeniously hewn so as to resemble a field-piece, was elevated upon a pair of wagon-wheels; and, brought up with due formalities, enforced, to the commander of the post, the propriety of surrendering at the first summons of the American colonel. This innocent piece of timber, thus brought to bear upon the eyes of the garrison, if not upon their works, was invested by the militiamen with such formidable power, that they were exceedingly glad to find a prompt acceptance of their submission. But the surrender was fatal to Colonel Rugely, as a hero and military man. His hope of becoming a brigadier was for ever cut off by his too ready recognition of this new instrument of warfare.

It was about this time that General Greene superseded General Gates in command of the southern army. He brought with him no troops and but a single aid. The returns of the troops in his command, six days after he joined the army at Charlotte,

10. What detachments were sent out by General Gates, and for what purpose? 11. When did Colonel Washington appear before the British post near Camden? 12. Who was in command of that post, and what is said of him? 13. What is said of the post, and how was it garrisoned? 14. What stratagem did Colonel Washington employ? 15. With what success? 16. What was the result to the British commander? 17. Who succeeded General Gates in command of the army? 18. What was the number of troops in the American army, six days after he took command?

gave but nine hundred and seventy continentals and one thousand one hundred and thirteen militia. The troops were without pay or clothing, tents or blankets. The British regular army in South Carolina, at this time, numbered five thousand men, exclusive of loyalists, and were so stationed as to cover the most important precincts in the state. They were thus enabled to overawe the populous settlements. The garrison at Winnsborough completed a chain of posts which the enemy had established, from Georgetown to Augusta, in a circle, the centre of which, equi-distant from Charlestown and Savannah, would have been Beaufort, in South Carolina. These posts consisted of Georgetown, Camden, Winnsborough, Ninety-Six, and Augusta. Within this circle was another chain of posts, consisting of Fort Watson, on the road to Camden, Motte's house, and Granby, on the Congaree. Dorchester, Orangeburg, Monk's Corner, and other places, were fortified as posts of rest, deposite, and communication. These stations were all judiciously chosen, as well for procuring subsistence as for covering the country.

The American army had been under march for Salisbury before the arrival of Greene. A command, under Colonel Morgan, had, as we have seen, penetrated South Carolina, pressing forward toward Camden, and occupying the very ground which had witnessed the defeat of Gates.

The exploit of Marion, in rescuing the American prisoners and capturing the British guards, made him particularly obnoxious to the British commander. Tarleton's success against Sumter, and the promptness and activity of his movements, pointed him out to Cornwallis as the proper officer to ferret out and destroy this wary partisan. Tarleton began the enterprise with a degree of wariness and art which was new to his practice. He fancied, at one time, that he had "the Swamp Fox" fairly in his meshes; but the British officer manœuvred in vain. Marion baffled and eluded him at all points, and his ad-

19. What is said of their condition? 20. What was the number in the British army, and how were they stationed? 21. Name the different posts. 22. What American officer had penetrated South Carolina, and was pressing forward toward Camden? 23. For what had Marion rendered himself obnoxious to the British commander? 24. Who was despatched by Cornwallis to destroy Marion? 25. With what success?

versary was compelled to leave him the undisputed master of the whole ground, while he turned his arms once more against Sumter, whose incursions had again become troublesome.

This daring captain, having recruited his command to an imposing force, advanced within twenty-eight miles of the British camp, at Winnsborough.

This audacity suggested to Cornwallis a plan of surprizing him in his encampment. Such importance was attached to securing his individual person, that an officer, with five dragoons, had it specially in charge to force their way to his tent, and take him, dead or alive. "The Game Cock," as Sumter was called by the Carolinians, was, in the language of Cornwallis, the greatest trouble which the British had encountered in the country.

The conduct of this enterprise was entrusted to a Major Wemyss, who approached the encampment of the American general with equal promptitude and caution.

Fortunately, Sumter had given more than usual strength to his advanced guard. His army had lain so long in their position, that he naturally expected attack. Colonel Taylor, by whom the advance-guard was commanded, had taken particular precautions. Fires had been lighted in front of his line, and his men were ordered, in case of alarm, to form so far in the rear of the fires, as to be concealed, while the approaching enemy would be conspicuous in their light.

The videttes and pickets did their duty, and the guard was ready to receive the attack. A murderous fire prostrated twenty-three of the British, as they reached the fires. The rest recoiled, then retreated for a hundred yards before they rallied. They were brought again steadily to the attack, and a close conflict followed; but the well-directed fire of the Americans completed what their advance guard had so well begun. The British were driven from the field, and found safety only in the darkness of the night. Wemyss fell into the hands of

26. Against whom did Tarleton next turn his arms? 27. What were Sumter's movements? 28. How did Cornwallis expect to secure the "Game Cock?" 29. To what officer was this enterprise entrusted? 30. What precautions had Sumter taken? 31. Describe the battle, and give the result.

the Americans, being wounded through both thighs, and deserted by his men in the precipitation of their flight.

Sumter, after this affair, left his position, and was pursued by Tarleton with the headlong haste which marked all the movements of that warrior. He came up with the American general at Blackstock's, on the 20th of November.

At this period, by the way, there were three distinct commands of the South Carolina militia; Marion, in the low country; Sumter, in the middle; Williams, in the upper; and, after his death, Pickens, assisted or seconded, by Colonels Clarke and Twiggs, of Georgia.

Blackstock's house, on the southwest bank of Tiger river, afforded a favorable position for the employment of a small force in battle. Sumter stationed his troops so as to avail himself of all its advantages. On this occasion, Sumter had with him, Clarke, Twiggs, and Chandler, of Georgia, and Colonels Thomas, Bratton, and Majors M'Call and Samuel Hammond, of South Carolina, who had joined forces with his some ten days before. Not doubting that the whole force of the British was upon him, he resolved to maintain his ground during the day, and, under cover of the night, escape across the river.

Tarleton's command consisted of his legion, a battalion of the seventy-first regiment, a detachment of the sixty-third, and a lieutenant's command of the royal artillery, with one field-piece. But, of this force, only four hundred mounted men had yet come up with the Americans.

As soon as Sumter made this discovery, his plans were changed; and he resolved to commence the attack and cut up his enemy in detail. Tarleton, supposing that he had the game in his own hands, had, immediately on arriving, secured an elevated piece of ground, in front of Sumter's position, and dismounting his men to relieve themselves and horses, prepared to await the arrival of his artillery and infantry.

32. What did Sumter and Tarleton? 33. When, and where, did Tarleton come up with Sumter? 34. Into how many commands were the South Carolina militia divided, at this time and who were the commanders? 35. How was Blackstock's house situated?—and what did it afford? 36. What officers had Sumter with him, at this time? 37. What did he resolve? 38. What was Tarleton's force? 39. What change now took place in Sumter's plans? 40. What did Tarleton?

But the assault of Sumter compelled him to take to his arms. The Americans descended from their heights, and poured in a well-directed fire upon the enemy.   They were met by the bayonet, and, being armed only with rifles, were compelled to retire.   The British advanced, but were met by a reserve of rifles, which prostrated many and repulsed the rest.   Tarleton, as he beheld his danger, commanded a second and desperate charge, directly up the hill; but the Americans stood firm, and received him with their rifles, under the united fire of which his men could not be made to stand.   Drawing off his whole force, he wheeled upon Sumter's left, where the ground was less precipitous; he was here met by a little corps of Georgians, about one hundred and fifty in number, who displayed the courage of veterans.   Clarke and Hammond, especially, distinguished themselves in this action.   But the pressure of Tarleton's whole force was too much for them to contend against.   They yielded, after a noble resistance, and gave way; but the timely interposition of the reserve, under Colonel Winn, and the fire from a company stationed at the house, determined the issue.   Tarleton fled, leaving near two hundred men upon the field of battle.   The loss of the Americans was trifling, but their brave commander received a severe wound in the breast, which kept him a length of time from service.   Twiggs succeeded to the command when Sumter was wounded.

The *army* of the South, when General Greene entered upon its command, was, in the language of his predecessor, "rather a shadow than a substance."   It consisted nominally of less than two thousand men.   One thousand of these were militia, and nine hundred continentals.   The first measures of Greene were to provide them with arms and clothing, and make such arrangements as would supply their future wants.   These were not of easy performance in a country where there was no real money, and nothing in circulation but a miserable paper currency, even then hopelessly irredeemable, and not less a jest with the Americans than a mockery with the British.

41 Describe the battle.  42. What was the result?  43. What was the American loss?  44. Who succeeded Sumter?  45. Of what did the army consist, when General Greene took command?  46. What were Greene's first measures?

But, whatever may have been the deficiencies and disadvantages of the service, the American general entered upon it with a manly determination to undertake its hardships with patriotic zeal, and to despond in nothing. He advanced toward the head of boat-navigation on the Pedee. The country in that neighborhood was fertile, and had not yet been traversed by an army of any magnitude. Here he sat down for a while, in order to recruit and exercise his little force; and here he matured his plans, perfected his intimacy with his officers, and drilled his raw militiamen. From this point he despatched his engineers to explore the country. The routes in all directions were carefully set down, and, with Governor Rutledge, of South Carolina, in his camp, he was not suffered to remain in ignorance of any matters which he deemed essential to his contemplated invasion of the state.

While Gates and Greene had been busy in the accumulation of an army, it must not be supposed that the little bands under Marion, and other partisan commanders, had been inactive. Marion, whose mode of warfare had acquired for him the *nom de guerre* of " the Swamp Fox," was never inactive. Hundreds of little successes, that do not properly belong to the main stream of regular history, yet concurred to render his career memorable, and to influence equally the hopes of his countrymen and the hostility of the enemy. His command was a peculiar one, being chiefly formed from the little and insulated section of country in which he lived. His warriors were his neighbors and friends, and the tie that bound them together brought into equal activity the duty of the soldier and the affections of the comrade. " Marion's brigade," was the extra military epithet which distinguished his command. It might contain ten men, or five hundred — it was still " Marion's brigade" — a membership in which had a sort of masonic value in the estimation of his followers, which amply compensated for all its privations and fatigues. Constantly active, it would be impossible for the pen of the historian to follow the progress of the little corps. Some of his exploits have been recorded. We can only glance at one or two more, in order to bring up our narration to the period of Greene's assumption of command over the southern army.

One of the first of his exploits was the surprise of a Major Gainey, at the head of a large body of tories, which he had collected between Great and Little Pedee. A second party of tories was defeated at Shepherd's ferry, near Black Mingo swamp. The tories were well posted to receive the attack, and a desperate conflict ensued. The parties were so near each other, during the greater part of the conflict, that the wadding of their guns continually struck on each side. Neither party had bayonets, and buckshot was quite as frequently used as ball.

This victory increased the " brigade " to nearly four hundred men, with which Marion marched upon Colonel Tynes, who had raised a large force of tories upon Black river. Tynes was surprised, several of his men slain, and his force dispersed, while Marion lost not a man. In all these marches and conflicts, the partisans lived entirely in the swamps, with no shelter but the forest, almost without blankets or clothing, commonly with no food but potatoes, and meat without salt. Marion himself, for a long time, had neither hat nor blanket.

The arrival of Greene abridged the independence of Marion's movements. His brigade constituted a portion of the men of the state, and was necessarily comprised within the command of that general. The activity, courage, and successful conduct of Marion, indicated him to Greene as one well calculated, by his knowledge of the country, for active employment; and Colonel Lee being joined to his " brigade," a combined attempt was made to surprise the British post at Georgetown. The town was entered, many were killed and taken; but the garrison remained firm, and the attempt was unsuccessful. The failure is ascribed to several causes; but the alarm of the guides, who

50. Whom did General Marion attack and defeat under Major Gainey? 51. What can you say of the conflict at Shepherd's ferry? 52. Of what number did Marion's " brigade " now consist? 53. Upon whom did Marion now march? 54. With what result? 55. How did the partisans submit? 56. What effect did the arrival of Greene have on Marion's movements? 57. What British post did they attempt to surprise? 58. With what success?

missed their way, and thus defeated the plan of co-operation between the several parties, is a sufficient reason. With this affair, which took place on the 25th of January, General Greene opened the campaign of 1781.

This failure was more than compensated by a brilliant event which happened a few days before, in the western extremity of the state, to which General Greene had detached Colonel Morgan with a strong force, with a view to his keeping down and restraining the brutal passions of the loyalists in that quarter. Morgan, shortly after his arrival, sent Lieutenant-Colonel Washington, with a regiment and two hundred horse, to attack a body of tories who had been plundering the whig inhabitants. Washington came up with them near Hammond's store, charged them vigorously and defeated them. General Cunningham, with a detachment of British militia of one hundred and fifty, was dispersed by a party under Cornet Simons, of Washington's command. These, and other successes, seriously excited the apprehensions of Cornwallis for the safety of the post at Ninety-Six; and he ordered Tarleton to throw himself at once across the path of Morgan.

With a force of twelve hundred men — five hundred of whom were the formidable legion which had been carrying terror and conquest through every quarter of the state for so long a time — Tarleton prepared to obey with his accustomed celerity. That there should be no chance for the escape of his prey, who lay on the west side of Broad river, it was concerted that Cornwallis should advance northwardly as far as King's Mountain, that Morgan's retreat might be cut off, and he compelled to fight. That Morgan should himself desire to encounter either of them, the British commanders do not seem to have suspected for a moment.

Instead of flying from Tarleton, however, Morgan advanced to the Pacolet to meet him. The Pacolet is a small river, fordable in many places. On the evening of the 15th, Tarleton put his troops in motion toward the head of the stream, as if

59. What event opened the campaign of 1781? 60. What events more than compensated for the failure at Georgetown? 61. What did Cornwallis? 62. What force had Tarleton? 63. What was Cornwallis's plan?

with an intention to cross it above the position which Morgan had taken, and thus place his adversary between his own and the main army under Cornwallis, which was only a day's march distant on the left. His stratagem took effect. Morgan made a corresponding movement; while Tarleton, silently decamping in the night, passed the river before daylight, at a crossing-place a few miles below.

Morgan then retreated precipitately, and before night regained a favorite position on Thicketty creek, where he determined to await the approach of the enemy. Tarleton supposing that his adversary was resolved on flight, hurriedly resumed the pursuit on the following morning. About eight o'clock, A. M., he came in sight of the Americans, and, instead of overtaking his adversary in the fatigue and confusion of a flight, he found him drawn up and ready under arms. Morgan's army had rested, breakfasted, and were refreshed. The British, on the other hand, had been five hours that morning on the march; but this difference was deemed unimportant to one who had hitherto known nothing but success. Tarleton, satisfied by the spirit and alacrity of his troops, prepared at once for battle.

Morgan had taken ground on an eminence which ascended gently for about three hundred and fifty yards, and was covered with an open wood. On the crown of this eminence were posted two hundred and ninety Maryland regulars, and in line, on their right, two companies of Virginia militia and a company of Georgians, making his rear line consist of four hundred and thirty men. This was commanded by Lieutenant-Colonel Howard. One hundred and fifty yards in advance of the line, the main body of the militia, about three hundred in number, all practised riflemen, and most of them burning with a keen sense of personal injury, were posted under the command of Colonel Pickens. In advance of the first line, about one hundred and fifty yards, were placed as many picked riflemen, scattered in loose order along the whole front. Those on the right were commanded by Colonel Cunningham, of Georgia, with a mixed command of Georgians and South Carolinians; those on the left by Major M'Dowal, of South Carolina. No partic-

64. Describe the movements of Morgan and Tarleton.

ular order was given to this desultory body; but they knew the service. "Mark the epaulette men," were the words of counsel which they whispered to one another.

In the rear of the second line, the ground descended, and then again arose to a height sufficient to cover a man on horseback. Behind this, the American reserve was posted, consisting of Washington's and M'Call's cavalry, one hundred and twenty-five in number. The advanced party were ordered not to deliver their fire until the British were within fifty yards, and, this done, to retire, covering themselves with trees and loading and firing as occasion offered.

When Tarleton beheld his enemy ready to receive him, he advanced to reconnoitre; but was prevented from doing so by the picked riflemen who were scattered along the entire front of the line. On this occasion they gave the cavalry a few discharges, which made them tremble at the deadly aim of the southern rifle. The British were formed when within three hundred yards from the front of Morgan's force, and soon after advanced with a shout, under the cover of their artillery, pouring in an incessant fire of musketry as they came. At the assigned distance, the militia delivered their fire with unerring aim; and "here," says Colonel Howard, "the battle was gained."

The assertion was justified by the spectacle of dead and wounded, commissioned and noncommissioned, who sank down under the deliberate and fatal discharge which first followed the advance of the foe. But this was not enough to repel the enemy under the excitement of battle and the goading of their commanders. The retreat of the militia quickened the advance of the British, who rent the air with shouts, as they fondly believed that the day was already won.

But the second line renewed the punishment which had followed from the fire of the first, and at this moment the fearful havoc which the riflemen had made among the officers rendered itself apparent in the confusion of the troops. Still they advanced; yet obviously with such hesitation, that Tarleton ordered the seventy-first regiment into line upon his left. His cavalry at the same time descended upon the Americans' right.

65. Describe the disposition of the American army for battle.

Morgan perceived this movement, and the necessity of covering his flank. In this crisis of the battle, Washington encountered the cavalry of Tarleton in a successful charge. The militia recovered, and, forming a new reserve, were ready to obey the command of Morgan to " give them but one more fire and make the victory secure." The bayonets of Howard's continentals were interlocked with those of the foe, and the day was won.

The concerted action of Morgan's whole force at this most important moment was the certain guaranty of victory. The enemy was within thirty yards, tumultuously shouting and advancing, when the final fire of the Americans was delivered. The survivors of the terrible discharge threw down their weapons and fell upon their faces.

Eight hundred stand of arms, two field-pieces, and thirty-five baggage-wagons, fell into the hands of the victors. The remains of the British cavalry were pursued for several miles by Washington; but the greater part of them escaped. Thus ended the great and well-fought battle of the Cowpens.

66. Describe the battle of Cowpens?

# CHAPTER VIII.

## FROM THE BATTLE OF COWPENS TO THE FLIGHT OF CORNWALLIS.

NEVER was victory more complete than this. Not a corps of the British retired from the field under command, except the remains of the cavalry who accompanied Tarleton himself. These were pursued by Lieutenant-Colonel Washington with his accustomed rapidity of movement — a rapidity which sometimes involved him in perils, when greater prudence, though less brilliant in its display, might have been better soldiership. Excited by the prospect of capturing the formidable cavalry-officer whose successes had hitherto been so uniform, and so productive of disaster to the Carolinas, Washington pressed forward with so much haste as to separate himself from the main body of his command.

Tarleton beheld this, and turned upon his pursuer. He was supported by two of his officers, one of whom crossed swords with the pursuing American. The blade of the latter, being of inferior temper, broke in the encounter, and left him at the mercy of the foe. At this moment, when a second blow would have brought him to the ground, a little henchman, not fourteen years old, who was devoted to his master, and carried no other weapon than a pistol at his saddle-bow, seasonably rode up and discharged its contents into the shoulder of the Briton. The arm of the assailant fell powerless at his side; but the other officer occupied his place. His sword was already lifted above the head of Washington, when the blow was broken by the interposition of the sword of Sergeant-Major Perry. A bullet

1. By what officer was Tarleton pursued in his retreat from the battle of the Cowpens? 9. Was Colonel Washington exposed to any particular danger during the encounter which took place?

from the pistol of Colonel Tarleton, aimed at Washington, brought the noble steed that bore him to the ground.

The fortunate approach of the Americans arrested the farther attempts of the Briton upon their leader. The moment was lost, and his flight was resumed. The British dragoons of Tarleton had really never fought well. They had repeatedly hacked to pieces a fugitive or supplicating militia ; but neither at Blackstock's, where they encountered Sumter, nor at Cowpens, where they met with Washington, did they maintain the high renown which they had hitherto acquired rather from good fortune than desert. The star of Tarleton waned from this moment. His operations grew limited in extent, and small in importance. His defeat on this occasion, with that of Ferguson at King's Mountain, were the first links in a grand chain of causes, which drew down ruin on the British interest in South Carolina.

Success did not lull Morgan into security. Not more than twenty-five miles from Lord Cornwallis, he naturally conjectured that his lordship would be in motion to cut off his retreat as soon as the intelligence should reach him of the defeat of Tarleton. He halted no longer on the field of battle than to refresh his men and secure his prisoners, who were five hundred in number, exclusive of the wounded ; and moved across Broad river the same evening.

His movements were necessarily slow, encumbered, as he was, with the wounded, the prisoners, and the captured baggage ; and he might have been easily overtaken and brought to a halt by a vigorous pursuit of the enemy ; but the good fortune which had attended him.through the conflict still clung to his standard.

Cornwallis, with a remissness which has been censured by Tarleton, hesitated to decide. In war, the delay of moments is the defeat of hosts. He stopped to destroy his baggage, and make some preparations which could have been reserved for another time, and which consumed two days, and thus lost a

8. What is said of the defeat of Tarleton at the Cowpens, and of Ferguson at King's Mountain? 4. What number of prisoners were taken by the Americans at the Cowpens?

prize, which, had he pursued promptly, he could scarcely have failed to secure.

He reached the great Catawba river just after the American general had passed in safety; but he no longer possessed the power to follow him. The swollen waters of the stream which barely suffered the passage of Morgan, rose up, foaming and threatening, in the face of Cornwallis. The Americans exulted in the conviction that a miracle had been performed in their behalf, like that which saved the Hebrews from the pursuit of the Egyptian tyrant. The British commander was not, indeed, swallowed up by the waters; but they stayed his march — they baffled his pursuit — and Morgan joined his commander, bringing off in safety the prisoners and baggage — the whole rich spoils of his valor and good conduct.

As soon as the Catawba was fordable, Cornwallis prepared to cross it, which he did successfully, though resisted by a part of Greene's army, under the command of General Davidson. It was a wise resolution on the part of the British general to attempt the passage in the night. A stream five hundred yards wide, foaming among the rocks, and frequently overturning men and horses in its progress, might, in daylight, have discouraged the hearts of his men. Nor would they then have been so safe from the unerring riflemen, who were posted among the trees and bushes which thickly covered the margin of the stream.

A sharp conflict, nevertheless, followed the attempt, in which many of the enemy, including Colonel Hale of the guards, were slain. Cornwallis himself had a horse shot under him, which barely survived to reach the shore, when he fell and expired.

General Davidson, in an attempt to change his position during the action, in order to occupy the front of the enemy, came between the light of his own fires and the advancing column of the British. A well-directed volley from them prostrated him with a number of his men. The militia became dispirited after this disaster, and precipitately retreated.

5. By whom was Morgan followed in his march to join General Greene, and how was the pursuit arrested? 6. Why did this circumstance prove particularly inspiriting to the Americans? 7. What did it enable Morgan to do? 9. As soon as the Catawba was fordable, whither did Cornwallis pursue General Greene?

A military race then began between the respective opponents, in which Cornwallis pursued Greene into Virginia. The British commander, content with this seeming success, and desiring to recruit his force for a more effectual prosecution of his march into Virginia, fell back upon Hillsboro, North Carolina, where he raised the royal standard and summoned the loyalists to rally beneath it.

To defeat this object, Greene recrossed the river Dan, and once more drew the attention of the British upon himself. A detachment of his force, under command of Pickens and Lee, fell in with a force of the loyalists, led by a Colonel Pyles, and cut them to pieces. Another body of tories, about the same time, were destroyed by the rash and sanguinary Tarleton, by whom they were mistaken for "rebels."

These disasters did not come singly, and their accumulation, with other circumstances, began to open the eyes of Cornwallis to his own danger. "He was surrounded," in his own language to the British ministry, "by inveterate enemies and timid friends;" and to fight and conquer Greene, became now as much a matter of necessity as it had before been one of choice. The Americans were gathering strength by daily accessions. The tories were growing cold in a contest which, however successful at first, had been pregnant with defeats and dangers; and the severe lessons which the British had received at King's Mountain and at Cowpens, had taught them to indulge in gloomy anticipations, which needed but the maturing influence of time for fullest confirmation.

Numberless minor events, small combats, and skilful manœuvrings, while they emboldened the Americans and their general, prepared the way for the more important issue which was to follow.

The two main armies, after various marchings and countermarchings, prepared to stake the issue finally on the sword. The scene of action was at Guilford Courthouse. The battle

9. Upon what place did the British general then fall back? 10. To prevent the tories from joining the British army, what movement was made by General Greene? 11. What service was now achieved by Colonels Pickens and Lee? 12. By whom was another body of tories about the same time destroyed?

was fought on the 15th of March, 1781. It was waged with great obstinacy and valor, and the victory remained long in suspense. Discipline, at length, achieved its natural triumph over the irregular force of the Americans.

Half of Greene's force were untried militia; but five hundred of his men had ever seen service. The veteran volunteers, under Pickens, had been despatched some time before to South Carolina, where they were imperatively demanded to meet the black brigades which the British were seeking to embody in that quarter; and the regular troops that remained, consisting of the infantry of the legion, a little corps of Delawares, and the first regiment of Maryland, formed the only portion of the American army that could be compared with the British. These did not exceed two hundred and eighty-one in number; yet, unassisted, they drove from the field, in the first instance, the thirty-third regiment, three hundred and twenty-two strong, supported by the yagers and light-infantry of the guards.

The Virginians behaved with no less valor, though with less experience. They maintained a long and arduous conflict with the whole British line, and only sunk at the push of the bayonet, for which they were neither prepared by practice nor the possession of the proper weapons.

The victory remained with the enemy; but the advantage with the Americans. The former lost six hundred and thirty-three men, killed, wounded, and missing; of these, one colonel and four commissioned officers died on the field; Colonel Webster, and several others, received mortal wounds; General O'Hara's recovery from his wounds was long doubtful; Colonel Tarleton, and General Howard, a volunteer, with twenty other commissioned officers, were wounded.

The victory must have been with the Americans, but for the unmilitary flight, in the beginning of the action, of the North

---

13. When was the battle of Guilford Courthouse fought? 14. Who gained the victory? 15. Of what was Greene's force composed? 16. Whither had the veteran volunteers been despatched?—and for what object? 17. What was the number of regular troops under Greene? 18. What did they accomplish? 19. What did the Virginians? 20. With whom did the advantage remain? 21. What loss was sustained by the British?

Carolina militia, and the second regiment of Marylanders. The loss of the Americans was about four hundred. Greene retired over Reedy fork, about three miles from the scene of action; while Cornwallis remained in possession of the ground, but too much crippled to pursue his enemy.

Three days after his victory, his lordship destroyed all his baggage, left his hospital and wounded, and fled toward the sea-coast, leaving the whole of the country behind him in the possession of the Americans. Greene pursued, but without overtaking the British; while Cornwallis, after a brief delay at Wilmington, hurried on to that junction with the British forces in Virginia, under Major-General Philips, and the traitor Arnold, which resulted in the siege and surrender of Yorktown, one of the most brilliant events in the progress of the war, and which greatly assisted to decide it. But these events must not be anticipated.

While these events were in progress in North Carolina, the whigs in South Carolina were everywhere gathering in arms. The absence of Cornwallis had withdrawn from the state that superior body by which he had held it in subjection. Pickens, with his brigade, was operating between Ninety-Six and Augusta; and Lee, with his legion, and a part of the second Maryland regiment, was advancing to co-operate with Marion.

General Sumter, though not yet fully recovered of his wounds received at Blackstock's, had drawn his men to a head, and had penetrated to the Congaree, which he crossed early in February, and appeared before Fort Granby. Such was the vigor with which he pressed the fort, that his marksmen, mounted upon a temporary structure of rails, had reduced the garrison to the last straits, when they were relieved by the unexpected approach of succor, under Lord Rawdon, who appeared on the opposite bank of the river.

Unable to contend with the superior force of the British, Sumter made a sudden retreat; and, two days after, captured an escort of the British regulars, going from Charlestown to Camden with stores, in wagons, which yielded a booty equally necessary to both parties. Thirteen of the British were slain, and sixty-six made prisoners; the wagons, containing a profusion of provisions, clothing, arms, and ammunition, fell into his hands.

Proceeding with his accustomed rapidity, Sumter swam the Santee river, with three hundred men, and appeared next before Fort Watson.

From this point he was again driven by Rawdon, who marched to its relief. He then retired to the swamps on Black river, where he remained to recruit, though not inactive, for awhile.

Emerging from this retreat, he was attacked, near Camden, by Major Fraser, at the head of a considerable force of regulars and militia; but the major was defeated after a severe handling, in which twenty of his men were slain. Sumter, after this event, retired to the borders of North Carolina, where he contrived to increase his force to three small regiments of state troops. His return, with that of the continental army, renewed the war in South Carolina with more regularity and vigor.

Marion had been as busy in his fastnesses as his great contemporary Sumter; and while Greene and the continentals gave full employment to the regular British army, his little brigade had met the tories in a spirit not unlike their own. Their savage murders, wanton excesses, and bitter cruelties — their house-breaking and house-burning — their blasphemies, impieties, and horrors — had put them completely out of the pale of military civilization. "No quarter to the tories!" became the cry of the brigade, when going into battle; and with this spirit, and guided by the skill and intelligence of their leader, the career of the partisans was as sleepless and rapid as its temper was now unsparing and vindictive. To conquer, merely, was not to complete the purpose for which they fought — to destroy, was their object, also; and so resolute had they shown them-

26. What service was achieved by General Sumter? 27. Driven from Fort Watson by Lord Rawdon, whither did Sumter retreat? 28. Emerging from this retreat, where was he attacked by Major Fraser? 29. Having defeated this officer, whither did Sumter retire? 30. How had Marion, meanwhile, been engaged?

selves, and so active and vigilant, that to root them out was as difficult as it had become desirable.

A new and well concerted attempt to annihilate this body, was arranged between Colonels Watson and Doyle. The former was to move down from Camden along the Santee — the latter was to cross Lynch's creek, and follow its course on the eastern bank. They were to unite their forces near Snow's island, which was the favorite hiding-place of the "brigade."

Marion heard first of the approach of Watson, and went out with his whole force to meet him. At Taucaw swamp, nearly opposite to the mouth of the present Santee canal, he laid an ambush for him, which he placed under command of Colonel Horry. At this time, he had but a few rounds of ammunition for each man. His orders to Horry were, to give two fires and retreat.

A second ambush was placed in a contiguous situation, which promised certain advantages. This was a party of cavalry, under the command of Captain Conyers. Horry's ambuscade gave its fires with great effect, but was compelled to retire. Watson, having made good his passage of the swamp, sent a detachment of cavalry, under Major Harrison, in pursuit of Horry.

This detachment was encountered by Conyers, who slew Harrison with his own hand. His party was dispersed, after suffering severe loss from the charge of Conyers.

Marion, too feeble to assail his opponent openly, continued in this way to embarrass his progress and weaken his force, until they had reached nearly to the lower bridge on Black river, seven miles below King's tree. Here Watson made a feint of taking the road to Georgetown. Too weak to detach a party to the bridge, Marion took an advantageous position on that road.

Suddenly wheeling, Watson changed his course and gained possession of the bridge on the western side. This gave him the opening to a very important pass, leading into the heart of

31. Where was the favorite hiding-place of his "brigade?" 32. Where did he encounter Colonel Watson? 33. In what manner did he harass that officer during his march to Georgetown?

Williamsburgh and to Snow's island. The river, on the west, runs under a high bluff; the grounds, on the east side, are low, and the stream, though generally fordable, was, at that time, swollen by freshets, so as nearly to reach the summit of the opposite shore. This prospect seemed to appal the British colonel. While he hesitated, the less wary partisan led the way for his troop, plunged in, and safely reaching the opposite banks, marched forward to occupy the eastern end of the bridge. Marion detached Major James, with forty musketeers, and thirty riflemen, under M'Cottry, to burn the bridge.

The riflemen were posted to advantage, and under cover, on the river bank. The attempt of the musketeers to burn the bridge, drew upon them the fire of Watson's artillery. Against this Marion had provided, and the artillerists of the enemy were picked off by M'Cottry's rifles as fast as they approached to apply their matches to the gun. The bridge was fired and consumed in the face of the enemy, who, baffled and harassed, turned from the pursuit of the wary partisan, and proceeded by forced marches to Georgetown.

But he was not suffered to leave behind him the foe whom his pursuit had seemed only to awaken. Marion hung upon his progress — now upon his flanks, now in front, and now in the rear — while his rifles exacted heavy toll from the enemy at every mile in their journey. Watson, at last, reached Georgetown in safety; but the implacable riflemen had followed his flying footsteps till the last moment. Never had man been more harassed; and the complaint of Watson, that Marion would not fight like a Christian and a gentleman, has passed, from its ludicrous solemnity, into a proverbial phrase of merriment in the South. Doyle, the coadjutor of Watson, was encountered in like manner, and with similar results. A single conflict drove him back to Camden, with a considerable loss in men, and a greater loss in baggage.

This affair was followed, on the part of the brigade, by a sharp conflict with a body of tories. These were routed, and their

84. What complaint did Watson make?  85. With what success did Colonel Doyle encounter Marion's brigade?  86. By what was this affair followed on the part of the brigade?

captain slain. A nephew of Marion also fell in the conflict. A second descent which Marion made upon Georgetown, about this time, was more successful than the first. It fell into his hands, but was afterward set on fire by an armed party from a British vessel, and upward of forty houses were reduced to ashes.

After the return of General Greene into South Carolina, which followed the flight of Cornwallis into Virginia, Marion ceased to act independently. The exploits of his brigade, no longer acting by itself, became merged in those of the liberating army.

87. What relation of the commander was killed in the conflict? 88. After Marion had succeeded in taking Georgetown from the enemy, what misfortune befel the town? 89. When did Marion cease to act independently?

# CHAPTER IX.

### BATTLE OF HOBKIRK'S HILL.

AT no period had opposition entirely ceased to the British arms in South Carolina. It has been by a singular mistake that this judgment has been given. She was struck down for a few weeks, but never subdued. In the worst hour of her misfortunes, there were still some noble bands of her sons, few in number, but fearless in spirit, that maintained her banner among the swamps and forests; always watchful of the occasion when to sally forth and wreak fearful vengeance on the invaders, in the moment of their greatest seeming security.

To the names of Sumter, Marion, and Pickens, may be added those of Harden, Hammond, Hampton, Huger, Horry, and others, who distinguished themselves from the beginning; and, in the course of the conflict, a new race of youthful warriors sprang up to take the places of those who had been slain, and afford a respite to the labors of others, who had kept the field from the first moment when the British cannon thundered in hostility upon her shores.

It does not fall within the plan of this work to record the smaller events, and assign the due praise to every young hero who acquired just renown in the service of his country. It is enough to say, that Carolina, from the opening of the campaign of 1780, became one vast and bloody battlefield, in which nearly all of her sons contended. Unhappily, they too often contended with one another; and it is with a sentiment of profoundest melancholy that we record the fact, that the direst issues that ever took place within her borders — the severest trials of strength, and the most fearful conflicts — were those in which

1. What names stand most conspicuous among the defenders of South Carolina?
2. What was the condition of the state from the opening of the campaign of 1780?

13*

her own sons were pitted against each other.  The invaders gained their chief victories by the arms of those who, though not always natives, had yet become citizens and the proper champions of the soil.

The flight of Cornwallis into Virginia enabled Greene to direct his undivided attention to the remaining enemy in Carolina, and on the 19th of April, 1781, he sat down with his main army before Camden.

On the 15th of the same month, General Marion, having the legion of Colonel Lee under his command, invested Fort Watson on the Santee.  This was a stockade fort, erected on one of the largest of the many ancient mounds which skirt this river. It was elevated about forty feet from the level of the plain, and far from any eminence which could command it.  Its garrison consisted of about eighty regulars and forty loyalists, commanded by Lieutenant M'Kay of the regular troops.  Unprovided as he was with artillery, it was impregnable to Marion.  Its steep sides and strong palisades discouraged any attempt to storm it.

One of the first efforts made to subdue it was by cutting the garrison off from Scott's lake, by which it was supplied with water.  From this danger M'Kay relieved himself by sinking a well within the stockade.  Thus foiled, and without artillery, the besiegers must finally have been baffled, but for one of those ingenious devices which are perhaps more readily found by a primitive than an educated people.

At a short distance from the fort there grew a small wood, which suggested the proper means of annoyance.  The trees were felled, and the timber borne on the shoulders of the men, was piled crosswise, under cover of the night, within a proper distance of the fort.  This enabled the assailants to command the fort, and with the dawn of day, when the light enabled the riflemen to single out their victims, the garrison found themselves overawed by the American rifles.  A shower of bullets drove them from their defences, and left them no alternative but submission.  The capitulation of the fort soon soon followed; and,

8. By what means did the invaders gain their chief victories ? 4. When did General Greene encamp with his main army before Camden ?  5. By whom was Fort Watson on the Santee invested ?  6. By whom was the fort commanded ?  7. By what means did General Marion force the garrison to capitulate ?

pushing his prisoners before him, Marion, after this success, hurried his force forward to effect a junction with Greene. The advance of Marion brought on the battle of Hobkirk's Hill.

Camden, before which the main army lay, is a beautiful village, situated on a plain covered on the south and east sides by the Wateree, and a creek which empties itself into that river. On the western and northern sides, it was guarded by six strong redoubts. It was garrisoned by Lord Rawdon with about nine hundred choice troops.

Hobkirk's Hill, where Greene took post, was about a mile and a half in advance of the British redoubts. It is a narrow sand-ridge of little elevation, which divides the head springs of two small branches, the one emptying into the Wateree river, the other into Pine-Tree creek.

The American force did not much exceed eight hundred men, and the strong defences of Camden, and his own want of sufficient artillery, were sufficient reasons to keep him from making any attempts upon that place. But this inferiority did not induce any timidity on the part of the American commander. Having made his arrangements and posted his sentinels with singular precaution, Greene neglected no occasion to seduce or provoke his enemy to come out from his defences and give him battle. The fall of Fort Watson, and the approach of the force under Marion to a junction with the main army, had the effect of bringing about Greene's object, and forcing Rawdon into the field.

On the 25th of April, Lord Rawdon, arming his musicians, drummers, and every person within his encampment by whom a weapon could be borne, sallied forth with great spirit to the attack.

It has been said by some writers, that Greene suffered himself to be surprised in this affair; but this is an error. The attack was made on the very quarter in which the American general was most prepared. The pickets behaved with the utmost coolness, gathering in the videttes, and forming with

8. How is Camden situated? 9. By whom was it at this time garrisoned? 10. How is Hobkirk's Hill situated? 11. What prevented General Greene from attacking Camden? 12. When was he attacked by Lord Rawdon?

great deliberation under Colonel Kirkwood's Delaware command. His position formed the American advance, and met the first shock of the enemy's charge.

Here the contest was maintained for a while with singular obstinacy, and this little squad retired slowly, fighting with resolute determination, step by step, as they receded before the accumulating pressure of the foe. Lord Rawdon's line was composed of the 13th regiment on the right, the New York volunteers in the centre, and the American loyalists on the left. The right was supported by Irish troops, and the left by a detachment under Captain Robertson.

The regiment posted with the cavalry was raised in South Carolina; so that on this bloody day, the number of European troops engaged was very small. Most of Rawdon's army were Americans by birth or immigration. Nearly one half of his troops were in reserve; the front which he advanced was comparatively small. He had, besides, taken a lesson from the American leaders, and employed flanking parties of picked loyalist riflemen, who moved abreast of his wing among the trees, and did much towards deciding the issue of the day. The fall of two of the best American officers in the beginning of the fight, was the cause of a most unfortunate disorder which followed among the troops.

The front of Greene's army presented his whole force. Two Virginia regiments, under General Huger, were posted on the right of the road; two Maryland, under Colonel Williams, on the left. The first Virginia, under Lieutenant-Colonel Campbell, was on the right of the whole; the second Maryland, under Lieutenant-Colonel Ford, on the left. The second Virginia, under Lieutenant-Colonel Hawes, and the first Maryland, commanded by Colonel Gunby, formed the centre.

Greene, conjecturing that the enemy knew nothing of his having artillery — which had reached him only a little time before the action — had closed the two centre regiments before it, so that it was completely masked. The effect may well be imagined, when these two regiments, suddenly retiring from the

18. What description of troops composed General Greene's army?

centre, left them free to vomit their showers of grape upon the dense ranks of the enemy preparing for the charge.

The confusion and dismay were conspicuous. The squadrons sank, and wheeled, and fled, beneath the terrible discharge; and nothing more seemed to be necessary than to give the command, to close upon their flanks with the regiments right and left, and cut them off from escape. The order was given. " Let the cavalry make for their rear; Colonel Campbell will wheel upon their left; Colonel Ford upon their right; the whole centre will charge — charge with trailed arms!"

Such were the commands of Greene, which his aids rushed to convey to the several captains. The roll of the drums announced their tenor, and Washington, at the head of his cavalry, disappeared among the trees which lay between his troop and the rear of the enemy.

The American general already believed his victory to be secure; but he had no ordinary adversary in Rawdon. With the quickness of instinct, this commander threw out his supporting columns, and the Americans, but a moment before in the fullest conviction that they had outflanked the enemy, were themselves outflanked. Their wings were enfiladed and their rear threatened.

At this crisis, when everything depended upon the greatest coolness and a composure which might look undaunted upon the scene, the first Maryland regiment, by excellence esteemed, in the language of Roman eulogium, the tenth legion of the American army — that band to which all eyes were turned for example, which had conquered the British with their own weapon, the bayonet, at the noble passage of valor at the Cowpens — which alone had fought half of the battle at Guilford, and obtained more than half of the triumph of that no less bloody day — now, unaccountably, shrunk away from the issue, in a panic which could not be overcome.

Greene, at this moment, was leading on the Virginian regiment of Campbell in person, on the extreme right, when he was called away by the confusion of the centre. Vainly, by voice and gesture, did he seek to restore their confidence, and bring them once more into the action. They heard and halted; but the

day was already lost.  They were already at the bottom of the
hill, and the cheers and clamors of the enemy now commanded
his attention in another quarter.

Urging his horse up the eminence, he saw for the first time
the utmost extent of his misfortune.  But a single regiment
remained entire ; his artillery was uncovered on the summit of
the hill.   To bring his troops off in order, and to save the artillery, were the only remaining objects ; and, amid a shower of
bullets, the American general delivered his commands with
composure, to draw off the right and left regiments and form
them on that of Gunby, which was now rallied; while their
retreat should be covered by the second Virginia.

This order, well executed, left to Greene the choice of deliberate retreat, or a renewal of the battle.   During its execution,
the main efforts of the British were to secure possession of the
artillery.   Horse and foot were ascending the hill, and the
matrosses were about to fly, when the American general applied his own hand to the drag-ropes.

This example was not to be withstood.  A little band rallied
to their rescue, bearing their loaded muskets in one hand while
applying the other to the ropes.  The fight was renewed in this
endeavor.

A British corps appeared on the hill, moving to the charge.
Dropping the ropes, the little troop, forming in the rear of the
artillery, met them with a fire which, repeated with deliberate resolution until escape was impossible, was terribly
destructive.

Thrice was the attempt renewed, and with the same effect.
The assailants were driven off with loss, until an overpowering
force of infantry and riflemen came to their assistance, and every
man of this gallant little band, but forty-five in number, was
either killed or taken.   The artillery now seemed lost ; but at
this crisis, Colonel Washington charged in upon the road, and
put an end to the strife around it.

This gentleman, in addition to the rescue of the artillery,

14. The battle being lost, what were now the only objects of the American commander ?   15. By whom was the artillery rescued ?   16. How many prisoners did he
take ?

captured more than two hundred prisoners. His humanity is alleged by the British to have been detrimental to his objects. A severe military judgment insists that he should have cut down instead of making captives. His prisoners encumbered his movements, and the time lost in taking them might have been of lasting benefit if it had been employed mercilessly upon the British rear.

Rawdon was not in a condition to pursue the Americans far. The latter halted at a distance of two miles to recover stragglers and take refreshment. At noon, the retreat was resumed, and the army finally encamped at Sanders's creek, about four miles from the scene of action, to which place Washington was ordered back to reconnoitre. As he proceeded in obedience to this order, he was told that Rawdon had returned to Camden, leaving Captain Coffin with his cavalry and a body of mounted infantry in charge of the field of battle.

This intelligence suggested to Washington the prospect of a new achievement. Retiring with his cavalry into a thicket on the roadside, he pushed forward a small detachment, with orders to approach under covert until within a short distance of the enemy's position. His stratagem produced the desired effect; Coffin's whole troop pursued and fell into the ambuscade. Washington rose from his hiding-place as they reached it, and the whole party were either cut to pieces or compelled to save themselves by flight. The field of Hobkirk thus actually remained in possession of the Americans.

The loss of the two armies in the main battle was nearly equal; that of the British, by reason of the artillery which the American brought into the field, being somewhat the greater. The event did not discourage the American commander, and its results thickened the difficulties which at this time began to encompass the British.

Very soon after the battle of Hobkirk, Greene detached a reinforcement to Marion on the Nelson's Ferry road, and on the

17. Where did Greene's army finally encamp? 18. Whom did Lord Rawdon leave in charge of the field of battle? 19. How did Colonel Washington dislodge him? 20. Which party suffered the greatest loss in this battle? 21. Soon after the battle of Hobkirk's Hill, what movement was made by General Greene?

third of May crossed the Wateree, and took such positions as would enable him to prevent succors from going into Camden from that quarter.

Rawdon, having received a considerable reinforcement under Watson, again sallied out on the eighth of May to bring the American general, if possible, to a second action. His only hope for the maintenance of the post, was in the defeat and destruction of the army under Greene. The latter was not ignorant of the straits to which his adversary was reduced, and all the efforts of Rawdon to force him into battle proved unavailing.

The British commander, baffled and disappointed, wreaked his vengeance upon the town which he had so long garrisoned, but which he felt himself no longer able to maintain. Camden was reduced to ashes, and amidst the shrieks of its people, and the "curses, not loud, but deep," of the loyalists whom he could no longer protect, Lord Rawdon prepared to descend the country. The fall of Fort Watson had broken the chain of communication with Charlestown, and Marion was even now busy in the leaguer of Fort Motte.

Having devastated the country, it no longer yielded support to Rawdon's troops. These the British commander resolved to save, though by the loss of the post and of the confidence of the tories. These miserable people, whose savage fury had so long hunted their countrymen with fire and sword, no longer protected from their vengeance by the arms of the British, were compelled to abandon their homes, and follow the fortunes of the enemy. They dared not await the justice of the Americans. Hundreds followed his lordship, scorned and despised by their allies and hated by their countrymen. Their history may be dismissed in this place. After sharing all the vicissitudes of an army retiring before a pursuing foe, they reached Charlestown, and built for themselves a settlement of huts without the lines. This hamlet, by a miserable mockery, was called Rawdontown. Here, men, women, and children were crowded together in a wretched condition of poverty and shame. They had dwelt happily on their farms near Camden; and perished in the utmost

22. Unable to force the Americans into battle, what was done by Lord Rawdon?
23. What became of the tories in the neighborhood?

destitution, utterly unnoticed and unassisted by those for whom they had sacrificed the ties of society, and all the first claims of country ; the victims equally of disease and want, they died, to use the emphatic language of that time, like " rotten sheep" upon the suburbs.

24. What was finally the fate of these wretched people ?

# CHAPTER X.

## TO THE SIEGE AND ABANDONMENT OF "NINETY-SIX."

THE breaking up of the British post at Camden, however unavoidable, was one of essential disservice to the British cause. From that moment the numbers of the Americans increased—arms in their hands and indignation in their hearts—following the footsteps of the retreating army, and wreaking vengeance at every turn, for the long suffering and cruel indignities which they had undergone. To Rawdon it seemed as if the fabled teeth of the dragon had been sown around him, so prolific on a sudden was the increase among his foes.

That this measure had become one of imperative necessity to the British commander, is unquestionable. With a strong enemy hanging upon his skirts — a dissatisfied population all around him — Marion and Lee, Sumter and Pickens, busy, with their accustomed promptitude, and operating upon the posts below, which connected him with Charlestown, and secured to him his only route of retreat to the seaboard — he had no alternative but to evacuate a station from which he had so long overawed the country, but which was now no longer tenable. The activity of the partisan bands below him, also, demanded his early succor for the several garrisons which they threatened. His own safety pressingly urged the propriety of his retreat.

Greene simply awaited the arrival of recruits from Virginia, when, it was evident to Rawdon no less than to his opponent, that all his stores and resources must fall into the hands of the Americans.

The hopes of the Carolinians grew doubly active at this period. The old revolutionary spirit, which had distinguished the people at the time of the battle of Fort Moultrie, seemed once

1. What effects followed the breaking up of the British post at Camden?

more to reanimate them. Squads of armed whigs sprang up simultaneously in every quarter of the state. Well mounted, and commanded by popular leaders, they seemed endowed with the attributes of ubiquity, and appeared to the astonished Britons to be everywhere at once. The very names of Marion, Sumter, and Pickens, were productive of momentary panic; and detachments from the troops of the two former generals, availing themselves of the flight of Cornwallis to Virginia, and the approach of Greene, carried their arms to the very gates of Charlestown.

Major Harden, a gentleman of Beaufort, whose name furnished one of the rallying sounds of the revolution, was a chief instrument in the hands of Marion for carrying out the bold and expert achievements which have crowned their names with a local celebrity as honorable as it is vivid and unperishing. With seventy select men, crossing the enemy's lines of communication, Harden ravaged the country, in the face of the foe, from Monk's Corner to the Savannah river. His force gathered as it went forward, and was quickly increased to two hundred men. With a rapidity of movement which baffled pursuit, he combined a readiness and valor which made him successful in every encounter. To entrap him, appeared as impossible as pursuit of him was vain. The Savannah no longer remained a boundary; but, throwing himself across from bank to bank, as circumstances required it, he became a terror to the loyalists of both provinces, extending his ravages from the seaboard to Augusta, and utterly defeating every attempt to accumulate a force against him. This duty achieved, he joined the detachment under General Pickens, who was then operating against Augusta, and Ninety-Six.

The fall of Camden led to the rapid overthrow of the enemy's chain of posts below, and completed the recovery of the state to within thirty miles of the sea. Greene, concluding, after the evacuation of this place by Rawdon, that it would be the enemy's object to withdraw his posts on the Congaree, and concentrate them below the Santee, despatched expresses to

2. What was done by detachments from the troops of Marion and Sumter? 3. Who made himself conspicuous against the invaders in the country from Monk's Corner to the Savannah? 4. What effects followed the fall of Camden?

Marion and Sumter to prepare themselves for such an event. He, himself, ordering the army to proceed by the Camden road for the Congaree, took an escort of cavalry and moved down in person to Fort Motte.

At M'Cord's ferry, he received the tidings of the capitulation of this place. Fort Motte lies above the fork on the south side of the Congaree. The works of the British were built around the mansion-house of the lady whose name it bore, and from which, in their savage recklessness of shame, the British officers had expelled her. It was a noble mansion of considerable value; but not of so much value as to abridge the patriotism of the high-spirited owner. Defended by a strong garrison, under a resolute commander, the fortress promised to baffle for a long time the progress of the besiegers. Under these circumstances, Mrs. Motte, who had been driven for shelter to a neighboring hovel, produced an Indian bow, which, with a quiver of arrows, she presented to the American commander.

" Take these," she said, while presenting them, " and expel the enemy. These will enable you to fire the house."

Her earnest entreaty that this course might be adopted, prevailed with the reluctant Marion. Combustibles were fastened to the arrows, which were shot into the roof of the dwelling; and the patriotic woman rejoiced in the destruction of her property when it secured the conquest of her countrymen. Such, throughout the dreary war of the revolution, was universally the character of the Carolina women. The sons fought; but who shall measure the aid and comfort and influence which the daughters brought to the conflict? This will need a volume to itself.

Driven out from their place of shelter, the garrison at Fort Motte was forced to surrender; and the force under Marion was ready for operation in other quarters. A portion of it, under Colonel Lee, was immediately despatched by Greene, as the van of the army, for the reduction of Fort Granby.

The fall of Fort Motte increased the panic of the British; and, two days after that event, they evacuated their post at Nel-

5. Where is Fort Motte situated? 6. By what means was the garrison forced to capitulate?

son's ferry, blew up the fortifications, and destroyed their stores. Fort Granby, after a brief conflict, was surrendered with all its garrison, consisting of nearly four hundred men. The terms afforded by Colonel Lee were greatly complained of by the Carolinians. These terms gave to the enemy the privilege of carrying off their baggage, in which was included an immense quantity of plunder. The approach of Lord Rawdon, with all his army, is said to have hastened the operations of Lee, and to have led to the liberal concessions which he made to the garrison ; but he has incurred the reproach of hastening the capitulation in order to anticipate the arrival of Sumter and the grand army. The siege had been begun some time before by Sumter, who had left Colonel Taylor, with a strong party, to maintain his position, while he made a sudden descent upon the enemy's post at Orangeburg, in which he was thoroughly successful. Sumter himself conceived that he had suffered injury by the capitulation, in which nothing was gained but the earlier possession of a post which could not have been held many days longer, and must have fallen, without conditions and with all its spoils, into the hands of the Americans. It was with bitter feelings that the whig militia beheld the covered wagons of the enemy — drawn by their own horses, which they knew to be filled with the plunder of their farms and houses — driven away before their eyes.

On the 11th of May, the garrison at Orangeburg, to the number of one hundred, with all their stores and a large supply of provisions, surrendered to Sumter after a spirited assault.

From Granby, Lee was sent to co-operate with Pickens against Augusta ; and, three days after the fall of the former post, his legion was arrayed before the walls of the latter.

Meanwhile, General Greene took up the line of march for Ninety-Six ; and, on the 22d of May, he sat down before that formidable station. The reduction of this place was an object of the greatest interest. The village of Cambridge — or, as it

7. Two days after the fall of Fort Motte, what was done by the British in that quarter ? 8. To whom did Fort Granby capitulate ? 9. What terms did he allow the enemy ? 10. Why did Sumter conceive himself injured by this capitulation ? 11. To whom did the garrison at Orangeburg capitulate ? 12. When did General Greene appear before Ninety-Six ?

was called in that day, the post of Ninety-Six — was at this time the pivot of very extensive operations. To possess it, therefore, was to give the finishing blow to the British strength in the interior of the state. The task of holding Lord Rawdon in check in Charlestown was confided to Sumter and Marion.

In the execution of this duty, they closed in upon him, until he established a line of fortified posts, extending from Georgetown, by Monk's Corner, Dorchester, &c., to Coosawhatchie. The British were frequently harassed by the partisans, who made incursions within this line; but the force of the assailants was not adequate to any serious attack upon any one of them, that of Georgetown alone excepted. This station having been left with a small garrison, and being separated from the rest of the line by swamps and water-courses of such magnitude as to prevent any sudden relief from reaching it, was attacked and carried. The British fled to their galleys, while Marion deliberately moved all the military stores and public property up the Pedee, demolished the fortifications, and returned, without loss, to his position in St. Stephens. The fall of the British forts at Augusta followed this event; and the leading object of General Greene was the prosecution of the siege of Ninety-Six.

This siege was one of the most animated occurrences of the American war. It lasted nearly a month. The place was remarkable on many accounts. It was the scene of the first conflict in the southern, and perhaps, in the revolutionary war. In this place, in the year 1775, began that sanguinary hostility between the whigs and tories, which afterward desolated the beautiful country around it.

A peculiar circumstance invited the hostile parties to this spot. It had been surrounded with a stockade as a defence against the incursions of the Indians, whose settlements were then in its near neighborhood. The stockade still remained.

13. By what name is the village situated at that place now known? 14. What advantage might be expected from the reduction of that post? 15. To whom had been confided the task of keeping Lord Rawdon in check in Charlestown? 16. Where had the British established a line of fortified posts? 17. Which of these posts was attacked by the Americans? 18. With what success? 19. What followed this event? 20. How long did the siege of Ninety-Six last? 21. On what account was this place remarkable?

and was improved and garrisoned by the British soon after they had obtained possession of Charlestown.   It made a chief point in their chain of military posts, and was trebly important as it maintained an open communication with the Indians, kept in check the whig settlements on the west, and covered those of the loyalists on the north, south, and east of it.   It was the most advanced post of the royal army, was a depot of recruits, and contributed to the support of Camden and Augusta, in the overawing influence which they maintained upon the population of the two states of South Carolina and Georgia.

At the time that Greene commenced his siege, the post was under the command of Colonel Cruger, with a garrison of near six hundred men — all native Americans.   Cruger himself was an American loyalist of New York, which state, with that of New Jersey, furnished the great body of his army.   These had enlisted at an early period of the war, and were considered among the best soldiers of the royal army.   The remaining portion of his force were riflemen recruited in the neighborhood — men, desperate from their social position, and marksmen of the first order.   This latter body were conspicuous in the successful defence of the place.

Cruger, on the approach of Greene, lost no time in preparing for his defence.   He soon completed a ditch around his stockade, threw the earth upon it, parapet height, and secured it within by traverses and coverts, to facilitate a safe communication between all his points of defence.   His ditch he farther secured by abbatis, and, at convenient distances within the stockade, erected strong block-houses of notched logs.   Within this post he was in possession of a very respectable battery, of a star shape, with sixteen salient and returning angles, which communicated with the stockade.   This battery was defended by three pieces of artillery, on wheel-carriages, which could be moved readily from one point to another.   On the north of the village extends a valley, through which flows a rivulet that supplied the garrison with water.   The county prison lying near

22. Why was it of peculiar importance to the British?   23. At the time that Greene commenced his siege, by whom was it commanded?   24. How many and of what description were his troops?   25. Who was Colonel Cruger?

was fortified, and commanded the valley on the side next the village. On the opposite side of the valley, and within reach of the fire from the jail, was a strong stockade fort with two block-houses, which covered the communication with the rivulet from that quarter. A covert way led from the town to the rivulet.

Greene, when he beheld the strength of the place, apprehended the failure of his enterprise; but this doubt did not discourage him from his design. He broke ground on the 23d of May, and by the 3d of June had completed his second parallel. The engineer of the American army was the celebrated Polish exile, Kosciusko. He has been reproached with the slowness of his operations. On completing the first parallel, a mine, directed against the star-battery of the enemy, was commenced under cover of a battery erected on his right. The work was pursued by the besiegers, day and night, without intermission. The troops labored alternately in the ditches, some on guard while others toiled, and even sleeping on their arms to repel the sallies of the besieged, which were bold and frequent, and resulted in long and spirited conflicts. The American works steadily advanced, however, in spite of these sallies; but a fierce strife followed every step in their progress, and not a night passed without the loss of lives on both sides.

As soon as the ground-parallel was completed, the garrison was summoned to surrender. The demand was answered with defiance, and the siege was pressed. With time to complete the approaches of the beleaguering army, the fall of the garrison had been certain; but the force of Greene was wretchedly inadequate. His recruits of militia from Virginia had failed to arrive; the Carolina troops were all actively engaged in keeping Rawdon in check below; while Cruger, with timely prudence, had incorporated with his army his negro laborers, and was farther aided from without by a marauding force under William Cunningham, which materially interfered with the supplies, the recruits, and general intelligence of the Americans.

Still the advance of the besiegers was such, that farther re-

26. Was the place strongly fortified? 27. Who acted as engineer in the besieging army?

sistance would soon have been temerity. The Americans had completed their third parallel, and, from wooden towers, the marksmen of the assailing army had succeeded in driving the British artillerists from their guns. To fire the houses of the garrison by means of burning arrows, such as had been employed in the capture of Fort Motte, was next resorted to by the Americans; but Cruger freed himself from this danger by promptly throwing off the roofs of his houses.

The works of the besiegers were so near completion, that a farther defence of the place was limited to four days. Besides the towers before spoken of, one of which was within thirty yards of the enemy's ditch, the besiegers had several batteries of cannon within a hundred and forty yards, one of which so completely commanded the " star " that the garrison were compelled to shelter themselves behind bags of sand, which increased its elevation by three feet. Through these sand-bags, apertures were left for the use of small arms by day, and the withdrawal of the sand-bags, left embrazures for the employment of the cannon by night.

Thus, for ten days, the besiegers and besieged lay watching each other. During this time, not a man could show his head on either side, without incurring the shot of the riflemen. Still the garrison, though greatly suffering from the American fire, maintained its defence with a constancy that reflects the highest honor on its commander. That Cruger must have surrendered, that it would have been a wanton sacrifice of life for him to continue a conflict in such circumstances, was inevitable, but that he had been strengthened in his resolution by advices which had reached him from without.

Rawdon, reinforced by three regiments from Ireland, had broken through the obstructions offered by the partisan forces under Marion, and was advancing by rapid marches to the relief of Ninety-Six.

This important intelligence had been conveyed to Cruger, and invigorated his defence. A woman was the instrument

28. How did the Americans endeavor to fire the houses of the garrison? 29. By what means did Cruger free himself from this danger? 80. How was Cruger animated to continue his resistance? 81. By whom was the intelligence conveyed to him?

employed by the British for encouraging Cruger to protract the siege. Residing in the neighborhood, she had visited the camp of Greene, under some pretence of little moment. The daughter of one tried patriot, and the sister of another, she had been received at the general's table, and permitted the freedom of the encampment. But she had formed a matrimonial connection with a British officer, and the ties of love had proved stronger than those of any other relationship. In the opportunities thus afforded her, she contrived to apprize the garrison that she had a communication from Lord Rawdon. A young loyalist received it from her lips, at a farmhouse in the neighborhood, and, under the fires of the sentinels, dashing successfully and at full speed by the pickets, he was admitted with hurras into the garrison.

This circumstance, and the approach of Rawdon, rendered it necessary to abandon the siege or carry the place by assault. By mid-day, on the morning of the 18th of June, the different detachments of the army were in readiness. On the American left, against the star battery, Lieutenant Duval, with a command of Marylanders, and Lieutenant Selden, with another of Virginians, led the forlorn hope. Close behind them followed a party furnished with hooks at the end of staves, and these were followed by the first Maryland and first Virginia, under Colonel Campbell, prepared for the assault. These were marched, under cover of the approaches, to within a few yards of the enemy's ditch. The posts, rifle towers, and advanced works of the besiegers, were all manned, with orders to clear the parapets of the garrison previous to the advance of the storming party. On the American right, against the stockade fort, Major Rudolph commanded Colonel Lee's forlorn hope, supported by the infantry of the legion, and Captain Kirkwood, with the remains of the Delaware regiment. Duval and Selden were ordered to clear away the abbatis, and occupy the curtain opposite them; then, driving off the enemy from the sides of the angle thus occupied, to open the way for the billmen to pull down the sand-bags. These overthrown, were to assist the party of Campbell in mounting to the assault.

A discharge of cannon, at noon, was the signal for the parties to move. A blaze of artillery and small arms, directed to the point of attack, covered the forlorn hope in its smoke. Under its shade, this gallant band leaped into the ditch, and commenced the work assigned them; but the enemy was prepared for them, and met the assault with valor and determination. Bayonets and pikes bristled above the parapet, and from the loopholes in the sand-bags, poured an incessant stream of fire, which swept the slender ranks of the assailants. The form of the redoubt gave the defenders a complete command of the ditch; and their coolness, and the comparative safety of their cover, enabled them to use it with complete success.

Under the cross-fire from opposite sections of the redoubt, the little band of Americans were mowed down with fearful havoc. Their leaders had both fallen, severely wounded, and two-thirds of their number lay bleeding and in death around them; yet was the strife maintained for near three-quarters of an hour, and the assailants, as if resolved on no other issues than death or victory, only retreated at length, at the express orders of their commander. In this conflict, they obtained possession of the curtain, and, in their retreat, though still under a galling fire from the garrison, they brought off the greater number of their wounded comrades. The attempt, by assault, was shown to be fruitless. Lord Rawdon, with twenty-five hundred fresh troops, appeared, soon after, in the neighborhood, and nothing was left to the American general but retreat. Had a few days of time been allowed to Greene's approaches on Ninety-Six, or had the supplies of militia promised from Virginia reached him, the prize for which he struggled must have been in his possession. Now, baffled, if not beaten, he fell back slowly and sullenly before the pursuit of Rawdon, until the latter, weary of a chase which promised to be hopeless, and, warned by circumstances which called him elsewhere, abandoned equally the pursuit and the country.

His march had served only to extricate Cruger from his immediate difficulty. The proofs were convincing, all around

him, that the day had gone by when a foreign foe could maintain itself among the recovering inhabitants. "Ninety-Six," in
defence of which so much blood had been already shed, was,
therefore, abandoned to the assailants, from whom it had been
so lately rescued; and piteous, indeed, was the misery of the
wretched loyalists, whom this abandonment virtually surrendered to the rage of the long-persecuted patriots. A fearful
day of retribution was at hand, which they did not venture to
await. At a season when their farms were most lovely in the
promise of a plenteous harvest, they were compelled to surrender them and fly.

Vainly did their chiefs expostulate with Rawdon against his
desertion of those who, to serve the cause of their sovereign,
had incurred the enduring hostility of their countrymen. But
the necessity was not less pressing upon the British general
than upon his wretched allies; and, with a last look upon their
homes, a mournful cavalcade of men, women, and children, prepared to abandon the fields of equal beauty and plenty, which
their treachery to their country had richly forfeited, but for
which they were still willing to perish rather than depart.

Sullenly the strong men led the way, while, with eyes that
streamed and still looked backward, the women and children
followed reluctantly, and with souls full of wretchedness and
grief. How bitterly in their ears, at such a moment, must have
sounded the notes of that drum and trumpet which had beguiled
them from the banners of their country to those of its invader?
What a pang to the bosoms of the fathers; what a lesson to
the sons, guiltless of the offence, yet condemned to share in its
penalties. Surely, when the barbarian drum again sounds to
war in Carolina, her children will find themselves all, with one
heart, united under the same banner.

86. What became of the loyalists in that neighborhood?

# CHAPTER XI.

**EXPEDITION TO THE LOW COUNTRY—SUMTER, MARION, ETC.**

THE retreat of the British from Ninety-Six, while it encouraged the whigs in that quarter, induced a very general apprehension that it would enable Lord Rawdon, by the additional force which it afforded him, to re-establish all the posts which he had lately lost to the southward of the Santee. After the flight of Cornwallis to Virginia, the British commanders in South Carolina had contracted their operations almost entirely within that extent of country which is enclosed by the Santee, the Congaree, and the Edisto.

Within these limits, after the late retreat of Greene, Rawdon had resolved to canton his forces, and the most eligible positions were examined with this object. But he soon found that the American general was not disposed to suffer the progress of this intention, without endeavoring to arrest or disturb it; and great was his surprise, accordingly, to hear that Greene, whom he had so lately driven before him, had faced about to give him battle upon the Congaree.

Having divided his force, and given one part of it to Colonel Stewart, who was stationed at Orangeburg, he felt himself unequal to the encounter; and, following the dictates of veteran prudence, he fell back before the approaching Americans, retreating hastily to this latter post, where he was sheltered on one side by the Edisto, and on the other with strong buildings, little inferior to redoubts. In the advance which Greene continued to make upon the retreating foe, an opportunity offered

1. What apprehension was excited by the reinforcement of Lord Rawdon's troops from the post at Ninety-Six? 2. After the flight of Lord Cornwallis into Virginia, to what part of the country did the British confine their operations? 3. What was Lord Rawdon surprised to find? 4. To what post did his lordship retire? 5. How was this post sheltered?

of striking a blow at his cavalry.    Rawdon had with him but a small number of horse ; his chief strength in this description of troops being engaged in distant operations.

Major Eggleston, with a strong body of the American cavalry, throwing himself in advance of the enemy, placed an ambush in reserve, and presented himself with a small number in view of the British.    This drew upon him, as was anticipated, an attack from the whole hostile cavalry.    His flight seduced them to the thicket where the rest of his troop was concealed, and their joint charges completely overwhelmed the foe.    Many were slain, and forty-five men and horse, with several commissioned officers, within a mile of the whole British army, fell into the hands of the Americans.    The flight of Rawdon to Orangeburg, stimulated by this event and the accumulating numbers and audacity of the Americans, was so precipitate, that more than fifty of the British army fell dead on the march, from fatigue, heat, and privation.

Greene encamped within five miles of Orangeburg, and offered battle to his antagonist.    Secure in his stronghold, Rawdon did not venture to sally out ; and the force of the American general was too feeble to justify an attack upon him in his works. Several efforts which he made with his cavalry, to arrest the approach of supplies to the British, having proved abortive, and tidings having reached him of the advance of Cruger with fifteen hundred men to the relief of Rawdon, compelled General Greene to retire from a position which he could not have maintained against his foe after the junction with Cruger.    A day before the junction was effected, he withdrew to the High Hills of Santee, while he meditated other modes for the expulsion of the enemy from the strong position which he had taken on the Edisto.

Having succeeded in driving Rawdon from Camden, by striking at the posts below, it was resolved to pursue a like plan of warfare, to compel the evacuation of Orangeburg.    In obedience to this resolution, Sumter and Marion, with their several

6. By what event was the flight of Lord Rawdon to Orangeburg stimulated ?   7. Where did General Greene encamp against him ?   8. How was he compelled to retire from this position ?   9. To what place did Greene withdraw ?   10. By what means did he resolve to compel the enemy to evacuate Orangeburg ?

commands, consisting chiefly of the state troops, and officered by those most able partisans, the two Hamptons, Taylor, Horry, Maham, Lacy, and others who had maintained the liberties of their country in the swamps, when they were too feeble to hold their ground in the field, were accordingly let loose, in an incursion into the low country, which drove the enemy in all quarters for safety into Charlestown, and, for a time, prostrated the royal power even to the gates of that place. This was the famous raid of the dog-days. It took place in midsummer, when the continentals dared not march.

While the partisans were sweeping down every path that led to the city, Greene, with the main army, pursued the road leading down the south side of the Congaree, and the east side of Cooper river.

Various little successes distinguished the progress of the partisans. Colonel Wade Hampton charged a party of dragoons within five miles of Charlestown, and appearing before the walls of the city, occasioned a degree of alarm in the garrison, which could scarcely have been justified by the appearance of the whole American force. The bells were rung, alarm-guns fired, and the whole force of the city confusedly gathered, and under arms.

In this foray, Hampton captured fifty prisoners, and after exhibiting them to the sentinels on the more advanced redoubts, coolly retired, without suffering interruption or injury. He also burned four vessels, laden with valuable stores for the British army. Lieutenant-Colonel Lee took all the wagons and wagon-horses belonging to a convoy of provisions; traversed Dorchester and the neighborhood, from which the garrison was expelled; and, meeting with Hampton, proceeded to rejoin the main body under Sumter.

Meanwhile, a detachment of Marion's men, under Colonel Maham, passing the head of Cooper river and Wadboo creek, penetrated below to the eastward of Biggin church, to obstruct

11. Who accordingly made incursions into the lower country? 12. What success attended them? 13. What road was meanwhile pursued by Greene? 14. What is related of Colonel Wade Hampton? 15. What was done by Lieutenant-Colonel Lee? 16. By whom was Biggin church garrisoned?

the retreat of the garrison at the church, by destroying the Wadboo bridge.

The church near Biggin bridge was a strong brick building, about a mile from Monk's Corner, where the British had a redoubt. The church covered the bridge, and secured the retreat at that point by way of the Corner. It was strongly garrisoned by Lieutenant-Colonel Coates, with a British force of nearly seven hundred men; and the detachment under Maham did not dare to advance with any confidence while unsupported by the main American force, under Sumter.

On the sixteenth of June, Sumter having collected the greater portion of his detachment, advanced to support Maham in his attempt upon the bridge. Reinforcing his troop with a detachmant under Colonel Peter Horry, the command devolved upon the latter officer, who at once proceeded to the destruction of the bridge. The cavalry of the enemy advanced boldly to defeat his purpose, but were received by the mounted American riflemen, who broke entirely through them, killing some, and taking a number of prisoners.

This defeat drew out the British in such force, that the party engaged in destroying the bridge was compelled to fall back upon the main body. Sumter, believing that the British had marched out to give him battle, retired behind a defile at a little distance in the rear, and prepared to receive the attack in the most advantageous position.

But the British colonel had no such purpose. In proportion as the confidence of the Americans rose in the conflict, that of the invaders invariably fell. The purpose of Coates was simply to wear out the day. With the approach of night, he accumulated the stores of the garrison within the church, and, having set fire to them, moved off on his flight to the eastward by Wadboo and Quinby.

The flames bursting through the roof of the sacred edifice, first informed Sumter of the flight of the enemy. The pursuit was

17. How is the church situated? 18. What was done by Colonel Maham with a detachment of Marion's men? 19. Who commanded the detachment that proceeded to the destruction of the bridge at Wadboo? 20. With the approach of night, what was done by Colonel Coates? 21. How did Sumter discover the flight of the enemy?

immediately commenced ; but, unfortunately, Lieutenant Single-ton, with a piece of artillery, was ordered to remain upon the ground, that he might not delay the movements of the infantry. Lee and Hampton led the pursuit, until, having passed the Wadboo, they discovered that the cavalry of the enemy had separated from the infantry, and had taken the route to the right.

Hampton diverged in this direction, urging his panting horses to the utmost, in the hope to overtake them before they could effect their passage of the river. In this he was unsuccessful, and he returned only to witness the equally fortunate escape of the enemy's infantry, the only remaining object of pursuit.

Marion's cavalry had joined the legion cavalry of Lee, and about a mile to the north of Quinby creek they overtook the rear-guard of the retreating army, consisting of one hundred men. The furious onset of the cavalry deprived them almost of the power of resistance. They threw down their arms with-out firing a gun.

Colonel Coates 'having passed Quinby bridge, had already commenced its demolition, and only awaited the passage of the rear-guard and his baggage to complete its destruction. The planks which covered the bridge were already loosened from their sleepers, and a howitzer, at its opposite extremity, was so placed as to protect the party engaged in throwing them off. As the rear-guard had been overcome without any fight, no alarm-gun had been fired, no express had been sent to apprize the British commander of his danger, and he was almost wholly unprepared for the defence. The panic by which he had lost one important part of his force, had nearly involved the anni-hilation of the remainder.

He happened, however, fortunately for himself, to be at the bridge when the American cavalry came rushing into view. His main body was at this moment partly on the causeway, on the south side of the bridge, and partly pressed into a lane be-

---

22. Did the Americans succeed in overtaking the enemy before they had crossed the river? 23. In what condition did they find Quinby bridge? 24. What had become of the rear-guard? 25. What was the situation of the British at the time the American cavalry approached?

yond it. Thus crowded, they were wholly disabled for immediate action. Coates, nevertheless, coolly prepared himself as
well as he might, to remedy the difficulties of his situation, and
make his resistance as effectual as possible. Orders were despatched to his troops on the advance, to halt, form, and march
up, while the artillerists were called to the howitzer, and the
fatigue party to the renewal of their labors for the destruction
of the bridge.

If the situation of the British was thus perilous, that of the
pursuing Americans for a time became scarcely less so. The
planks sliding into the water, and the open jaws of the howitzer,
ready to send destruction into their crowded ranks, left them
little time for deliberation. Pressing upon each other, a dense
mass upon a narrow causeway, they felt that the withdrawal of
the enemy's fatigue party from the destruction of the bridge
would be the signal for applying the lighted port-fire to the
howitzer. A moment longer, and the iron hail would have
mowed down their columns.

The front section of the American force was led by Captain
Armstrong, of Lee's legion. He saw the danger, and availed
himself of the single moment that was left him. Dashing over
the bridge, he drove the artillerists from the gun. Lieutenant
Carrington followed; the third section advanced, but faltered.
Maham, at the head of Marion's men, feeling the halt, charged
by the legionary cavalry; but the death of his horse arrested
his progress. Captain M'Cauley, who led his front section,
pressed on, passed the bridge, and joined in the fierce melee,
hand to hand, that was going on upon the causeway beyond.

This narrow passage was now crowded, and a conflict, no less
confused than desperate, followed their encounter. Some of the
working party, snatching up their guns, delivered a single fire
and then fled. Two of Lee's dragoons fell dead at the mouth
of the howitzer, and several were badly wounded. Still the
others remained unhurt. Coates, with his officers, covered by
a wagon, opposed them with their swords, while the British

26. What was the condition of the pursuers? 27. Who led the front section of the
American force? 28. What was done by this officer? 29. By what other officers was
he followed? 30. Did their men succeed in crossing the bridge?

infantry hurried forward to find an opening in which they might display.

Lee meanwhile had arrived, and was engaged with Maham and Dr. Irving, his surgeon, in repairing the bridge, so as to enable the rest of his force to cross to the relief of the few brave men who had effected the passage, while yet the planks remained upon the sleepers.

At this moment, Armstrong and M'Cauley discovered themselves to be alone. Their men had failed to cross the bridge while the passage was available, and, of the few by whom they had been followed, but a single soldier remained. Coates and his officers occupied the causeway, protected by a wagon in front, and, until the plank which he had succeeded in casting from the sleepers could be restored, they could hope for no assistance from their countrymen. Had they been promptly followed, the enemy might have been cut in pieces. Now, they beheld nothing but the seeming certainty of their own fate.

The resolution of these brave men, in this predicament, was equally prompt and decided with that which had involved them in it. They knew that they should be safe from the fire of the enemy in front, as long as Coates and his officers were in the rear; and boldly urging their way through the confused bodies still flying along the causeway, they rapidly passed over it, gained the woods, and, wheeling to the left, escaped without hurt, within the shelter of the forest.

Colonel Coates, having succeeded in throwing the plank from the bridge, and thus briefly delaying the advance of the cavalry, retired to the Shubrick plantation adjoining, and took post under cover of its numerous buildings.

At three o'clock, the detachment of Sumter reached the ground. He found the enemy drawn up and ready to receive him. As the American force consisted chiefly of riflemen and cavalry, and very few had bayonets, it would have been madness to advance directly to the attack. The precedent of King's Mountain furnished the partisan with his order of battle.

81. Finding themselves at length alone, how did they escape from their dangerous situation? 82. Whither did Colonel Coates retire? 83. By whom was he here encountered?

His own brigade, led by Colonels Middleton, Polk, Taylor, and Lacy, were ordered to reach and occupy a line of negro houses.

Marion's brigade, at that time, very much reduced, was thrown into two divisions, and ordered to advance on the right of the enemy, having no shelter but fences, and these within short gunshot of the house which the British occupied.

The several parties moved to the attack with alacrity. Sumter's brigade soon gained the negro houses in their front, and from these directed their rifles with great effect. Colonel Thomas Taylor, with a small command of forty-five men, pressed forward to the fences of the enemy's left, from whence he delivered his fire. This drew upon him the British bayonet, which compelled his retreat.

Marion's men, as they beheld this, with the coolness and intrepidity of veterans, rushing through a galling fire, extricated Taylor, and, from the imperfect covering of the fences, continued the fight until not a charge of ammunition remained among them. All who fell in the action were of Marion's command.

The British maintained their defence from within the houses, and from a picketed garden, till the sun was down. The Americans were then drawn off, after a conflict of three hours, in which they lost forty men, killed and wounded. The British loss was seventy killed; their force nearly doubled that of the Americans, and were chiefly composed of Irish troops, but for whose inexperience in the use of firearms, the loss of Marion's men must have been infinitely greater than it was. Sumter was compelled to forego any farther attempts upon his foe, as, at the close of the engagement, there was not a single charge of powder among his men.

The British lost, in the several engagements, apart from the slain and wounded, the numbers of whom could never be accurately known, nearly two hundred prisoners, including nine commissioned officers, a large quantity of valuable stores, wagons, and horses, and — a prize no less rare than valuable in the

84. What colonels were under Sumter's command? 85. What of Marion's brigade? 86. What of Colonel Taylor and his command? 87. How was he extricated? 88. What was the American loss? 89. What the British? 40. What the relative force engaged? 41. Why was Sumter compelled to abandon the attack? 42. What losses did the British meet with in the several engagements?

eyes of the starving Americans — seven hundred and twenty guineas, taken in the paymaster's chest, with the baggage at Quinby bridge.

The expedition of Sumter, though not as successful as it might have been — for Coates's whole force might have been captured — was of the highest service, as it inspired the country with a wholesome confidence in its native valor. The troops actually engaged in the attack on Colonel Coates, were almost exclusively South Carolina militia, and they displayed, with the vivacious audacity of the partisan, the firm, collected resolution of the drilled veteran.

Marion's men amply demonstrated, when they brought off Taylor's division from the British bayonet, under the heaviest fire from their pickets, that nothing was wanting but military constancy, and the weapons of soldiers, to meet the best appointed troops of Europe.

43. What was the effect of Sumter's expedition on the country? 44. What is said of Marion's men?

# CHAPTER XII.

RESTORATION OF CIVIL AUTHORITY — EXECUTION OF HAYNE.

THESE events, while they led to the concentration of the British forces, allowed a breathing spell to the Americans. Greene had retired to the High-hills of Santee, where the condition of his army, two-thirds of the men of which were sick, rendered repose absolutely necessary. But this repose did not imply idleness. To discipline his troops, no less than to restore the sick, was a leading object of the commander. His mind was occupied with the necessity of grappling, on better terms of equality, with the two able British generals with whom he had already tried his strength.

To drive Rawdon to Charlestown, and confine him within the limits of that city, under the control of a respectable force, would enable him to turn his arms against Cornwallis, and detain or, at least, contribute to the detention, of that formidable commander in Virginia. Such was his desire; but the business on his hands proved too various, and his resources too few, for its performance; and, fortunately for the cause of American liberty, Cornwallis found other foes, too numerous for his safety or escape, in the state which he had invaded.

While Greene lay at the Hills, Marion, with his brigade, traversed the Santee with a success and an activity that did not suffer diminution because of the intense heats of August. He was still the same cautious but enterprising, bold, yet vigilant captain — always in motion, and always successful, that he had ever shown himself from the first. His contemporary, Sumter, at the same time, with no less activity, returned to the Ninety-Six district, where the sanguinary war of whig and tory

1. Whither did Greene retire? 2. What was the condition of his command? 3. How was his mind occupied? 4. How was Marion occupied? 5. How Sumter?

had been renewed among the inhabitants, with a ferocity commensurate to the forbearance which they had so long shown of necessity, and to that hatred which was not naturally the consequence of their adverse principles.

With the lawlessness of professed banditti, the several parties ravaged the possessions of their opponents, sparing no plunder and hesitating at no crime. To suppress these parties, overawe discontents, and capture the ringleaders, gave full employment, for some time, to the arms of this active partisan. The wretches thus captured, would have been subjected to vindictive and summary justice, by the arm of martial law, but for the re-establishment of civil power in the state, from which it had been withdrawn during the presence everywhere of the British forces.

The return of Governor Rutledge to the state, and the restoration of the regular authority, together with the arrival of a reinforcement of troops from North Carolina, contributed to strengthen Greene's army, and encourage him in the hope that he should be able to pursue his objects, and press the British downward to their sole stronghold in the city. The only enemy of force before him, was Colonel Stewart, who had been left by Lord Rawdon in command, at Orangeburg. Sumter's incursion into the low country had drawn his lordship with some precipitation down to Charlestown, where he only remained long enough to sully his military honors by numberless acts, equally sanguinary and shameful.

The reverses of the British arms had embittered the temper of their leaders, and they seemed to think that, in deeds of cruelty alone could they lessen the mortification of defeat. One of these deeds, as it has already received the general reprobation of the American world, and as it indicates the temper in which the invaders of Carolina treated and beheld her sons, should receive particular attention. This was the wanton execution, without trial and against law, of a noble Carolinian, taken in arms against the enemy, and hung by the joint com-

6. With what parties had the latter to deal, and what is said of them? 7. What contributed to strengthen and encourage Greene? 8. What enemy was before him? —and where was he in command? 9. What did Lord Rawdon in Charlestown? 10. What deed of the British, and under whom executed, that has received the reprobation of the American world?

mand of Lord Rawdon and Lieutenant-Colonel Balfour, who held the post of commandant of the city.

Colonel Isaac Hayne was a planter of South Carolina, of good nurture and family, and highly esteemed among his countrymen for his amiable manners and unblemished character. During the siege of Charlestown, he commanded a troop of horse, and served his country, at the same time, as a senator in the state legislature. His corps of cavalry, which operated in the rear of the British army, and not within the city, did not share in the general captivity of the citizens in the fall of Charlestown, but was supposed to be included in its terms of capitulation. After that event, opposition, for a brief space, being overawed throughout the state, this little corps, like nearly every other of the same kind, was disbanded, and Hayne returned with his family to the privacy of his plantation.

The British traversed the state, which was, at length, declared to be conquered ; and the complete defeat of Gates at Camden, almost made it so, for a time. A military government had been established over it immediately after the reduction of Charlestown, and successive commandants were appointed for the administration of its affairs, whose powers were left undefined, and were, indeed, dictatorial.

Among these commandants, the most conspicuous was Lieutenant-Colonel Balfour. He was a vain man, proud of his authority, and solicitous of its exercise — a sycophant to the great, and a tyrant to the humble. By the subversion of every trace of the popular government, without any proper civil establishment in its stead, he contrived, with the aid of a few coadjutors, to concentrate in his own person all powers, whether legislative, judicial, or executive, and exercised over the citizens a like authority with that which he possessed over the military. For the slightest offences, and on pretexts the most idle and insufficient, they were imprisoned in places the most loathsome. Some were incarcerated in the vaults beneath the Exchange,

11. Who was Colonel Isaac Hayne ? 12. What troops did he command ? — and in what other way did he serve his country ? 13. What kind of government was exercised over the state at the time ? 14. Who was Colonel Balfour ?

then termed the provost; some were hurried on board the prison-ships, denied to see their friends and families, and deprived not only of their accustomed comforts, but of those necessaries which health and decency equally demanded.

The fortune of war had thrown nearly five thousand of the Carolina troops into the hands of the British, and these were made to endure all the evils and hardships which it was in the power of vain insolence, malignant hostility, blind prejudice, or the accustomed arrogance of British officers toward their colonial dependents, or captives, to display. Under a policy no less short-sighted than inhuman, which so generally marked the proceedings of the British commanders in America, they determined to break the spirit of the people to the will of their sovereign, and enforce, at the point of the sword, submission to their exactions.

Instead of seeking, by measures of judicious indulgence, to beguile the Carolinians from those principles which had produced their disaffection to the royal authority — a course which might have had the desired effect, when we regard the closer sympathies which had distinguished the Americans of the southern colonies, and particularly South Carolina, with the mother-country, and the absence of any of those rival interests which lay at the foundation of the quarrel between England and the northern colonies — the unwise representatives of British dominion in Carolina, clothed in a little brief authority, to which their conduct proves them to have been unaccustomed, exasperated the people by their insolence, and provoked them to desperation by their unnecessary annoyances and injuries. Considering the whole state as subdued and freed from the wholesome fear of retribution, which might have induced them to pause in their progress of injustice, they, soon after the reduction of Charlestown, began to act toward the inhabitants as rebels out of the pale of all indulgence, and only to be brought back to their duty by the scourge and sabre. Nor did they content themselves with administering to the supposed offenders the penalties of treason with their own hands. The bloody conflicts between the

15. What course did he pursue toward the inhabitants and prisoners? 16. What error did the British officers commit?

whigs and tories, which had begun in 1775, were renewed ; and, under British sanction and encouragement, the monstrous cruelties and crimes which distinguished that fratricidal warfare from 1775 to 1780, had become faint impressions to those which followed that period.

No language can do justice to, and visit with proper execration, the doings of that dismal civil war, which desolated the fair fields of Carolina, and deluged her dwellings with the tears and blood of her children. The ties of nature, of society, of neighborhood, were torn apart and trampled. Friendships and fellowships were sundered with the sword. Father and son stood with confronting weapons in opposite ranks, and brothers grappled in the gladiatorial embrace of the savage, goaded to constant strife by the shouts and rewards of the British conqueror. Under their favoring countenance, people of the worst character emerged from their hiding-places in the swamp; men of all sorts of crimes; thieves and murderers; blood-painted and gallows-branded wretches, who needed but the halloo of the savage huntsman to spring upon the track of the unhappy fugitive. Hundreds of refugees from Florida hounded at their heels. These drove the patriots from their hiding-places and country, ravaged their possessions, burnt their dwellings, abused their women, slew their children, and converted the sweetest homes of happiness into places of sorrow or the most savage solitude. In the single district of Ninety-Six, there were no less than fourteen hundred widows and orphans made by this savage warfare.

There was but one mode left for safety to those unhappy Carolinians, who, still devoted to their country's liberties, were yet liable to be torn and tortured through the bosom of their exposed and suffering families. This was to accept of the protection of British power against the aggravated excesses of their own infatuated countrymen. This protection was granted only to those who claimed it as British subjects.

To this wretched necessity, Colonel Hayne was soon reduced. A mean artifice of a British officer seduced him from his plan-

17. What is said of the effects of that civil war ?  18. What mode was left for safety to the patriots ?  19. Who, among others, was reduced to this necessity ?

tation to the city, where he was closely imprisoned, and obtained his release from this duress, at the call of a dying wife and children, only by subscribing a declaration to the British crown. This he did, though not without expressly excepting to that clause which required him with his arms to support the royal government. His exception was replied to in language which might have soothed most minds, though, perhaps, it should not, strictly speaking, have satisfied any. He was verbally assured that such services would never be required at his hands.

"When the regular forces of his majesty," were the words of the British officers, "need the aid of the inhabitants for the defence of the province, it will be high time for them to leave it." But they required this aid much sooner than they imagined.

The approach of Greene with his continentals — the sudden uprising, almost at the same moment, of Marion, Sumter, Hampton, Davie, Harden, and a hundred other fearless partisans — their strange successes — their rapid movements, whether in assault or retreat — the partial defeat of Cornwallis — his flight to Virginia, and those crowding necessities which drove his successor, Lord Rawdon, from Camden to the seaboard — exasperated the passions of the British as much as they alarmed their fears.

Hayne, having made his peace with the British government on the only terms which they would admit, had scarcely returned to his plantation, where he received the last breath of a dying wife, and buried a second of his children, when he was peremptorily required to join the British standard.

His resolution was that of the patriot. Forced to draw the sword, he drew it in behalf of his country. He repaired to the American camp, recruited his troop, and commenced a career which was destined to be as short as it was spirited. By a sudden dash, which he made upon the quarter-house, an outpost of the enemy in the immediate neighborhood of Charlestown, he succeeded in making General Williamson a prisoner.

20. How was he seduced from his plantation? — and how was he released? 21. To what clause did he except in the declaration of allegiance? 22. How was he replied to? 23. What were the words of the British officers? 24. What were the events which exasperated and alarmed the British? 25. What farther of Colonel Hayne? 26. Whom did he make prisoner?

This man was a traitor to the state, and his life was forfeited to the gallows. To rescue him from this probable fate, the British commandant in Charlestown ordered out his whole cavalry, which succeeded in overtaking the party of Hayne, dispersed it, and rescued Williamson. Colonel Hayne, unfortunately, fell also into their hands.

He was carried to Charlestown, and kept in close custody until Rawdon, leaving Stewart at Orangeburg, arrived in the city. He was then brought before a court of inquiry. The members of the court upon this examination were not sworn, nor were the witnesses; yet, in consequence of this examination, "Lord Rawdon and the commandant, Lieutenant-Colonel Nesbitt Balfour, resolved upon his execution, for having been found under arms, and employed in raising a regiment to oppose the British government, though he had become a subject, and accepted the protection of that government after the reduction of Charlestown."

Such were the terms and reasons for this sentence, which was ordered to be carried into effect two days after. This sudden, unlooked for, and unjust sentence, was equally unexpected by the prisoner himself and by the citizens. It was not supposed that a mere court of inquiry could be resolved into one of final trial and condemnation. The men of the city pleaded in his behalf, the women petitioned in person, and implored on bended knees for remission of the sentence; but Rawdon and Balfour were inexorable.

The hurts of vanity, the disappointments of ambition, the defeat of all their plans of conquest, and the constant advance and frequent successes of the victorious Americans, made them vindictive and merciless. Perhaps, too — though this is not suffered to appear in the proceedings — Hayne was only a chosen sacrifice to the manes of Major André. Balfour endorsed one of the petitions, offered in behalf of Hayne, with the two words; "Major André." The unhappy man was less moved than his fellow-citizens and friends. He saw and conversed with them

27. What of Williamson? 28. How was Williamson rescued? 29. Who was taken prisoner? 30. What sort of trial had Colonel Hayne? 31. Who resolved upon his execution? 32. When was it ordered to take place? 33. Who pleaded in his behalf?

with Christian cheerfulness, and the resolute bearing of the soldier.    To a friend, the evening before his death, he declared himself to be " no more alarmed at the thoughts of death than at any other occurrence which was necessary and unavoidable." He requested the existing authorities to accommodate the mode of his execution to a soldier's feelings ; but this was denied him.

The proceedings in his case were obviously parallel to those of André.    Attended by thousands of spectators, gloomy and sad as by an impending calamity to themselves, he walked to the place of doom.    His carriage was firm, manly, and unostentatious.    To his eldest son, a boy about thirteen years of age, on the morning of the fatal day, he delivered all the papers which were connected with his fate, and gave his final instructions as to the disposition of his remains.    Ascending the fatal eminence of death, he parted from his friends with the simple assurance that he would endeavor to show them "how an American should die ;" and, with that unshaken resolution which had distinguished his deportment throughout the painful scene, he himself gave the signal which hurried him into eternity.    He died in a manner becoming the martyr to his country's freedom.    His heroism in death, extorted from his enemies the confession that " if he did not die in a good cause, he must, at least, have acted from a persuasion of its being so."

The execution of such a man as Colonel Hayne, under such circumstances, and with so little show of justice, was not an event to escape the consideration of the American general, or to pass from the memories of the Carolinians.    Unsatisfied by the explanations that were offered by the British commander, Greene declared his purpose of retaliation on all such British officers as should fall into his hands — a declaration which was induced by the voluntary self-devotion of all the officers of the southern army.    These brave men met together and addressed to him a memorial, in which, after declaring what had reached their ears of the enormous cruelties practised by the British, and of the bloody execution which has just been recorded, they recommend measures of immediate retaliation by a similar treatment

84. Describe the execution.   85. What did Greene declare to be his purpose ? — and why ?   86. How was this declaration induced ?

of all British subjects — avowing their perfect readiness to abide by a recommendation which, in the event of capture, at once placed themselves entirely without the pale of mercy from the enemy.

" But," concludes this noble document, " we had rather commit ourselves to the most desperate situations than prosecute this just and necessary war upon terms so dishonorable."

Fortunately for the cause of humanity, but a little time elapsed after this when the policy of the war rendered unnecessary the adoption of such rigorous measures. Still the American general wore the countenance of one who was inflexible in his determination. A very few days after the execution of Hayne, Marion's cavalry captured three British officers with an enemy's party ; and the affair of the Eutaw, which will be recorded in the next chapter, placed in the hands of Greene a prisoner sufficiently distinguished to awaken all the apprehensions of Balfour for his safety.

87. With what words did the memorial of the officers conclude?

# CHAPTER XIII.

### BATTLE OF EUTAW.

COLONEL STEWART, whom Lord Rawden had left in charge of the British army, had been watched by the American general with intense anxiety. In command of nearly three thousand troops, he was too strong to apprehend any assault from a force so poorly provided, and so feeble in most respects, as that of the Americans; and, but for discontents among his men, and the great fatigue to which his new Irish regiments had been subjected before reaching him, he would have been in good condition to turn upon the steps of Greene.

Some weeks elapsed, however, before Stewart was ready for a movement of any kind, and during this time the American general was held in suspense as to his future objects. Not doubting, however, that the necessity of providing for his army would carry his adversary to the banks either of the Congaree or Santee, measures were taken for the removal of all the provisions upon the northern side of both these rivers. This measure was chiefly executed by the brigade of Marion. This proceeding necessarily increased the resources of the American, while diminishing those of the British army.

When Stewart moved, he took post amidst the hills near the confluence of the Wateree and Congaree. Here the two armies lay in sight of each other's fires; but the heat of the weather precluded operations of any kind, and, as if by mutual consent, their swords remained undrawn in their scabbards for a season. The intervention of two large rivers secured them equally from

1. Who had been left by Lord Rawdon in command of the British army? 2. What was the number of Colonel Stewart's troops? 3. What prevented him from immediately attacking General Greene? 4. What measures were taken by the Americans for diminishing the resources of the enemy? 5. When Colonel Stewart moved, where did he take post?

sudden attack, and their labors were confined to the watching of each other's movements, to the capturing of convoys, and the conquest of detachments and foraging parties.    In this service, the Americans soon proved their superior activity.

Greene, speaking of his cavalry in these expeditions, asserts them to be unexcelled by any in the world.    Washington was detached down the country, across the Santee, and soon made himself felt in the capture of two bodies of the enemy's horse. Lee, crossing the Congaree with his cavalry, penetrated between the main body of the British army and the post at Orangeburg, and, in sight of the latter place, drove in, dispersed, and captured several of their detachments.    No inequality of numbers seems, at this time, to have impaired the confidence of our partisans in themselves, or lessened their courage ; and such was their audacity, that the enemy was compelled to send out large detachments from his main body for the protection of his convoys. For every wagon load of provisions, he paid the price in blood.

Equally active with these officers were Marion, Maham, and Harden, in covering the country below.    The embarrassments produced by these united operations, the great difficulty of procuring provisions, and the necessity of lessening his main army, to strengthen his posts below, in order to cover his communications between Orangeburg and Charlestown, rendered the position of the British commander particularly uncomfortable.

A movement of Greene, and the concentration of most of the detachments of the Americans, at a general rendezvous, determined the movements of Colonel Stewart.    Falling back upon his reinforcements and convoys, he took post, forty miles from his late position, at the Eutaw springs.

He was followed by Colonel Lee, who was pushed forward to watch his movements, while General Pickens, with the state militia, advanced with a similar object, in the neighborhood of

6. In what service were the American cavalry unrivalled ?   7. What was done by Colonel Washington ?   8. What was achieved by Colonel Lee ?   9. What other officers were equally active in covering the country below ?    10. How was the position of the British commander rendered particularly uncomfortable ?   11. What circumstance determined his movements ?   12. Where did Colonel Stewart take post, and by whom was he followed ?

the enemy's post at Orangeburg. The main army of the Americans, meanwhile, crossed the Congaree, moving slowly down the south bank, toward the post at Motte's, where Greene, having resolved upon a discontinuance of the pursuit, determined to await the progress of events.

This resolution, as it seemed to indicate a want of confidence in the American commander, encouraged the British. Halting upon his ground at Eutaw, Stewart prepared to meet and fight his enemy. Withdrawing the garrison from Orangeburg (which he established at Fairlawn), he called in to his aid that which had been maintained at the latter post as a foil to Marion. This movement he was enabled to make in consequence of the disappearance of the "Swamp Fox," who, in one of his secret expeditions, had rapidly crossed the country to Pon Pon, where Colonel Harden was closely pressed by a British force of five hundred men.

To pass through both lines of the British communication with Charlestown; to surprise, defeat, and disperse this force, under Major Fraser, numerically superior to his own; to return by the same route, pass the Santee, put his prisoners in safety, then advance upon the Eutaw, in order to a closer co-operation with the army under Greene; was but the work of a few days and of ordinary labor, with this able warrior. The junction of Marion with Greene, preceded by a brief interval of time the advance of the American commander upon the foe.

The memorable battle of Eutaw Springs was fought on the eighth of September, 1781. The number of the Americans, rank and file, was about two thousand. That of the British was something more than two thousand three hundred. The day was fair, and intensely hot; but the battle opened in a wood, the shade of which afforded some relief to the combatants.

At four o'clock in the morning, the American army moved in four columns from its bivouac. The state troops of South Carolina, with Lee's legion, formed the advance, under com-

13. What movement was made by the main body of the Americans? 14. What was done in the meantime by Marion? 15. When was fought the memorable battle of Eutaw Springs? 16. What was the number of the Americans? 17. What number of men had the British? 18. Where and when did the battle commence? 19. What troops formed the advance of the Americans?

mand of Colonel Henderson. The militia of South and North Carolina, under Marion, followed next. Then came the regulars, under General Sumner. The rear was closed by Washington's cavalry, and Kirkwood's Delawares, under Colonel Washington.

So completely had the detached parties of the Americans cut off those of the British, that the advance of their army was unsuspected. The only patrol had been captured during the night; and so entirely secure did Stewart esteem himself in his position, that an unarmed party of an hundred men had been sent out to gather sweet potatoes.

Two deserters from Greene's army conveyed to the British commander the first intelligence of the approach of the Americans, and Captain Coffin, at the head of his cavalry, was sent out, as well to recall the potato " rooting party," as to reconnoitre the Americans and cover the party. The American advance, when encountered, was immediately charged by Coffin, with a confidence which showed his ignorance of its strength, and of the greater force of which it was the precursor. He was repulsed; the firing alarmed the potato-diggers, who all fell into the hands of the Americans.

In the meantime, Stewart pushed forward a detachment of infantry, to keep the Americans employed while he prepared for battle. But Greene, persuaded by the audacity of Coffin that the whole British force was at hand, proceeded to form where the encounter took place.

The column of militia, when displayed, formed the first line; the South Carolinians in equal divisions on the right and left, and the North Carolinians in the centre. Marion commanded the right, Pickens the left, and Colonel Malmedy the centre.

Henderson, with the state troops, including Sumter's brigade, covered the left of this line, and Lee, with his legion, the right. The column of regulars also displayed in one line. The North

20. Which followed next? 21. What officer commanded the regulars? 22. How was the rear closed? 23. How were the British prevented from gaining information of their approach? 24. What party first fell into the hands of the Americans? 25. When the battle was formed, what officers commanded the militia of North and South Carolina? 26. How was the left of this line covered? 27. How the right? 28. By what officers were the regulars commanded?

Carolinians, under General Sumner, occupied the right; the Marylanders, under Colonel Williams, the left; the Virginians, the centre, under Colonel Campbell. The artillery, consisting of four pieces, was equally distributed with the two lines. Washington's cavalry, under cover of the woods, formed the reserve. In this order the Americans advanced to the battle.

When the first line reached the advances parties of the British, it was ordered to move on in order, driving them before it. In this manner, firing as it advanced, it went resolutely forward, while the enemy sunk back and found shelter in their own line.

About two hundred rods west of the Eutaw springs, the British army was drawn up in a single line, extending from the Eutaw creek beyond the main Congaree road. The creek covered their right; the left was supported by Coffin's cavalry and detachment of infantry, held in reserve under cover of the wood. The ground on which the British army was displayed was altogether in wood; but, at a small distance in their rear was a cleared field, extending west, south, and east from the dwelling-house, and bounded north by the creek flowing from the springs.

This creek is a bold one, having a high bank, thickly bordered with brush and undergrowth. From the house to this bank ran a garden inclosed with palisadoes, and the windows of the house, which was two stories high, with garret rooms, commanded the whole surrounding fields. The house was strongly built of brick, and surrounded with various offices of wood, one of which, a barn of some size, lay to the southeast, a small distance from the principal building.

The Americans approached from the west. Their large superiority in cavalry made the house a point of great importance to the British commander, who gave orders to Major Sheridan to occupy it at the first symptom of defeat, and to cover the army from the upper windows.

29. What artillery had the Americans? 30. What officer commanded the cavalry in reserve? 31. Where was the British army drawn up? 82. How were they protected? 33. What was in their rear? 34. How was the garden situated? 85. Describe the house? 86. What orders were given respecting it by the British commander?

On the right he had made a like cautious provision.   Major Marjoribanks was posted in the thicket bordering the creek, with three hundred picked troops, to watch the flank of the Americans, should it be opened at any time to attack.   The British artillery was posted in the main road.

The disappearance of the skirmishing parties from the main opposing bodies, was the signal for a desperate and steady conflict.   The militia of the first American line rushed with shouts into the hottest of the enemy's fire, even after their artillery had been demolished.   Their valor and unflinching perseverance amidst the continual falling of their comrades around them, was the admiration of both armies.   They did not falter until it was impossible for human courage longer to continue a conflict which human wisdom could no longer approve.   They had fired seventeen rounds before they hesitated, and were then succored by the North Carolinians, under General Sumner.

With the appearance of Sumner's relief, Colonel Stewart brought up the infantry of his reserve into line on his left, and the struggle between these fresh troops began with renewed fury.   At length Sumner's brigade, after sustaining the conflict with numbers far superior to their own, fell back also.

Elated at this result, and conceiving the victory to be now sure, the British rushed forward in pursuit, and their line became deranged in consequence.

At this important crisis, the American commander issued his orders to Colonel Williams, who remained in command of the second line, to advance and sweep the field with his bayonets. This order was promptly obeyed; the two brigades received it with a shout, and advanced with a degree of impatience which scarcely heeded the deliberate and measured guidance of their officers.   When within forty yards of the enemy, the Virginians of the line delivered a destructive fire, and the whole body, with trailed arms, rushed forward to the charge, through showers of

---

87. What provision had he made on the right?   88. How was the British artillery posted?   89. What was the signal for a desperate conflict?   40. What is said of the militia of the first American line?   41. What did Sumner's brigade?   42. With what effect on the enemy?   43. What order was given by the American commander, at this crisis?

grape from the British artillery, and seemingly unmoved by the stream of fire that blazed incessantly before them.

The advanced left of the enemy recoiled beneath the desperate resolution of this charge. Their disorder became visible, and was confirmed by the prompt movement of Colonel Lee. Wheeling the legion infantry round from its position on the extreme right, he poured in upon the British left a close enfilading fire, and their confusion became irretrievable.

The centre and right of the British army still remained much more numerous than the American, and awaited the threatened charge with a constancy that seemed unshaken. But the disorder and flight of the left had its effect upon the other divisions of the army ; and the pressure of the fugitives from the left upon the centre, imparted a portion of their panic to the rest of their companions. The advance of the Marylanders, at this lucky moment, helped to increase the confusion of the foe. The former delivered their fire with deliberation and fatal effect, and along their whole front the enemy yielded.

Completely triumphant, as they now supposed themselves, the Americans pressed forward to prevent the British from rallying, and to cut them off from the brick house, to which the fugitives naturally turned their eyes. Successful in this, the victory would have been complete. The great loss which the enemy had sustained must have compelled his surrender, unless he could secure this shelter, which was now his object. It was in striving to defeat this object that the Americans sustained their greatest loss ; and the affair which so far had promised a glorious victory, ended in the complete disappointment of the conquering army, and the temporary defeat of its proudest hopes.

At this stage of the battle, Marjoribanks still stood firm in the thickets which covered him. General Greene saw that he must be dislodged from a position which would soon enable him

44. How was this order executed? 45. What was the effect on the British? 46. What confirmed their disorder? 47. Which part of the enemy's line first gave way? 48. What effect was produced by their disorder and flight upon the other divisions of the army? 49. What was the effect of the advance of the Marylanders? 50. Believing themselves to be now completely triumphant, to what did the Americans direct their efforts? 51. Could they have attained this object, what must the British have been compelled to do? 52. How did the Americans meet with their greatest loss ?

to renew the fight with disadvantage to the Americans. Colonel Washington, with his cavalry, was despatched to this duty; but, on attempting a charge, he found that he could not penetrate the thicket with his horse. An attempt to gain the enemy's rear, brought upon him a destructive fire, which slew many of his men and horses, and drove the rest in confusion.

He was succeeded by Colonel Hampton; and Kirkwood's infantry, with their bayonets, rushing, at the same time, to revenge their companions, succeeded in expelling the British from this strong position. But Marjoribanks retired slowly, still holding on to the thickets, and making for a new position, of nearly equal strength, behind the palisadoes of the garden.

Here the British army had partly rallied, though nothing could well exceed the alarm in their encampment. Everything was given up for lost. The commissaries destroyed their stores; the numerous retainers of the army, mostly loyalists and deserters, who dreaded falling into the hands of the Americans, seizing the horses wherever they might be found, fled in terror, carrying consternation where they went, even down to the gates of Charlestown.

Their alarm might not have been groundless, had it not been for the misfortunes of the Americans, in the losses of Washington's cavalry, and the rash pursuit, by the infantry, of the disordered British. So severely had Washington's command suffered in the affair with Marjoribanks, that but two of his officers could return into the action. The colonel, himself, had his horse shot under him, and owed his life to the clemency of a British officer.

By the time that Marjoribanks had gained the palisadoes, Sheridan had thrown himself into the house, and some of the routed companies from the British left, had made good their retreat into the picketed garden, from the intervals of which they could fire with security and effect.

53. On what duty was Colonel Washington despatched? 54. With what success did he attempt this? 55. Who succeeded in expelling the British from their strong position? 56. Whither did Marjoribanks retire? 57. What is said of the alarm, at this time, in the British encampment? 58. What was now the state of Washington's command? 59. By the time that Marjoribanks had gained the palisadoes, what had been done by Major Sheridan, and by some of the routed companies?

The whole British line was now in full flight before the American bayonet. Their retreat lay directly through their own encampment, where their tents were all standing, and a thousand objects scattered around in grateful profusion, which, to the famished troops of Greene, were too tempting to be withstood.

Fatigued, and almost naked, panting with heat, and suffering from thirst — at the same time believing their victory to be secure — the pursuing Americans fell into acts of insubordination, to which the fire of the British from the contiguous houses eminently contributed. The shelter of the tents, from this fire, became an excuse, of which these brave men did not scruple to avail themselves. And here happened one of those miserable reverses which so often baffle equally the calculations of wisdom and the deeds of valor. Here the American line got into irretrievable confusion. Its officers, nearly abandoned by their soldiers, became conspicuous marks for the British party, who now poured their fire from the windows of the house. In vain did they seek to rescue their men from the baneful consequences which had followed their entrance into the encampment. They had dispersed without order among the tents, had fastened upon the intoxicating liquors, and had now become utterly unmanageable.

The British officers availed themselves promptly of this miserable condition of things. Marjoribanks and Coffin made simultaneous movements; the one, from his thicket, on the left; the other, from the wood, on the right of the American line. Greene soon saw the dangers which threatened him, and issued orders to Lee, of the legion, to fall upon Coffin. In the absence of Lee, who had probably disappeared in pursuit of fugitives, Major Eggleston, with a detachment of the legion cavalry, proceeded to obey, but was repulsed by Coffin, who immediately after hastened to charge the rear of the Americans, now dispersed among the tents.

Here, however, he encountered Hampton, and, by him, was successfully charged and beaten in turn. A sharp fight resulted

60. In what direction did the British line retreat? 61. How did their pursuers fall into confusion? 62. What excuse can be made for their insubordination? 63. What advantage was taken by the British of this state of things? 64. What officers opposed this movement?

in Coffin's retiring from the conflict.    A moment after, the command of Hampton was almost annihilated by a fire from the picketed garden, where Marjoribanks had concealed himself. This skilful officer, to whom the British army chiefly owed its safety, having scattered the cavalry of Hampton, proceeded to the performance of another movement, which was decisive of the strife.

The British artillery, which had been captured by the Americans, had been brought up and opened upon the brick house, where the enemy were strongly sheltered.    Unfortunately, in the hurry of the fight, the pieces had been brought too near the house, and were commanded by its fire, which very soon killed or disabled all the artillerists.    Marjoribanks, as soon as he had scattered the cavalry of Hampton, sallied into the field, re-captured the pieces, and hurried them under cover.    Then, being reinforced by parties from the house and garden, he charged the Americans, scattered among the tents, and drove them before him.    They found safety only in the cover of the wood, where the army of Greene had rallied; and the British, too much crippled to venture into conflict beyond the shelter of the houses, slowly fell back upon their position.

Thus ended the severe battle of the Eutaw, in which both parties claimed the honors of the victor.    There is no difficulty in settling the question between them.    The British were driven from the field of battle at the edge of the bayonet, and took refuge in a fortress.    So closely had they been pressed, and so narrow was their escape, that a forward party of the Americans were only prevented from entering with them by a precipitate closing of the doors in the face of some of their own officers and men, who were taken prisoners in consequence, and interposed by the captors as shields for the protection of their persons, while retreating under the mouths of the musketry which lined its windows.

The Americans were simply repulsed from a fortress to

65. To whom was the British army chiefly indebted for its safety, on this memorable day ?  66. What was, at this time, the situation of the British artillery ?   67. What was achieved by Marjoribanks ?  68. Where did General Greene's army rally ? 69. Why were they not pursued by the enemy ?   70. Which party claimed the victory in the battle of the Eutaw ?  71. Did the British remain masters of the field of battle ?

which they had driven their enemy in fear and with great slaughter. That the Americans should have completed their victory by taking the house, is undeniable. This must have been the case, had they not yielded to the temptation presented to their wistful eyes by the unknown luxuries of a British encampment. The spoils of the enemy proved more fatal to their virtue and, in consequence, to their victory, than his weapons had done to their lives. The reproach of losing a victory within their grasp, is greater than if they had suffered defeat. The last may be due to fortune, to unequal strength, to a thousand influences beyond the courage, the conduct, or the skill of man. The first can only arise from his wilfulness, his vices, or his misconduct.

That the Americans fought well, and conquered while they fought, is undeniable; that they did not complete their conquest, is a reproach, painfully increased in its severity, by the reflection that their failure was followed by an unhappy loss of valuable lives, which, otherwise, might have united in the shout of triumph with the survivors. Among these victims was the gallant Colonel Campbell, who fell a moment before the final charge of the Americans which drove the British from the field at the point of the bayonet. The shouts of victory revived him in his dying moments. He demanded the cause of the shouting, and being told that the enemy was in full flight and utterly routed, exclaimed, with the holy satisfaction of the patriot soldier, "I die contented." These were his last words.

The battle of Eutaw is one over which hangs much confusion and doubt. The results are undoubtedly what we have given The details are subjects of considerable question. The partisans of the South were especially dissatisfied with the reports of the affair. That they did their duty well is undeniable. They make, however, an unfavorable report of the performances of other parties of whom the official report speaks favorably. It is very certain that, in the management of the conflict, there were many mistakes, if not much bungling.

72. What prevented the Americans from taking the house? 73. What is a just subject of reproach against them? 74. What American officer fell during the shouts of victory? 75. Being told that the enemy were in full flight, and utterly routed, what did he exclaim? 76. What is said of the battle of Eutaw?

# CHAPTER XIV.

MARION, PICKENS, MAHAM, SUMTER, CUNNINGHAM — THE
"BLOODY SCOUT" — THE MOUNTAINEERS — DORCHESTER
— PROGRESS OF THE AMERICANS.

IN this severe engagement, the Americans made five hundred
prisoners; and, if farther proof were needed to establish their
claim to victory, it was found in the events of the succeeding
day. Colonel Stewart, leaving his dead unburied, and seventy
of his wounded to the humanity of Greene, breaking the stocks
of one thousand stand of arms, and destroying his stores, abandoned his position, and retreated with precipitation before his
enemy.

The Americans advanced within five miles of him, to Ferguson's swamp, where he made his first halt. It was Greene's
intention to have renewed the action the next day; and he
despatched Marion and Lee to watch the line of communication
between the Eutaws and Fairlawn, where the British had a
strong force, under Colonel M'Arthur, in order to prevent the
junction of this body with the enemy's main army. The simultaneous movements of the two corps, that of Stewart and
M'Arthur, enabled them to meet at mid-distance, and to out-
number the American detachment. By this movement, their
junction was secured the evening of the day after the battle,
and their retreat immediately continued.

Greene pressed the pursuit during the whole of one day, but
without success. The escape of Stewart was secured, for the
time, and the American general was compelled to forego his

1. How many prisoners were made by the Americans in the battle of Eutaw?
2. What farther proof can you adduce to establish the claims of the Americans to the
victory? 3. Where did the British general make his first halt? 4. At what place had
he another strong force? 5. How did General Greene endeavor to prevent the junction of this body with the enemy's main army? 6. How was his design defeated?

object, and yield his earliest attention to the prisoners and wounded in his hands.

But, though Stewart succeeded in escaping from his pursuers, the British power in South Carolina was completely prostrated by the battle of Eutaw. He had lost in killed wounded, and missing, nearly one half of the force which he brought into action. The British regulars lost something more than this, in the failure of their charm of power—their reputed invincibility. Their regulars had been foiled with their own peculiar weapon, the bayonet; and, perhaps, almost entirely owed their safety to the sharp shooting of loyal Americans, by whom their ranks were too much filled from the beginning; and who, in almost all their victories, made a numerous and efficient part of their armies. By a very inferior force had they been driven from the field, and their courage fell in proportion to the daily increase of confidence in their own prowess, on the part of the Americans. Nothing seemed wanting to make the American soldiers as good as any in the world but a moderate length of practice, and frequent exercise in actual conflict.

The losses of Greene had also been severe in a very great degree. His officers, in particular, had suffered dreadfully, chiefly in consequence of their exposure from the fire of the house, in their vain attempts to rescue the intoxicated soldiers from the British tents, and in the equally vain effort of the cavalry to force their way through a dense thicket, lined by British bayonets. Thin as the American regiments had ever been, they were always deficient in' officers. In this bloody affair, no less than sixty-one had been killed and wounded. Twenty-one of these, including Colonel Campbell, had died upon the field of battle.

The loss of British officers was, also, very severe, but less than that of their enemies. Major Marjoribanks, who had so highly distinguished himself during the day, died of fever, on the march to Charlestown. The spot where he lies buried is still shown upon the roadside. To the descendants of his enemies he is indebted for a tomb, covering his remains. The rest of the British wounded narrowly escaped capture by Marion. This vigilant and ever-restless captain, understanding that they had been shipped at Fairlawn, for Charlestown, descended the country rapidly, by night, and would have intercepted them, but for a slave of one of the plantations, who gave intelligence of his movements to the British camp. This brought out a strong detachment against him, and he was compelled, in turn, to steal away and avoid interception.

Returning from the pursuit of Stewart, Greene recrossed the Santee, and resumed his position at the Hills. Feeble as his army had ever been, it was now destined to become still more so. His militia soon left him. Of the North Carolinians, but one hundred remained, and their term of service was near expiring.

Marion, Pickens, and Hampton, with the South Carolina militia, were necessarily detached to cover the country; and, with the continentals alone, he had to discharge all the painful and fatiguing services required by six hundred wounded, half of whom were prisoners.

Exposure in the swamps, at a sickly season of the year, had brought upon his army the diseases of the climate; and, without medicine or comforts, of any kind, the whole camp exhibited a scene of the utmost misery and destitution. Numbers of brave fellows perished in a condition of wretchedness, only surpassed by such as distinguished the plague-hospitals of the East. Ten days after the battle of Eutaw, the American general would have found it impossible to muster, at headquarters, a thousand men fit for action.

Meanwhile, intelligence reached the South that Cornwallis contemplated a return from Virginia to Carolina by land. A movement of Colonel Stewart, about this time, seemed to confirm the truth of this intelligence. That officer, having recruited his army by all the available troops which he could gather from

12. How did the rest of the wounded escape capture by Marion? 13. Returning from the pursuit of Stewart, where did Greene encamp? 14. In what condition was his army? 15. Ten days after the battle of Eutaw, how many men, fit for action, could he have mustered? 16. What intelligence, in the meanwhile, reached the South? 17. What movement was made by Colonel Stewart?

below, and having strengthened his cavalry until it became far superior to that of the Americans, once more advanced to the Eutaws.

This movement served to drive the several American detachments of Marion and Hampton across the Santee; and, had the British continued their advance with vigor, it is not improbable, in the reduced and miserable condition of Greene's army, that they would have regained the ground, if not the influence, which they had lost in the late affair.

But it was remarked that they no longer acted with their ancient vigor. They had lost the assurance of victory, which their first successes had inspired, and which had made them confident. They now exhibited a readiness to flee, on the first show of danger, as much like, and as little creditable, as that which had distinguished and disgraced the conduct of the American militia when taking their first lessons in warfare.

The audacity which they had lost seemed now to be the characteristic of the Americans. The detachments of the latter presented themselves before their strong holds, taunted them by the boldest daring, but failed to bring them forth. Maham, of Marion's brigade, while, at a subsequent period, the British lay at Monk's Corner, captured one of their posts, and took eighty prisoners, in the face of their whole army.

The advance of the British to the Eutaws did not result, on their part, in any increase of vigor or activity. Its command had devolved upon a Major Doyle (afterward a general in the British service in India), during the illness of Colonel Stewart, who was suffering from a wound received at Eutaw.

This officer took post at Fludd's plantation, three miles above Nelson's ferry. His army, recruited from the British and loyalist forces in Charlestown, was still more than two thousand men, not including a body of three hundred, stationed at Fairlawn, under Major M'Arthur. This force, so superior to that of Greene, gave to the enemy the undivided command of the

18. What effect had this movement on the Americans? 19. What change in the conduct of the British army is noticed at this time? 20. What is said of the Americans? 21. What was done by an officer of Marion's brigade? 22. Upon whom had the command of the British army now devolved? 23. From what cause? 24. Where did Major Doyle take post? 25. What was the amount of his army?

country to the south of the Santee and Congaree, and westward to the Edisto.

But this superiority was not of long continuance. The diligence of Greene and his officers, and the patriotism of the soldiers, served to sustain them in their position, amid every form of privation and suffering, and gradually to restore their strength. The army was recruited by Colonels Shelby and Sevier, with five hundred men from the mountain region, and the infantry received an accession of one hundred and sixty recruits from North Carolina. The artillery destroyed in the battle of Eutaw had been replaced from Virginia; the wounded survivors had been recovered, and the cavalry — that most essential part of an army in a level and thinly-settled country — was rapidly accumulating under the several commands of Sumter, Marion, Horry, Maham, Hammond, and others. In two months from the battle of Eutaw, the American general was in a capacity to act. Marion, having under him Sevier, Shelby, Horry, and Maham, with their respective divisions, was ordered to operate between the Santee and Charlestown. Sumter, with his brigade of state troops, and some companies from his militia-brigade, was ordered to take post at Orangeburg and defend the country against the loyalists from the city; while Pickens, with two regiments, maintained the frontier from the Indians, and covered it against the predatory warfare which still raged in that quarter.

The commands of Sumter and Marion crossed the rivers in the beginning of November, and advanced upon the enemy. The former soon fell in with a strong party of the loyalists under General Cunningham, who had advanced upon Orangeburg, and one of his officers, a Major Morris, suffered himself to fall into an ambuscade, in which he sustained some loss. The forces of Sumter and Cunningham, being nearly equal, operated as mutual checks upon each other. Cunningham, who had issued from Charlestown on a predatory expedition in to the upper

26. What part of the country was he thus enabled to command? 27. How was General Greene's army soon after recruited? 28. When did he find himself in a capacity to act? 29. What officers were ordered to act between the Santee and Charlestown? 30. Where did Sumter take post? 31. Where was Colonel Pickens stationed? 32. When did Sumter and Marion cross the river and advance upon the enemy? 33. What party did Sumter encounter?

country, was checked in his progress; while Sumter, to continue this restraint upon his enemy, and maintain himself in safety, fell back for the present, and secured himself by a careful selection of position.

It was about this period that a foray was undertaken by William Cunningham, who, by his savage ferocities, had acquired the *nom de guerre* of " Bloody Bill," which is generally known in Carolina tradition as the " Bloody Scout." Cunningham made his way with a force of two or three hundred men from the city to the interior, taking advantage of the temporary absence from the route of any large party of the Americans. His own force was broken up into small parties, the better to elude detection. Their rendezvous was appointed at Rogue's Ford, on the Edisto, from which point they spread themselves on every hand.

Though scattered in small bands, they were yet easily got together, and were always prepared to act in concert. They took the interior country by surprise, and marked their silent and rapid progress everywhere by massacre. They gave no quarter. Their prisoners, where they met resistance, were hewn to pieces after conflict. But, in most cases, they found only defenceless people in their houses, unprepared for combat — unapprehensive of danger. The men were commonly shot or cut down; the women experienced various brutalities; boys of fifteen were hewn to pieces; horses and all moveable property carried off, and when not moveable, burned. The horrid massacres, on Cloud's creek, of Turner's troop — at Edgehill, of Hayes' party, where scores of men were butchered at the same moment after capture — are still reported with shuddering by the people of the regions where these terrible atrocities were committed.

Nor did they spare the isolated residence which offered no resistance. The detailed crimes of this " bloody scout," as still dwelt upon by the preserving tradition, would crowd a volume. The deed done — men slain, horses stolen, houses burnt — the

34. Who undertook a " foray " about this time? 35. What was his *nom de guerre?* 86. Where did the several parties under his command rendezvous? 87. How did they mark their progress? 38. How did they dispose of their prisoners? 89. Describe their progress. 40. At what places were horrible massacres committed?

marauders sped in search of newer victims, from house to house
— never lingering long in one spot, lest the avenger should rise
upon them.

He did finally rise.   The country was roused, and hurried
on the track of the desperadoes.   Scores of small parties, led
by outraged fathers, sons, brothers, were soon upon their heels,
and but few escaped.   Those who did were indebted for their
safety rather to the speed of their horses than their own skill
or valor.   Cunningham himself escaped and survived the war,
returning finally to Europe.   But, in all the region of country
thus ravaged, he remains to this day the proverbial monster.
His deeds were indignantly repudiated by the British General
Leslie, and by General Cunningham, the representative of a
remote branch of the same family.

To return to the affairs below.

The progress of Marion was arrested for a while, in consequence of his encountering, at Wantoot, the whole army of
Stewart, who was at this time busy ravaging the country, laying in provisions for sustaining a siege in Charlestown, and accumulating that plunder with which their fleet of three hundred
sail was laden when they subsequently took flight from the
waters of Cooper river.

About this time, the news was received, by both armies, of
the fall of Cornwallis in Virginia.   To the British in Carolina,
it was ominous of that fate which the unrelaxing energies of
Greene, and the determined valor of the troops under him,
seemed resolved to hasten; and, in anticipation of this event,
the British commander, as if no longer confident in his arms,
was preparing to convert his soldiers into mere marauders.   In
the short period which followed the return of Major Doyle with
the British army to the Eutaws, he had succeeded in plundering
the country, on the Santee and Congaree, of every negro, and
of almost everything else in the shape of property that could
be carried away.   But that Marion and Hampton guarded the

41. What did they do where no resistance was offered ?   42. Did the avenger arise ?
43. With what success ?   44. What became of Cunningham ?   45. What is said of
him ?   46. How was the progress of Marion arrested ?   47. What news was received
about this time ?   48. How had Major Doyle been employing his army ?

opposite banks of these rivers, their ravages would have extended far beyond these comparatively narrow limits.

The intelligence of the surrender of Yorktown reached the camp of Greene about the last of October. The day was observed as a jubilee in camp, and the grateful tidings gave a new impulse to the desire of the American general to cross the rivers which separated him from his enemy, and drive him down to the sea. This object had now become one of infinite importance, in order that the elections might be held as generally throughout the state as possible for the legislature. The re-establishment of the civil authority was of the last importance to the country, as well as to the army. The former was without laws, and had been exposed to a jurisdiction as various and wild as the passions of the several and conflicting parties by whom, at successive periods, it had been held in possession. The latter was suffering from every species of want.

" Our situation," says Greene, in a letter immediately after the battle of Eutaw, " is truly deplorable in the quartermaster's and ordnance departments. We have no ammunition and not half tents enough ; few camp kettles, and no axes, and, until very lately, no canteens."

Add to this, the want of clothes to cover their nakedness, the want of salt to season their food, and the want of physic to heal their sick, and the patriotism of the American general and his troops will derive its highest honors from their condition.

On the 18th of November, the camp at the Hills was broken up, and the American army again put in motion. As the route to be pursued led the army off from the support of Marion, who was charged with guarding its left while on its march, Captain Eggleston, with the legion, and a detachment from the Virginians, was despatched to strengthen him. The main army took up the line of march on the route by Simmons' and M'Cord's ferries, through Orangeburg, to Riddlespurger's ; thence by the Indianfield road to Ferguson's mill, where that road crosses the

49. How was the news of the surrender of Yorktown received in the American camp ? 50. What was now the desire of General Greene ? 51. Why was this object of great importance ? 52. What had been for some time the condition of the country? 53. What were the wants of the army ? 54. When was the American army again in motion ? 55. What route did the main army pursue ?

Edisto — the intention of the American general being apparently to gain a position on Four Holes, for the double purpose of covering the country beyond him, and controlling the movements of the enemy on his right. Another object in this movement was to intercept the flight of the British to Savannah — intelligence having been received by Marion, from Charlestown, that such was their intention.

It was in the confident belief that the force of Marion was adequate to keep in check that of the enemy under Stewart, that Greene ventured to place himself in a position which left him particularly exposed to an attack from Charlestown. To the great astonishment of Marion, no less than of the commander-in-chief, the mountaineers under Shelby and Sevier — upon the strength of whose reinforcement he had ventured into the field — on a sudden deserted him, after three weeks' service. This desertion was, with some probability, attributed to the departure of their colonel, Shelby, who had obtained leave of absence. Something, too, has been said of the service not being sufficiently active for their habits; but reasons such as these furnish a poor apology for soldiers, who, in the cause of their country's liberty, should be well pleased to encounter any sort of service which it may be the policy of their commander to impose. But they were restless, impatient, and naturally desirous of reaching their homes, and with nothing to do but watch and wait events, it was, perhaps, natural that they should be restive.

Marion had endeavored to find them sufficient employment. He had approached and defied the enemy, but could neither tempt nor provoke him to leave his encampment. With numbers decidedly inferior, the brave partisan was chagrined to find it impossible to bring the British into the field; and the only services in which he was able to employ his mountaineers were in attacks on the post at Fairlawn, and on the redoubts at Wappetaw. Detachments of about two hundred of them, supported by Maham's cavalry, were, in both instances, commanded by

56. What was the intention of the American general? 57. What other object had he in view? 58. Why did Greene venture to place himself in danger of an attack from Charlestown? 59. How was this object defeated? 60. What excuses have been assigned for the desertion of the mountaineers? 61. How had Marion endeavored to employ them?

Shelby. Wappetaw was abandoned at their approach. The attack at Fairlawn was made while the enemy lay at Wantoot. In passing this post, Marion showed himself; but did not succeed in decoying the British cavalry into the field. At Fairlawn, the attack was successful; the place surrendered at discretion, and the whole garrison, with three hundred stand of arms, stores, and provisions, fell into the hands of the Americans. The house with its contents, and the abbatis, were committed to the flames.

The desertion of the mountaineers, who formed so large a portion of Marion's command, might have been of the most pernicious consequence to the several divisions of the American army, but for the alarm which the movement of Greene across the Congaree had occasioned in the mind of Stewart.

Greene had advanced too far to recede; Marion had passed the Santee, and any disaster to him would have compelled an immediate retreat of the main army, to avoid worse consequences. The ignorance of the British commander of the real condition of his foe, and, perhaps, a consciousness of his own weakness — of which the Americans were equally ignorant at the time — by prompting his retreat toward Charlestown, induced Greene to undertake an enterprise calculated to confirm the enemy's fears of the American strength, and, by forcing him into Charlestown, without risking an action, to get the entire command of the state.

With this object, he left the army on its march, under the command of Colonel Williams; and, at the head of two hundred cavalry, and as many infantry, moved briskly toward Dorchester. The cavalry consisted of Lee's and Washington's, and one hundred men drawn from the command of Sumter. The infantry were those of the legion, and detachments from the lines of Maryland and Virginia. The command of this detachment was given to Colonel Wade Hampton.

Greene flattered himself with the hope of being able to sur-

62. What success did they meet at Fairlawn? 63. What prevented the evil consequences which might have arisen from the desertion of the mountaineers? 64. What movement was now made by General Greene? 65. With whom did he leave the main army? 66. What officer commanded the advanced guard of the American detachment?

prise the post at Dorchester; but the enemy received notice of his approach, and lay upon their arms all night.  Not seeing the Americans appear as soon as they expected, the British sent forth a party of fifty for intelligence.  Hampton's advanced guard encountered the party, and but few were suffered to escape.  So close was the pursuit of the survivors pressed to the enemy's post, that the whole cavalry of the British army, which, with a strong detachment of infantry, had been sent to reinforce that post, issued out to charge the pursuing party.

To cut off this corps, was a leading desire with Greene, and he saw their approach with the most pleasurable anticipations.  But they recoiled and fled from the fierce onset of Hampton's horse.  Twenty or thirty were slain, wounded, or taken; and such an alarm did the presence of Greene in person excite among them, under the belief that his whole army was at hand, that the garrison at Dorchester, during the night, destroyed everything — threw their cannon into the river, and made a rapid retreat to Charlestown.  Greene did not dare to pursue, for the infantry of the enemy alone exceeded five hundred.

This manœuvre had all the effect which was intended.  The panic of the enemy increased, their outposts were all abandoned, and their whole force concentrated at the quarter-house, about six miles from Charlestown.  Here, where the isthmus is narrow, the fugitives were halted and joined by General Stewart, who, meanwhile, had been hurrying with all speed, by another route, toward the city.

General Leslie, who now succeeded Stewart, made every preparation for immediate attack.  The fears of the fugitives from Dorchester had magnified the force of Greene to something more than three thousand men, at a time when that commander could not muster at headquarters more than eight hundred.  The force under Leslie was scarcely less than five thousand; yet he deemed it necessary, in the general panic, to

67. Did Greene succeed in surprising the enemy at Dorchester?  68. What was the result of this attack?  69. What was the number of the enemy's infantry?  70. What was the effect of Greene's manœuvre?  71. Who had now succeeded General Stewart?  72. To what number was the American force magnified by the fears of the fugitives from Dorchester?  73. What was the actual number?  74. What was the amount of General Leslie's force?

resort to a measure which must sufficiently have testified his own fears, while it awakened, to the keenest poignancy, those of the remaining inhabitants. He embodied in regiments the numerous slaves who had been drawn from the neighboring plantations, and crowded into the city as a part of that plunder with which the providence of the British commanders had prepared to console themselves for a flight which now appeared to be inevitable.

75. To what measure did he, in the general panic resort?

# CHAPTER XV.

### CIVIL GOVERNMENT RE-ESTABLISHED — WAR SUBSIDES.

DRIVEN in from all their outposts, the British were confined in their operations, to the city, the Neck, and the neighboring islands. The object of General Greene, and all that he could effect, in the thin and unprovided condition of his army, was attained; and Governor Rutledge convened the legislature of the state at Jacksonborough, a little village on the Edisto river, about twenty miles from the sea, and thirty-five from the city of Charlestown.

This event, which once more restored the forms of civil government to the state, after an interregnum of nearly two years, took place in January, 1782. It was originally arranged by the governor and common council to convene it at Camden; but General Greene, after his excursion to Dorchester, having reconnoitred the country between the Edisto and Ashley, and found it possessed of sufficient military advantages to admit of his covering Jacksonborough with his little army from danger and insult, warmly recommended the adoption of the latter place in preference to all others for the assembling of the delegates; since the re-establishment of the civil authority so near the British garrison would, more conclusively than any other event, short of the absolute expulsion of the foe, confirm the evidence of a complete recovery of the state.

The army, in the meantime, took post at the plantation of Colonel Skirving, six miles below Jacksonborough, and on the road leading to Charlestown.

1. To what parts of the state were the British now confined? 2. Was the object of General Greene now attained? 3. When did this event occur? 4. Where had the governor and common council arranged to convene the legislature? 5. Why did General Greene recommend Jacksonborough? 6 Where did the army take post?

But, before the place could be put in perfect security, Greene conceived it necessary to drive the British from John's island, one of the inner chain of islands which stretch along the coast from Charlestown to Savannah, separated from the main by creeks and marshes, and from each other by estuaries of the rivers, generally denominated sounds and inlets. John's and James's islands, with the city and the Neck, were now the only footholds left to the British, of all their conquests in South Carolina.

On John's island, which is secure, fertile, and extensive, they maintained a force of five hundred men, under Colonel Craig. The island was also guarded at all accessible points, by galleys carrying heavy guns. These galleys, at a favorable time of the tide, might easily approach Jacksonborough, which is not beyond striking distance from John's island; while the communication with Charlestown being open through James's island, made it easy for the British, unperceived, to throw reinforcements into the former.

Greene resolved, if possible, to drive the enemy from this important position. It was soon ascertained, not only that the island was accessible, but that the British, unapprehensive of danger, were comparatively unprepared for attack.

Laurens and Lee, knowing the desire of Greene, and having examined the approaches, solicited his permission to enter upon the undertaking. Their plan was to pass by night between the galleys, and surprise the force under Craig. There was one point between the Stono and Edisto, at which the island was formerly connected with the highland by a piece of hard marsh. To complete the inland communication between Charlestown and Edisto, by the way of Stono, a canal had been cut through this marsh, and was known by the name of New Cut. At low water this is fordable, and to guard this pass the British had moored two galleys at convenient distances; but to avoid exposure from

7. What was necessary to be done to put the place in perfect security? 8. What were now the only footholds left to the British, of all their conquests in South Carolina? 9. How is John's island situated? 10. What force had the British at this place? 11. How was the island farther guarded? 12. Why did General Greene resolve to drive the enemy from John's island? 13. Who solicited permission to enter upon the undertaking? 14. What was their plan? 15. What was the situation of the galleys?

grounding, they were placed in positions which were necessarily somewhat remote; and this circumstance suggested the project of passing between them.

Greene sanctioned the plan of these enterprising young officers, and the night of the 13th of January was fixed on for its execution. The main army moved on the 12th to Wallace's bridge, with the view of diverting the attention of the enemy from the real point of attack; while two light detachments, under the command of Laurens, crossing the country from Ashley river, waded the north branch of the Stono, and advanced to New Cut, which is at the head of the southern branch.

The rest of the army was put in motion after dusk, and advanced to cover and support its detachment. Greene himself reached the Cut before the time of low water, at which period alone the canal is fordable.

Here he found his attacking party in strange embarrassment. The detachments of Lee and Laurens, forming separate columns on the march, had been led, the first by Lee, and the second by Major Hamilton. Lee's column was in advance, and Laurens, as commander of the whole party, accompanying it in person. But Hamilton, through the desertion of his guide, lost his way to the ford, and his column was completely lost to the enterprise.

The time for striking the blow had passed. The first column had crossed over to the island, but was necessarily recalled before the height of the returning tide should prevent its retreat. The opportunity was thus lost of cutting off, by complete surprise, a force of five hundred of the enemy.

But the object could not be relinquished, and Greene ordered a boat on wagons from the Edisto, determined on forcing his passage to the island. The artillery was then brought to bear upon the galleys, and drove them from their stations, while Laurens, passing the Cut, penetrated to the encampment of the enemy.

16. When was the attempt made? 17. Who commanded the two columns of the attacking party? 18. Which column succeeded in crossing the Cut? 19. What prevented Major Hamilton's from crossing? 20. Defeated in their intentions of cutting off the enemy by surprise, what was done by General Greene?

But the latter did not wait for the assault. The alarm occasioned by the narrow escape of the morning, convinced him of the insecurity of his position; and taking counsel from his apprehensions rather than his valor, Major Craig had already commenced his flight, in anticipation of the attack. A few prisoners only rewarded the rapidity of Laurens's movements; but the main object of Greene was attained, and without loss.

This event completed the security of Jacksonborough, and left the government of the state, assembled within its walls, free in the unrestrained and fearless execution of the arduous and solemn duties devolving upon its hands.

The assembly met and formed a quorum on the day for which the members were summoned. The proclamation of the governor precluded all persons from suffrage and membership who had placed themselves under British protection, or were in any manner obnoxious to popular odium or suspicion. None but true and tried men were present, and these were mostly veterans — the brave men who had sustained the conflict with unremitting valor and unfailing fortitude from the beginning. But very few were present who had not drawn their weapons in the strife; and many appeared on this occasion, clad in armor, who had stolen a brief respite from the labors of the field, that they might assist in the no less arduous toils of council. All had suffered, and many of them severely. A nobler assembly — one more distinguished for faith, integrity, wisdom, and valor — was never yet convoked in the cause of a nation.

The proceedings were opened by a speech from Governor Rutledge, distinguished by the accustomed energy of manner and force of matter which characterized that orator. In the course of this speech, he gave a brief glance at the history of the war in the state. A portion of his picture we transfer to our pages, as summing up, briefly, a thousand details which a more particular narration would make too voluminous for our limits:

" The enemy," said he, " unable to make any impression upon

21. What was his success? 22. What benefit resulted from this expedition? 23. What persons had been by the governor's proclamation precluded from suffrage or membership in the new legislature? 24. Of whom was the assembly composed? 25. How were the proceedings opened?

16

the northern states, the number of whose inhabitants, and the strength of whose country, had baffled their repeated efforts, turned their views towards the southern, which a difference of circumstances afforded some expectation of conquering, or, at least, of greatly distressing. After a long resistance, the reduction of Charlestown was effected by the vast superiority of force with which it had been besieged. The loss of that garrison, as it consisted of the continental troops of Virginia and the Carolinas, and of a number of militia, facilitated the enemy's march into the country ; and their establishment of strong posts in the upper and interior parts of it, and the unfavorable issue of the action near Camden, induced them vainly to imagine that no other army could be collected which they might not easily defeat.

"The militia commanded by the brigadiers Marion and Sumter, whose enterprising spirit and unremitting perseverance under many difficulties are deserving of great applause, harassed and often defeated large parties ; but the numbers of these militia were too few to contend effectually with the collected strength of the enemy.

" Regardless, therefore, of the sacred ties of honor, destitute of the feelings of humanity, and determined to extinguish, if possible, every spark of freedom in this country, they, with the insolent pride of conquerors, gave unbounded scope to the exercise of their tyrannical dispositions, infringed their public engagements, and violated the most solemn capitulations. Many of our worthiest citizens were, without cause, long and closely confined, some on board of prison-ships, and others in the town and castle of St. Augustine ; their properties disposed of at the will and caprice of the enemy, and their families sent to a different and distant part of the continent, without the means of support. Many who had surrendered as prisoners of war were killed in cold blood ; several suffered death in the most

26. By what means did he state Charlestown had been reduced ? 27. What effect was produced by the fall of Charlestown ? 28. What induced the enemy to suppose the state conquered ? 29. Who commanded the militia which still endeavored to contend with the British ? 30. How did the enemy treat many of our worthiest citizens ?

ignominious manner, and others were delivered up to savages, and put to tortures under which they expired.

" Thus the lives, liberties, and properties of the people were dependent solely on the pleasure of British officers, who deprived them of either, or all, on the most frivolous pretences. Indians, slaves, and a desperate banditti of the most profligate character, were caressed and employed by the enemy, to execute their infamous purposes. Devastation and ruin marked their progress and that of their adherents ; nor were their violences restrained by the charms or influence of beauty and innocence. Even the fair sex, whom it is the duty of all, and the pride and pleasure of the brave, to protect — they and their tender offspring were victims to the inveterate malice of an unrelenting foe. Neither the tears of mothers, nor the cries of infants, could excite in their hearts pity or compassion.

" Not only the fearful habitations of the widow, the aged, and the infirm, but the holy temples of the Most High, were consumed in flames kindled by their sacrilegious hands. They have tarnished the glory of the British arms, disgraced the profession of the British soldier, and fixed indelible stigmas of rapine, cruelty, perfidy, and profaneness on the British name !

" But I can now congratulate you, and I do so most cordially, on the pleasing change of affairs which, under the blessing of God, the wisdom, prudence, address, and bravery of the great and gallant General Greene, and the intrepidity of the officers and men under his command, has been happily effected. His successes have been more rapid and complete than the most sanguine could have expected. The enemy, compelled to surrender or evacuate every post which they held in the country, frequently defeated and driven from place to place, are obliged to seek refuge under the walls of Charlestown, and on islands in its vicinity. We have now the full and absolute possession of every other part of the state, and the legislative, executive, and judicial powers are in the free exercise of their respective au thorities."

*31. Upon what were the lives, liberties, and property of our people made dependent ? 32. What buildings were committed to the flames ? 33. Repeat the congratulatory paragraph of Governor Rutledge's address.

The governor proceeded to recommend the embodiment of a regular force of state troops, and a re-organization of the militia. Another important matter which he suggested for their consideration was, " the conduct of such of our citizens as, voluntarily avowing their allegiance, and even glorying in their professions of loyalty and attachment to his Britannic majesty, have offered their congratulations on the successes of his arms, prayed to be embodied as royal militia, accepted commissions in his service, and endeavored to subvert our constitution and establish his power in its stead ; of those who have returned to the state in defiance of a law by which such return was declared to be a capital offence, and have abetted the British interest ; and of such whose behavior has been so reprehensible that justice and policy forbid their free readmission to the rights and privileges of citizens."

" The extraordinary lenity of this state," continues this address, " has been remarkably conspicuous.  Other states have thought it just and expedient to appropriate the property of British subjects to the public use ; but we have forborne to take even the profits of the estates of our most implacable enemies."

Governor Rutledge concluded with recommending immediate attention to the currency, which had become worthless as a tender, and proposed to repeal the law from which it drew the legal sanction to its circulation.

The legislature proceeded to business in a spirit corresponding with that which the governor's speech had shown.  Laws were passed for confiscating the property of certain persons, and banishing them from the state ; for amercing the estates of others of whose personal services the country had been deprived.  The preamble to the act of confiscation, relating the reasons which justified the measure, declared it to be a measure of retaliation for like confiscations made by the British authorities of the property of the patriots.  But the most efficacious reason for the adoption of this measure, was the necessity of

84. What did the governor proceed to recommend ?  85. What other important matter was suggested for their consideration ?  86. What did the governor, in conclusion, recommend ?  87. What laws were passed by this assembly, respecting certain persons ?

the case. The state was wholly destitute of funds; no immediate resources could be had either by loan or taxation, and the estates of the loyalists presented the only means for establishing a fund upon which to build a temporary credit. The indulgence of the state authorities, subsequently released the rigor of this act in the case of many of the individuals upon whom it bore, whose names were stricken from the records which chronicled their shame and forfeiture.

The legislature, among other acts, originated a bill for vesting in General Greene, in consideration of his services, the sum of ten thousand guineas — a gift which furnished an example to the states of Georgia and North Carolina, which they promptly followed. The former voted him five thousand guineas, and the latter, twenty-four thousand acres of land.

Governor Rutledge was succeeded in the executive chair of South Carolina by John Matthews (1782). The office was tendered first to Christopher Gadsden, who declined it because of his infirmities and age.

The military operations of the opposing forces seemed almost entirely suspended during the session of the legislature. The British were paralyzed, and never ventured from the cover of their stronghold, and the Americans were too feeble to attempt them there. The fall of Cornwallis, however, brought to Greene a small portion of the army which had been employed against him, under the command of the famous General Wayne, and he was enabled to assume a more active character in his operations.

He despatched Wayne, with a detachment, to Georgia; and this general, by a series of small but sharp engagements, succeeded in circumscribing the movements of the British in that state to the limits of Savannah, as Greene, in South Carolina, had forced them within the walls of Charlestown.

---

88. What necessity existed for the adoption of this measure? 89. What compensation was voted to General Greene? 40. How was the example of South Carolina, in this respect, followed by Georgia and North Carolina? 41. Who succeeded General Rutledge in the executive chair? 42. To whom had the office previously been tendered? 43. Why was it declined by him? 44. What was the condition of the opposing forces, at this time? 45. What accession to his army did Greene now receive? 46. What did General Wayne achieve in Georgia?

The subsequent evacuation of Savannah filled the Carolinians with a lively hope that their chief city would, also, soon be rescued from the hands of the enemy. The British garrison, at Savannah, however, was added to that of Charlestown; while Wayne, having completed the duties upon which he had been sent to Georgia, re-united his division to the main army, under Greene.

The successes of Greene's detachments, operating on his left, were not so brilliant as those of Wayne. The brigade of Marion suffered some reverses, which were due only to a want of strength. The country, from the Edisto to the Santee, became thrown open, in consequence, for a time, to the ravages of the enemy; and a party of loyalists, under the command of William Cunningham — familiarly known by the epithet of "Bloody Bill Cunningham" — escaped from the lower country, and ascended the Saluda, with a body of three hundred horse. But we have already despatched this history in preceding pages.

This movement was made in concert with the Cherokee Indians, and demanded all the vigilance of Pickens, who held watch upon the borders. Rapid as was the progress of this marauding party, their tracks were made everywhere in blood. But the whig hunters turned out with spirit, and under popular leaders, the tories were routed and dispersed. A portion of them fled to the Cherokees, and drew upon the savages another chastisement, such as had already more than once thinned their warriors, destroyed their villages, and diminished their hunting-grounds.

The daily extension of General Greene's troops to the southward and eastward, and the contraction of his cordon around the land limits of the British, soon began to be felt by General Leslie, their commander. His foraging ground became too small to yield a subsistence to the large numbers of horses which had accumulated within his lines, in consequence of his calling in his detachments, and he was reduced to the necessity, in order to relieve himself of this difficulty, of putting two hundred of these animals to death.

An alarm excited in the American camp, on the rumored approach of the enemy with strong reinforcements, led to an order to Marion to repair to headquarters with all the force he could gather. This command was promptly obeyed; but a detachment of mounted infantry was left at Monk's Corner, to watch the motions of the enemy, who, by means of Cooper river, had free access in their boats and galleys to that neighborhood.

To destroy this detachment, in Marion's absence, a force of three hundred and fifty men were transported by water from Charlestown. The sudden return of Marion, with all his brigade, from the camp of Greene — an event quite unexpected by the enemy — enabled him partly to defeat their enterprise. His force did not equal that which was arrayed against him, but he, nevertheless, resolved upon attacking it. In order to detain the enemy, he despatched Colonels Richardson and Sevier, and a part of Maham's horse, with orders to throw themselves in front of the British, and engage them until he should come up with the main body. The order was gallantly executed. The British advance was charged and driven near St. Thomas's musterhouse, by Captain Smith, of Maham's cavalry, and their leader, Captain Campbell, with several others, fell in the flight. Unhappily, the pursuit was urged too warmly. The pursuers were met by Captain Coffin, who, at the head of his cavalry, charged and dispersed them in turn. This event left Marion too weak to hazard an engagement, while the enemy were very well content to continue their march without attempting to force him to it.

The British expedition, by the timely interposition of Marion's force, resulted in nothing more than their capture of a small number of cattle, with which they retired across Wappetaw to

53. To what was General Leslie compelled by the restriction of his limits? 54. Where was a detachment of Marion's mounted infantry stationed? 55. What attempt was made to destroy this force, during Marion's absence? 56. How was their enterprise partly defeated? 57. How did Marion endeavor to detain the enemy? 58. By whom was the British advance put to flight? 59. What officer fell in the flight? 60. What resulted from the pursuit being too warmly urged? 61. What did the British achieve by this expedition?

Haddrell's point, where, and at Hobcaw, they had established posts to facilitate the movements of strong parties which were continually alert in procuring provisions, the want of which was now seriously felt in the garrison.

The brigade of Marion had always been one of the most efficient in the service, at once remarkable for the vigilance and the valor of its officers and men. Unhappily, however, a question of precedence with respect to rank, arose between two of the former, both of them highly distinguished as leaders, and particularly esteemed by their commander. These were Colonels Horry and Maham.

During the absence of Marion, in attendance upon the legislature, the command was given to Horry; upon which preference — a preference due to the seniority of the latter as an officer — Maham separated his corps from the brigade, which lay at Wambaw, posted them higher up the river, and then proceeded to the legislature, of which he, also, was a member.

In this affair, Colonel Maham was unquestionably in fault. Greene and Marion endeavored to reconcile the discontented officer, but without success; and while the dispute was pending, and, perhaps, in consequence of the withdrawal of Maham's horse from the command of Horry, the latter was surprised by a strong detachment of infantry, artillery, and cavalry, under Colonel Thompson — afterward more renowned and generally known as Count Rumford — and the brigade dispersed.

On hearing this intelligence, Marion put himself at the head of Maham's regiment, which he had reached but a few hours before, and hurried on toward Wambaw, the scene of the surprise, to check the enemy and collect the fugitives. Arrived within five miles of the British, he halted to refresh his men and horses, and while the latter were unbitted and feeding, the whole of the enemy's cavalry made their appearance.

62. Where had they established posts for the procuring of provisions? 63. How had Marion's brigade always ranked? 64. Between which officers did a dispute arise? 65. From what cause? 66. Where was General Marion? 67. To whom was the command given during Marion's absence? 68. What did Maham, in consequence? 69. Who was in fault in this affair? 70. Who attempted to reconcile the quarrel? — and with what success? 71. What happened to the brigade, during the absence of Maham's corps? 72. When intelligence of this misfortune reached Marion, what movement did he make? 73. How was he surprised?

If the Americans were unprepared for the encounter — and it was Maham's opinion, that a charge of the British, if ordered immediately on coming into view, would have dispersed the regiment — the enemy seemed as little disposed to take advantage of their surprise. Seeing that they not only halted, but exhibited appearances of indecision and alarm, Marion, though with a force only half as numerous, resolved to attack them.

The indecision of the British had allowed the Americans full time to mount their horses and recover; and they moved to the extremity of a lane, through which they were to issue, with a firm and fearless countenance. Though greatly fewer in number than the foe, the Americans were better mounted; and frequent exercise and repeated successes had inspired them with a confidence in themselves, which almost made them heedless of any odds. But they were destined, by one of those counter events, which disturb and defeat equally the hopes and the calculations of men, to lose "a glorious opportunity," in the language of Marion, "of cutting up the British cavalry."

The front section was led by an officer of approved courage, who, in a very recent affair, had signally distinguished himself. It is Napoleon, however, who says "that every man has his moment of fear;" and it was, seemingly, at some such unlucky moment that the leading officer was required to begin the battle. He led his section forward, until, emerging from the cover of the lane, at its extremity, and in the face of the foe, instead of charging boldly before him, he dashed aside into the forests on his right, and drew after him the whole regiment in irretrievable confusion.

Vainly seeking to arrest their flight, Marion' himself was borne away by the crowd, and narrowly escaped falling a victim to their miserable panic. Many of the fugitives had to quit their horses, and disembarrass themselves of their boots and armor, to pass a deep creek which lay in their way.

It was fortunate that some alarm prevailed in the hostile ranks. The British were doubtful of their victory; and, ap-

74. Upon what did Marion resolve? 75. From what cause was the attack unsuccessful? 76. What happened to Marion? 77. How did the fugitives escape? 78. What was the condition of things in the British command?

prehensive of ambuscade, did not pursue with promptness and resolution.   They suffered some precious time to elapse before they moved in pursuit; and but few of the Americans were killed or taken.   They were no less confounded at their blood-less victory than was Marion mortified at a defeat so shameful.

Marion's force thus dispersed, was, however, not annihilated. This brave partisan possessed, in a singular degree, the love and confidence of his countrymen, and the men who followed him 'were generally of that elastic temper which no reverses can subdue, and no defeat keep inactive.   Wherever he made his appearance known, his recruits rapidly gathered around him ; and, falling back upon the Pedee, he collected the scat-tered fragments of Horry's brigade, and withdrew, till better times, to the Santee.   The triumph of the enemy was but of short duration.   Colonel Thompson retired before a detach-ment from Greene's army, under Colonel Laurens, and took post at Cainhoy, where he was too strongly posted to appre-hend any attack in his position from the American detachment.

Laurens returned beyond the Ashley, where Greene, from want of resources of all kinds, troops, ammunition, and provi-sions, was compelled to remain comparatively inactive.   The subsistence of the southern army, for the last eighteen months of the war, had been derived altogether from South Carolina. Even the detached army, under Wayne, in Georgia, was sup-plied with provisions from the sister-state.   Without regarding the amount of her quota, South Carolina took it upon herself to supply the troops; and, at the close of the war, she was found to be the largest creditor-state in the Union.   When it is considered how many years she had been the seat of active and unremitting warfare, and how long she had been engaged in supporting two armies, in spite of the interruption of her agriculture, and the devastation of her plains, it will rather be matter of surprise that it should have been done at all, than that it should not have been done in better manner.   The greater wonder is, how any soldiers could be kept together

79. His force thus dispersed, whither did he retire? 80. What reverse did the enemy experience?   81. Why was General Greene now comparatively inactive?   82. How had the southern army been supported for the last eighteen months of the war? 83. How was the state situated at the close of the war?

under circumstances such as those which prevailed in Greene's army.

He writes, about this time, to the president of congress, " we have three hundred men without arms, and more than a thousand so naked for want of clothing, that they can only be put on duty in cases of desperate necessity. Men in this situation, without pay or spirits, it is difficult to tell what charm keeps them together. I believe that it is nothing but the pride of the army and the severity of discipline that supports them under their sufferings."

The South has reason to be proud of such soldiers; and the wonder how they should have triumphed finally over the wealth, the valor, and the strength of Britain, and her thousand mercenaries, becomes proportionably lessened in the contemplation of a record such as this.

The only relief for the army in this deplorable condition, was derived chiefly from a specific contribution, voluntarily yielded by the inhabitants — a source of relief, by the way, which, throughout the war, brought its small, but timely, aid frequently for its temporary preservation. In addition to this, a contraband trade was opened with certain merchants in Charlestown, and carried on with the concurrence of the governor and council, through the medium of an agent near the army, and under the keen and vigilant eyes of Colonels Lee and Laurens, by which, in return for rice, such goods as answered the more pressing wants of the Americans, were furnished from the city. The removal of the army, upon the adjournment of the legislature, down to Bacon's bridge, at the head of Ashley river, facilitated this trade by opening a boat-communication with the city. The produce from these arrangements, though small and precarious, somewhat relieved the distresses of the army. To its general good behavior and unshaken integrity, under such heavy wants as it had been compelled to endure, we must record one sad and singular exception.

No longer able to meet the Americans in the field, the Brit-

84. In what matter did General Greene describe the condition of his troops? 85. What relief had the army from this destitution ? 86. What other expedients adopted for their relief? 87. How was this trade facilitated ?

ish employed another agent of warfare, which they have, perhaps, been as little reluctant to use as other and far less civilized nations.   This was corruption.   The near neighborhood of the American army, within twenty miles of the city, suggested to the enemy a design of working upon its distresses, and fomenting those discontents which they well knew must arise in every body of men, whose condition is such as that of the American army.   An emissary had succeeded in tampering with the soldiers of the Pennsylvania line, five sergeants and twelve soldiers of which had been bought over to the purposes of the enemy.

Had the zeal of these wretches, in behalf of their new employers, not prompted them to make an experiment on the fidelity of the Marylanders, the most fatal consequences might have ensued to the whole army.   But the sound principles of these long-tried and noble fellows sustained them against temptation. Their integrity, the quick ears of one of their camp-women, and the vigor and vigilance of Colonel Harmer, furnished the evidence for fastening the crime upon one Gornell, their leader. His arrest, and that of four other sergeants, was the signal for the flight of twelve of the same line, who broke away and escaped to the enemy on the very night on which he was taken.

The plot had been rapidly ripening.   Symptoms of mutiny had appeared in the American camp, and the movements in that of the enemy were conclusive of a scheme of simultaneous operation between the foe and the insurgents.   The American commander acted with decision.   His outposts were soon moved to headquarters, Marion recalled from the Santee, and the army held in constant readiness for battle.   Gornell, the ringleader of the mutineers, was tried and condemned; and with his execution, and the close confinement of his four confederates, every appearance of mutinous temper ceased in the encampment.

With this attempt terminated all serious efforts of the British against the main body of the southern army.   The day of their power was rapidly passing away; and the resolution of

88. What was attempted by a new agent of the enemy?   89. How was the plan discovered?   90. How did the American commander act?   91. How was the ringleader of the mutineers treated?

the British parliament, to withdraw their forces from America, and put an end to a war in which they had lost an empire, and incurred, with the shame of such a loss, the worse reproach of having, in the progress of the warfare, lost their reputation for justice, magnanimity, and the noblest qualities of a civilized and Christian people, prepared the way for the evacuation of Charlestown.

When the vote of the British parliament for discontinuing aggressive war in America was communicated to General Leslie, he proposed to General Greene a cessation of hostilities, and that he should be permitted to receive and purchase from the planters such supplies as he might need or desire.

Greene referred the first proposition to Congress; to the second he gave a flat refusal — declaring his resolution to prevent all supplies from going into Charlestown, except so far as his contracts for clothing made it necessary. To this refusal, Leslie replied by a threat of taking his provisions by force, and commenced his operations for that purpose.

Greene, accordingly prepared to oppose him. Marion was ordered to strengthen himself, so as to meet the enemy in the quarter where he commanded; while a strong detachment was formed, under General Gist, to cover the country lying south and west of the position of the army. Gist's brigade comprised the cavalry of the legion, and that of the third and fourth Virginia regiments, under Colonel Baylor; the infantry of the legion, the dismounted dragoons of the third regiment, the Delawares, and one hundred men from the line, under Major Beale. The whole of the infantry was placed under command of Colonel Laurens. Thus prepared for all events, Greene flattered himself that he should be able to neutralize the efforts of Leslie, and laugh at his threatenings. Some glimpses, at this time, of a gentler influence than that of war, began to prevail in the American camp.

The arrival of General Greene's wife, who joined her hus-

92. What resolution was now passed by the British parliament? 93. For what did this resolution prepare the way? 94. What proposal was then made by General Leslie? 95. What was the reply of General Greene? 96. What determination did Leslie then express? 97. Under whose command was placed the infantry stationed for the purpose of defeating his intention?

band on the 28th of March, contributed to enliven the monotony of an army in a state of inactivity. The presence of the Americans in force, necessarily brought back the planters and their families, who dwelt in the neighborhood. These were wealthy and hospitable, and the gratitude which they felt for their deliverers delighted to show itself in the generous forms of convivial entertainment. A gallant passage from Johnson's narrative of the events of this period, may fitly conclude this chapter.

"In modern ages and nations"— he might have said, in all ages and most nations — "the transition from war to love has ever been direct and uniform. The army abounded in gallant young officers, and the country in wealthy, elegant, and accomplished women. The laurels of the former were readily laid down at the feet of the latter, and received with approving smiles. Those who had reconquered the country, were liberally admitted to a participation in its wealth and treasures; the feudal service exacted was a willing submission to that power which conquers all. Many were the matrimonial connections to which this period gave rise, between the officers of the army and the heiresses of Carolina and Georgia; and it is needless to add that they yielded a valuable acquisition, both to the population and the society of the country."

98. How was the monotony of the American camp now enlivened ?   99. Repeat the extract from Johnson's narrative.

# CHAPTER XVI.

MARION — LAURENS — EVACUATION OF CHARLESTOWN.

THE military events of this period were rapidly drawing to a close. They involved no affairs of leading importance. Early in April, Marion recrossed the Santee river with a small force of two hundred militia and Maham's horse, reduced to one hundred and twenty. It was General Greene's wish that he should take post as near as possible to the enemy, in order to straighten his limits beyond Cooper river, and to enable Colonel Laurens to pass the Ashley, and close upon the enemy between the latter river and Goose creek. But, not being able to mount his infantry, it became necessary to take post on the Santee, at a point which would enable him to effect the double purpose of securing a retreat, and forming a junction with any party when necessary, either at Huger's bridge, over the west branch of Cooper river, from which he was twenty miles distant, or at Strawberry ferry, which was twenty-five from his position. His cavalry, meanwhile, patrolled the country within view of the enemy's posts at Haddrell and Hobcaw, to check the incursions of the British in that quarter, and obtain the earliest intelligence of their movements.

To relieve himself once more from a neighbor who had always proved so troublesome, General Leslie prevailed upon a Scotchman, under the feigned character of a deserter, to penetrate the country into the settlements of the Scots loyalists, and persuade them to make such movements as would recall Marion to that quarter. The unfortunate agent, on his return from this

1. What movement was made by Marion in the month of April? 2. What was the desire of General Greene? 3. Not being able to mount his infantry, where did he take post? 4. How far distant was he from Cooper river? 5. How far from Strawberry ferry? 6. How was his cavalry meanwhile engaged? 7. How did General Leslie contrive to remove Marion from such close neighborhood to his army?

duty, was intercepted and executed by Marion. But he had done his work; the loyalists were excited, and under Major Gainey, of Pedee, a tory leader of considerable local celebrity, appeared in arms.

Taking command of Maham's cavalry, Marion proceeded to meet Gainey, who was an old and well-known opponent; and one, like himself, who had a high reputation for his adroitness as a partisan warrior. Colonel Maham was too sick to accompany his command, and was left at his own place, attended by a small guard. Here he was captured by a daring young loyalist, named Robbins, who had made a circuit and penetrated nearly sixty miles into the country with this object. Robbins was one of Cunningham's men, and Maham, from the known hostility of the loyalists to him, expected nothing but death at his hands. But Robbins, not having his superior with him, exhibited the natural generosity of a brave man, and parolled the sick captive to his own house.

The rapid progress of Marion, and his sudden appearance before Gainey, convinced the latter that his movement was not likely to be attended by any favorable results; and the willingness of Marion to spare the unnecessary shedding of blood, facilitated a pacification between the parties, and led to the renewal of a treaty of neutrality, to which Gainey had bound himself the year before. To this treaty, Marion added a clause, permitting such of the loyalists as wished it, to retire with their property from the country. These terms the tories were very ready to accept. They saw that they were about to be abandoned by the British, and yielded with the best grace to the necessity that pressed upon them.

This insurrection had scarcely been quelled before the partisan was summoned back to his former position. His absence had left the British at liberty to renew their depredations between Cooper and Santee rivers; and his infantry, under Colo-

8. What was the fate of his emissary? 9. Under what leader did the tories rise in arms? 10. What movement was then made by Marion? 11. Why did not Colonel Maham accompany him? 12. What misfortune befell him at this time? 13. How was Colonel Maham treated by his captor? 14. What was the issue of Marion's appearance before Major Gainey? 15. What clause was added to this treaty by Marion?

nel Ashby, had been compelled to retire before a superior foe. He was joined on his route by a newly raised corps, under Major Conyers, and, but for this timely aid, must have reached his position alone, for the rapidity of his movements had broken down the corps of Maham, which he left behind him to recruit.

At Murray's ferry, he halted to collect his militia and await the arrival of his weary cavalry. Here he consolidated the two commands of Maham and Conyers, and about the middle of July recrossed the Santee, at the head of a respectable body of horse and about three hundred dismounted cavalry. With these he took post on the Wassamasaw; but had scarcely done so before he was compelled, by the movements of General Leslie, to move immediately to Georgetown, against which place it was apprehended that a numerous fleet of small vessels, convoyed by galleys and armed brigs, and conveying eight hundred men, which issued late in July from Charlestown, was intended to operate.

To this place Marion hurried with his usual speed and spirit; but the enterprise of the enemy was directed to another point, and he succeeded in sweeping from the banks of the Santee more than six hundred barrels of rice. Again was the force of Marion set in motion and thrown over the Sampit, to prevent the advance of the British upon Georgetown. In this he succeeded; but it was utterly impossible to annoy them in their movements up the South Santee, and upon those plantations which they could plunder in safety, under the guns of their galleys.

At their departure, he once more returned across the Santee, and took post at Wadboo, as the return of the enemy's fleet to Charlestown suggested the probability of their attempting some similar enterprise upon another of the rivers communicating with that city. Here a party of his infantry drew upon themselves the attention of the British. They believed the infantry

16. What had occurred in the meantime to his infantry which had been left under Colonel Ashby? 17. What reinforcement did Marion receive on his route to rejoin the main army? 18. With what force did he recross the Santee? 19. Why did he move immediately to Georgetown? 20. Whither was the enterprise of the enemy directed? 21. What did he succeed in taking from the Santee? 22. What success attended Marion's farther movements? 23. Where did Marion now take post? 24. With what object?

to be isolated.   Knowing their cavalry to be with Marion, and ignorant of the rapidity of his return, they supposed him to be still at Georgetown.   Major Fraser, at the head of above one hundred British dragoons, advanced to surprise this party.

It was not without some uneasiness that Marion prepared to receive the enemy.   The greater part of his force, at this time, consisted of what were termed, in the language of that day, *new-made whigs*.   They were men originally tories, who, in consequence of a judicious proclamation of Governor Rutledge, which offered pardon to all who would join the American forces within a limited time, had deserted from the British.

But his uneasiness was misplaced.   There could not have been a description of men more deeply interested in securing themselves against the British sabres.   Not one of them, if taken, would have escaped military execution.   Instead, therefore, of surprising the Americans, Fraser found them drawn out and ready to receive him.   His charge was met with firm nerves and the keenest aim.   A single fire terminated the action; and it is seldom that a single fire has done equal execution on a like number of men.   One officer, eight men, and five horses were killed; three officers, eight men, and a number of horses wounded and taken.   The Americans sustained no loss in men, but a very severe loss in ammunition.   The driver of the wagon which contained it, or his horse, took fright during the engagement, and made off in a direction which revealed its flight to the enemy, by a small detachment of whom it was captured.   Unhappily, Marion was destitute of his cavalry, who were then patrolling the country below, and cavalry alone could have retrieved his loss.   Five of his men, armed with the broad swords of the slain British, and mounted on as many captured horses, resolved upon the effort.   They succeeded; but the prize was again wrested from their hands before they could reach the infantry, by the return of the enemy in force.

25. What did the British suppose to be the condition of Marion's command ? — and where did they suppose it was? 26. Who advanced to surprise him? — and with what force? 27. How was Marion's army at this time constituted? 28. By what means had they been induced to join the American army?   29. What was the result of Major Fraser's attack?   30. How many of the enemy were killed, wounded, or taken?   31. What loss was sustained by the Americans?   32. How did they lose their ammunition?   33. How was the wagon rescued?   34. By what means was it recaptured?

"It was certainly," remarks the historian, "the distinguishing attribute of Marion, always to extract good service from the militia. They thought themselves invincible under him; and in the present instance, he declares that not a man faltered; that he even had to check their anxiety to move out into the open field and receive the charge of the cavalry. But Marion's coolness never deserted him; in the absence of his cavalry, a defeat would have been converted into a rout, and both corps would have been sacrificed in detail."

Had his cavalry been present, the assailants must have been utterly cut to pieces. In an hour and a half after they had moved off, Major Conyers arrived with his horse, and went instantly in pursuit. But Major Fraser had by this time formed a junction with a detachment of infantry which had advanced to his support; and, without ammunition, Marion was forced to retire once more toward the Santee.

Greene, with half his army on the sick-list, could give him no succor. Gist was employed upon the Combahee, in protecting that river from the foraging parties of the enemy; and partial, indeed, would have been the securities of the American army, were it not that the troops of the British in Charlestown and the vicinity were in not much better condition.

But events were approaching — brought about by the steady adherence of the Americans to their resolution of independence, in spite of privation, danger, and every form of suffering — which were at length calculated to give them relief from present evils, and a triumphant solace for all the past. Early in September, Sir Samuel Hood arrived, with a convoying fleet, to cover the evacuation of the British from Charlestown. Major Fraser was recalled to the city, and Marion resumed his station at Wadboo. The light brigade, under General Gist, took a position, soon after it was formed, in advance of the army near the Stono. Colonel Laurens, who had been charged with con-

85. Repeat what is said of Marion. 86. What prevented the British from being cut to pieces in this battle? 37. Why was Marion finally forced to retire? 38. What prevented General Greene from assisting him? 39. How was General Gist employed? 40. What occurred early in September? 41. Major Fraser having been recalled to the city, where did Marion resume his station? 42. Where was General Gist's brigade stationed? 43. What post was assigned to Colonel Laurens?

ducting the intercourse with the corps of intelligence in Charlestown, had a guard assigned him, and placed himself without the pickets of the brigade and near to Wappoo creek.

When General Gist was ordered to the southward, to protect the country on the Combahee from the foraging fleet of the enemy, General Greene did not think it advisable to withdraw Laurens from a post so highly confidential and important; and, accordingly, issued no orders to the latter to join his brigade.

But the ardor of Laurens was not to be restrained when the prospect was open for active operations against the foe.   When made acquainted with the orders of Gist, "to strike at the enemy wherever he might meet them, he resolved to share in the enterprise; and, rising from a sick-bed, he hurried after the brigade, which he overtook on the north bank of Combahee river, near the ferry.   Colonel Laurens solicited from his commander an opportunity for immediate enterprise; and, fatally fortunate in his application, he obtained his wish.

The enemy had landed from their boats on the opposite side of the river, and the cavalry, under Major Call, had been ordered round by Salkehatchie bridge, to join the militia who had collected in that quarter.   Twelve miles below the ferry, on the north side of the Combahee, the extreme end of Chehaw neck approaches the bed of the river, which generally, between these points, is bordered by extensive swamps and rice-fields.   At this point, General Gist had ordered a work to be thrown up, for the purpose of annoying the enemy in their retreat, and the command of this post was conferred on Laurens.

With fifty infantry, some matrosses, and a howitzer, he moved down the river on the evening of the 26th of August, near enough to take post at Chehaw point by the dawn of the following day.   At the place of Mrs. Stock he spent the night, in the enjoyment of company, and in the utterance of feelings and sentiments which heighten the melancholy interest of the fatal

44. Eager to engage in active operations against the enemy, where did Colonel Laurens join the brigade?   45. What request did he make of his commander?   46. Where had General Gist thrown up works for the purpose of annoying the enemy in their retreat?   47. To whom did General Gist entrust the force sent against the enemy? 48. What was the amount of this force?   49. When did Colonel Laurens set out to take the command of his post at Chehaw?   50. Where did he spend the night?

event which closed his adventure. The warm hospitality of the lady of the mansion, and the blandishments of female society, beguiled the time, and the company did not separate until two hours before the hour when the detachment was set in motion. The expected conflict was the subject of conversation, and the apprehensions of the ladies were soothed by the pleasant indifference with which he spoke of the event.

At three o'clock he commenced his march, mounted and at the head of his detachment, altogether unsuspicious of danger, when the enemy was discovered. They had probably received some intelligence of the march of the detachment; and, landing on the north bank of the river, and pushing into the road that communicates with the point, they had formed an ambuscade in a place covered with fennel and high grass, and were completely concealed from sight, until they rose to deliver their fire upon the unsuspecting Americans.

With the discovery of the British, the decision of Laurens was promptly taken. He saw that his only alternative against a shameful surrender, or a more dangerous if not more shameful retreat, was an energetic charge. This he instantly ordered, and, with characteristic courage, led the way.

He fell at the first fire; so did Captain Smith of the artillery; and the men were thrown into confusion, and fled. The howitzer fell into the enemy's hands, who pursued the flying infantry about a quarter of a mile, when they were met by General Gist. The pursuers fell back and drew up under cover of a wood, near the edge of the river. An attempt to dislodge them before the infantry came up, failed, and was attended with some loss. Their front was covered by logs and brush, so as to be inaccessible to cavalry, and in infantry they were superior to Gist's command.

The loss of the British on this occasion is unknown. That of the Americans was very serious for so small a force; and in the death of Laurens the army lamented a tried and gallant soldier; the country an unshrinking, unsleeping patriot. Greene, in a letter, speaks of him in this language:

51. How was he surprised on his march the next day by the enemy? 52. What was the fate of Colonel Laurens? 53. What other officer likewise fell? 54. By whom were the flying infantry met in their retreat? 55. Which party suffered the greatest loss in this engagement? 56. What character is given of Colonel Laurens?

"Poor Laurens has fallen in a paltry little skirmish. You knew his temper, and I predicted his fate. The love of military glory made him seek it upon occasions unworthy his rank. The state will feel his loss."

His body was deposited in the earth at the plantation of Mrs. Stock, "where," says the biographer of Greene, "a small enclosure of the simplest structure seems to excite, not answer, the inquiry, 'What undistinguished stranger lies buried here?'"

From the Combahee river, the British passed into the Broad, successively ascending the streams which communicate with that river, and carrying off all the provision and live stock which they could collect. From thence they put into Port Royal, and laid the islands of Beaufort and St. Helena under contribution. It was in vain that Greene, with the feeble army which he commanded, sought to cover and protect these places. A country of vast extent, intersected with streams and marshes, easy of entrance, and quite as easy of egress, was liable to insult at a thousand quarters, to which the guardian eye could not extend nor the guardian wing give shelter. Still, the attempt was everywhere made, with a promptness and energy which only needed corresponding resources to have been everywhere successful.

General Gist pursued the British with all diligence to Port Royal ferry, where he found two of their galleys. Having opened a field-piece upon them, he soon compelled them to slip their cables and attempt to make off. In this attempt one of them, the Balfour, of two double nines, ran aground, and was abandoned by her crew. They spiked her guns and scuttled her before their departure; but their work was performed with too much hurry to be effectual. She was easily repaired; and under the command of Lieutenant Adams, with a picked crew of twenty-five men, did excellent service afterward in defending these waters from the picaroons which at that time infested them.

Gist rejoined the main army after the expulsion of the British

---

57. From the Combahee river, whither did the British pass? 58. What did they effect there? 59. Whither did they pass from thence? 60. Why could not General Greene protect these places? 61. Whither did General Gist pursue the British? 62. How did he become possessed of one of their galleys? 63. To what service was it afterward applied? 64. What is further said of General Gist?

from Beaufort, and his brigade, from this period to the close of the war, remained inactive; and the same may almost be said of the entire army, with very few and unimportant exceptions.

The British had retired under the guns of their redoubts, and no longer sought occasion for conflict. Their operations were confined chiefly to the collection of cattle and provisions for their contemplated voyage. The Americans traversed the Neck in the face of their fortifications, and Kosciusko, the famous Polish exile, who had succeeded to Colonel Laurens in the command of the advanced light troops before the enemy's lines, still farther abated their desire for adventure by the audacity of his frequent approaches.

The last blood shed in the American war was that of Captain Wilmot, of the Americans, who, with a small command, continued to cover John's island, and watch the passage by the Stono. Impatience of inactivity, and a love of adventure, led Wilmot frequently to cross the river, and harass the enemy's parties on John's island. In one of these excursions, undertaken in conjunction with Kosciusko, against a party of the British woodcutters, he fell into an ambuscade and was killed.

Meanwhile, General Leslie was pressing his preparations for the final evacuation of Charlestown. Greatly constrained and distressed in that limited position by the cordon which, in spite of all his weakness, the American general had contrived to maintain around his foe, Leslie adopted a series of providential measures which somewhat lightened his embarrassments. He relieved himself of great numbers of unnecessary consumers in the garrison, by suffering the loyalists to leave his camp and make their peace with their countrymen — a privilege of which hundreds readily availed themselves.

Another measure, of equally good policy, was his expulsion from the city of all those who were alleged to favor the American cause. This measure was ingeniously calculated to furnish

65. To what were the operations of the British now chiefly confined? 66. Who had now succeeded Colonel Laurens in the command of the American light troops? 67. Whose was the last blood shed in this war? 68. Where was Captain Wilmot stationed? 69. What were the circumstances of his death? 70. What preparations was General Leslie now making? 71. How did he relieve his garrison of several hundred unnecessary consumers? 72. What other similar measure did he adopt?

a pretext to many, who, having neglected to avail themselves of the benefits of the governor's proclamation, were necessarily dependent only on the mercy of the country.    The harsh command of expulsion from the British camp, seemed to give them some claim to the indulgence of their countrymen.

Having levelled the walls of the town and of Fort Johnson, the British commander opened a communication with General Greene, apprising him of the intended evacuation, and proposing terms in order that his departure might be a peaceable one.    An arrangement accordingly followed, by which the Americans were to take possession as the enemy's rear-guard retired ; the former pledging themselves to forbear all hostile attempts upon the movements of the British, on condition that they should do no injury to the city.

On Saturday, the 14th of December, 1782, this event took place.    The morning gun was the signal for the British rear-guard to abandon their advanced redoubts.    General Wayne, at the head of three hundred infantry, the cavalry of the legion, a detachment of artillery with two six-pounders, having been detached from the American army, had crossed Ashley river the night before, and was stationed in readiness to follow the enemy's movements.

At the sound of the morning gun the two parties were put in motion, at an assigned distance asunder of two hundred yards. They moved down the King-street road, till they had passed the lines, when the British filed off to Gadsden's wharf, where they embarked in boats which awaited them.

" It was a grand and pleasing sight," says General Moultrie in his memoirs, " to see the enemy's fleet, upwards of three hundred sail, lying at anchor from Fort Johnson to Five Fathom Hole, in a curve line, as the current runs ; and what made it more agreeable, they were ready to depart."

73. Having levelled the walls of the town, and of Fort Johnson, what communication was made by the British commander to General Greene ?  74. What arrangement was effected between them ?  75. When was Charlestown evacuated by the British ? 76. Who commanded the American detachment which entered the city as the enemy retired ?  77. What was the stipulated distance between his troops and the British rear ?  78. By what route did the enemy retire ?  79. What does General Moultrie say of the fleet ?  *

The reluctance of the one party to leave, and the impatience of the other to succeed them in the possession of the city, led the British, now and then during the march, to cry aloud to General Wayne that he was pressing too rapidly upon them. On such occasions, the halt imposed upon the Americans was a short trial of their patience.

Well might the Carolinians be impatient to behold those dear homes from which they had been so long exiled. Wayne moved forward, and halted on the south side of Broad street, nearly opposite to Church. In the rear of the American advance, came the governor of the state, attended by General Greene, and escorted by two hundred cavalry. His council, and long troops of officers and citizens, followed on horseback. Smiling faces and joyful voices saluted the deliverers as they came. The balconies and windows were crowded with the aged men, the women, and the children, who for nearly three years had wept with apprehension and sorrow the absence and the loss of dear sons, affectionate brothers, and warm friends. Their tears now were those only of joy and of triumph. " God bless you, gentlemen; God bless you, and welcome, welcome home."

Such were the sweet words which hailed the long-banished citizens, and the long-suffering soldiery of Greene. In tears, in silence, and on bended knees, the full hearts of the rescued citizens found utterance that blessed day. The state was at last free from the defiling presence of the invader, never, we trust, to suffer again from his painful scourge and humiliating arrogance and footstep !

80. Can you describe the entrance of General Wayne ?

17

# CHAPTER XVII.

### CLOSING SCENES OF THE WAR — PEACE OF PARIS — SUMMARY.

THE day after the restoration of Charlestown to the American authorities, the British fleet put to sea. If the joy of the Carolinians was great in once more resuming possession of their metropolis, the sorrows of the British on leaving it were comparatively greater. It had been for more than two years the scene in which they had played their several parts of power without restraint. Every passion of the tyrant had they shown in turn; haughty scorn, contemptuous hate, reckless lust, and griping and grinding avarice. They had trampled upon its sensibilities, shed its best blood in wantonness, and gleaned it of its treasures. The last lingering hour of their stay was distinguished by the ravages of a spirit still as greedy of gain as they had shown at their first coming. Thousands of slaves, stolen from the plantations, swelled the flying train of the British officers. For these the spoilers ultimately found a profitable market in the West Indies. The share of Lieutenant-Colonel Moncrieff, alone, is stated to have been no less than eight hundred negroes.

But this last robbery of the invaders sinks into insignificance, when compared with their frequent plunder of the same species of property during the first year of their conquest. It has been computed that South Carolina, alone, lost by these robberies no less than twenty-five thousand negroes. The losses of Georgia and North Carolina were proportionately great.

The reluctance of the invaders to leave the metropolis of Carolina, showed itself even more conclusively in the number

1. When did the British fleet put to sea ? 2. How did they dispose of the negroes ?
3. How many slaves were stolen from South Carolina by the invaders?

of deserters whom they left behind them. Hundreds emerged from cellars, chimneys, and other hiding-places, as soon as the certain absence of their army made it safe to do so. Scarcely a Hessian went back but under compulsion; and thousands prepared to encounter every danger of ill treatment from a people whom they had wronged, rather than return to a standard to which they had been sold by their mercenary sovereigns.

Among the deserters, the Irish were particularly numerous. Their desertions were so frequent, long before the war had been brought to an issue, that their officers ceased entirely to confide in them; and it is not improbable that the inactivity of General Stewart when at Orangeburg, and the subsequent imbecility which seemed to mark the proceedings of the commander while in garrison, arose rather from doubts of the fidelity of the troops than from their sickness or any other of the alleged causes.

The treaty of peace between the respective commissioners of America and Great Britain, very happily, soon followed the evacuation, and relieved the country from other evils, scarcely less serious than those which came with a state of actual warfare. The southern army, thrown for its support entirely upon South Carolina, soon exhausted the few remaining resources of the province, and the patience of the people. The state became indignant at this charge, when it was known how much it had already contributed, and how much more than any of its sisters it had suffered for three tedious years.

The army, seemingly abandoned by Congress, and having got from South Carolina all that she was able to give, proceeded to collect its food at the point of the bayonet. The state authorities — John Mathews being governor — became alarmed and angry; and their resolution to prevent the exercise of any further purveyance, increased the rage and suffering of the starving soldiery.

General Gist, who was in command at James's island, could no longer restrain his men. The cavalry at the Eutaw broke

4. What circumstance shows the reluctance of the British soldiers to depart? 5. Which of the troops were most forward to desert? 6. What event followed the evacuation of Charlestown? 7. How did the southern army proceed to collect food, after the resources of South Carolina failed?

out into actual mutiny, and were brought back to their duty only by the eloquent entreaties and reproaches of their commander. To such a height did the discontents arise, that General Greene, on one occasion, was compelled to select and draw out in order of battle, from the sound parts of his army, a sufficient force to keep the rest in subjection. These were all continental troops. The militia had been disbanded some time before without pay, and with a very cavalier disregard to their services and sufferings. The tidings of peace, as they led to the disbanding of the army, relieved the fears of the country, and in some degree the sufferings of the soldier. He could now return to those homes and happy anticipations from which the calls of his country had so long withdrawn him. He had reason to rejoice in the beams of peace, though it is feared that thousands who survived the strife, received but a small share of the blessings for which they strove in war. A tardy justice on the part of the nation has sought to compensate them for their wounds and sufferings; but the secret consciousness of their desert has been, perhaps, their greatest and best reward.

Provisional articles of peace were signed at Paris on the 13th of November, 1782, by which the king of Great Britain acknowledged "the United States of New Hampshire, Massachusetts, Connecticut, Rhode Island, New York, New Jersey, Pennsylvania, Delaware, Maryland, Virginia, North Carolina, South Carolina, and Georgia, to be free, sovereign and independent states; that he treated with them as such; and for himself, his heirs and successors, relinquished all claims to the government, proprietary and territorial rights of the same."

The termination of the revolutionary war, resulting as it did in the unrestrained and individual sovereignty of the several states engaged in it, left South Carolina free to the adoption of her own plans of government, her laws and domestic policy. Her people, with that elastic temper which had distinguished

8. To what measure was General Greene compelled? 9. What is said of the disbanding of the militia? 10. How were the sufferings of the soldiers at last relieved? 11. When were provisional articles of peace signed? 12. What was then the number of the states? 13. Name them. 14. What declaration was made with regard to these states by the king of Great Britain? 15. What was South Carolina now free to do?

them from the beginning, soon set themselves to .work to repair the disasters occasioned by the long and painful conflict which has been just recorded, and to remedy those defects in their social and political condition which it developed.   In this object it was fortunate for the country that the moderation with which the republicans regarded and treated the loyalists, led to the hearty co-operation, in all leading respects, of these lately hostile parties.   The greater part of the exiled tories were permitted to return, by legislative enactment, and, under some temporary disabilities and small fines, were restored to citizenship. Though laboring under an immense debt, the state generously restored to the late owners half a million of pounds sterling of confiscated property in actual possession.

The history of that common bond of union, by which South Carolina became one of a community of states, must be looked for in another volume.   To new-model the constitution of the state, in conformity with that of the United States, a convention of her people was called in 1790.   The constitution then adopted recognised the following elements: that all power comes from the people, and is to be exercised for their benefit; that they are bound by no laws but such as are sanctioned by their representatives; that all are equally subject to the laws; that no freeman can be taken, or imprisoned, or deprived of his property, or exiled, or in any manner destroyed or deprived of life, liberty, privilege, or possessions, but by the judgment of his peers, or by the law of the land.   It also guarantied freedom of conscience in matters of faith and religion.

These principles of liberty and equality which pervade the constitution, are impressed upon the laws of the state, which were made in compliance with them.   Under these laws the people have prospered, and have been blessed with great increase for the last seventy years.   A mild and indulgent government, with small taxation; a fruitful country, and the production of commodities which form the staples of consumption for

16. In what manner were the loyalists treated by the republicans?   17. What property did the state restore to them?   18. For what purpose was a convention of the people held?   19. In what year was it called?   20. What principles were recognised by the constitution then adopted?   21. What has been for seventy years the condition of this state?

millions, and the use of which is rapidly increasing, encourage the citizen in his labor and reward him for it. But few interruptions have occurred in the progress of the state to prosperity. Religion and education have kept corresponding pace with the progress of agriculture among the people. Public works of great value and cost, in every section of the country, mark the watchful care of an intelligent legislature.

The numbers of the people of South Carolina, which in 1765 were but one hundred and twenty-three thousand of all descriptions, are now (in 1859) about seven hundred thousand; and this increase has been constant and progressive, though thousands of her sons have colonized the rich fields of Alabama, Mississippi, and the fertile regions beyond.

Nor is the prosperity of South Carolina marked only by affluence in wealth and increase of numbers at home. Her sons have always held a leading rank in the estimation of the Union. Their counsels have been no less acknowledged for, than distinguished by, wisdom. Their character has been unexceptionable and blameless. Spotless in integrity, they have not been wanting in that honorable ambition which seeks the high places of responsibility; and in stations of the highest trust they have shown themselves equally adequate to their tasks and worthy of their honors. Her jewels, indeed, have been always as brilliant as they were numerous; and though one of the smallest states, in a territorial point of view, in the Union, her moral weight has ever given her a distinguished attitude in the councils and performances of the whole country. Her chronicle of great names is unusually copious. Her Draytons, Pinckneys, Rutledges, Middletons, and Gadsdens, as educated men, no less than statesmen and patriots, were always in the first rank; and the long list which follows, and which should be fixed firmly in the memory of her sons, is of itself a column of glory to her name which shall for ever preserve it, amid all the vicissitudes of power, and in defiance of all the

22. How is the labor of the citizen encouraged and rewarded? 23. What was the population of the state in 1765? 24. What is it now (1859)? 25. How have Carolinians always ranked? 26. How does South Carolina compare with the other states in extent of territory? 27. What position has she procured by her moral weight? 28. Who are named among her statesmen and patriots?

devastating effects of time. Moultrie and Marion, Sumter, Laurens, Horry, Pickens, Williams, the Hammonds, and hundreds more, who distinguished themselves equally in civil and military affairs during the war, were all remarkable men; and, more recently, the names of other renowned and mighty men furnish a record as glorious, which fully proves that the example of the past has not been chronicled in vain.

One lesson, in chief, may be gleaned, among many others, from this imperfect story of the past. It is that which teaches the citizen to cling to the soil of his birth in the day of its difficulty, with the resolution of the son who stands above the grave of a mother and protects it from violation. This will be a safe rule for the citizen, whatever may be the cause of war or the character of the invader. Opinion hourly fluctuates and changes; public policy is of all things the most uncertain and capricious; and the pretexts of ambition suggest a thousand subtle combinations of thought and doctrine, upon which the human mind would depend with doubt and difficulty.

But the resolves of a decided majority, in all questions of public expediency or policy, assumed as the voice of the soil, would be the course equally of patriotism and safety. This rule, preserved in memory and maintained as a principle, would unite a people and make them invincible. The thunders and the threatenings of the foe would die away, unharming, in the distance. Unanimity among our citizens will always give them unconquerable strength, and invasion will never again set hostile foot on the shores of our country.

29. Who were conspicuous in the field? 80. What lesson may be learned from this history? Repeat the concluding paragraphs.

# BOOK VI.

## SUPPLEMENTARY.

—•—

## CHAPTER LAST.

### FROM THE CLOSE OF THE WAR OF THE REVOLUTION TO THE PRESENT TIME — 1782 TO 1860.

WITH the exciting issues, doubts, dangers, trials of strength and passion, which constituted the chief interest in that long narrative of war through which we have gone, we have no more to deal. Such crises, in the affairs of a people, are, perhaps, ordeals of training and preparation; ordeals of fire; by which they are to be at once purified for a great service, and a goodly development of moral strength and stature. It is, perhaps, essential to every people, that they should, at some period or other, go through some such ordeal. At all events, whether necessary or not, such has usually been the great necessity of every great nation, at some early era in its progress. Even if the Deity does not decree the necessity, as one of his own chosen and imperative processes for trying the strength and sinews of his people, it is yet very certain that, in the avarice, insolence, and restless ambition of men, there will be found always some portions of the human family prepared to make war a human necessity! Nations are required to accept it as one of the evil conditions inseparate from the assertion of their rights, their liberties, and independence.

From the record comprised in the preceding pages, we have seen that no people of this country — perhaps, of any country — no state in this Confederacy — ever bore up more manfully, under such an accumulation of evils, than did the little state and people of South Carolina. One of the feeblest of the British colonies in America, with a small and scattered population, easily accessible to the invader from the sea; bordered, in the interior, by vast wildernesses, filled with savage men; her own population, in large proportion, foreign by birth, and totally incapable of realizing, for themselves, that idea of independence of all foreign rule, which constituted the chief dream, desire, and earnest purpose of her leading native intellects; it may readily be conceived that her trials would be, in the last degree, severe; her fortunes liable to every sort of caprice; her plains overrun; her sons overpowered; her homes despoiled; and that there must be moments of exhaustion, of extreme and accumulated misfortunes, when her constancy would be shaken, and when her heart would sink within her, almost hopeless of the future, and disposed to doubt the legitimacy of her desire to maintain herself a sovereign and independent state. But she survived these despondencies; strove through all; and emerged, finally, from the trial, bleeding at all her veins, but with the grand passion of her soul attained! She had won her liberties by her constancy and faith; her valor, and the patriotic pride, which enabled her to endure privation without complaint, and to meet danger and death without a fear.

She is compensated. The danger is passed; and she is now required to meet more arduous necessities, if not more perilous, by endeavoring to establish her liberties, on a firm foundation, consistently with the enlarged and growing civilization of the age, chastened by the recognition of the paramount claims of morals and religion.

The history of her progress, in this duty, is one not calculated to enlist the active sympathies of those who desire the excitements of war, and revel only in the strong interests and crises which belong to the violent collision of hostile passions.

As one of the confederated states of the great American Confederacy, South Carolina can assert no exclusive right to the achievements of the nation; and these, luckily for the national happiness and security, have been conquests of peace and society, rather than of anarchy and war. Whatever have been the trials and troubles of the Confederacy, she has shared them only as one of many; and the details which belong to our common history, as a nation, must be sought for in other volumes. In her individual career, however, or in the part she has taken in the affairs of the Confederacy, it will be found that she has been invariably true to the great principles which actuated her throughout the Revolution, and from the earliest periods of her colonial foundation.

She has taken a patriotic share in the burdens of the nation; she has contributed some of the bravest soldiers, the ablest statesmen, and the noblest warriors, to its fields and councils, and has never shrunk from any social or national responsibility; has kept faith with her sister sovereigns, and has maintained a proverbially jealous watch over the common constitution of the country, which the wisdom of her great revolutionary sires contributed to devise, as embodying the best securities equally of state and people.

Nor has she been heedless of those interests of morals, education, and social virtue; manners, conduct, and society; which, perhaps, constitute more precious securities, for human liberty, than law has ever been able to devise. Her progress in civilization, in arts, and arms, is to be found written on her fields and cities, as well as in the records of the national performance. She has been steadily advancing in all those pursuits which are found to bring prosperity to a people, and to train them to a due sense of their social responsibilities, their vital duties, and interests.

But, before this progress could be well begun, she had domestic troubles to overcome, which were of a sort to vex the human and social sense almost to despair; and, at times, to render faint the hopes and energies of the best statesmanship. Covered with scars and glory, with scores of able and thoughtful leaders, military and civil, the termination of the Revolutionary war found her a wreck in fortune, and with a country most terribly demoralized by the progress of a long war, which had witnessed the total ruin of all her homesteads, and the disruption, everywhere, of the bonds of society. Wild passions had been let loose, and had fed on blood and rapine, for too long a season to be soon brought into subjection. The peace with Great Britain brought no absolute peace to her scattered communities, which sometimes glared on each other with the eager ferocity of the tiger. Lawless men traversed her forest-paths, for a time, with violence and impunity. Desperadoes, whom war and rapine had taught all their lessons, raged, torch in hand, around quiet and defenceless habitations. The old feuds of whig and tory were still unsatisfied. Old revenges were perpetually rising up to renew the bloody scenes of former seasons; and, in some instances, the loyalist, notorious for crimes committed during the war, though discharged by court and jury, has been seized upon by a still infuriated people, and dragged, in the very presence of the judge, to the halter and the tree, allowed " short shrift," and shorter cord, and launched into eternity, in spite of the general amnesty proclaimed by the government. It required many years before the wild passions which had been stimulated by the bloody civil feuds of the Revolution, could be restrained by the arm of law, or subdued and soothed by the gentler offices of religion.

But we must proceed to illustrate this summary by details. We have seen that John Rutledge, governor and dictator of the state, during the most arduous period of the struggle in the war, gracefully yielded up his trust, in 1782, at the convention of the General Assembly at Jacksonboro. He could then properly do so, the war being entirely at an end. The venerable patriot, Christopher Gadsden, was chosen to succeed him.

This brave old man declined the office, pleading his age and growing infirmities. He had shown himself one of the most forward, persevering, and earnest of the great men of the Revolution; had commanded in the military, led in the council, and was one of the prisoners of war to the British, under the capitulation of Charlestown. Violating his securities as such, the British governor in Carolina put him in close imprisonment, with forty of the chief citizens of Charlestown, with whom he was sent to the castle of St. Augustine. These citizens were kept as hostages for the good behavior of the rest of the people, who were suspected of insurrectionary movements. Here, at St. Augustine, with his health suffering from close confinement,

1. When and where did John Rutledge resign his office of governor ? 2. Who was chosen to succeed him ? 3. What is said of Gadsden ?

in his old age, Gadsden amused himself by a study of the He-
brew language.   When restored to his home, in the decline of
life, he might well reject the office tendered him, on the plea
which he made for refusing it.   The tribute was due to his
noble character and great services.

John Mathews was chosen to the office.   He, too, had shown
himself a patriot of the Revolution ; was a man of ability, with
a stern sense of what was due to the dignity of the state.   He
was soon after embroiled in a controversy with General Greene,
representing the army, as we have glimpsed at in preceding
pages.   Abstractly, the governor was right, and the course
which he took, in resisting the exactions of a soldiery who were
no longer necessary to the country, was required by his oath
of office as governor of the state.   But the case was an exceptional one, and required some allowances.   The army should
have been disbanded, like the militia, with the withdrawal of
the foreign enemy.   But, while the militia were sent adrift, at
the various places where the peace found them — not permitted
to behold the pageant, when the British withdrew, and the
Americans marched into the city — the continentals were not
to be so summarily dismissed.   There were large arrearages to
be paid them, for which Congress had made no preparation.
They were destitute of means.   The granaries of South Carolina had been their only source of supply for three years, and
South Carolina was measurably exhausted.   She had no money
— no means of raising it.   To support the soldiery, her only
process was to drag the provisions from the stores of her own
citizens ; and these, drained of their supplies during the war,
were naturally tenacious of all that the British had left them.
Governor Mathews had no right to assess the citizens for the
support of the soldiery, and, as governor, that which he might
not do himself, he was bound to see should not be done by any
other authority.   For the details of the controversy between
himself and Greene, see Johnson's life of that general.

The assembly which elected Mathews governor, proceeded

4. Who succeeded Gadsden ?  5. What is said of him ?  6. In what controversy
was he embroiled ?  7. What was the condition of the continental troops ?  8. What
resources had South Carolina at this time ?   9. What did the assembly proceed
to do ?

to supply all the vacancies in the different departments of office, and to re-establish all the branches of civil government. The governor was empowered, as had been his predecessor, to " do all matters and things which are judged expedient and necessary to secure the liberty, safety, and happiness of the state." The times were still too unruly — the British were still present — and the dictatorship was a necessary adjunct of the duty of an executive.

Laws were passed for the confiscation of the estates of tories, and for banishing from the country such as were active and decided friends of the British ; also, for amersing the estates of others, who were less offensive, and in lieu of their personal services, which had been withheld from the country. Two hundred and thirty-seven persons, or estates, were included in the first of these classes, and forty-eight in the last. From these numbers, it may be conjectured with some safety, what was the real proportion of the old or native population which was found wanting to the country in the day of her trial. These enactments were afterwards modified or repealed, by the terms of the evacuation of Charlestown, as may be seen in previous pages. The mood of the conquerors naturally became more indulgent to the vanquished, in proportion as they felt the security of the infant republic.

In 1783, Benjamin Guerard, of Charlestown, was made governor. He, too, had been a tried patriot during the Revolution. During his administration, Charlestown was incorporated, and called " *Charleston.*" The town of Stateburg was founded about the same time, by General Sumter ; and — a more significant beginning — cotton began to be cultivated for export, though still on a limited scale.

In 1785, William Moultrie was elected to the executive chair ; of him and his revolutionary career, we have already made full report. Moultrie, like Gadsden, had been kept as a British

10. What laws were passed affecting the tories ? 11. How many persons or estates were included in these two classes ? 12. Was there subsequently any modification of these laws ? 13. Who succeeded Mathews as governor ? — and when ? 14. What is said of him ? 15. What noticeable event occurred during his administration ? 16. What town was founded by General Sumter ? 17. Which of the great staples began to be cultivated about this time ? 18. Who was the next governor ? — and when was he elected ? 19. What had been his fate during the war ?

prisoner, almost from the fall of Charlestown to the close of the war. The South had constant reason to complain, that in the exchange of prisoners with the enemy, the North had the preference always. See, on this subject, Graydon's (Pennsylvania) Memoirs. Moultrie's own Memoirs of the Revolution are of great value, as the evidence of an eye-witness of most that he relates, and frequently as a most conspicuous actor in the event.

We are told that during this administration the Methodists first made their appearance in Carolina as a religious fraternity. It is probable that some few of them had been in the state before, and, indeed, as far back as the time of Wesley, in Georgia. The town of Columbia was located during Moultrie's term, and ordered to be laid out as the seat of government of the state, which it continues to be — a beautiful situation on the banks of the Congaree, approached on every hand by railroads, and remarkable for its polish, intelligence, and growing population. It is the seat of the State College also, of the Lunatic Asylum, the Theological College, and several other educational establishments.

Thomas Pinckney, of Charleston, was elected governor in 1787. He, too, had distinguished himself in the Revolution, and had been severely wounded in the battle of Camden. He was subsequently a major-general in the armies of the United States in Florida and Georgia; but his merits did not solely lie in the military line. He had been educated in Europe, and was one of the best read and most accomplished scholars of his day in Carolina. At the opening of the Revolution, he, with his brother, Charles Cotesworth, and; indeed, most of the sons of the wealthier families in South Carolina, were educated at British schools and universities; and it is probable that few men on the American continent could approach them in the profundity, grace, and finish, of their acquisitions. Subsequently, Charles Cotesworth was, with many, a favorite candidate for the presidential office.

20. Of what had the South reason to complain? 21. When did the Methodists first make their appearance as a religious sect in South Carolina? 22. What town was located during Moultrie's term? — and what is said of it? 23. What state institutions are located here? 24. Who was the next governor? — and when was he elected? 25. What is said of him? — what of his brother?

During Mr. Pinckney's administration, the Instalment law of the state was passed; the last attempt in South Carolina, says the chronicler, to interfere between creditor and debtor. The last instalment was made payable March 25, 1793. Clermont parish was established in the same year.

In 1789, Charles Pinckney succeeded as governor. He was of Charleston, a man of brilliant abilities, and subsequently the American minister to Spain. The state records were removed to Columbia this year. That town was gradually taking form and seeming. The first session of the assembly met there in January, 1790; and there the present constitution of the state was ratified, June 3, of the same year.

Meanwhile, the population of the whole state had been growing with remarkable increase, especially in the upper country. New settlers came from Pennsylvania, from Virginia, and North Carolina; British traders began to re-occupy the old places, and, the rancor of civil strife having subsided, the banished royalists reappeared in familiar haunts, without having the terrors of the halter in their eyes. When, in 1790, the census of the United States was taken, the population of South Carolina had reached a fraction less than 250,000. The white population had swollen to 140,178. The slaves and free colored were 108,900.

In 1792, Arnoldus Vanderhorst, of Charleston, was made governor. He, also, had distinguished himself as a patriot and soldier of the Revolution.

During his administration, the law was passed abolishing the old British statute, the right of primogeniture, and an equal distribution was granted of the property of intestates. The Roman Catholics were organized into a church, May 2, 1791. The Orphan House Asylum, a noble charity, was established

26. What measures were passed during his administration? 27. Who succeeded him? — and when? 28. What is said of Charles Pinckney? 29. When was the present constitution of the state ratified? — and where? 30. What is said of the increase of population in the state? 31. What was the whole number of inhabitants in 1790? 32. How many whites? 33. How many blacks? 34. Who was elected governor in 1792? 35. What is said of him? 36. What important law was passed during his administration? 37. When were the Roman Catholics first organized into a church in the state? 38. What institution was established in Charleston at this time?

(1792) in Charleston, where it now maintains and educates some three hundred orphans, of both sexes.

The year 1791 was distinguished in South Carolina, by the visit of General Washington, making the tour of the Southern states. He was received with heartfelt enthusiasm; visited the public and military works; and expressed the warmest gratification at what he saw. On leaving Charleston, for Savannah, he was escorted by Governor Vanderhorst, Generals Moultrie, Pinckney, and many other eminent citizens.

In 1792, the city of Charleston was fatally visited by yellow fever, which held sway for nearly four months, and carried off one hundred and sixty-five victims, mostly foreigners. The Instalment law expired with the last payment, March 25, 1793. In this year, the Santee canal, uniting the Santee with the Cooper river — a stupendous work at that period — was begun.

In 1794, William Moultrie became, for the second time, governor of the state. The year was noted for a large increase in the cultivation of cotton.

The 27th of February, of the year 1795, was marked by the death of the famous partisan, General Francis Marion. He died at his residence, St. John's parish, in his sixty-third year. His biography has been frequently written. His performances are well known, and constitute a history of which his country will long be proud. Retiring from the field at the close of the war, he did not wholly withdraw from the public service. He continued to hold a commission in the militia of the state. He represented his parish in the senate. In 1790 he sat as a member of the convention for forming the state constitution. In 1794 he resigned his military commission. The simple tomb which covers his remains at the family homestead was reared by a private citizen. There is no public monument yet raised in his honor, by the state which he contributed, as much as any man, to pluck from the control of the invader.

39. What distinguished individual visited the state in 1791? 40. How was he received? 41. By whom was he escorted when he left Charleston? 42. What fearful epidemic visited Charleston in 1792? 43. What was the number of its victims? 44. What public work was begun in 1793? 45. Who was elected governor in 1794? 46. For what was this year noted? 47. What notable event occurred in 1795? 48. What is said of Marion?

In 1796, Charles Pinckney again succeeded to the office of governor. In 1798, Edward Rutledge, one of the signers of the Declaration of Independence, became the governor. In 1799, the yellow fever again raged in Charleston, but with less fatality, and still its subjects were mostly foreigners. The legislature, during this administration, established the office of comptroller-general. About the same time the state was newly districted or divided off into counties, districts, and parishes. These were twenty-four in number, as follows: Beaufort, Charleston, Georgetown, Orangeburg, Camden, Cheraw, Ninety-Six, Pinckney, and Washington *districts.*

The *parishes* and *counties* were: St. Helena, St. Luke, Prince William, St. Peter, St. Philip, St. Michael, St. Bartholomew, St. John (Colleton), St. Andrew, St. Paul, All Saints, Prince George, Frederick, Louisburg or St. Matthew, Orange, Lexington, Winton, Clarendon, Clermont, Salem, Richland, Fairfield, Chesterfield, Darlington, York, Chester, Union, Spartanburg, Pendleton, Greenville, Abbeville, Edgefield, Newberry, and Laurens. Three years after this period, another organization of the sections of the state took place, by which its grand divisions were made to embrace twenty-eight districts, as follows:—

*Lower Districts.* — Beaufort, Charleston, Colleton, Georgetown, Williamsburg, Marion, and Horry.

*Middle Districts.* — Barnwell, Edgefield, Orangeburg, Newberry, Lexington, Richland, Fairfield, Sumter, Kershaw, Darlington, Chesterfield, and Marlborough.

*Upper Districts.* — Abbeville, Laurens, Union, Chester, Lancaster, York, Spartanburg, Greenville, and Pendleton. The last district has recently been divided into two separate districts, one of which is called Pickens, the other Anderson. Still more recently, Sumter has been divided into two also — Sumter and Clarendon. It seems probable that other like divisions of other

49. Who was elected governor in 1796? 50. Who in 1798? 51. What happened in Charleston in 1799? 52. What public office was established during this administration? 53. How was the state districted? 54. Into how many districts? 55. Name them. 56. Name the parishes or counties. 57. What division subsequently took place? 58. Into how many districts was the state then divided? 59. Name the parishes in the Lower district? 60. In the Middle district? 61. In the Upper district? 62. Which of these districts have recently been subdivided? 63. What is probable with regard to others?

districts will take place, several of them being quite too cumbrous for the convenience of the people, retarding the operation of law, and baffling the objects of education.

In 1800, John Drayton, son of William Henry, of Revolutionary memory, became governor. He was a man of letters, and has left us several valuable volumes of a public character; one, a body of "Memoirs of the Revolution in South Carolina," in two volumes; and a single volume, "A View of South Carolina." He was a close, circumspect, and industrious compiler, and his notes are useful and authoritative.

During his administration the *county* courts were abolished, and *district* courts substituted in every district.

In 1801 the Santee canal was finished and went into successful operation. In the same year the South Carolina college was established by the legislature as a public institution, supported by the government. To this college the state appropriates some twenty-five thousand dollars per annum. It is on an extensive plan, with numerous buildings, and possesses a fine library, which receives annual additions to a large amount from legislative appropriations.

At this period the United States census made the population of South Carolina to consist of a total of three hundred and forty-five thousand, five hundred and ninety-one; of which one hundred and ninety-six thousand, two hundred and fifty-five were whites, one hundred and forty-six thousand, one hundred and fifty-one slaves, and three thousand, one hundred and eighty-five free blacks and colored; showing a considerable increase over the preceding census, though the drain by emigration to the southwest had already been begun.

James B. Richardson, of Sumter, a planter, and son of the Revolutionary General Richardson, was elected governor in 1802. We only note, during this period, that vaccination was

64. Who was elected governor in 1800?   65. What is said of him?   66. What changes were made in the courts during his administration?   67. What public work was completed in 1801?   68. Where was South Carolina college established, and how is it supported?   69. What amount does the state contribute annually for its support?   70. What was the population of the state at this time?   71. How many whites?   72. How many blacks?   73. How many free blacks?   74. Who was elected governor in 1802?   75. What noticeable events occurred during his administration?

first introduced into South Carolina by the celebrated Doctor Ramsay. The cotton-culture continued to increase and expand.

Paul Hamilton succeeded as governor in 1804. He was the friend and counsellor of Isaac Hayne, the martyr in the Revolution, and himself a Revolutionary personage of great influence. In September, of this year, Charleston was visited by a dreadful hurricane, which destroyed a vast amount of property, and for a time threatened the whole city. — The debts due the state were ascertained to amount to seven hundred and thirty-four thousand, seven hundred and fifty-five dollars.

Charles Pinckney was again made governor in 1806. During his term, the right of suffrage was accorded by the legislature to all white citizens, without requiring a property qualification.

In 1808, John Drayton was again elected governor.

In 1810, Henry Middleton, of Charleston, of one of the famous old colonial and Revolutionary families, succeeded to Drayton. In this year the population of South Carolina, by the United States census, made a total of four hundred and thirteen thousand, five hundred and fifteen; namely, two hundred and fourteen thousand, one hundred and ninety-six whites; one hundred and ninety-six thousand, three hundred and sixty-five slaves; and four thousand, five hundred and fifty-four free blacks and colored — an increase in ten years of some sixty-five thousand. We note the greater proportionate increase of the slave population.

In 1811, a general free-school system for the education of poor children was established for the first time. We shall note, hereafter, the result of the working of this system, and indicate equally its defects and benefits.

In 1812, Joseph Allston, of Georgetown, became the governor. This gentleman was a man of large abilities. He was

76. Who was elected governor in 1804? 77. With what calamity was Charleston visited in September of this year? 78. What amount of debt was due the state at this time? 79. Who was made governor in 1806? 80. What important act was passed during his administration? 81. Who was made governor in 1808? 82. Who in 1810? 83. What was the population at this time? 84. The number of whites? 85. The number of slaves? 86. The number of free blacks? 87. What was the increase in ten years? 88. What was established in 1811? 89. Who was made governor in 1812?

intimately concerned and active in the political parties of the nation, and will long be remembered as the husband of the beautiful, accomplished and charming, but unfortunate, Theodosia, the favorite daughter of Aaron Burr. Her fate, for she disappeared at sea, is still a mystery. She is thought to have fallen a victim to some one of the many piratical vessels which infested the gulf of Mexico for so long a period.

Several important events took place in South Carolina during Governor Allston's administration. The bank of the state was established in Charleston. Subsequently, branches of it were created at Columbia and Camden.

It had become necessary to ascertain and fix the boundary line between the two Carolinas, and commissioners from North and South Carolina were appointed by the respective states. They proceeded to their survey with due diligence, and finally agreed upon the line. This, however, seems to have been arbitrarily resolved upon, and without proper regard to the configuration of the country. It should have followed the summits of the Apalachian, or Blue-Ridge chain, wherever this rose between the two states. The result of the present arrangement is to throw certain portions of North Carolina on the South Carolina side of the chain; and thus, while the convenience of business and a market would lead the people to the villages of the southern, the arbitrary enactment of law compels them to cross the mountains of the northern, state. Of the mountain region of South as well as North Carolina, no portion of the United States can exceed the beauty, salubrity, and fertility. It constitutes the Helvetia of the country.

The geographical designation of South Carolina is as follows:—

South Carolina is situated between thirty-two degrees, four minutes, thirty seconds, and thirty-five degrees, twelve minutes, north latitude, and one degree, thirty minutes, and six degrees, fifty-four minutes, west longitude, from the capital at Washington, or seventy-eight degrees, twenty-five minutes, and eighty-three degrees, forty-nine minutes, west longitude from Greenwich. From the closest computation which has been made, South Carolina contains 30,213 square miles, or 19,435,680 acres; and averages in length one hundred and eighty-nine miles, and in breadth one hundred and sixty miles.

Her present limits are included within the following lines :—

Beginning at a cedar stake, marked with nine notches, on the shore of the Atlantic ocean (Goat island), about one mile and a quarter east of the mouth of Little river, and running thence north forty-seven degrees, thirty minutes west, ninety-one miles, seventeen chains (along the line run in 1764), to a light wood post (the northeast corner of the state); thence south eighty-nine degrees, five minutes west, sixty-five miles, forty chains, to the end of the line run in 1764; thence north two degrees, fifteen minutes east, seven miles, fifty-nine chains, to a marked sweet gum, designating the southeast corner of the Catawba Indian boundary-line (being the intersection of the five-mile creek); thence north forty-one degrees west, thirteen miles, eight chains, to a marked hickory, about one third of a mile beyond Thomas P. Smith's house; thence south fifty-two degrees west, seven miles to the Catawba river (near the mouth of White's branch); thence north three degrees west, up the Catawba river, about seven miles, to where it intersects the line run in 1772 (which commences at the mouth of the Little Catawba river); thence along the said line, due west sixty-four miles, forty chains, to a stone near the Tryon mountain, marked 'S. C.,' which designates the termination of the line run in 1772. Here the commissioners appointed by the legislatures of North and South Carolina, to establish the north boundary line between the two states, set up a stone in 1813, marked 'N. C. and S. C., September 15th, 1813,' and thence continued the line due west four miles, twenty-two and a half chains, to a rock marked 'S. C, and N. C. ;' thence south twenty-five degrees west, twenty-nine and a half chains, to a chestnut on the top of the ridge, dividing the waters of the north fork of Pacolet river from the waters of the north fork of Saluda river; thence along the said ridge (keeping on the summit of the same all the way) until it intersects the Cherokee Indian boundary line (in a straight line near thirty miles, and following the ridge fifty miles), where a stone is set up and marked ' S. C. and N. C., 1813 ;' thence south sixty-eight degrees, fifteen minutes west, eighteen miles, thirty chains, to the intersection of the thirty-fifth degrees north latitude, which is marked on a rock in the east branch of Chatooga river, with ' latitude 35° A. D. 1813' (all which aforesaid lines divide this state from North Carolina) ; thence down the Chatooga river to its junction with the Tugaloo, where it is called the Toruro river (general course southwest twenty-nine degrees, distance in a straight line twenty-five miles) ; thence down the Tugaloo and Savannah rivers, to the intersection of the same with the Atlantic ocean (general course southeast forty degrees, distance in a straight line two hundred and twenty-six miles), all which divide this state from Georgia ; thence along the seacoast, including all the islands adjacent, to the place of beginning (general course northeast fifty-four degrees, thirty minutes, one hundred miles in a straight line).

An event of national interest occurred during Allston's administration. The aggressions of Britain upon our commerce aroused the indignation of the American people, especially of the south ; and on the eighteenth of June, 1812, the Congress of the United States declared war against Great Britain. In this declaration the patriotism of South Carolina, represented by such men as William Lowndes, John C. Calhoun, and Langdon Cheves, was actively influential. They were the most earnest pleaders to the nation for the assertion of its rights. The war was of brief duration, lasting about two years. In this time, apart from the usual unfavorable effects of war upon commerce, South Carolina suffered little from its influence. Occasional descents were made upon her coasts by the British cruisers, and the entrances to the several ports of Charleston, Beaufort, and Georgetown, were sometimes obstructed by their frigates.

In South Carolina a becoming spirit was manifested to meet

95. Describe her present limits. 96. What event of national interest occurred during Allston's administration ? 97. What part did South Carolina and her representatives take in this discussion ? 98. Who were her representatives at this time ?

the enemy in the event of invasion, which was anticipated from the same force which penetrated to Washington. Fortifications were raised in and around Charleston; and such places along the coast as were more accessible for the landing of an enemy, were put in a condition for defence and manned with troops.

In Charleston, the spirit of individual enterprise and valor kept equal pace with that of the public authorities. A number of private armed vessels were sent forth, which did immense injury to the commerce of Great Britain, and sent in numerous prizes. One or two events, occurring in shore, along the Carolina coast, were particularly brilliant, and surpassed by no exploits during the war. Among these was the defence of the schooner Alligator, in January, 1814.

This vessel was commanded by sailing-master Basset, and lay abreast of Cole's island. Observing an enemy's frigate and brig just without the breakers, and suspecting that an attack would be made upon him during the night, Mr. Basset made his preparations to receive the enemy accordingly. Six boats were discovered pulling up with muffled oars, and under cover of the marsh, at about eight o'clock in the evening. They were hailed and fired upon. A general discharge of grape and musketry from both sides followed, and was continued for half an hour.

The assailants were beaten and driven off with considerable loss. The Alligator had two men killed and two wounded. Her force was but forty men, while that of the British was near one hundred and forty. A large cutter of the enemy was shortly after picked up on North Edisto, supposed to have been one of the boats used on the occasion by the enemy. The bodies of an officer and a common seaman were found near it; the former, besides other wounds, having lost an arm. The Alligator was afterward sunk in a squall, while lying in Port Royal sound, off the island of St. Simons. Seventeen of her crew and two officers perished.

In August, 1813, the Decatur, a private armed vessel of

Charleston, mounting seven guns and commanded by Captain Diron, being on a cruise, discovered a ship and schooner, and stood toward them. She was soon abreast of the latter, which hoisted English colors and fired a shot, but without effect. After much manœuvring, and the ineffectual exchange of several shots, together with a broadside, the two vessels came into close action, and a severe fire of musketry ensued. Captain Diron prepared to board, and succeeded in doing so.

The resistance of the British was desperate. Firearms became useless, and the fight was carried on with the cutlass. The captain and chief officers of the enemy were killed, her decks covered with the dead and wounded, and her colors were finally torn down by the Americans.

The prize proved to be the Dominica, of fifteen guns, with a crew of eighty men. She suffered a loss of thirteen killed and forty-seven wounded; among the former was her commander. The Decatur had but four killed and sixteen wounded. The king's packet, Princess Charlotte, which had sailed under convoy of the Dominica from St. Thomas, remained an inactive spectator of the bloody contest, which lasted an hour. At its close she made sail to the southward. The Decatur had suffered too greatly in rigging to pursue. The same active cruiser, shortly after, captured and brought into Charleston, the British ship London Trader, mounting several guns, and having a valuable cargo of sugar, coffee, cotton, rum, and molasses.

August 18, of the same year, the British, in boats, made a descent upon Dewees's island, burnt some small craft, and ravaged several of the seashore plantations. They visited Capers's and other islands, and carried off the live stock and provisions. On the 22d of the same month, they landed in force on Hiltonhead, in Beaufort, and repeated their plunderings. These places were all defenceless, with no fortifications, and a population too sparsely settled and few of numbers to offer resistance.

On the 27th and 28th of the same month, a dreadful gale raged along the coast, in which Charleston, Beaufort, Sullivan's

103. Describe the fight of the Decatur? 104. What the name of her prize, the number of her men, and her guns? 105. What was the loss on board the Decatur? 106. What further success had this privateer? 107. What happened on the 18th of August of this year? 108. What on the 22d? 109. What on the 27th and 28th?

island, Georgetown, Edisto, Goose creek, and other seacoast settlements suffered great loss in life and property. The British suffered, also. Their sloop-of-war, Moselle, was wrecked and went to pieces in Broad river. In October, of the same year, Charleston was blockaded by the enemy, who made many prizes of vessels with rich cargoes.

In 1814, David R. Williams, a planter of the upper country, and a gentleman of high reputation and popularity, became the governor.

The coast of Carolina was still watched closely by the British frigates, while their barges continued to harass the shores and plantations whenever there was plunder to be got, or the country ravaged with impunity. They were sometimes caught in the act, and made to pay its penalties. On one occasion (January, 1815), while Captain Dent, who commanded at Charleston, was at the North Edisto, he obtained information that a party of the enemy belonging to the British ship Hebrus, was watering on a neighboring island. He directed Mr. Laurence Kearney to proceed outside with three barges, to cut off their retreat, while a detachment of militia advanced upon them by land.

The frigate was at anchor, out of gun-shot. Seeing the design of the Americans, she fired guns and made other signs of recall, when two of the boats pulled toward her, and a tender that contained a strong party attempted to run out also.

The wind shifted at this time, bringing the Hebrus to windward of the American barges, but the tender to leeward of them. Kearney, regardless of the frigate and of the two boats, directed his aim at the tender. The Hebrus made the greatest exertions to save her. Shot were fired at her own cutters to drive them back to the assistance of the tender, and a third boat was also despatched to her succor. The fire of the frigate was also opened upon the American barges, and with such effect, that a shot took off the head of a man at Mr. Kearney's side.

110. What loss did the British sustain in this gale? 111. What happened in October of this year? 112. Who was made governor in 1814? 113. To what annoyances were the Carolinians subjected from the enemy at this time? 114. Who was in command at Charleston in January, 1815? 115. What enterprise did he direct against the British ship Hebrus? 116. Describe this battle.

But the gallantry of this officer effected his object. He laid the tender aboard and captured her directly under the guns of the frigate. The launch of the Hebrus was also taken. The tender, beside other arms, had a carronade and six brass swivels in her. Forty prisoners were made on this occasion and brought into South Edisto. A few days later, the same gentleman, in the launch of the Hebrus, with a crew of twenty-five men, went out and captured a tender belonging to the Severus; in which were forty men. The coast of Carolina was thus distinguished throughout the whole period of the British blockade, by numerous other events, marked by like gallantry and success, which, if they were small of importance, were still fully significant of the spirit and promptness, the vigilance and determination, of the people. The achievements of the British, hovering along the coast with a strong squadron, were of no more imposing character. They made no formidable demonstration upon any point capable of defence, and confined their efforts wholly to midnight forays along the exposed islets, and to the capture of sluggish merchant-vessels. With the close of this year (1814), the war was at an end.

The treaty of peace, between the United States and Great Britain, signed at Ghent, December 24, 1814, relieved the shores of Carolina from the presence of an enemy which had kept them on the alert and anxious for a long space of time. The commerce of Charleston frequently suffered, meanwhile, from the British cruisers. But the spirit of the people was good; the old spirit of Seventy-six had fully revived in 1812, to meet the ancient enemy; and numerous descendants of old revolutionary heroes were to be found volunteers in the field, and present in Canada, Florida, Georgia, Louisiana — wherever the enemy threatened — as well as at home.

Nor should it be forgotten that the Carolina boy, who incurred the blows of the British officer at Waxhaws, for refusing

117. What was the number of prisoners taken? 118. What further capture did Mr. Kearney make? 119. What did the British accomplish on the coast in numerous midnight forays? 120. In what year was the war brought to a close? 121. Where and when was the treaty of peace between the United States and Great Britain signed? 122. From what was Carolina, in consequence, relieved? 123. What is said of the spirit and conduct of the people?

to clean his boots, was the commander-in-chief, who, at the bloody plains of New Orleans, washed out long scores of recorded vengeance, sworn for satisfaction fully thirty years before. Hayne, Hampton, Hamilton, Laval, and many other South Carolinians, most of whom could trace back their blood to revolutionary stock, distinguished themselves during the war.

In 1816, Andrew Pickens, of Edgefield, a revolutionary name of great distinction — was made governor of South Carolina. During his term, the legislature seriously addressed itself to the business of internal improvement, commencing with liberal appropriations of money. It is much doubted, however, whether this was always expended wisely. The engineering science of the state was then but rudely and imperfectly developed; and there is always apt to be fatal facility in the expenditure of money when it issues from the treasury of a people, and is not guarded by the jealous vigilance of individual interests.

The village of Moultrieville (Sullivan's island) was incorporated during this administration. The church of St. Paul, in Charleston, was consecrated. The summer of 1817, in Charleston, was marked by the fatal prevalence of yellow fever, of far more than customary severity.

In 1818, John Geddes, of Charleston, a popular favorite and lawyer, was elected to the executive chair. The period was distinguished by the increasing rancor of parties, then distinguished by the names of Republican and Federalist. The former gained the ascendency in the election of Geddes. But the party lines thus drawn, however stringently, and supported with whatever degree of tenacity, were destined to be soon obliterated, and to give place to others, which fused and absorbed all the old distinctions.

Cheraw, on the Pedee, during the administration of Geddes, grew into a commercial town of considerable importance.

In 1820, Thomas Bennett, of Charleston, a gentleman of

124. Who are named as particularly distinguishing themselves in the war? 125. Who was made governor in 1816? 126. To what did the legislature of the state address itself during his administration? 127. With what success? 128. What noticeable events occurred in 1816 and 1817? 129. Who was elected governor in 1818? 130. For what was this person distinguished? 131. What place grew into a commercial town of importance in this term? 132. Who was elected governor in 1820?

wealth and great popularity — a mechanic and large proprietor — was elected governor of the state. His administration was marked by an event of very painful interest to the inhabitants of Charleston. A bold, but wholly unsuccessful scheme of insurrection among the negro population, was devised by one Denmark Vesey, a mulatto, from the island of St. Domingo, who, having been a spectator, and, possibly, a participator of the insurrection in the island, had brought with him a taste for its horrors to Carolina. His plans were marked by considerable judgment and intelligence, due, no doubt, to his previous experience. As it is always easy to persuade the ignorant and dissolute that they are badly governed, Vesey succeeded in corrupting a number of the negroes, and employed them in the dissemination of his scheme. The appeals were made to their appetites and passions. They were promised the plunder of the city, and the gratification of all their lusts. But, fortunately, through the fidelity of some native slaves, the plot was discovered; the citizens took up arms; the ringleaders were seized and the design defeated without bloodshed. The principal negroes concerned were tried before a court constituted for the purpose, and a certain number were convicted. Vesey, the chief conspirator, with thirty-four others, the most prominent, and against whom the evidence was decisive, was hung; a like number were transported from the state, while about twice the number, who had been arrested also, were acquitted. Four white men, foreigners, were indicted as privy to and participants in the conspiracy. They were found guilty of misdemeanor, and sentenced to fine and imprisonment.

John Lyde Wilson, an eminent lawyer, of Georgetown, succeeded to Bennett as governor, in 1822. During his term of office, the low country was ravaged by a destructive hurricane, which destroyed several lives and much property. Charleston suffered especially. In 1823, the Medical College of South Carolina was incorporated. It has, since that day, attained a

---

188. What painful event occurred during his administration? 134. How did Vesey lay his plans? 185. How was the plot discovered and defeated? 186. What was the fate of Vesey and the other conspirators? 187. Who was elected governor in 1822? 188. What noticeable events occurred during his administration?

distinguished rank among the sister schools throughout the Confederacy ; and remains still one of the most flourishing of all southern institutions of like kind.

Richard I. Manning was elected governor in 1824. This gentleman was a planter of Sumter district, and the son of a brave captain of the Revolution. In the same year, the courts of law of South Carolina were newly modelled by the legislature.

This year was distinguished in South Carolina by the visit of Lafayette, to the state, in his circuit through the Confederacy. There were special reasons why this visit should occasion special gratification in South Carolina. It was upon her shores that he had first landed, nearly fifty years before, in his chivalrous sympathy with the American cause. It was by a son of South Carolina, Francis Huger, assisted by Bollman, a German, that he had been rescued from the dungeons of Olmutz — a brief period of liberty only, since he was soon recaptured. Lafayette, revisiting South Carolina, had the satisfaction of being welcomed by Huger, no longer a youth, and their interview, which was long and private, may well be supposed to have had a touching interest for both. The visit of Lafayette to South Carolina was hailed by the people with great enthusiasm and many honors.

On the 16th of August, 1825, General Charles Cotesworth Pinckney died, covered with years and honors. This gentleman, as we have shown in previous pages, had been one of the most firm, consistent, and able of the revolutionary leaders in South Carolina. Educated at Westminster (England), he began the practice of law, in Carolina, in 1770, but was soon called from the courts of law to the fields of strife. A captain at the opening of the Revolution, he soon rose to the colonelcy of the first regiment of South Carolina infantry. After the battle of Fort Moultrie, and when his own state had been temporarily freed from the invader, he joined the northern army, and became an aid-de-camp to Washington. He was present, in this capacity, at the battles of Brandywine and Germantown. When

139. Who was elected governor in 1824 ?   140. What is said of him ?   141. For what events was this year distinguished ?   142. How was Lafayette received in South Carolina ?   143. What distinguished individual died in 1825 ?   144. What is said of him ?

the tide of war again flowed south, he returned to Charleston, and was soon actively engaged in the several conflicts in Georgia and Carolina, which terminated in the fall of both their capital cities. At the final investment of Charleston, he had command of Fort Moultrie; on the abandonment of which he joined the garrison of the city, and was conspicuous among its defenders. With its surrender, he became a prisoner of war. After the war was over, he was made major-general of the militia of the lower division of the state. A favorite of Washington, and a strong advocate of the political principles of that great man, he was tendered, at successive periods, the judgeship of the supreme court; the secretaryship of war, and that of state; but he declined them all. He was a member of the convention which framed the Constitution of the United States, and subsequently contributed greatly to its adoption in the convention of his own state, which deliberated on this compact. Appointed minister to France, at the period of our national difference with the French Directory, he resented the attempt to corrupt him; and when insolently required, on behalf of his country, to pay tribute to France, as represented by this Directory, his reply became memorable, and an American proverb, which was echoed by the voice of war throughout the Confederacy. "Millions for defence," said Pinckney, "but not a cent for tribute!" Returning home, he was named by Washington as major-general of the armies of the United States. His whole career was marked by usefulness and honor. Of pure nature, fine education, classical purity of style and thought, his success as a lawyer was due rather to his virtues and to his intellect than to his eloquence. Eloquence he did not affect; but his argument was always just, well and logically reasoned, lucid, direct, and simply proper and to the point. His sense of justice and benevolence was acute and tenacious. He refused all compensation for his services from the widow and the orphan. Polished in manners, pure of life, he lived and died a Christian.

In 1826, John Taylor, of Richland, a gentleman of wealth and a planter, became the governor of the state. The adminis-

145. Who was elected governor in 1826? 146. What particularly distinguishes this administration?

tration of this gentleman was distinguished by the first legislative demonstration of South Carolina, of her hostility to the tariff laws of the United States. On the 12th of December, 1827, the legislature passed resolutions which denounced them as usurpations of the rights of the state.

In the same period, the Commissioners of Free Schools reported the establishment of eight hundred and ninety-two schools, of this character, within the state, in which eight thousand eight hundred and thirty-four pupils were taught, at an annual cost of thirty-six thousand five hundred and eighty dollars.

In 1828, Stephen D. Miller, of Sumter district, was elected governor. The Free-School report for this year lessened the number of public schools to eight hundred and forty, but increased the number of pupils to nine thousand and thirty-six; the annual appropriation for whom was also increased to thirty-nine thousand seven hundred and sixteen dollars. The legislature again passed resolutions against the United States tariff laws, and entered a protest, December 19, 1828. The excitement on this subject was hourly increasing within the state.

In 1830, James Hamilton, jr., of Charleston, a distinguished lawyer, and a man of various abilities, who had succeeded to William Lowndes as the representative for Charleston, in Congress, was made governor. He was an ardent opponent of the tariff laws; and, like a large proportion of the chief men of South Carolina, urged their veto by the sovereign interposition of the state. This period was distinguished by the great debate in Congress, ostensibly on the resolutions of Foote, respecting the public lands, between Hayne, of South Carolina, and Webster, of Massachusetts (January, 1830). The true issues in this debate involved organic topics of the constitution — the rights of the States, and of the Confederacy, respectively; the one party (state rights) claiming the Federal Union to be only a

147. What was the number of free schools in the state at this period? — of pupils? — the annual cost? 148. Who was elected governor in 1828? 149. What changes were noticed in the School reports? 150. What further action was taken by the legislature on the subject of the tariff? 151. Who was made governor in 1830? 152. What is said of him? 153. For what was this period distinguished? 154. What were the true issues involved in this debate?

creature of the states, with limited powers not subject to consideration; the other, substantially asserting the control of the states by the Congress, and representing the Federal Union as a creature of the people at large — of the whole confederacy. It seems proper, in this place, to show what was the position taken by South Carolina.

1. She contended that the bond of Union was a compact between the states, and called the Constitution. 2. That this was a compact between sovereign equals, in which they pledged themselves to forbear the exercise of their sovereign power over certain defined objects, and to assert jointly their sovereign power over other equally specified objects, through the agency of a general government. For external purposes, these powers were to be exerted jointly; for internal purposes, or state matters, to be exerted separately.

3. That the Federal Constitution was a compact jealously devised; cautiously guarded by limitations and specifications, conceding power to the general government only in certain respects, which were all declared, and reserving all other powers, not enumerated in the instrument, to the exercise of the individual states.

4. That, in forming the constitution, the states divested themselves of none of their sovereignty; that the constitution is a power of attorney, under which the functionaries of the general government, as the agents of the states, are to do the duties assigned them by the paramount authority, the states.

5. That, as the Congress of the United States is but the agent of the states, the refusal of the states, or any of them, to recognise the law passed by the Congress is an inherent right of the principal. That it is an absurdity to talk of a state rebelling against the general government. The superior can not rebel against the inferior — the principal against the agent.

6. That each state has the right of a veto on any act of Congress which it shall deem unconstitutional. That unconstitutional laws are null and void *ab initio*.

7. That, in virtue of her sovereignty, the state is the judge of her own rights, and is bound to her people to protect them against the usurpations of Congress by *nullifying* the unconsti-

155. What position did South Carolina take in this debate?

tutional law, and relieving her citizens from all obligations to obey it. This is by *nullification,* or the interposition of the *state veto,* uttered in its sovereign capacity.

Such were the principles upon which Hayne relied in his great contest with Webster, who represented the centralization of the confederacy, or rather the utter absorption of the states individually, in the power of the general government.

He argued that the constitution was not formed by the states in their sovereign capacity — that it is not a compact between the states, but that it is a government formed by the people of the whole, as one massed and common population, having no individual existence as communities, but resolved into one promiscuous nationality : that the individual sovereignty of the states was a thing secondary to the national confederacy ; and that in any issues between the parties, any questions of right, or rule, or separate jurisdiction, the supreme court was the sole arbiter between the parties.

To all this South Carolina, through Mr. Hayne, Mr. Calhoun, Mr. M·Duffie, and other chosen representatives, replied, that, with respect to the parties to the constitution, Mr. Webster was at deadly issue with all history, and they referred to the record. They said that such doctrines resolved the government into a consolidated power, fatal to the rights of the several parties making it ; that it subverted all the fundamental principles of constitutional liberty ; that the term sovereignty, as applied to them, would be, if such doctrines were true, a sheer absurdity ; and that their securities, as separate communities, separate in any measure, would be just as absurd ; that the supreme court, which is insisted upon as the common arbiter, the court of dernier resort, is itself the creature of the general government, appointed by its executive, and living by its authority ; that the previous experiences of this judicial tribunal has shown it to be itself usurpative constantly, by implication and construction, seeking the increase of its own power, enlarging that of the federal government, and abridging, with stealthy but continued industry, the securities and rights of the states as individuals. To close,

156. What was Mr. Webster's argument ? 157. How was he answered by the representatives of South Carolina ?

South Carolina asserted, as she had done at the beginning and as the justification of her resort to the state veto, the authority of such states as Virginia and Kentucky. In the resolutions of the former state, as reported by Madison, one of the best authorities upon the constitution, it is said: "The constitution of the United States was formed by the sanction of the states, given by each in its sovereign capacity." And we may add, they took their own time about it, consenting or adopting severally, at distinct periods, in state convention, and in frequent cases reluctantly, and with strong minorities opposed. In South Carolina there was the opposition and negatives of several able men — Rawlins Lowndes, for example. In regard to the doctrine of the veto, or state interposition, to arrest federal usurpation, the resolutions of Virginia declare, "that where resort can be had to no common superior to the authority of the parties, the parties themselves must be the judges, in the last resort, whether the bargain made has been pursued or violated."

The "Kentucky resolutions" spoke in language yet more decided. They say "that the government, created by this compact, was *not* made the exclusive or final judge of the extent of the powers delegated to itself, since that would have made its discretion, and not the constitution, the measure of its powers; but that, as in all cases of a compact among parties having no common judge, each party has an equal right to judge for itself, as well of infractions, as of the mode and measure of redress."

The resolutions of Kentucky say further:—

"That the principle and construction contended for by several of the state legislatures, that the general government is the exclusive judge of the powers delegated to it, *stop nothing short of despotism;* since the discretion of those who administer the government, and not the constitution, would be the measure of their powers."

Upon these authorities, equally lofty and lucid, South Carolina built her argument, and asserted her sovereign right to interpose with her veto and arrest the operations of a law of Con-

158. What do the Virginia resolutions declare?    159. What do the Kentucky resolutions declare?

gress, upon her people, which she deemed to be unjust and usurpative.

And it was upon these organic issues that Hayne and Webster, contended, representing severally the state-rights doctrines, and those of the federal or consolidation-government party.

The debate was a protracted one, and brought forth, to their fullest extent, the respective powers of the two great champions. The state-rights party held and believed that the argument was with Hayne, and that it was unanswerable. The federal party held otherwise, of course. Hayne was an adroit and able debater; lucid, logical, with a well-balanced mind; graceful and impassioned as a speaker; sweet and winning in his eloquence, and wonderfully persuasive in manner.

Webster, on the other hand, was one of the most remarkably-endowed men whom New England has ever produced; broad-fronted in opinion; stern and inflexible of doctrine; powerful in exhortation, in assault as in defence; a classical scholar, of large reading and pure style; simple, bold, and capable, because of a fine imagination, to rise into flights of grandeur and eloquence, which few men could equal or approach. It was admitted that his powers were never more severely tried. It is asserted that his logic was not equal to his eloquence. It is claimed by South Carolina that Hayne's argument is irrefutable, and that it required all the dialectic skill of Webster, all his adroitness as politician and lawyer, all his eloquence as a classical scholar and highly-endowed imaginative thinker — not to answer, but to obscure and slur over the question.

We have stated enough for the historical clues to this argument at large. The student must seek its further exposition elsewhere. It is left for us briefly to state, that even in South Carolina there was a large party opposed to the extreme measures which were contemplated by the majority. This party, claiming equally to be of the state-rights doctrine with the party of nullification — recognizing the *right* of secession from the confederacy on the part of a state no longer sure of its rights within it — were yet incapable of recognizing the right of nulli-

160. What is said of this debate? 161. What of Colonel Hayne? 162. What of Mr. Webster? 163. What is claimed by South Carolina in regard to this debate?

fication ; that is, the forbidding of one or more laws of Congress while still remaining an integral of the Union.   And in the local contest of parties, both became heated to such a degree as to threaten the country with civil war.   Their respective numbers may be rated, that of the nullification party at thirty thousand, that of the Union party at fifteen thousand.

The leaders on both sides were remarkably-endowed men. On the one side were arrayed such men as Calhoun, Hayne, M'Duffie, Hamilton, Trumbull, Preston, Cooper, Hammond, Harper, Smith (Rhett) Elliott, and many others equally enthusiastic and perhaps able; on the other were Poinsett, Huger, Petigru, Legaré, Grimké, Lee, Drayton, Johnson, Elliott, Memminger, Cunningham, Richardson, Perry, etc.   In the course of the conflict, talents were developed, of the political sort, such as will always illustrate this period in a remarkable manner.   The controversy shed a light over the hitherto neglected characters of the constitution, which we believe will, in great degree, affect the judgment of future times.   Among the pamphlets of value, close argument, and admirable eloquence, may be mentioned that of Trumbull on the side of state-rights, and that of Hurlbut on the side of union.   The Union party argued rather against the wisdom and policy of extreme measures than upon the organic principles.   It is not easy to show, however, to what extremes the parties went, and how often they forgot the argument in the bitterness of the controversy. Happily these conflicts are over, and were passed without bloodshed, though frequently on the verge of it, especially in Charleston.

The nullification party was successful, triumphed everywhere at the ballot-box, and had the destiny of the state in its hands. The rest rapidly followed.   On the 17th of December, 1830, South Carolina made a formal declaration of state-rights principles, and enacted an ordinance to nullify the operation of the act of Congress imposing duties, etc.

164. What is said of the two parties in South Carolina?   165. What their relative numbers?   166. Who were the leaders of the party of nullification?   167. Who of the Union party?   168. Who wrote and published pamphlets on this question?   169. What was the result of the conflict?   170. Which party triumphed at the ballot-box? 171. What ordinance was enacted on the 17th of December, 1830?

John C. Calhoun succeeded to Robert Y. Hayne in the senate of the United States, and in 1832 Hayne was made governor of the state.

The nullification, by the sovereign authority of South Carolina, of an act of Congress, which forbade the obedience of its citizens to the federal authority in all matters involved in the said act, called forth from Andrew Jackson, then president, a proclamation denouncing the ordinance of nullification, and commanding the obedience of her citizens to the federal law.

This proclamation was promptly answered by Hayne as governor, with another asserting the sovereignty of the state, and calling upon the citizens to be firm in its maintenance. The proclamation of Jackson was denounced in South Carolina as the sublime of despotism, and as a total surrender of all the rights and securities of the states to a consolidated and central usurpation. The state prepared for invasion. The president, a man of notorious will and great determination, having at the same time a personal feeling of hostility — an absolute quarrel, indeed — with some of the chief men of South Carolina, prepared to coerce it, and armed vessels were already sent to the port of Charleston to enforce the revenue laws and compel the submission of the community.

Meanwhile, the preparations of the state went on; troops were organized; large supplies of cannon and other weapons of war, with the necessary munitions, were bought; and a call was made for volunteers. Even out of the limits of the state, it was understood that more than fifty thousand men had volunteered to maintain South Carolina; while it was also reported that quite as many had volunteered to the president, to enable him to subdue the disaffected state. It is quite probable that both accounts are exaggerated. To attempt to coerce a state into the confederacy must be the signal for the subversion of it.

172. Who succeeded Hayne in the senate? 173. Who was made governor in 1832? 174. What proclamation by the then president of the United States was made in consequence of the course of South Carolina? 175. How was this proclamation answered by Governor Hayne? 176. How was the proclamation of the president received in South Carolina? 177. For what did the state prepare? 178. What is said of the president and his measures? 179. What preparations did the state make? 180. What number of volunteers were reported on both sides? 181. What is said of any attempt to coerce a free state into the confederacy?

Free states are not to be cemented into sisterly harmony by blood and fire!

Fortunately for the country, the crisis was such as to compel a pause in the action of the stronger power in Congress. A compromise measure was introduced, by which the tariff was to undergo such a degree of modification, within a limited period of time, that Mr. Calhoun and the representatives from South Carolina declared themselves satisfied. The compromise was probably the fruit of wisdom and moderate counsels; but it has proved a delusion, and might as well have been a *ruse de guerre*, so far as regards the permanent settlement of the question. The fatal policy which drove South Carolina to the final issue is still to too great a degree the policy of the majority in Congress. Its fruits will probably develop themselves in future mischiefs which will find no remedial agency. But it is not our province to anticipate.

On the 1st of June, 1832, General Thomas Sumter died near Bradford Springs at the advanced age of ninety-eight. His military career and great Revolutionary services have already been reported in previous pages. After the Revolution, he was for many years a representative in Congress and senator from South Carolina. In these situations he always commanded the highest respect. He was a true and fearless patriot, a brave soldier, and a partisan general of brilliant abilities.

In 1834 George M'Duffie, of the middle country, became governor of the state. Mr. M'Duffie was one of the ablest statesmen and orators that our country has produced. Classical and finished of style, of extensive reading and most vigorous thought, he possessed a bold, vehement, and powerful utterance, which would justify us in describing him as the Demosthenes of the country.

1834—'6. The annual report of the commissioners of free schools, for 1835, made the number of schools seven hundred and nine, in which eight thousand, four hundred and seventy-five pupils were taught, at an annual cost of thirty-three thousand, six hundred and thirty-one dollars.

1836. Pierce M. Butler, of the middle country, was elected governor. This gentleman came of old Revolutionary stock, and was himself distinguished as a public-spirited and able citizen. He crowned his distinctions finally, in after days, by dying bravely while leading on a South Carolina regiment against the enemy on the field of Churubusco.

During his administration, the report of the free-school commissioners made the number of schools six hundred and ninety five, and of pupils six thousand, seven hundred and eighteen — a considerable diminution from previous returns, which we are to ascribe in part to the increased prosperity of the people, the increase of private schools, and the better capacity of the people to sustain them. But the annual appropriation of the state for their support remained unchanged — thirty-three thousand, six hundred and thirty-four dollars.

During the same administration, a charter was granted of the Great Western railroad, designed to connect the city of Charleston with the states of Ohio and Kentucky, and, through them, with the great valley of the Mississippi. To this railroad the state of South Carolina made large appropriations. She had already contributed largely to the railway connecting Charleston with Augusta, Georgia, one of the first of such enterprises in the Union, and at one time the longest continuous line of railway in the world.

In 1838, Patrick Noble, of Abbeville, one of the most eminent citizens of the upper country, was elected governor. He dying in office the second year of his term, was succeeded by the lieutenant-governor, B. K. Hennegan. During the legislative session of 1839, the committee reports made an exhibit of the condition of the banks of the state of South Carolina, as follows :—

189. Who was made governor in 1836? 190. What is said of him? 191. What was the report of the free-school commissioners during his term? 192. What great work was chartered by the state during this administration? 193. What was the action of the state in aid of this work and another of similar kind? 194. Who was elected governor in 1838? 195. What is said of him? 196. Who succeeded him? 197 During this legislative session, what important report was made?

| BANKS. | 1839. | Capital. | Circulation. | Deposits. | Specie. |
|---|---|---|---|---|---|
| Bank of Charleston, . .●. | July 1 | $2,938,125 | $761,826 | $698,902.12 | $516,762.33 |
| B'k of the State of S. C. | Oct. 1 | 1,156,318.48 | 563,270 | 612.289.45 | 291,180.40 |
| S. Western Railroad B'k, | Oct. 1 | 1,361,421.78 | 419.130 | 69,072.61 | 185,001.03 |
| State Bank.......... | Oct.16 | 1,000,000 | 125,762 50 | 70,607.48 | 21,352.68 |
| Merchants' B'k, Cheraw, | Oct.31 | 480,000 | 410,159 | 28,024.30 | 83,782.65 |
| Bank of Camden.. .... | Oct.31 | 315,940 75 | 272,950 | 46,867.65 | 70,704.44 |
| Bank of Georgetown. | Nov.1 | 200,000 | 173,666 | 29,729.89 | 46,775.88 |
| Commer'l B'k, Columbia | " 5 | 800,000 | 436,760 | 58,622.70 | -184,667.34 |
| Union Bank ... .... | " 5 | 1,000,000 | 84,696 67 | 198,122.23 | 83,090.56 |
| Bank of South Carolina | " 6 | 1,000,000 | 346,395 | 183,150.10 | 81,346.06 |
| Planters' & Mechan. B'k. | " 8 | 1,000,000 | 458,935 | 355,006.03 | 168,061.44 |
| Bank of Hamburg...... | " 12 | 438,500 | 495,545 | 60,857.98 | 123,388.75 |
| Totals. .......... | | 11,610,805 01 | 4,499,095 17 | 2.401,252.04 | 1,856 143.56 |

In order that the reader and student may compare the progress for himself, of twenty years of these institutions within the state, we add the last exhibit (October, 1859) of their condition, and of the circulation and capital thus invested within the limits of the state. It will be seen that the number of banks has been increased from twelve to twenty, from 1839 to 1859 : —

| Banks. | Discount. | Deposits. | Circulation. | Specie. |
|---|---|---|---|---|
| Camden. . . | 266,477.28 | 26,063.03 | 130,616 | 36,877.32 |
| Charleston. | 2,107,184.97 | 613,633.89 | 841,345 | 645,350-36 |
| Chester. . . | 232,185.64 | 44,892.19 | 443,520 | 62,715.77 |
| Commercial | 821,259.83 | 170,593.30 | 332,020 | 111,204.75 |
| Exchange. . | 317,537.24 | 69,125.15 | 453,605 | 46,253.20 |
| Far. & Ex. . | 841,112.35 | 93,457.65 | 532,755 | 134,702.23 |
| Georgetown | 165,555.99 | 73.454.60 | 143,835 | 45,399.64 |
| Hamburg. . | 229,513.86 | 53,501.89 | 621,347 | 121,098.79 |
| Merchants'. | 213,864.78 | 28,954.70 | 281,207 | 52,555.01 |
| Newberry. . | 163,145.73 | 44,323.75 | 355,782 | 61,280.22 |
| People's. . | 892,945.10 | 135,607.84 | 329,775 | 198,738.83 |
| Planters'. . | 56,880.40 | 29,567.35 | 240,965 | 24,479.90 |
| Pl'rs & Mec' | 903,003.63 | 139,275.11 | 147,490 | 88,586.48 |
| S. Carolina. | 1,016,893.09 | 198,135.63 | 93,912 | 50,569.95 |
| S. W. R. R. | 736,581.25 | 405,276.53 | 293,255 | 82,481.04 |
| Bank State. | 2,342,718.98 | 739,707.32 | 1,402,182 | 440,518.03 |
| Col. Branch. | 880,060.14 | 287,858.32 | ........ | 13,067.53 |
| Cam.Branch | 236,373.72 | 11,961.19 | ........ | 3,109.44 |
| State . . . . . | 574,704.82 | 210,259.54 | 308,240 | 135,812.50 |
| Union. . . . . | 881,656.77 | 174,065.39 | 158,320 | 40,000.00 |
| Total . . . . | 13,879,655.57 | 3,551,714.38 | 7,110,173 | 2,394,800.99 |

198. How many banks were there in the state at this time ? 199. What was their total capital ? 200. Circulation ? 201. Deposits ? 202. Specie ? 203. What is the present number of banks (October, 1859) ? 204. What is the amount of capital ? 205. Circulation ? 206. Deposits ? 207. Specie ?

The aggregate results are as follows : —

| LIABILITIES. | | RESOURCES. | |
|---|---|---|---|
| Capital | $14,962,062.34 | Specie | $2,394,800.99 |
| Circulation | 7,110,173.37 | Real Estate | 759,020.57 |
| Profits on hand | 2,068,020.98 | Bank Notes | 317,422.00 |
| Due Banks | 2,596,432.37 | Due from Banks | 1,211,359.41 |
| Deposits | 3,551,714.38 | Discounts | 13,879,655.57 |
| Due State | 3,208,798.23 | For'n Exchange | 378,378.76 |
| Other items | 1,475,00 | Domestic Ex. | 7,404,802.02 |
| | | Bonds | 1,067,455.41 |
| | | Stocks | 1,892,627.73 |
| | | Surplus Debt | 1,454,810.89 |
| | | Branches | 1,537,804.67 |
| | | State | 281,473.37 |
| | | Other items | 919,065.28 |
| | $33,498,676.67 | | $33,498,676.67 |

During the same session of the legislature (1839), the returns of the state census made the free white population of the state as follows : —

| | | | |
|---|---|---|---|
| Spartanburg | 17,847 | Darlington | 6,029 |
| St. Philip & St. Michael | 15,661 | Lexington | 5,846 |
| Edgefield | 15,069 | Colleton | 5,845 |
| Abbeville | 14,006 | Richland | 5,773 |
| Anderson | 12,839 | Lancaster | 5,509 |
| Greenville | 12,556 | Chesterfield | 5,413 |
| Laurens | 12,382 | Marlborough | 4,119 |
| Pickens | 11,491 | Kershaw | 3,947 |
| York | 11,173 | Horry | 3,930 |
| Barnwell | 10,978 | Williamsburg | 2,687 |
| Union | 10,873 | Georgetown | 2,014 |
| Chester | 9,349 | St. James, Goose Creek | 1,302 |
| Fairfield | 9,152 | St. John's, Berkley | 812 |
| Sumter | 8,916 | St. John's, Colleton | 679 |
| Marion | 8,291 | St. Stephen's, | 390 |
| Newberry | 8,286 | St. James', Santee | 283 |
| Orangeburg | 7,392 | | |
| | | Total | 250,839 |

We find, too, same year, that the Committee on Education reported the number of free schools at eight hundred and thirty-two, the pupils at eight thousand eight hundred and sixty-seven, and the annual cost of their tuition at forty thousand three hundred and twenty-six dollars and twenty-nine cents. The parishes of Prince William, St. James, and Santee, are not included in

208. What was the number of free white inhabitants in the state in 1839 ? 209. What was the school report ?

this report; and the census is probably defective in many respects.

In 1839, there was a lively agricultural movement in the state; a great state agricultural convention was held at Columbia, in which most of the districts were represented by the leading men of each. This movement led to district or county societies, which have no doubt largely contributed to thorough tillage in the state. We may say, in passing, that South Carolina has brought the finest staples of the East — rice and cotton — to the highest degree of cultivable perfection, far beyond anything known to the countries in which these staples originated.

In 1840, John P. Richardson, of Sumter, was elected governor. Mr. Richardson had been one of the leaders of the union party, and it is in proof that the strifes of party, occasioned by the question of nullification, was at an end, in the fact of his election. He had been a member of Congress; had come of Revolutionary stock, and was a man of acute intellect and high ability. He was a planter.

During this administration, the state sustained the loss of one of her most distinguished representative minds, in the death of Robert Y Hayne, who died prematurely of fever, in the fiftieth year of his age, and in the very maturity and. harvest of his powers.

Robert Y. Hayne, boasting a peculiar Revolutionary celebrity, was born at St. Paul's parish, in 1791. He was early marked for distinction; became a successful lawyer; then attorney-general of the state; a speaker of the house in the General Assembly of South Carolina; a representative; then senator in Congress, where he distinguished himself as the champion of the South, in the great debate in Congress, the issues being the rights of the South — the rights of the states — as against the usurpations of the Federal Government, involving side issues which enlisted, pro and con, all the several sections of the country. Contending with one of the most singularly-endowed men that

---

210. What important movement was made in 1839? 211. What is said of the results of this movement? 212. Who was elected governor in 1840? 213. What is said of him and of his election? 214. What important event took place during his administration? 215. What is said of General Hayne?

any country has ever produced, General Hayne bore himself not merely valiantly, but brilliantly; and whatever may be the decision, popularly, in respect to the comparative powers of the two combatants, it will be safe to say that the rights of the South suffered no injury in his hands. The palm of superior eloquence and power might be with his opponent, while the argument and the truth belonged to him.

We have already indicated, in some degree, his progress. He left Congress and became governor of the state. Our political strifes, temporarily quieted by the *Compromise Act* bill, and it being desirable to inaugurate a more liberal and enlarged policy for the city of Charleston, he became the mayor of that city. Subsequently, when the policy of the state sought to extend her communication by railroad with the West, he accepted the presidency of the Charleston, Louisville and Cincinnati railroad, and died of fever at Asheville, North Carolina, while in the prosecution of his official duties. A public monument has been contemplated to his memory, but, as usual in democracies, nothing has been done; the living candidates for popular favor putting aside the claims of the past, for, as Shakspeare hath it, "The present eye praises the present object," and "Things in motion sooner catch the eye, than what not stirs." A democracy, by an inevitable law of nature, must degenerate into an ochlocracy; since the tendency, once begun, to go down, has a momentum that can never arrest itself, and only stops at the foot of the hill!

Richardson, as governor of South Carolina, was succeeded by James H. Hammond, of Barnwell in 1842. Governor Hammond had distinguished himself as an able partisan in the nullification campaign. He was of that party; had been an editor of a political newspaper, and was an aide to Governor Hayne. He became subsequently a brigadier-general of state militia, and was for a time member of the house in Congress. A gentleman of large wealth, he had travelled in Europe. While in the gubernatorial chair, he answered the letters of

216. What office did he accept when he left Congress? 217. What office did he subsequently fill? 218. Of what public work did he after this accept the presidency? 219. Where did he die? 220. What is said about a monument to him? 221. Who succeeded Richardson as governor in 1842? 222. What is said of him?

Clarkson on slavery, in an able pamphlet. A planter, he introduced large and useful improvements in agriculture, and established an extensive drainage of swamp lands. With a mind naturally well endowed, improved by collegiate education and travel, he was soon distinguished as one of the ablest intellects in the state. His executive career was marked by a bold grasp of the public necessities, and by a judicious management of state affairs. He is now (1859) one of the state senators in Congress.

The year 1843 was distinguished for South Carolina by the death of Hugh S. Legaré, one of her most eminent statesmen and literary men. He died at Boston, June 16th, of that year, while secretary of state of the United States under President Tyler. His life had been distinguished by public services and by masterly achievements in letters. In the former, he had served South Carolina in the legislature, as attorney-general, and in the house of representatives in Congress. He had served the nation at large as *chargé d'affaires* at Brussels, one of the most brilliant courts in Europe, and died while in the performance of the duties of secretary of state, having succeeded Mr. Webster in Mr. Tyler's cabinet. As a man of letters, he was recognised as one of the most brilliant classical scholars in the whole country, familiar not only with the Greek and Latin, but with all the continental languages of Europe, and as familiar with their respective literatures as with their languages. He was one of the founders of the Southern Review, and one of its most frequent and brilliant contributors. He contributed also to the pages of the New York Review, and other publications of like order. Several of their most profound and elaborate papers, upon topics of ancient learning, with analyses of the ancient orators, as well of themselves as orators and men, and of their characteristics as writers. He was himself one of the most accomplished of public speakers, at once closely argumentative and brilliant. A collection of his writings has been made which might receive much additional value by the publication of a great deal which has been omitted. His mortal remains, originally committed to the vault of a friend in Boston, have been recently brought home and deposited at Magnolia cemetery, near Charleston, where, by a private subscription among his admirers, a graceful monument has been raised to his memory.

James H. Hammond, as governor of South Carolina, was succeeded, in 1844, by William Aiken, of Charleston, a planter of great wealth, who had previously served in the legislature as representative and senator, and subsequently as a representative in Congress.

In 1846, David Johnson, one of the judges of the superior courts of the state, an eminent lawyer of the upper country, was elected governor of the state. His administration was marked by the formation of the Palmetto regiment, and by its achievements in the war with Mexico. This noble regiment consisted of between eleven and twelve hundred men, mostly young men, the average age of the members not exceeding twenty-three. They were chiefly of the native population, and of good families — no mercenaries seeking pay and plunder, but ardent young volunteers, eager for distinction in war, and chivalrously seeking glory near the flashing of the guns.

The regiment distinguished itself, second to none, in most of the affairs which marked the march from Vera Cruz to the conquest of the capital of Mexico. They won credit at the siege of Vera Cruz ; suffered terribly on the march to Alvarado ; were put in charge of Puebla ; were in the several battles of Contreras, Churubusco, Chepultepec, and at the gates of the city ; and it was the flag of the regiment that first waved over the walls of the conquered city of the Montezumas. But the regiment suffered, among the worst, in all these actions. Colonel Butler, its commander, was slain at its head while leading the charge. Lieutenant-Colonel Dickinson, succeeding to the command, perished shortly after in like manner ; but their followers gallantly avenged them. The remnant of the regiment returning to Carolina, covered with bloody laurels, scarcely

229. Who was elected governor in 1844? 230. What is said of him? 231. Who was elected governor in 1846? 232. For what was his administration marked? 233. What was the number of men in the Palmetto regiment? 234. What is said of the men?

numbered three hundred men. The state awarded a medal to each of the survivors.

Whitemarsh B. Seabrook, a planter of Edisto island, succeeded in 1848 as governor of the state. Mr. Seabrook was an able writer, especially on agricultural subjects. He had been indefatigable in the maintenance of the agricultural society, and in the promotion of all objects tending to improve the culture of the state.

He was succeeded by John H. Means, of Fairfield, in 1850. His administration was marked by the demise of John C. Calhoun, at Washington, March 31, 1850. Mr. Calhoun is idenfied with the political history of South Carolina from the war with Great Britain in 1812 — a term of nearly forty years. He was one of the most brilliant statesmen, not only of South Carolina, but of the confederacy, and a worthy successor of the celebrated John Rutledge. As an orator, perhaps, he did not rank, though his vehemence and intensity, his rapidity of thought, intuitive conception, and subtle analysis, was in proof of that rare faculty of imagination, which sometimes looks like inspiration, and which possesses several of the most remarkable qualities of eloquence; intensity that glows like passion; vehemence which declares for truth; rapidity like the lightning, as pure, subtle, direct, and instantaneous, which is the sign of power; and all blended, working like passion, and disdaining all the minor arts of fancy. His history must be sought in other volumes; but, from the close of 1812 to that of 1850, it was, in brief, the history of South Carolina. He was her ruling spirit — the embodiment of her thought and policy. He died in the harness; literally falling, death-stricken, at the moment when, in debate in Congress, he was asserting the violated rights of his people, and the outraged and endangered securities of the whole nation, no less than of the South; since the aggressions of one section upon another can not fail to provoke resistance, and the whole fabric of union is necessarily endangered in the collision! This is, in brief, the history of all the confederacies that the

285. What were the achievements of the regiment? 236. What were its losses? 237. What did the state award each of the survivors? 238. Who was made governor in 1848? 239. What is said of him? 240. Who succeeded him in 1850? 241. For what was his administration marked? 242. What is said of Mr. Calhoun?

world has ever known; the aggressions of large states upon smaller — of the commercial upon the agricultural, which is the usual history, compelling the revolutions in which disintegration follows, and commotion, and anarchy, and war; cupidity prompting the desire of conquest wherever spoil is to be reaped, though to the utter ruin of all the parties!

John L. Manning, a wealthy planter of Sumter, succeeded to Means as governor of South Carolina in 1852. Mr. Manning had previously represented his district in the state senate.

To him succeeded James H. Adams, of Richland, a wealthy cotton-planter also, whose administration was chiefly marked by his recommendation that the slave-trade be reopened, as essential to furnishing the adequate labor to the South; a measure highly desirable, no doubt, to the industry of the South, but which seems to be impracticable in the present confederacy, in consequence of the prejudices of the North, and its numerical superiority in Congress.

Robert F. W. Allston, an eminent rice-planter of Georgetown, succeeded Adams in 1856 as governor of the state.

In 1858 he was succeeded by William H. Gist, of Union district, a popular man, a lawyer, and for many years a representative in the senate of the state. Mr. Gist is still (1859) governor of the state.

In the close chronicling which we have accorded to our progress as a state and people, omitting all minute details, we are of opinion that we have grasped all the most important *facts* in the history of the state from the close of the Revolution. But facts do not severally constitute truth; and in history it demands the grouping of all the essential facts in the progress of a people, in order to a just comprehension of their civilization and their just claim to rank in the estimation of mankind. In such a work as the present, such a grouping is impossible, involving as it would, not merely a vast accumulation of details, but a philosophical investigation into causes, and a just deduction from these of their legitimate effects. And such investigation would

243. Who was elected governor in 1852? 244. Who succeeded him? 245. For what was his administration chiefly marked? 246. Who was next made governor? 247. Who was elected governor in 1858?

imply argument and speculation, both of which would be improper here. All that is left to us accordingly to do, is to report briefly, in summary, the present condition of South Carolina; and it will be for the reader or student to make his own comparisons, of this present, with that past, of which we have given him, in preceding pages, ample materials for judgment.

South Carolina, a small colony, settled by the English on the borders of the Atlantic on one side, and an immense wilderness on the other side, in the interior of North America, was enfeebled equally by the smallness of her population, the poverty of her individual people, and the selfish and ignorant policy of a foreign government. But the soil was fertile; the situation good; the colonists hardy and courageous; and possessed with a stern English sense of right and independence. As they grew, they thought; and very soon they began to assert their rights. Before many years, they threw off the government which had failed to do them justice; which was, in fact, an obstacle to their development; and required to be put on a footing with the rest of the British people, under the immediate control of the crown.

In this they exhibited a courage, a firmness, a character, which found their proper representatives in a strong body of very able men.

But they were neither sufficiently advanced in power, in population, in wisdom — nor had they suffered the necessary degree of injury from the foreign government — to think of, or assert, their absolute independence. That was to come with their continued growth, and required a few more seasons. And it did come; and with the seasons, the men!

We have said that the Revolution, which entirely freed them from foreign dominion, was probably premature. But this could not be said of them had their population been long enough upon their soil to become homogeneous. The Revolution was *not* premature, as respects their resources in the one most essential respect. They were in possession of the necessary degree and development of a native intellect for a native government! They were in possession of an adequately-endowed race of great men, equal to their defence in war, and to their government in times of peace. And this is the best argument for the independence of a people. The native civilization had so far advanced, that Britain herself could not, in 1776, have produced abler men for command of armies, or for statesmanship, than could the state of South Carolina. Certainly, in the whole thirteen colonies, none took higher rank in either province; and had the population been homogeneous — had not the state been one-third filled with a new and foreign people — full of natural prejudices in favor of the old and against the new — she, alone, single-handed, could probably have maintained the contest with all the forces that were brought against her.

It is scarcely probable that, with an united people, the enemy could ever have penetrated her forests, or taken possession of her cities.

Up to this period, her civilization had made rapid progress in all *material* respects. She had become a successful cultivator of rice and tobacco, great staples and in large demand; her trade flourished; she had begun to build shipping and to create a native commerce. She had begun to cultivate, equally, the products of the East and the South; the rice of China, the cotton of India, the olives and the wines of France and Italy. She was in the possession of a soil and climate favorable to all these objects of culture.

The historian who should properly and philosophically write the history of South Carolina, with regard to *all* her acts, would need to go into a survey of her peace, her prosperity, her growing opulence, her improved civilization, her refinement — wonderful for a new state — as shown by her settlements upon the Ashley, the Cooper, the Santee, and other rivers, in 1776, and to contrast these regions and her general condition, *then*, with that which they displayed when she emerged from the war of the Revolution; covered with wounds, and weeds, and ruin! bleeding and impoverished; her fields laid waste; her cultivation at an end; her roads unsafe; her territories, far and near, covered with hostile factions — desperate people; and, in brief, the whole work of civilization, law, society, requiring to be begun anew!

But it *was* begun; and with the same virtuous energy which

19

had marked the same people in their previous labors. Gradually, order, and civil liberty, and law, were restored to their supremacy. Gradually, culture, and education, and civilization, made their way to ascendency. Roads were laid out; bridges built; towns and villages started up in the wilderness; and still there were great, commanding minds, to retrieve the past; to mould the future; to seize upon the helm, and guide the ship of state, in safety and dignity, to her proper harborage, and anchor her firmly, where the winds and waters would break upon her, however violently, in vain!

But, before this condition could be reached, she had to traverse a wide sea of uncertainty and doubt. She entered the confederation of her sister states, against the warnings of some of her great men, and, perhaps, with some general misgivings. But she was naked, poor, struggling with disaster and debt; and, still present to *her* eye, as to that of all the other states, was the dread, the danger, of foreign invasion — an ever-present fear, after the late experience of a seven years' war — prompting all of them to concessions, in behalf of a general union, in which, alone, could safety be hoped for, at that early period.

Some of these concessions were unfortunate, and may now almost be considered fatal. One of these, which allowed other states to decide upon the representative *status* of her population, and to accord to her negroes an inferior representation to the negroes of the northern states, was a monstrous, if not a fatal error. Another was that of cutting off the slave-trade, which alone could supply an agricultural people, in a tropical region, with its adequate proportion of physical labor. But for the dread of foreign aggression, neither of these concessions would have been made! The result of the Confederacy, by natural laws, was to abridge the independent energies of the southern states; to cut off trade, and disparage their capacity for commerce and manufactures.

But the war of 1812, with Great Britain, found South Carolina faithful to her sister states. She was one of the most urgent, though at the sacrifice of her most precious interests, for the declaration of defiance to a power which outraged the flag of the Confederacy, and treated the national character with scorn. She was still represented by a race of great men. Calhoun, Cheves, Lowndes — these are national names that can not die; inseparable from all that is great and glorious in our second war for independence, as the war of 1812 has been so happily styled.

And they survived this war, and continued, some of them, for a long time, to be the great men of South Carolina! and to these names were added others, noble followers in the wake of these, or gallant companions, who have maintained the high rank of the state in the Confederacy, and at home, till the present hour!

And the population and civilization of the state have continued to grow till the present hour! The fields are fertile; the productions of the earth are multiplied; there are goodly staples which the culture of our people send forth abundantly for the supply of foreign countries. There are commerce and trade in full activity; there are profitable manufactures; there are precious ores, gold, silver, copper, iron, in our mountains, which are delved for with energy and industry. A thousand miles of railway are to be found penetrating to our most remote districts. They stretch from the seaboard to the mountains; from Charleston to Augusta; to Columbia and Camden; to Greenville, Anderson, Pendleton, York, and reach and unite with the railways of Georgia and North Carolina. The *material* progress of the state has advanced wonderfully; and grand structures, for public use, and public works of rare magnificence; and noble charities; and cities growing from wood to brick, and from brick to granite and marble, declare for an intelligence which is as brave and enterprising as it is sleepless and well-directed!

Nor have the spiritual and nobler elements of our nature been denied their proper aliment and nurture. Religion, everywhere, in all precincts, continues to build her temples to the living God; there are arts which humanize and spiritualize, which adorn and beautify a race, and of all these there are living representatives. Education, in its simplest and in its profoundest forms, is everywhere at hand, to train and tutor the intellectual man to the just development of his intellectual attributes. Since 1810, the state has made large appropriations to the education of the poor. For fifty years she has endowed and supported a college for the more ambitious. And sects and sections have shown themselves emulous in this work; and there is now a score of similar institutions, all according equal collegiate advantages to those who would aspire greatly. In respect to the popular education, the most extraordinary efforts, and the largest appropriations, have recently been made; and, in some sections, such as Charleston, the progress has been beyond all estimation. Some of the ablest minds of the state have devoted themselves to this work, with a zeal, an energy, an intelligence, that promises the grandest results. Hitherto, it must be admitted, the popular or free-school system of the state, yielded no results commensurate with the appropriations and efforts made. It may be well to say here, that the reasons for this failure are evident enough upon reflection. In countries purely agricultural, especially where the culture is of staples, implying a demand for large bodies of land, the sparseness of the population is necessarily unfavorable to education. The poor can not send their children from any distance to a school — this is a physical impossibility; and it is a pecuniary impossibility that any state should be able to build and establish a school at every man's door! Here is the whole difficulty. It follows that agricultural communities can never enjoy the same advantages of education which are possessed by such as are commercial and manufacturing. It follows, too, from the same cause, that communities purely agricultural can never exhibit the same degree of intellectual activity with communities commercial or manufacturing, or where the population is sufficiently dense to enable the community to meet the expense of good and continuous tuition. For the secret of intellectual activity lies in continual attrition; the constant contact and friction of rival minds. These are the natural disadvantages of purely agricultural states.

But the civilization of South Carolina has led her to great sacrifices and continued efforts to overcome these natural difficulties; and, with the gradual increase of her population, and the diversification of her employments, we have every reason to hope and believe that she will never be deficient in the men who are to wield her power, assert and maintain her arguments, and defend her rights.

Hitherto, she has always been strong in her strong men! It is with a mournful pride that we refer to the great names, in recent periods, which she has possessed and lost. Calhoun, M'Duffie, Cheves, Hayne, Hamilton, Cooper, Drayton, Legaré, Grinké, Elliot — these are names of men equal to all the exigencies of a people, and capable of conferring fame upon any annals. They are gone! and South Carolina stands upon the threshhold of a new era, and, we trust in God, a yet superior progress! Let us hope that each season shall produce its proper men. May that Providence that has great states and cities in its keeping, crown her with increase, and raise her to heights, in the future, commensurate with the noble elevations of the past; to all virtuous achievements; to all grandeur, consistent with what is good, and noble, and pure, and true. and wise, and honorable!

**THE END.**

# THE ROMANCES OF WM. GILMORE SIMMS.

From the North American Review, October, 1859.

" THE Cassique of Kiawah" is the most recent in the series of novels that Mr. Simms has given to the public, and, in artistic skill and vivid narrative, is hardly inferior to the best of its predecessors. The series numbers now no less than eighteen; all, or nearly all, of which we have read, usually as they first appeared, and several of them more than once; and, though there are very great differences in their merits, we have read none of them without interest, and most of them with great satisfaction. Indeed, in our own deliberate opinion, since the demise of Cooper, there is no one who can be reckoned his superior among American novelists.

The scene of Mr. Simms's novels is laid, uniformly, we believe, at the South, and frequently in South Carolina. The localities are all familiar to him, and his historical researches have informed him of the events, habits, and manners of former times. To singular felicity in the choice of his subjects, Mr. Simms adds many other excellencies. He has evidently a thorough mastery of the resources of the English language; yet, we do not always approve his selection of words; and, while his sentences are usually well constructed, and often with peculiar skill, they sometimes betray extreme carelessness. In higher qualities, also, we find him irregular; yet, we recognise in his writings, in a superlative degree, the power of picturesque description, the imaginative conception of character, the nice delineation of its delicate shades, the ability to deal with subtile and violent passions, and the skilful arrangement and development of intricate plots. The range of the characters he presents to us reaches from the highest to the lowest, including almost every variety; and he seems to be equally at home with them all. They are all genuine flesh and blood; and we become interested in them, as though they had been our friends and neighbors, so natural and living are their movements and speech before us. The graceful and delicate forms of human feeling are treated with entire appropriateness; yet, the genius of Mr. Simms leads him rather to sketch the darker and more agitating passions. Revenge, fraternal hatred, and the like, often form the groundwork of his plots, and, in most of his works, stand out quite prominently on the canvass. The writings of Mr. Simms are worthy of a more extended notice than we can now give them. We hope to be able, at some time, to present to our readers a careful and adequate review of his merits. We invite them now to the perusal of his novels, with the assurance that they will find themselves amply compensated by the pleasure they can not fail to find in it. To those who can not read them all, we scarcely know how to indicate a proper selection. " Charlemont," " Beauchampe," and " Confession," are, in our judgment, of least interest and least worth. To those who are fond of deep excitement, of rapid shifting of scene and interest, and of the tumultuous and wild in human character, we commend " Richard Hurdis" and " The Scout," or, which is its better name, " The Black Rider of the Congaree." " The Yemassee" is full of life and action, and is a touching tale of Indian treachery and fidelity.

The half dozen designed to illustrate the Revolutionary period at the South, namely, " The Partisan," " Mellichampe," " Katharine Walton," " Woodcraft," " The Forayers," and " Eutaw," should all be read in connection, both as illustrating one another, and because, in the successive works, we have the same characters, in part, continued and developed. Among those characters, too, there is one on which the author seems to pride himself, as being the creation of his own brain. We mean " Captain Porgy," who, like Cooper's Leather Stocking, or Shakespeare's Falstaff, was thought to be too good to kill off in a single book. We can not but think the development of this character, on the whole, as awkward as his own protuberant person, though we are very little disposed to quarrel with a hero, from whose conversation we have gathered so much philosophy, and with and at whom we have so often laughed.

Those readers who are acquainted with the early history of Carolina, and the famous constitution framed for the infant colony by John Locke, will remember the title " Cassique"—derived from the natives, indeed, but appropriated by him to one of the higher orders of his projected aristocracy. The red men of that region gave the name "Kiawah" to the Ashley river, on which the city of Charleston now stands. The romance before us is named from one of its principal characters, who, by virtue of that office, occupied a large tract of land on the river. His brother, the other leading personage of the tale, is introduced to us as the captain of the Happy-go-Lucky, a buccaneer somewhat of the Drake and Cavendish school, with perhaps a higher order of sentiment and more refinement than they had. The time of the action is 1682, just when privateers had been declared pirates, and much of the plot turns on this change of public policy. Its main interest, however, arises from the fact that the elder brother had wooed and married the maiden to whom the younger had been betrothed. Under the management of an ambitious and unscrupulous mother, she had been induced to transfer her allegiance, though not her affections, from a lover whom she was taught to believe no longer living. It will be seen at once that this contrast in the interests of the brothers, and the likeness and unlikeness of their characters which their common blood and different position would generate, must needs furnish a skilful writer with many scenes of the intensest dramatic interest, and that the proper unravelling of such a skein would call for no slight exertion of genius. We must say that, in our opinion, Mr. Simms has achieved this difficult task with remarkable success. The proprieties of characters and position are everywhere preserved, and all the violent contrasts that face us at the outset are perfectly harmonized in the consummation. The scene changes from the deck and cabin of the privateer to the swampy and wooded banks of the Ashley; from the low drinking-houses to the fashionable saloons and masquerades of Charleston; from a naval engagement on the coast to an Indian assault and massacre at the barony of Kiawah. Of course a great many subordinate personages are introduced, all of whom are skilfully drawn and effectively handled. The wife of the cassique, so deeply loved by both the brothers, though not often presented to the reader, makes on him the impression of a saintly purity and loveliness, which is finely contrasted with the hard and unfeeling selfishness of her false and scheming mother. Zulieme, the child-wife of the rover, is totally unlike them both. She is, indeed, the original character of the book—a fine creation of the author; yet so naturally conceived, and all her peculiarities so ably sustained, that we seem to have known her well already, and can only wonder that we never before met her in the regions of fiction. She has all the truth and affection of a wife, with the simplicity and wondering ignorance and changeful moods of a spoiled, pouting child. The combination is wrought with great skill, and Zulieme is, of his female characters, on the whole, the author's masterpiece. But there is hardly any character introduced that is not well drawn. The governor of the colony, timid and covetous, a confederate with the free-trader; the ambitious and treacherous lieutenant, who would supplant his chief; the two sprigs of nobility from England, conceited, yet brave and manly; the female would-be leader of fashionable society, unprincipled and vain; the coarse, vulgar, desperate, murderous pirate; the Indian boy, Iswattee—all of these are drawn with a fulness and accuracy of delineation that leave little to be desired for the completeness of the picture With this skill in portraiture is combined a constant onward movement in the action of the piece, and passions, vehement and tender, are so blended with changing scenes and interest, that he who has once been engaged in its perusal will hardly feel disposed to lay the book aside until he has read it to its close.

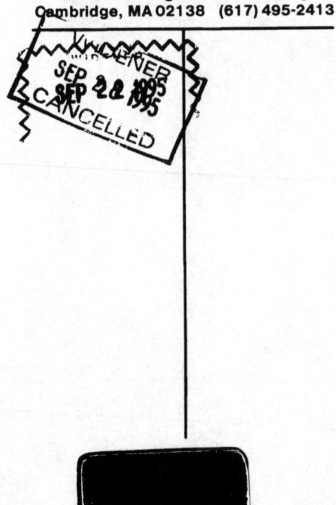

Check Out More Titles From HardPress Classics Series In this collection we are offering thousands of classic and hard to find books. This series spans a vast array of subjects – so you are bound to find something of interest to enjoy reading and learning about.

Subjects:
Architecture
Art
Biography & Autobiography
Body, Mind &Spirit
Children & Young Adult
Dramas
Education
Fiction
History
Language Arts & Disciplines
Law
Literary Collections
Music
Poetry
Psychology
Science
…and many more.

Visit us at www.hardpress.net

CPSIA information can be obtained
at www.ICGtesting.com
Printed in the USA
BVHW081616220819
556561BV00018B/3917/P